Hugh Sebag-Montefiore

BARNES
&NOBLE

NEW YORK

For Aviva Burnstock, my wife,
and for Saul and Esther, my children

This 2007 edition published by Barnes & Noble, Inc.,
by arrangement with John Wiley & Sons, Inc.

ISBN-13: 978-0-7607-9118-9
ISBN-10: 0-7607-9118-X

Printed and bound in the United States of America

1 3 5 7 9 10 8 6 4 2

Contents

Illustrations follow page 146

Illustrations

v

Enigma wheels (the author; photographs taken at Bletchey Park, thanks to assistance from Tony Sale and John Gallehawk, as were the other photographs of Enigma apparatus taken at Bletchley Park listed below)

The *Polares* (Alec Dennis)

Frank Birch (Diana Justus)

Peter Twinn (Peter Twinn)

The *Krebs* (Eric Tubman)

Harry Hinsley (his son Hugo)

The *Lauenburg* (Sir Ludovic Kennedy and the Imperial War Museum)

The *Lauenburg* being sunk (Sir Ludovic Kennedy and the Imperial War Museum)

Fritz-Julius Lemp (Herbert Langsch)

U-110 (Sir Barry Sheen)

Allon Bacon (the Bacon family)

David Balme (David Balme)

Enigma machines (the author; photographs taken at Bletchley Park)

Rolf Noskwith (Rolf Noskwith)

Leslie Yoxall (Leslie Yoxall)

Jack Good (Professor Jack Good)

The *Geier* and the *Ashanti* (Reg Swann)

Norman Denning (his daughter Jill)

Mark Thornton (Robert de Pass)

William Prendergast (Robert de Pass)

U-559's conning tower (Robert de Pass)

Tony Fasson (his sister Sheena d'Anyers Willis and Stephen Wood, Keeper of the National War Museum of Scotland)

Ken Lacroix (Ken Lacroix)

Friedrich Bürgel (Friedrich Bürgel)

U-744 (Lorne Edwards)

U-505 (Wayne Pickels)

Paul Paillole and General Lewis (Paul Paillole)

Acknowledgements

This book would never have been written had it not been for the publication of Robert Harris's novel *Enigma*, and the West End production, and TV adaptation, of Hugh Whitemore's play *Breaking The Code*. These two dramas, which are both based on what happened at Bletchley Park during the Second World War, not only fascinated me, but popularized the Enigma story, and showed that there was a market for more books on the subject.

Three historians have also been an inspiration: firstly, the late Sir Harry Hinsley, who not only played such an important part in the breaking of the Naval Enigma, but who also masterminded the production of, and co-wrote, the official five volume history *British Intelligence in the Second World War*. Critics of these volumes complain that they are full of useful facts, but fail to describe the colourful characters who took part in the exciting events described. However Sir Harry more than made up for that when he was interviewed by me, generously holding nothing back for his own private use, even though he was in the process of writing his autobiography. Secondly, I am indebted to David Kahn, whose *Seizing The Enigma* is the best history book about the Naval Enigma captures to date. He also gave me any help he could when I was searching for Germans who were on captured German ships and U-boats. Thirdly, I would not have been able to find so many previously unpublished sources for this book had it not been for the help of Ralph Erskine, a retired barrister, who has become the leading expert on the Naval Enigma. I am also grateful to Stephen Budiansky whose book *Battle of Wits: The Complete Story of Codebreaking in World War II* is the most comprehensive account to date in relation to the American role in breaking the Enigma.

The four historians mentioned above only represent the tip of the iceberg. The following historians have been just as generous with their time and expertise: Ralph Bennett, the writer of several books about Ultra, including *Behind The Battle*, the late Clay Blair, whose two volume *Hitler's U-Boat War* has raised the standard of dramatic writing in books about U-boats to new heights, Gilbert Bloch, the French expert on Enigma, Alec Douglas, the writer of the official history of the Canadian Navy during the Second World War, Captain Bernard Edwards, an expert on convoy victims, the Polish Enigma experts Jozef Garlinski and Władysław Kozaczuk (the writer of *Enigma: How the German Cipher Machine Was Broken, and How It Was Read By the Allies in World War Two*). Also, Timothy Mulligan, the archivist and historian who works at the National Archives in Washington, Dr Axel Niestlé and Professor Jürgen Rohwer, the German U-boat specialists, Dr Berthold Sander-Nagashima, a historian at the Militärgeschichtliches Forschungsamt, Professor Alberto Santoni, the Italian expert on Enigma intelligence, Roger Sarty, Director of Historical Research at the Canadian War Museum, Hugh Skillen, the organiser of Enigma Symposiums, Professor Jean Stengers, an expert on the French and Polish contributions in the Enigma story, Alan Stripp, one of Sir Harry Hinsley's co-editors of *Codebreakers*, the first book in which a collection of cryptographers explained how the Enigma code was broken, and Dr Yves Tremblay and Jean Morin, from the Directorate of History and Heritage, National Defence, in Canada. Professor Colin Burke, the first historian to describe in detail the American contribution to the breaking of the Enigma code, which he did in his book *Information and Secrecy*, and Stephen Budiansky, the writer of *Battle of Wits: The Complete Story of Codebreaking in World War II*, also kindly made available or explained some of their best source material relating to the US and Enigma.

I am equally indebted to the following historians, librarians and editors who assisted me or have permitted me to use their collections: Professor Andrzej Ajnenkiel of Wojskowy Instytut Historyczny, Warsaw, Axel Betten and Stefan Kühmayer of Deutsche Dienstelle Wehrmacht Auskunft Stelle, Berlin, Margaret Bidmead of the Royal Navy Submarine Museum, Gosport, David Brown and Jock Gardiner, historians, Kate Tildesley and Bob Coppock, foreign document curators, and Jenny Rate, Admiralty Librarian at the Naval Historical Branch of the Ministry of Defence, Helmut Döringhoff of Bundesarchiv Militärarchiv in Freiburg, Germany, Michael Gray, an editor at Navy News, Jenny Hill at the National Maritime Museum,

Acknowledgements

Greenwich, Volker Hogrebe of Verbandzeitschaft des Deutschen Marinebundes, Grzegorz Kowalski of Centralne Archiwum Wojskowe, in Poland, Christine Lecuyer at the Department of Veterans Affairs, Canada, David Prior at the House of Lords Record Office, Hans-Jürgen Schneider of Verband Deutscher U-Bootfahrer, Claire Sibille of the Service Historique de l'Armée de Terre at the Ministère de la Défense in France, Andrzej Suchcitz at the Polish Institute and Sikorski Museum in London, John Taylor and William Cunliffe at the National Archives in Washington. The assistance Horst Bredow gave me at the U-boat Archive at Altenbruch, near Cuxhaven in Germany, and which Graham Smith gave me at the Naval Manning Agency in Portsmouth, deserve a special mention; without their help it would have been impossible to have discovered so much about what happened on board the U-boats which were captured along with their Enigma codebooks, and aboard the British ships which captured them.

When I started writing this book, I was not intending to describe in detail any of the techniques used by the Bletchley Park cryptographers to break the code. However I changed my mind after talking to the following Bletchley Park veterans, whose previously unpublished accounts represent an important part of the Enigma history: Professor Jack Good, Rolf Noskwith, Richard Pendered, and Professor David Rees. I also received assistance from other Bletchley Park cryptographers including: Mavis and Keith Batey, Derek Taunt, Peter Twinn and Leslie Yoxall. Much of the detail about codebreaking techniques which are covered in this book would not have been included had it not been for the efforts of Sir Michael Alexander, the son of Bletchley Park cryptographer Hugh Alexander. Others, including Ralph Erskine, have lobbied the government in an attempt to persuade them to declassify Hugh Alexander's history of what went on in Hut 8, the Naval Enigma hut, during the war, but it was only thanks to Sir Michael's persistence that his father's history was released in time to be referred to in this book. As readers will see, it is one of the most important sources I have consulted.

The interviewees and document contributors mentioned in the Notes relating to each chapter have also made very important contributions. Their testimony and documents, in many cases never previously revealed in a published work, can now be taken into account whenever history books describe how the Enigma cipher was broken. I cannot mention them all, but the following were particularly important: David Balme, the sub-lieutenant who courageously climbed down inside the U-110 to recover the Enigma codebooks, Kenneth Lacroix, the only man who climbed down into the captured U-559 who has lived to tell the tale of what happened inside, Paul Paillole, the head of French Counter-Intelligence during the war, who has spoken frankly about how the French helped to break the Enigma in the first place, and how subsequently their action gave the Germans the opportunity to find out about the Allies' Enigma secret, and Gisela Schmidt, who bravely decided to reveal everything she knew about her father Hans Thilo Schmidt, in spite of the pain suffered through describing such tragic memories.

I have been helped by the following researchers, and advisers: Michaela von Buchholtz, Captain Ireneusz Goreczyn, Defence Attaché at the Polish Embassy, Jürgen Uchtmann, Military Attaché at the German Embassy, Tina and Marina Aurich, Laura Dalla Costa, Charlotte Gardille, Tina and Pia Gottschaller, Verena Gutscher, Christa Haiml, Elke Helmts, Christina Hucke, Lesley Hussell, Sabine von Laufen, Astrid Lehner, Justyna Naglic, Magda Pekalska, Roland Preuss, Katarzyna Psoda, Tony Sale and John Gallehawk, from the Bletchley Park Trust, Priska Schmückle von Minckwitz, Peter Sheridan, Ulrike Stratmann, Veronika Thieme, Agnieszka Trzcinska, Daniela Weippert and Iris Widmer. Clive Wolman and John Standing, the actor, whose real name is Sir John Leon (he has inherited the title which has come down from Sir Herbert Leon), told me about Bletchley Park's and the Leon family's history, as did Penelope Oldham, Veronica Ashbrooke, and Lord Fanshawe.

Peter Wright and Rod Gilchrist, editor and deputy editor of the *Mail On Sunday*, showed great patience and flexibility when I took time off from projects I was working on for them in order to complete this book.

Lastly I should mention my agent, Mike Shaw from Curtis Brown, who encouraged me to write this book in the first place, Ion Trewin, the managing director of Weidenfeld & Nicolson who commissioned it in spite of the number of books about Enigma written before, and Benjamin Buchan, my chief editor, who has advised me wisely on what I should leave out from my first draft, and what I should insert into my final manuscript. Margaret Body was the copy-editor; her job would have been even more difficult had it not been for the painstaking efforts of my wife, Aviva Burnstock, and my parents April and Stephen Sebag-Montefiore, who kindly waded through my first draft so they could advise me on what to change.

Introduction

Lots of books have already been written about Enigma, and they all have one characteristic in common. They all say that it was thanks to the brilliant codebreakers at Bletchley Park that Britain managed to read Nazi Germany's most secret messages. But what has been written has given a false impression about how the code was really broken.[1] The codebreakers did of course make a vital contribution. But they would never have achieved what they did if some of the Enigma codebooks and manuals had not first been captured by spies and ordinary British seamen who risked, and some times lost, their lives in the battle for the code.

The very first capture of Enigma documents occurred long before the outbreak of the Second World War. Hans Thilo Schmidt, the so-called 'Enigma spy', handed over some Enigma manuals to the French Secret Service in 1931. Subsequently, after war was declared, more Enigma codebooks and apparatus were captured in a series of hit and run raids on German U-boats and trawlers that were carried out by the British, American and Canadian Navies. It is these 'pinches' - as they were nicknamed by the Bletchley Park codebreakers - and the resulting breaking of the all-important Naval Enigma code which form the core of this book.

The Enigma spy, Hans Thilo Schmidt, has been mentioned in history books before. Paul Paillole, the head of French Counter-Intelligence during the war, described Schmidt's espionage for the French Secret Service in his book *Notre Espion Chez Hitler* which was published in France in 1985. But more information has become available since then: Paillole wrote about Schmidt without hearing the testimonies subsequently provided by British codebreakers. These accounts make a case for saying that, without Schmidt's assistance, Army and Air Force Enigma messages would not only never have been read regularly by the Allies before the war,[2] but they would also, after the outbreak of hostilities, not have been read until June 1940 at the earliest, and possibly until the end of 1941.[3] This would probably in its turn have delayed the date when Naval Enigma messages could have been read by the Allies.[4] (These dates are explained in Notes 3 and 4 to this Introduction.) Paillole was also denied access to Schmidt's family, so he was not able to write anything about Schmidt's private life, nor could he pinpoint what happened to Schmidt after he was arrested by the Gestapo. Schmidt's daughter, Gisela, told me the whole heartbreaking story, and it is revealed for the first time in this book.

The captures at sea have also been written about before. The classic books on this subject are *The Secret Capture* by Stephen Roskill and *Seizing the Enigma* by David Kahn. However both were written without the aid of crucial sources that have become available following their publication, such as the recently declassified 'The History of Hut Eight 1939-45' by Patrick Mahon (hereafter referred to as 'History of Hut Eight'), and Hugh Alexander's 'Cryptographic History of the Work on the German Naval Enigma', which describe in graphic detail how British codebreakers, including Alan Turing, joined forces with the Royal Navy to break the code being used by Nazi Germany's U-boats. These official accounts of how the Naval Enigma cipher was broken lay hidden away in the British and American archives for over fifty years. Until December 1999, the History of Hut Eight could only be inspected in Washington; it was not available in England, and the 'Cryptographic History of Work on the German Naval Enigma' (hereafter referred to as 'Alexander, *Naval Enigma History*') was not declassified anywhere until December 1999. These histories, together with other documents unearthed in the Naval Historical Branch of the Ministry of Defence in London, which reveal exactly what Engima documents were captured, have enabled me to give a more complete description of how the Naval Enigma was really broken.

It is worth pointing out that no single capture of material enabled the codebreakers to break the Naval Enigma once and for all. The early captures only gave the codebreakers some of the answers they needed, and even the later captures only showed Bletchley Park how to read German messages until the next change in Enigma procedure. That explains why so many captures were necessary for Naval Enigma to remain an open book to Britain and its Allies. So describing the battle to break the code is like commentating on an evenly matched boxing match, with first one man and then the other pinning his opponent against the ropes and attacking him mercilessly until the next change in fortune. A chronology of the events relating to the breaking of the code has been placed at the end of this book in order to help the reader see where each of the captures figures in the Enigma history, and how it helped the codebreakers.

One of the interesting questions which is answered by this new look at the captures at sea is who was at fault on the German side. When attempting to fathom why it was that so many German codebooks were captured, it is easy to assume that panic and shell shock amongst the German sailors and submariners was the predominant reason. After all, who could blame them for forgetting about the encrypting machines and codebooks as they struggled to escape from U-boats which were being attacked at point blank range by Allied warships? However, interviews with German crewmembers from the captured U-boats reveal a different story. The main problem was that the U-boat commanders had not been trained properly on how to dispose of the encrypting machines and codebooks when forced to abandon ship. They thought they were acting correctly when they attempted to sink their U-boats without first destroying all Enigma paraphernalia or throwing it into the sea. But they were wrong, and much of the blame for this should be laid at the door of the German Naval Command which should have insisted that all Enigma material was destroyed or thrown overboard before any German U-boats were scuttled by their crews. It should have been obvious that there would be occasions when a U-boat commander would abandon ship after attempting to open the diving tank vents only to find that the U-boat did not sink because the levers operating the tanks had been damaged during the attack, thus rendering the Enigma machine and codebooks liable to be captured – which is exactly what happened.

This culpable failure by the German Naval Command would not have mattered so much if they and their cipher security advisers had had the foresight to adapt the Enigma machine so as to make life difficult for codebreakers, even following the capture of the codebooks. But no adequate contingency plan seems to have been put in place at the design stage. So, for example, the German cipher experts unwisely allowed each of the wheels which could be used inside the Enigma to be given different characteristics: each wheel when placed inside the Enigma machine had a different 'turnover position'; in other words it turned over the wheel placed next to it at a different position in the former wheel's cycle.[5] This was the very feature which eventually helped Alan Turing to crack the Naval Enigma cipher once some of the codebooks were captured. All he had to do to know which wheels were in the machine – one of the crucial questions to be determined when breaking the Enigma – was to identify the position at which the wheels in the machine were turning over the wheels next to them. This was one of the points which is revealed in the recently declassified 'History of Hut Eight'.

Another factor which should have minimised the effect of the Enigma machine and codebooks being captured was the German Naval Command's reaction when there was evidence suggesting that this might have happened. It would not have been difficult to devise a test to check whether the Enigma was compromised. For example, a message could have been sent out on the Naval Enigma networks announcing a rendezvous of U-boat tankers at a remote spot not normally frequented by Allied ships. If Allied ships had then turned up at the spot on the date and at the time specified in the message, the Germans could have been pretty sure that Enigma was compromised. But no such step was taken, and so the British and American codebreakers carried on reading German messages unchecked.

The Germans certainly tried to make their Naval Enigma cipher more secure in the course of the war. Their decision to use a fourth wheel after 1 February 1942 'blinded' Bletchley Park for ten and a half months. However even that measure was blighted by an elementary mistake. The security of the four-wheel Enigma was dependent on two codes, the short weather report code and the short signal code used by the U-boats, remaining out of Allied hands. After the codebooks for these codes were captured in October 1942, the four-wheel Enigma cipher was read. The Alexander, *Naval Enigma History*, states that weakening Naval Enigma's security in this way was an act of 'extreme folly'.[6] That was only half the story. Documents uncovered in the course of researching this book show that the German willingness to close their eyes to what was happening at times bordered on stupidity. Even when the British armed forces made - mistakes, such as infamously allowing the battle cruisers *Gneisenau* and *Scharnhorst* to escape from France in February 1942, the German admirals used this as evidence to confirm that Enigma could not have been compromised. They could not imagine how the British could have failed to intercept these ships if they were reading Naval Enigma signals. This kind of approach meant that when Allied operations went wrong the Allies were in a no-lose situation. Paradoxically, the greatest threat to the Allies winning the war at sea was the danger that they would sink too many ships too quickly, thereby alerting the German Naval Command to the possibility that this was because its ciphers were being read.

All this assumes that Naval Enigma was a vital cog in the Allied war machine. But was it? It was certainly responsible for winning individual victories, such as the stunning decimation of the Italian Fleet at Matapan in March 1941 and the sinking of the *Scharnhorst* in December 1943. According to the official history *British Intelligence in the Second World War* written by a team led by Sir Harry Hinsley, Enigma's greatest contribution to the war at sea occurred when it helped Britain to defeat the U-boats in the Atlantic between October and November 1941. 'The growing expertise of the OIC, (the Operational Intelligence Centre within the Admiralty), in evasive routing, based on the reading of the Enigma, was a fundamental cause' of the U-boats' defeat according to Hinsley and his colleagues, even if other factors such as the diversion of U-boats from the Atlantic to Norway and the Mediterranean played their part as well.[7] That victory alone would have been enough to have made the long drawn out struggle to break it worthwhile. If sinkings of merchant ships supplying Britain had increased proportionately with the number of new U-boats coming into service during the second half of 1941 and the early part of 1942 – as would probably have been the case had Enigma not been broken – who knows what might have been the result?

Enigma's role in May 1943 in warding off the renewed assault by U-boats in the Atlantic was also important, but 'it was only one of the factors underlying the success of the Allied offensive' at sea according to the official historian.[8] More warships and aircraft, better radar and a willingness to attack the U-boats rather than wait to be attacked by them were all equally, if not more, instrumental in the defeat of the U-boats during 1943. On the other hand, Hinsley and his colleagues believe that the Allied invasion of France would probably have had to be delayed to 1946 if the breaking of the Enigma had not contributed to the comprehensive defeat of the U-boats by the beginning of 1944, the year when the invasion, codenamed Overlord, was actually undertaken.[9] So the breaking of the Naval Enigma is thought to have enabled the Allies to end the war two years earlier than would have been the case without it.[10]

Shortly before this book was first published as a hardback in

England, the controversial Holywood film *U-571* was released; it was controversial because it showed the Americans capturing an Enigma from a U-boat, whereas in real life, as has been indicated above, it was the British who made the most crucial captures. Since then the newspapers have been full of reports telling 'the true story'. However in doing so another injustice has been perpetrated, and this time it is the Americans whose role has been unjustly downgraded. They did play an important part in the breaking of the Enigma code in that they were able to produce and manufacture machines which could break the Enigma regularly even after the Germans added the fourth wheel to their cipher machines. Although the American machines were only produced after May 1943, by which time the German U-boat threat to shipping in the Atlantic had temporarily abated, the Naval Enigma code still had to be broken if the Allies were to win the war without unacceptable loss of life at sea. So the machines produced were very important. The British engineers had been unable to design equivalent machinery which was reliable. That is why in this new edition of my book I have written a fuller account describing what the Americans did, and the obstacles that were put in their way.

The new material about Naval Enigma in this book should not obscure the fact that there were difficulties in researching it. Sir Harry Hinsley, who played such an important role in breaking the Naval Enigma code, died after I had interviewed him for the first time, but before I could see him again. Fortunately, his son Hugo put me in touch with Jonathan Steinberg, a history don at Trinity Hall, Cambridge, who had interviewed Hinsley in depth shortly before he became ill. The tape of this interview, which Steinberg so generously lent to me, helped mc to fill in many of the gaps which had been left as a result of Hinsley's tragic and premature demise.

I encountered a different problem when I was attempting to find the family of Rodolphe Lemoine, the spymaster who had run the Enigma spy, Hans Thilo Schmidt, during the 1930s. The surviving Lemoines would, I hoped, give me some clues which might enable me to find Hans Thilo Schmidt's family. The high point of my search came when I rang the number given in a French telephone directory for a G. Rolf Lemoine and was told by the lady who claimed to be his wife that her husband was indeed Rodolphe Lemoine's son Guy. Unfortunately, he was away in Paris, she told me, but he would arrive home soon. But each time I phoned there was another excuse why he was not there. Further enquiries unearthed the fact that she was living in an old people's home. 'She suffers from delusions,' the receptionist told me. 'She thinks she has a husband, but really she is alone.' Fortunately, this setback was not disastrous, since I did eventually manage to find Hans Thilo Schmidt's daughter by following up another lead.

Although I started this Introduction by stating that I wanted to correct the mistaken impression that the codebreakers broke the Enigma by themselves, I do not want to minimise their involvement. So this book is not exclusively about the 'pinching' of the Enigma codebooks and manuals by spies and the Navy. Even after the codebooks were captured, the Bletchley Park codebreakers still had to use their ingenious methods, many of them invented by Alan Turing and his colleagues, to read the German encrypted messages. Some of their most important techniques are explained in Appendices at the end of this book. Because there are some limited descriptions of the codebreaking techniques in the main text itself, and because it is easier to follow these descriptions if a summary of the defined terminology is available, I have listed some of the most important definitions in a restricted Glossary which is also at the end of this book.

I must confess that there is an additional reason for my wishing to research the Enigma story. Bletchley Park, the house in Buckinghamshire where the Enigma code was broken by Britain's codebreakers, used to be owned by my great great grandfather, Sir Herbert Leon. He was a stockbroker who later became a Liberal MP at a time when Gladstone was prime minister. He and his second wife, Fanny, lived at Bletchley Park from the early 1880s until his death in 1926. The house and its surrounding estate was eventually sold off by the Leons, following Fanny's death, in 1937. My father, Stephen Sebag-Montefiore, has often told me about the strange Victorian time warp he entered when, as a young boy, he was taken to Bletchley Park by his parents to visit the Leons. A family pilgrimage was made every Christmas. He remembers above all else that the house was always humming with servants. There were no less than forty gardeners. You could go to sleep at Bletchley Park with the flower beds ablaze with yellow daffodils, and wake up in the morning to find that the same beds had been transformed into a sea of red tulips.

My father also remembers that the Leons loved horses. On Boxing Day all of their guests were expected to attend the lawn meet in front of the house. The riders would first congregate in the Bletchley Park stable yard opposite the Cottage where Dilly Knox's section would one day break into the Italian Naval Enigma. It was a memorable and colourful event with the pink coats worn by the huntsmen set off by the darker habits worn by the women who rode side-saddle. As the Leons and their descendants sat in their saddles during those Boxing Day meets in the early 1930s, sipping sloe gin from the glasses handed to them by the Bletchley Park butler, neither they - nor my father watching from the sidelines - realised that they were witnessing what would turn out to be the end of an era. Like all Anglo-Jewish families they would have been horrified if they had known about the Holocaust which was about to sweep across Europe, but how pleased they would have been if they had known that one day their estate would be used in an operation which would make such a great contribution towards the saving of the nation and the winning of a world war.

Prologue

A graveyard in a forest south of Berlin - January 1999

I was standing in the middle of a clearing in a pine forest just outside Berlin when I realised that I must have found what I had been seeking. For months I had been hunting for some concrete evidence about the Enigma spy, Hans Thilo Schmidt. He was the German Defence Ministry Cipher Office executive who in 1931 gave the French Secret Service their first clues on how to break the Enigma code. Now I was almost sure that I had literally stumbled upon his last resting place. My feet were embedded in a springy, mossy mound, and the ground where I was standing was soft and swelling, as if the body hidden down below had loosened the earth while trying to push its way out.

It was exactly as it had been described to me. Behind the mound stood a solitary gravestone. I had to hack away the undergrowth and branches surrounding it before I could see that it was no longer the pristine white tablet, garlanded with flowers, it had been when last seen by my informant. It was already beginning to turn green, thanks to a coating of mould. But it bore the words 'Johanna Schmidt Geb. Freiin Von Könitz *27.12.1857 + 24.10.1928'. That was Hans Thilo Schmidt's aristocratic mother, who had been born a German baroness, in spite of the fact that her mother was English. Hans Thilo Schmidt's own grave under the mossy green mound was unmarked.

Before I tracked down his daughter, Gisela, I had had serious doubts about whether this man, who was said to have played such an important role in the Enigma saga, had ever existed. So little was known about him. My worries were only allayed after his daughter told me about the grave, showed me her documents, and told me her sad story. That begged another question. Should Hans Thilo Schmidt be revered as an unsung hero, or had he just spied for the money? He had not exactly given the Enigma cipher to the Allies. He had sold it to them for a lot of money, and his original act of treachery had taken place two years before the Nazis seized power. So no one could say that he had, in the first place at least, been motivated by a desire to overcome the evil regime. His desire to destroy the Nazis only developed later. That made him a flawed hero, the codebreaking equivalent of Oscar Schindler, who, like Hans Thilo Schmidt, was perfectly prepared to put his own life on the line as long as he made a handsome profit, and seduced a lot of women, in the process.

Schmidt was eventually betrayed to the Germans by the one of his French spymasters. But what happened next has been shrouded in mystery. Was he tortured by the Gestapo after his arrest in March 1943? Was he shot? Or did he kill himself? Even the French Secret Service which ran him as its most treasured spy did not know what happened to him at the end. His daughter was able to fill in some of the gaps. She also told me that she had only seen the grave in the forest once since that terrible day in September 1943 when, with tears streaming down her cheeks, she had watched her father's coffin being lowered into the ground. In her mind's eye, she could still see the words he had written to her shortly before he poisoned himself with the cyanide which she had helped to procure.

After finding the gravestone, I sought out the little cottage which serves as the administration centre for the graves dotted around the forest. It was there that I at last found the written proof I needed that Hans Thilo Schmidt had really been buried where his daughter said. A clerk handed me a formal document certifying where Hans Thilo Schmidt had been buried and when, and who had paid for the flowers which had once decorated his gravestone. The document contained a poignant reminder that he was abandoned and forgotten. No one had tended the grave since flowers had last been placed on it more than fifty years ago.

The German military cemetery near Stafford – 12 February 1999

Five hundred miles to the west of Berlin, in the German military cemetery at Cannock Chase in Staffordshire, are the graves of twenty-five more men who died while fighting in the battle for the code. These men were once part of an elite fighting force which manned the German U-boats during the Second World War. Their U-boat was the *U-33*, which was sunk on 12 February 1940 while attempting to lay mines in the Firth of Clyde, one of Britain's busiest estuaries, off the west coast of Scotland.

Every year on 12 February, the anniversary of their death, flowers are laid beside their gravestones. The flowers provide a shocking splash of colour in this bleak and desolate spot where the groups of identical grey granite rectangular gravestones are lined up in rows as orderly as soldiers standing on parade. No one at the cemetery knows who pays for the flowers. Even the cemetery administrator can only say that the order comes from somewhere in Germany.

There used to be another gravestone which commemorated the death of Max Schiller, a twenty-sixth member of the crew, but it was quickly removed during the late 1970s after Schiller turned out to be alive. He is now an old age pensioner living near Annan in Dumfriesshire. He will never forget the hours he spent in the sea following the sinking of the *U-33*. It was the worst day of his life.

None of these vigorous young men was prepared for the terror they experienced when their U-boat was spotted by HMS *Gleaner*, a British anti-submarine vessel. They had heard the sound of the British ship's asdic sonar beam searching for them under the water; it was as if gravel was being sprinkled on the outer shell of their submarine. Then their blood froze, as deafening explosions from the depth charges dropped above their heads were accompanied by what felt like violent blows from a huge hammer striking the submarine's hull. The bangs were so loud that they left even the bravest men feeling disoriented and out of control. So who could blame one of the officers for pleading with Max Schiller, who was just eighteen years old and the youngest in the crew, to sit beside him because he thought he was going to die? And who could have guessed that the fear of being killed by the depth charges combined with the shock of being immersed in the freezing waters of the Firth of Clyde after abandoning the U-boat would cause another member of this elite force, who had Enigma wheels in his pocket, to lose his mind temporarily. It was just unfortunate, as far as Nazi Germany was concerned, that the Enigma wheels which this man had been told to drop into the sea were said to be still concealed in his clothing when he was rescued, and so were effectively handed to the British without their even having to board the sinking submarine.[1]

Bedrule church in the Scottish Borders, 30 October 1998

There is no special ceremony or floral tribute to mark 30 October, another important anniversary in the Enigma story, at the tiny church in the parish of Bedrule, in the Scottish Borders, near Jedburgh. But inside the church the searcher can find a black metal memorial on the north side of the nave, bearing the words:

> In loving memory of Francis Anthony Blair Fasson, Lieutenant, GC, RN. Killed in Action in an Enemy Submarine in the Mediterranean 30 October 1942.

Under the plaque a more detailed explanation can be found in a modest wooden frame:

> 'At 1550 hours, on 30 October 1942, HMS *Petard*, of which Lieutenant Fasson was First Lieutenant, commenced a hunt for a German U-Boat in the Eastern Mediterranean. At about 2200 hours, following a search in company with other destroyers, U-559 had surfaced and was being abandoned by its crew.
>
> In a gallant attempt to recover Top Secret enemy code books, Lieutenant Fasson and Able Seaman Colin Grazier stripped off their clothes and swam across to the U-559. With the help of a very young NAAFI Assistant, 16 year old Tommy Brown, the attempt was partially successful, but the seacocks had been opened. U-559 sank taking Lieutenant Fasson and Able Seaman Grazier with it. Both were awarded the George Cross posthumously for reasons that could not be revealed at the time.'

This brief prosaic account barely does justice to what was one of the most courageous and significant acts of the Second World War. To dig up the details of the heroic story it was necessary to travel down to London so that I could look up the documents stored in the Public Record Office near Kew Gardens. There I found an account of what happened which is infinitely more stirring than what is revealed on the wall of the Bedrule church. The codebooks which Tony Fasson and his assistants recovered on that dark night contained the key to the Enigma code being used by the German U-boats, in the Atlantic as well as in the Mediterranean, in their attempt to bring Britain and her American ally to their knees.

The codebreaker boffins working at Bletchley Park, near what is now known as Milton Keynes, just could not break Germany's Naval Enigma code using brainpower alone. Without the codebooks Britain might have been starved into submission as her Atlantic lifeline was cut off by the German U-boats. But with the codebooks in Britain's hands everything changed. All of a sudden those eerie morse code messages, which for so long had been the harbingers of night attacks on Britain's defenceless merchant shipping, became welcome tell-tale clues enabling the convoys to avoid the deadly 'sea wolves'.

The Honours and Awards Committee, sitting in 1943, stated that Fasson's – and Grazier's – 'gallantry was up to the Victoria Cross standard'.[2] It was only with reluctance that the Committee went on to say that Fasson and Grazier were not eligible for the Victoria Cross 'because the action was over and the service cannot be held to have been in the face of the Enemy'. Instead they were both awarded a George Cross and Tommy Brown was awarded a George Medal for heroism not in the face of the enemy.

*

Behind all of these deaths, graves and medals lies an almost incredible story. It is the story of how Enigma was broken and how it remained an open book to the Allies for a substantial part of the Second World War. Contrary to what many people still believe, it is not a story of one solitary genius breaking the Enigma code through brainpower alone, although the famous mathematician Alan Turing did indeed play a starring role. Nor were the men mentioned in this Prologue the only ones who risked their lives in their bid to see that the code was broken. It is a long-running saga involving a large cast of charismatic, courageous and eccentric characters, many of whom would never have been allowed to perform the functions they carried out in today's more security-conscious society.

But courage and brilliant brains would not have been enough to have ensured that the code remained broken over such a long period. Luck, and mistakes by both sides in the conflict, also played an important part in the story. By analysing these mistakes, lessons can be learned which should be remembered long after all the heroes and geniuses mentioned in this book are forgotten.

The Betrayal

Belgium and Germany

1931

On Sunday 1 November 1931 Hans Thilo Schmidt, a forty-three-year-old executive at the German Defence Ministry Cipher Office in Berlin, took a step from which there was no turning back. He booked into the Grand Hotel in Verviers, a small Belgium town on the border with Germany, for his first meeting with a French Secret Service agent. Schmidt had been contemplating making this move for months. During June 1931 he had paid a visit to the French Embassy in Berlin to find out who he should contact in Paris if he wanted to sell some secret documents to the French government.[1]

Three weeks later he had followed up the advice given by the Embassy staff and had written a letter to the French Deuxième Bureau, the umbrella organisation which on France's behalf carried out many of the task performed in Britain by MI 5 and MI 6.[2] In his letter he explained that he had access to documents which might be of interest to France, and he specifically mentioned that he was in a position to hand over the manuals for a coding machine which had been used in Germany since June 1930. If the Deuxième Bureau was interested he was happy to meet up with its representative in Belgium or Holland, he wrote. It was in response to this letter that the meeting in Verviers had been arranged, and the scene was set for Schmidt's first act of treachery.

In normal circumstances Schmidt would probably never have considered becoming a traitor. He was just an average man from an upper-middle-class background with no political agenda or burning ambition to be successful. Although his mother had been born a baroness, she was not rich. She had lost her title when she had married Hans Thilo's father, Rudolf Schmidt, a university history professor. Hans Thilo's circumstances had improved a little in 1916 when at the age of twenty-eight he had married Charlotte Speer, the daughter of a well-to-do hat-maker. Charlotte's mother's family business, C.A. Speer, ran a shop in Potsdamerstrasse in Berlin which was the place for smart Germans to go for their umbrellas, walking sticks and of course their hats. The profits from this shop helped to pay for Hans Thilo and Charlotte's wedding present, some land and a house in Ketschendorf, a rural area, now part of Fürstenwalde, just outside Berlin.

But then came the galloping inflation and the economic downturn which forced the Speers to close their shop. All of a sudden Hans Thilo's prospects looked far from rosy. He was fortunate that his father and his brother, another Rudolf, were prepared to help him out with his domestic expenses. Hans Thilo and Charlotte had two children by the time the economic depression began to bite and, although he had his job in the Cipher Office thanks to an introduction arranged by his brother, his salary was barely enough to keep himself, let alone his young family.

His first act of betrayal had nothing to do with matters of state. He betrayed his wife by having an affair with his maid. Presumably Hans Thilo must have hoped that his wife would never find out what went on when she was out of the house. But if he wanted to be discreet, he certainly went about it in a half-hearted way. His children, Hans-Thilo the younger and Gisela, knew exactly what was going on. They quickly realised that they had to tip-toe around their small Ketschendorf house in case they barged in on something which they and their father might have found extremely embarrassing. Sometimes they could hear the sound of their father and the maid making love in the spare room when their mother was out shopping. It was to be the first of many such affairs. His children at first had no idea whether their mother knew about her husband's philandering. They suspected that she did not. But they did notice that from time to time one maid would disappear only to be replaced by a more ugly substitute. Then their father would start off another seduction ritual until the next maid disappeared.

Hans Thilo's extramarital affairs were not confined to his maids. He also had sexual encounters when he stayed the night in Berlin; he claimed that he had to work late in the office. His sister Martha would try to cover his tracks when Charlotte, his wife, attempted to ring him at Martha's flat where he was supposed to be staying. 'He has just gone shopping,' Martha would tell Charlotte. But Martha's excuses gradually wore a bit thin, and Charlotte must have soon realised that she could not believe a word Martha said. The relationship between the two sisters-in-law took a turn for the worse after they fell out over the clothes Martha gave Charlotte for Christmas. Charlotte was far from being the neat gazelle-thin princess Hans Thilo coveted. She ate for comfort because of her unhappy marriage and put on weight. Martha, who either was not very sensitive or perhaps wanted to make a point, always insisted on giving her stockings and dresses that were several sizes too big. To Charlotte this appeared to be a not very subtle hint that she was too fat, and there were furious scenes every Christmas. Charlotte complained to her husband about the insults she was forced to endure.

But these rows were nothing compared to those which occurred when Charlotte confronted Hans Thilo about his love affairs. He would try to reassure her by saying, 'Mutzipuss, you are the only one I really love. The other women mean nothing to me. I've tried to stop having affairs, but I just can't help myself.' Her response was that if he could not help himself, she could – by hiring uglier maids. At this he would sigh philosophically, and say, 'That would not do any good. The uglier they are, the more grateful they are for my taking an interest in them.' Their children guiltily listened to all this through the thin plaster walls which ensured that no one in the house had any privacy. They felt they were implicated in their father's treachery, since once the rowing had stopped, he would try to explain to them why he behaved as he did. 'It's just that I love women,' he would tell them. 'I love them so much that I wish I had been a woman myself.'

Hans Thilo loved fantasising. 'When you grow up, people will not drive to each other's houses,' he told his children. 'They will fly from house to house. You will see people on the moon, and everyone will have their own wireless with pictures.' The dream world he conjured up for them was all part of his charm. Everyone who heard him talking in this way was amused. Except for Charlotte. Every now and then she would threaten to leave him so that she could make a new start with someone who really loved her. After one such threat, Hans Thilo decided to move out of their Ketschendorf house so that he could live permanently in Berlin. His sister Martha even went so far as to find him a girlfriend, someone who, she said, would look after him properly. However, even this crisis passed after Gisela and Hans-Thilo the younger urged their parents not to split up.

It was Hans Thilo's inability to resist temptation at work which turned him into a traitor. In the Cipher Office where he worked ciphers were made up for the German armed forces. These were kept in a locked safe. However, thanks to his brother Rudolf, who had been head of the Cipher Office between 1925–8, Hans Thilo was the trusted assistant to Major Oschmann, his brother's successor. As a result he often had access to the safe where the ciphers were stored. It did not take a genius to realise that these ciphers would fetch a lot of money if they were offered to another country, and Schmidt eventually decided to exploit his money-making opportunity. That is how it came about that he made contact with the French Secret Service.

The Deuxième Bureau's secret agent who had been entrusted with the task of ensnaring and tempting Schmidt into a life of espionage was a larger than life character who went under the name of Rodolphe Lemoine. In fact Lemoine was not his real surname. Like many spies, he enjoyed having as many aliases as possible. His real surname was Stallmann. Lemoine was his French wife's surname. He had married her in 1918 after moving to France from his native Germany. However, when he was working under cover for the Deuxième Bureau, he used the codename Rex. Whoever was responsible for allocating the codenames must have had a sense of humour, perhaps spotting that Lemoine lived like a king – usually at the Deuxième Bureau's expense. When he went out on an assignment he would stay at the best hotel in town and book the most expensive suite. His informants were invariably softened up with champagne and encouraged to smoke the large cigars which Lemoine himself favoured. Or perhaps it was because he looked like a king or at the very least a medieval pope. Lemoine was a huge bear of a man. When he met Schmidt for the first time he was sixty-one years old and his powerful charismatic personality was accentuated by his large shaven head and piercing blue eyes which looked out from behind round-rimmed spectacles. Once you were caught in their hypnotic gaze it was hard even to think of escaping.

As soon as Hans Thilo Schmidt was shown into Lemoine's opulent hotel suite in Verviers in November 1931, Lemoine began to put into practice the procedure which had been honed by similar encounters over the years. At all such meetings a subtle form of jostling for position has to take place before both sides settle down to the serious business of hammering out a deal. In order to take control of the situation, Lemoine wanted to frighten Schmidt just a little before befriending him. So Schmidt was asked what he would have done if the official to whom he had spoken at the French Embassy in Berlin had taken him to be an agent provocateur and had handed him over to the police. This suggestion had the desired effect and Schmidt, who was obviously very tense, said that if Lemoine was going to talk like that there was no point carrying on with the meeting.

But Lemoine could not let the matter rest there. He had to make it clear to Schmidt that the French Secret Service could not possibly take on a new recruit unless it was convinced that he was genuine. Lemoine had to know why Schmidt was willing to become a traitor. It was then that Schmidt told Lemoine about his financial difficulties and his feeling that his country could not expect him to be loyal if it failed to look after him. He might have added that he had trained as a chemist; so it should have been easy for him to find a well-paid job if the government had been running the economy properly.

Once Lemoine heard this, he knew exactly how to deal with Schmidt. He would offer him fabulous amounts of money for any valuable documents which he could produce. In short, he would play Mephistopheles to Schmidt's Dr Faustus. By the end of their first meeting, Lemoine and Schmidt had come to an understanding. Schmidt was to bring the best documents he could lay his hand on to their next meeting and Lemoine would tell him then how much they were worth.

Lemoine was not to be disappointed. On Sunday 8 November 1931, the two men met again at the same hotel. During the meeting, Schmidt produced two documents out of his brief case which made Gustave Bertrand, the 34-year-old code expert accompanying Lemoine, gasp with disbelief. For they were nothing less than the manuals explaining how to operate the top secret Enigma machine being used by the German Army. When Bertrand heard Schmidt go on to apologise for not bringing along the list of current Enigma settings, he knew that he was on to a potential goldmine as far as France's security – and his own career – was concerned.

As soon as he was alone with Lemoine, Bertrand suggested that they should pay Schmidt 5000 Reichsmarks for what he had brought. It was difficult for Bertrand, when he was interviewed about this meeting several years later, to remember exactly what Lemoine then told him. But in substance it was something like this: 'We must catch him once and for all now. Let me offer him twice as much as you are suggesting, that is 10,000 marks [about £20,000 in today's money]. And I would like to offer him the same again if he carries on helping us.' Bertrand, who was by this time metaphorically rubbing his hands with glee, quickly agreed to what Lemoine was saying. So while Bertrand took the Enigma manuals up to his hotel room so that they could be photographed, Schmidt was signed up as a Deuxième Bureau spy. The deal he agreed was both exciting and terrifying. It would enable him to earn large amounts of money. But as Lemoine told him, once he was in, there was no way out. The French Deuxième Bureau would never let him go.

Back in Paris, Bertrand showed his photographs to the cryptographic specialists. Although he was in charge of the cipher section in the Deuxième Bureau, he was not a hands-on cryptographer himself. The cryptographers must have felt that Bertrand and Lemoine had been taken in, because they reckoned that the documents provided by Schmidt would not enable them to break the Enigma code; the manuals explained how to encipher a message, but they did not enable a cryptographer to read Enigma messages. Bertrand was very disappointed, but he and his superiors agreed that they should get a second opinion from the cryptographic experts in Britain.

Wilfred 'Biffy' Dunderdale, the man who was running the British Secret Intelligence Service's French station during the 1930s, was to be the go-between. Like Lemoine, he was a cosmopolitan man of independent means. Lemoine's money came from his father, a jeweller in Berlin; Dunderdale's father was a shipping magnate. Biffy Dunderdale, who was just thirty-one years old when he was approached by Bertrand, would later play a significant role in making sure that Bertrand's Enigma secret ended up in Britain without the Germans discovering. But that was later. In 1931, even he was powerless to help. All he could do was to send the copy photographs to London and then relay back to Bertrand the British cryptographers' verdict. They agreed with their French counterparts that Schmidt's documents would not enable them to crack the Enigma.

Bertrand's response was to ask the head of the Deuxième Bureau if he could show the documents to his opposite number in Poland who, long before Bertrand had met up with Hans Thilo Schmidt, had mentioned the Poles' inability to read the impenetrable code being used by the German Army. When the answer came back in the affirmative, Bertrand booked his ticket to Warsaw.

2

The Leak

Poland, Belgium and Germany

1929–38

Two years before Bertrand went to Warsaw with his Enigma manuals, the Polish Army's Cipher Bureau had found itself caught up in its own drama relating to an Enigma cipher machine. On the last Saturday in January 1929 an alert customs officer working in Warsaw had been about to process a heavy box when his suspicions were aroused by a request from the Germany Embassy. Apparently the box had been sent to Poland by mistake and a German Embassy official was requesting that it should be returned to Germany immediately. When the box was opened, an Enigma machine was found inside.

The Polish General Staff's Cipher Bureau quickly called in two engineers to examine it. They were Ludomir Danilewicz and Antoni Palluth, two of the proprietors of the AVA corporation, a Warsaw-based communications company which had established close links with the Cipher Bureau. The examination of what turned out to be a commercial Enigma cipher machine went on throughout Saturday night and Sunday, the two men only returning to their homes on the following Monday. By that time the Enigma had been packed up again and was on its way back to the German company in Germany. As far as is known no one there ever suspected that it had been opened.[1]

There is no official record available for public scrutiny which confirms that the examination of the Enigma in the customs warehouse heightened the Polish Secret Service's interest in the cipher machines being used by the German armed forces at the end of the 1920s and the beginning of the 1930s. But a private account written by Leonard Danilewicz, another AVA partner, suggests that the findings made by his brother Ludomir and Antoni Palluth did indeed lead to an attempt being made to read some Army Enigma messages.[2]

According to Leonard Danilewicz, the attempt to decipher the messages was carried out using strips of white celluloid marked with squares in which the letters of the alphabet were inscribed. Using these strips, it was possible to trace the path taken by the electric current as it passed through the wheels inside the Enigma machine. However this attempt to decipher the German Army's secret messages came to nothing, which was not surprising since, as the Poles discovered later, the Enigma wheels used by the armed forces included different internal wiring to that used inside the commercial Enigma wheels.

During the same month, January 1929, Lieutenant Maksymilian Ciężki, the 30-year-old head of the Cipher Bureau's German section, turned up at the Mathematics Institute at the University of Poznań, a town west of Warsaw, to set up a cryptology course. While he was at the university, he interviewed some of its cleverest students and invited twenty of them to attend a series of lectures on how to break codes.[3] The Enigma cipher was never mentioned, but Marian Rejewski, Henryk Zygalski and Jerzy Różycki, the three students who were eventually employed by the Cipher Bureau, later found out that both Ciężki and Palluth, who also taught on the course, had tried unsuccessfully to read some Enigma messages.[4]

By December 1931, when Bertrand turned up in Warsaw with his photographs of the Enigma manuals, the best of the cryptology course students were already working on simpler ciphers in a cellar in the basement of the Poznań army command post which had been commandeered by the Cipher Bureau. It was known as the 'Black Chamber', a rather pretentious nickname in the eyes of the students.[5] They were not told about Bertrand's December 1931 meetings with Major Gwido Langer, who was the 37-year-old head of the Cipher Bureau in Warsaw. In the course of the meetings Bertrand had handed over the photographs of the Enigma manuals to Langer. After a quick consultation with his codebreaking experts, Langer had told Bertrand that the manuals contained some very important information which would assist the Poles. The manuals revealed that the German Army had adapted the commercial Enigma machine which the Poles had already inspected. But the photographs furnished by Bertrand were not quite enough to enable the cryptographers to read the Enigma messages. Langer asked Bertrand whether his source might be able to procure a copy of the Enigma settings which were currently in use.[6]

Shortly after Bertrand's visit to Warsaw the setting instructions which Langer had requested were handed over to Bertrand at another meeting with Hans Thilo Schmidt in Belgium. The documents were quickly sent to Warsaw in a diplomatic bag and handed over to Langer. Further settings were handed over to the Poles in May and September 1932. But even then Bertrand received no confirmation from Poland that there was any prospect of the Polish cryptographers breaking the code. By the time Bertrand travelled to Warsaw again in September 1932, he was having to face up to a growing crisis which was brewing within his own country's intelligence service. For Bertrand and Lemoine were not the only secret agents meeting up with Hans Thilo Schmidt. After the first meetings they had been accompanied by André Perruche, who worked for the Service de Renseignements department of the Deuxième Bureau (the French equivalent of MI6). Unlike Bertrand, he was not solely interested in ciphers. He had to look at the wider picture encompassing all Franco-German relations.

Perruche believed that Schmidt's information about Germany's rearmament plans was far more important than the cipher documentation which might or might not lead to the reading of some Enigma messages. The rearmament intelligence could usually be sent in a normal letter as long as it was written in invisible ink, and it could be sent without Schmidt having to cross international frontiers with incriminating documents in his briefcase. In other words the intelligence could be acquired more safely than the ciphering documents. Although Schmidt had been given a camera so that he could photograph documents himself, that did not avoid the risk that he would be caught crossing the German border with the photographs. By May 1932 Perruche had already received a number of such letters from Schmidt. Most of the information came from Schmidt's brother Rudolf, whose high-flying Army career made him an insider.[7]

In May 1932 Perruche asked Louis Rivet, the deputy chief of the Deuxième Bureau's SR-SRL intelligence service, the umbrella organisation which was responsible for both Perruche's and Bertrand's sections, as well as counterespionage, to stop Schmidt travelling abroad so frequently. Notwithstanding Bertrand's objections, Rivet agreed with Perruche, and arrangements were made for Lemoine to set up a safe way of communicating with Schmidt in Berlin. Henceforth it was to be used whenever possible.[8]

This put-down concentrated Bertrand's mind wonderfully. He had to try to bring the Enigma project to a head once and for all. His first attempt to move things along took place in Warsaw in September 1932. As he handed over a third list of Enigma settings, he explained that he was more than a little worried that no progress had been made. But Langer merely asked him to be patient a little longer and promised that Bertrand would be the first to find out when they managed to construct an Enigma machine, which had to be done before the Enigma messages could be read.[9] So Bertrand left Warsaw once more with nothing to show for his trip.

Bertrand's second gambit was made at the end of October 1932 during his next meeting with Hans Thilo Schmidt. The meeting was held at the Hotel d'Angleterre in Liège in Belgium. In the course of the meeting Bertrand asked Schmidt whether the Enigma documents which he was handing over were definitely for the up-to-date Enigma model. It was the first time that he had raised the question whether Schmidt was being paid for nothing. Schmidt countered that he was not a crook, and a serious argument was only averted thanks to Lemoine, who did not translate into German Bertrand's most cutting comments. In an effort to calm everyone down Perruche suggested that Bertrand and he should go out of the room. Lemoine was left behind to restore the peace with Schmidt. Fortunately, some soothing words, coupled with the 5000 marks retainer which Lemoine proceeded to hand over, appeared to have the desired effect.[10]

But the money which Lemoine handed over so liberally ended up by creating another problem for the Deuxième Bureau. Hans Thilo Schmidt had used it to improve his lifestyle dramatically, and his French spymasters were concerned that this could lead someone to ask questions about where the money had come from. When he turned up to their meetings, he now wore elegant flannel suits and smart shirts and ties rather than the shabby attire in which he had originally presented himself. His family had also noticed a difference. He began to take his wife, Charlotte, away on expensive holidays. During the summer of 1932, they left their son and daughter at a children's home run by a Jewish couple, who had not yet been affected by the Holocaust that was brewing in Germany, while Schmidt and Charlotte spent six weeks travelling around Czechoslovakia. Their holiday included a trip to the mountain resort of Spindermühle, now known as Spindleruv Mlyn, a place which Schmidt later nominated for one of his meetings with the French secret agents.

Other rendezvous locations were identified by Schmidt, as he and his wife went on sightseeing tours around Europe. They particularly liked going on skiing trips to Switzerland, where they could use the brand new wooden skis purchased by Schmidt at great expense. If anyone had been observing Schmidt closely, they would have reported that, on the one hand, he and his wife appeared to have made, or inherited, a lot of money and were using it to bankroll a second very lavish extended honeymoon and, on the other hand, he was still visiting the nightspots in Berlin by himself as if he was a carefree bachelor. Lemoine eventually advised him to settle down a little so that he would attract less attention.[11]

But settling down involved Schmidt spending more money. He decided to enlarge his house at Ketschendorf, and he also set up a small factory with just a handful of employees which could produce fat for local soap-producers. Unknown to his children, this was to be a front for all the money he was being paid by Lemoine. What they did notice was that he did not seem to spend much time working at the factory. If anything, Charlotte Schmidt spent more time there than her husband, which was of course partly explained by the fact that he had a regular job at the Cipher Office. It was Charlotte who had to drive the vanloads of fat to their best client. The fat was extracted from animal bones picked up from the local butcher each week by one of Schmidt's factory workers. Gisela and Hans-Thilo the younger also noticed that, unlike most businesses, their father's factory did not seek to make as much money as possible. Some of its practices would not have been out of place in a charity. For example, Hans Thilo Schmidt carried on paying his staff, even when he allowed them to take lengthy breaks from work.

Another device which covered up how Schmidt came to be earning so much money was set up with the assistance of Lemoine and Guy Schlesser, another agent who worked alongside Perruche in the Service de Renseignements section of the Deuxième Bureau. Schmidt had devised a new method of making soap, and under a bogus contract, he was to be paid a royalty in return for allowing his process to be used by a soap manufacturer based in France.[12]

Schmidt's children thought that his growing prosperity should have made him more relaxed. But instead his success appeared to have hardened his heart. He had always been an indulgent father when they were young. Then all of a sudden he began to become impatient and intolerant. Gisela never forgot an incident that typified his new frame of mind. She and her brother had been looking for some stationery on their father's desk. During their search she picked up a white envelope, inside which was another black cardboard envelope suitable for protecting photographs. When Schmidt discovered they had taken it, he became apoplectic with rage in a way they had never seen before. He made them swear that they would never interfere with what was on his desk again. At the time Gisela and her brother were terrified by the way their father had shouted at them. It was only later, after they found out about his dealings with the French, that they understood why he had been so angry.

The envelope incident was not the only occasion when traces of Schmidt's double life appear to have affected his behaviour at home. He and Charlotte would talk together in French – presumably to hide what they were talking about from their son and daughter. But when Gisela asked for some help with her French homework both parents denied being able to speak or read any French. It was as if they did not want anyone else to know. Another inexplicable mystery was the way Hans Thilo and Charlotte Schmidt refused to tell their children where they had been on holiday. On one occasion they came back from a holiday saying that they had been to Denmark. But they had brought back the skeleton of a sea horse which the children felt must have come from another country. Gisela risked her father's wrath by looking through his desk drawers again, and found a card from a hotel in Algeria. After another trip to Switzerland, her parents claimed that all the snapshots they had taken had been stolen. So there was nothing to show where they had been.

But one aspect of Schmidt's life never changed. In spite of his attempt to be a better husband, he could never quite manage to be absolutely faithful to his wife. His house became a domestic version of a knocking shop. On the one hand there was the father carrying on as before. On the other hand there was his twelve-year-old son who, encouraged by his father, also began to have affairs with the servants. Once that occurred, Gisela could no longer discuss what was going on with her brother. It was something which the men in the family were allowed to do, but which was certainly not permissible for any of the women. Gisela had to be content with having chats with her father about who she was going to marry. He took on board the fact that she was not interested in men who were in the Army, and encouraged her to marry an upstanding professional man such as a doctor. He assured her that he had enough money to set a doctor up in a good practice, if she ever found the right man. The advice he gave his son was of a much more earthy nature. Schmidt told Hans-Thilo the younger which nightclubs to visit if he wanted to pick up women. But he advised him to watch out for the beautiful transvestites who often frequented the places he was recommending.

Hans-Thilo the younger was blond, and his father was keen that he should be forewarned so that he could repulse any homosexual advances.

It is not clear whether Schmidt intended to use his children in order to pass himself off as a good Nazi. As far as Gisela can remember, he never positively told his son to join the Hitler Youth. Her father never talked about politics at home at all. It was just that it seemed the obvious thing for Hans-Thilo the younger to do if he wanted to please his father. Hans Thilo the older acted as if he was a committed member of the Nazi party. This was more important than ever after January 1933 when Hitler finally took over the reins of power in Germany. Schmidt's highly placed contacts at the Cipher Office had warned him that the Nazis intended to set up a new organisation, the Air Ministry's Forschungsamt (Research Office), which would be permitted to tap the phones of anyone who was acting strangely. 'Never talk about politics, even in private,' Schmidt would advise his children. 'Someone is always listening.'

After the Nazis came to power, the Deuxième Bureau once more attempted to reduce the risks which Schmidt was taking on its behalf. In 1936 Perruche and Guy Schlesser, who for a time took over as Schmidt's principal Deuxième Bureau contact, insisted that Schmidt should not meet French secret agents outside Germany except in an emergency. This effectively meant that Bertrand's regular supply of Enigma settings would have to be sacrificed so that Schmidt was free to concentrate on the German Army's movements and invasion plans.[13]

On 1 October 1936 Rudolf Schmidt became a general. Thanks to Rudolf's quick promotion and his willingness to talk to his brother about his job, Hans Thilo Schmidt was able to reveal how quickly the Germans were rearming themselves, how they were adopting new tactics involving the use of armoured divisions to blast their way through their enemies' defences and, most important of all, when they were about to invade another country. In January 1936, for example, Schmidt was able to warn the French about Hitler's plans to invade the Rhineland, which duly occurred two months later.[14]

But ironically, it was the Deuxième Bureau's concern for Schmidt's safety and the emergency procedure set up by Perruche and Schlesser to enable him to communicate with his French spymasters without leaving Berlin which was to lead to quite the opposite result to that intended. Schmidt was told that if he needed to contact the French quickly, he should telephone Georges Blun, a French journalist based in Berlin. If Schmidt slipped into the conversation the words 'Uncle Kurt has died', Blun would know that Schmidt needed to see him immediately. Both men would then go to the waiting room in the Charlottenburg railway station in Berlin.

At 8 a.m. on 6 November 1937 Blun received the pre-arranged signal and hurried to the agreed meeting place. By 11 a.m. the document which Schmidt had handed to Blun was being put into the hands of the French Ambassador, André François-Poncet. It was only then that the procedure which had been so carefully worked out broke down.[15] The document was Schmidt's account of a secret meeting between Hitler and some of his highest ranking generals and admirals which had taken place the day before. According to Schmidt, Hitler had decided to expand Germany at its neighbours' expense. He was prepared to use force if necessary. Austria and Czechoslovakia were to be his first targets.

François-Poncet should have sent Schmidt's report to Paris in a diplomatic bag. He had already been warned, thanks to intelligence provided by Schmidt, that the Germans had in the past been able to penetrate the diplomatic cipher which the French Ambassador was using to communicate with his political masters in Paris. The cipher had been altered since then, but it should have been obvious that the Germans would try to break it again, which they duly did. So the telegram which François-Poncet sent was intercepted by the Air Ministry's Forschungsamt and read. Perruche, Lemoine and Bertrand were only to find this out when they met up with Schmidt in Switzerland eleven days later. Their meeting was a stormy affair. Schmidt was furious that François-Poncet had referred to the Hitler meeting in a vulnerable telegram. Fortunately, his contacts in the Forschungsamt had told him that it had been intercepted before he had passed on the extra details of the meeting given to him by his brother. He was prepared to hand this document over to the French agents, but he wanted their assurance that none of his information would ever be sent to France via the French Ambassador again.

The document which he proceeded to hand over could not have been clearer. For it consisted of a map of Europe with dates written on each country indicating when it was scheduled to fall under the control of Nazi Germany: Austria in spring 1938, Czechoslovakia in autumn 1938, Poland in the autumn 1939. . . . Once again Rudolf Schmidt was Hans Thilo's source. Rudolf had been told what had been discussed by Colonel Hossbach who was writing up the minutes of the meeting. Rudolf, who was shocked by Hitler's plans, had then discussed the details with his brother.

The one aspect of the affair which may never be explained, now that François-Poncet is dead, is why the French Ambassador sent the telegram which he did send. According to the book *Notre Espion Chez Hitler* by Paul Paillole – who worked alongside Schlesser in the Deuxième Bureau – the document Schmidt gave the Ambassador was so shocking that François-Poncet decided he should tip off Paris immediately about what had taken place the day before. The account given in Paillole's book however does not explain why François-Poncet's telegram to the French Minister of Foreign Affairs on 6 November 1937 was so vague. It stated:

> Yesterday afternoon an important meeting took place in the Reich's Chancellery which was attended by a large number of generals and admirals . . . [including] General Goering.
>
> The newspapers have not reported it and it is difficult to know what this long meeting was about. I have been told that it was about raw materials and the difficulties which the shortage of iron and steel impose on rearmament . . . But it would be astonishing if that was all that was being talked about when so many high-ranking officers were summoned to the Chancellery.[16]

At first sight the telegram did not appear to serve any purpose. One might have expected François-Poncet either to have spelt out the details of the meeting being described, so that the French government could have done something about it quickly, or he should not have sent any telegram at all, in case it compromised the security of France's most important secret agent. But Paillole's book does quote the minutes of a meeting which was convened on 9 December 1937 by Admiral Wilhelm Canaris, the head of the German Abwehr (the German Army's Secret Service), to look into the leak. The minutes described what at least one general believed had happened: 'General Beck believes that François-Poncet knows his diplomatic code has been cracked. The last sentence of his cable suggests that he knows more than he is saying and that he will send his full report by courier.'[17]

A photograph of the full minutes of the 9 December 1937 meeting in Canaris's office was handed to Schlesser when he met Schmidt in Bern, Switzerland in January 1938.[18] Schmidt told Schlesser that his position as the liaison man between the Cipher Office and the Forschungsamt enabled him to monitor how the investigation into his own leak was progressing. But for Schlesser, who could read between the lines of the superficially helpless comments made by the people reporting back to the head of the German Secret Service, the minutes of the meeting must have made chilling reading. The Canaris report stated that 'On the day after the [5 November] meeting François-Poncet correctly reported what had been discussed . . . Everyone present [at the Canaris meeting] was asked if they had any idea who was responsible for the indiscretion. No one had any idea . . . Canaris reminded everyone that the main object of the meeting was to find out at any cost who passed the information to François-Poncet.'

After this French slip-up, new procedures were laid down governing how Deuxième Bureau agents could keep in touch with Schmidt.[19] No French agent was allowed to meet Schmidt in Germany. He was to use a new kind of invisible ink when writing to his spymasters, and all his letters were to be sent to new addresses, one of which was in Geneva. Most important of all, as far as Bertrand was concerned, Schmidt was to be encouraged to leave his position at the Cipher Office so that he could move to the Forschungsamt. He would then be able to see what happened as the investigation into the 6 November 1937 leak progressed. But in spite of all of these precautions Schlesser must have realised, as he read through the material handed over to him and passed them on to his colleagues in Paris, that the documents which their super-agent could supply to them in future – and the days of his life – might soon be numbered.

3

An Inspired Guess

Poland

1932

By 1938 most of the Deuxième Bureau staff who knew about Hans Thilo Schmidt had come to the conclusion that his documents would never lead to the breaking of the Enigma code. So that same year, as a last resort, a plan was devised in Paris which it was hoped might resolve the Enigma problem once and for all. The plan envisaged French agents, with contacts inside the Abwehr, letting it be known that Enigma messages were being read. The idea was that such a move would force the Germans to use a new cipher, which might be easier to break.[1]

It is not absolutely clear whether this plan was ever approved in the higher echelons of the Deuxième Bureau. Perhaps the French Secret Service bosses merely considered it a legitimate ruse which could be used against the Poles, rather than the Germans, in order to force the Polish Cipher Bureau to reveal whether they were near to breaking into the Enigma code.[2] Whatever the motive behind the formulation of the plan, it must have horrified Langer when it was put to him during 1938. He persuaded Bertrand not to put it into operation in the short term, on the grounds that the Poles would soon be in a position to report to the French and the British on how their research into Enigma was going. But what Langer failed to do was to admit that he had broken his promise to keep Bertrand informed if Enigma was ever broken. The Polish cryptographers had, in fact, not only broken into Enigma, but had been reading it for more than five years!

The break into Enigma had been achieved in an atmosphere of growing tension and extreme secrecy. The Polish codebreakers' families may have known that their husbands and sons were working for the government, but none of them heard anything about the groundbreaking work relating to Enigma. When Antoni Palluth, one of the Poznań cryptology lecturers, slipped his revolver into his pocket each month and went off to Nazi Germany on another secret mission, it would have been hard for him to tell his wife Jadwiga that he was going on a normal business trip. So when she waved goodbye to him, she always did so with great emotion, as if it were for the last time. Given his expertise in radio, it did not take her long to guess that he was liaising with Polish agents who needed to have radio equipment to communicate with their spymasters in Warsaw.

Back in Warsaw, Palluth did not attempt to conceal the fact that he was helping the Polish Secret Service. He would work a normal day at his AVA radio company, before speeding away in the General Staff's black limousine for another evening of top secret moonlighting. Hours later he would return to his Warsaw flat, escorted by a soldier. Palluth would often be carrying a briefcase handcuffed to his wrist. He was then expected to work on the German coded messages in the briefcase until the early hours of the morning. Sometimes he was forced to ask his wife to guide him up to their bedroom after he had literally been blinded through overwork. In the morning the soldier always returned to pick up the documents before it was time for Palluth to go to his AVA office once again.

But Palluth, for all his expertise at cracking some of Germany's simpler codes, had no success when it came to Enigma. The Enigma problem was eventually handed down to three of the mathematics students from Poznań University who had once been Palluth's pupils. Jerzy Różycki, the youngest of the trio, was not even twenty when Palluth's cryptology course was set up. He was an extrovert who appears to have found it hard to observe the secrecy rule imposed on him when he was signed up by the Cipher Bureau. When he went home, he would kiss his mother and say, 'My beautiful mother, it's so sad that you'll never be able to be proud of me.' She wondered whether he was referring to the time when she had caught him as a precocious four-year-old, surreptitiously helping his older brother with his mathematics from under the table. Then, she had said to him, after she had finished scolding him, 'One day you'll be a great man, and I'll be very proud of you.' His wistful comments, now he was grown up, led her to believe he was concerned that he was not able to live up to her high expectations.

It is interesting to note that whatever security vetting was carried out by the Polish Cipher Bureau, it was not put off Różycki because of his dissolute family background. Bebenek Różycki, Jerzy's father, was a heavy drinker, a gambler and a womaniser, attributes which were less frowned upon in the Ukraine, where his family had once been aristocratic landowners, than in Poland. Perhaps the vetting committee was swayed by one of Różycki *père*'s good points. He was exceptionally lucky, which led his Polish friends to say of him, 'Bebenek could jump into the water stark naked, and still come up wearing a tuxedo.'

Marian Rejewski and Henryk Zygalski, the other two mathematicians who had been asked to work on Enigma, were very different. They were solid, down-to-earth characters, born in the west of Poland, an area once under Prussian rule. History does not relate why it was that out of the three mathematicians Maksymilian Ciężski selected Rejewski to make the first mathematical assault on the elusive Enigma cipher. Perhaps it was because Rejewski was the oldest of the trio – he was twenty-three in 1929 when he attended his first lectures on the Cipher Bureau's cryptology course – or perhaps it was because he had received better reports from his university professors. Or perhaps it was because everyone agreed with Marian's father, a cigar merchant, who told everyone that his son was a genius, and that Marian was clever enough to break through the barriers which, under Prussian rule, had prevented Polish people taking up the most prestigious positions in the law and the civil service.

After the last of the three mathematicians had completed his studies at Poznań University, all three moved to Warsaw in the autumn of 1932 so that they could work part time for the Cipher Office. It was then that Ciężki sought out Rejewski and asked him if he would mind putting in a few extra hours in the afternoons. When Rejewski agreed, Ciężki told him that he must not tell his two colleagues and proceeded to give him some of the information which he had collected about Enigma.[3] Much of it had been taken from the Enigma manuals which Hans Thilo Schmidt had given to Bertrand in 1931.[4]

These manuals[5] made it clear that an Enigma was used to scramble the letters making up the words in a message before it was sent out in morse code by a radio transmitter. So, for example, if a German wanted to send a message saying 'Hitler ist in Wilhelmshaven', the Enigma operator would tap the H key on his keyboard and write down on his notepad which bulb on the Enigma's lightboard lit up. And so on for each letter of the message. Schmidt's manuals also explained how an Enigma machine produced the cipher text. (See the simplified representation of the path taken by the electric current inside an Enigma machine in Diagram 1 on page 35.) Hitting a key on the Enigma keyboard released an electric current which ran to a series of scrambling elements – including a plugboard and three wheels. The scrambling elements diverted the current away from its original course. The current would then hit a 'reflector' end disk which would send the current back through the same scrambling elements again, though on a different course, and the current would finish up by lighting a bulb marked with one of the letters of the alphabet.

The scrambling elements were the most important parts inside an Enigma. The way they were set determined what cipher text was produced. The plugboard, one of the scrambling elements, looked like a telephone switchboard. The settings lists which Schmidt passed to the French Secret Service specified how all Enigma operators and receivers during a particular quarter should set the plugs connecting the plugboard sockets. These socket settings were referred to in the German manuals as the Steckerverbindungen.

The second scrambling element described in Schmidt's manuals was a series of three movable wheels, which could be rotated individually or together around a horizontal axle, like a series of bicycle wheels.[6] On the right face of each wheel, there were twenty-six pins, which served as current entry points, when the current was going from right to left through the wheels; on the left face of each wheel, there were twenty-six flat contact plates, which served as current exit points when the current was going from right to left. If the current, going from right to left, emerged at a contact plate on the left face of, say, the wheel placed inside the Enigma on the right, it flowed into the pin sticking out from the right face of the middle wheel, which was touching the contact plate in question, and then carried on flowing through the middle and left wheels. When, on the other hand, the current flowed from left to right through the wheels, the function served by the pins and contact plates was reversed; the contact plates became the entry points into the wheels, and the pins became the exit points. Inside each wheel there were twenty-six wires which connected the twenty-six electric current entry points on the right face of each wheel with the twenty-six exit points on the left face of each wheel. A typical internal wire would connect up an entry point on the right face of the wheel, say the one labelled J, with an exit point labelled with a different letter, such as X. So if ever the current went in at J on the right face, it was diverted to come out of the left face at X. If this diversion occurred inside the wheel

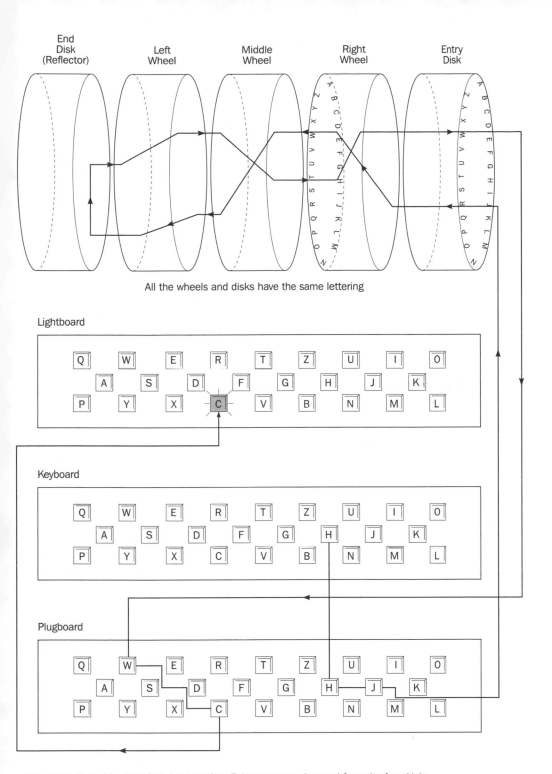

End Disk (Reflector)   Left Wheel   Middle Wheel   Right Wheel   Entry Disk

All the wheels and disks have the same lettering

Lightboard

Keyboard

Plugboard

Note. Wheels in this simplified drawing of an Enigma are as observed from the front/right.

The H keyboard key is tapped and the current goes to H in the plugboard then to J in the plugboard, then to J in the entry disk's right and left faces. Then after going through the wheels, it is reflected back to W on the entry disk. It then goes to W in the plugboard, then to C in the plugboard, then to C in the lightboard.

placed on the right side of the Enigma, and if the middle wheel was lined up with the right wheel, so that X on the left face of the right wheel was lined up with X on the right face of the middle wheel, the current would enter the middle wheel via the X pin, and then would be diverted again, as it passed through the wire inside the middle wheel connecting the X pin on the middle wheel's right face with the relevant contact plate on its left face. The same would happen inside the wheel placed on the left, and then the current would go into the reflecting end disk which was referred to in German as the umkehrwalze (the reflecting wheel). Each current entry point on the end disk's right face was connected to a different current exit point on the end disk's right face. So that if, for example, the current went into the end disk at L, it would bounce back out of its right face at, say, G, and it would then go back through the three wheels, going from left to right, being diverted again as it went through each wheel.

The wheel on the right turned anti-clockwise one twenty-sixth of a revolution each time a keyboard key was pressed. This meant that if an Enigma operator pressed the H key on the keyboard twice consecutively, the current would go into the right wheel's right face at a different point on each occasion, it would follow a different pathway through the wheels, and it would usually light up a different letter. Any one of the three wheels could be placed on the right, middle or left. The wheel order to be used by all Enigma operators, which might be, say, wheel 1 on the right, wheel 3 in the middle, and wheel 2 on the left, was, like the plugboard socket connections, specified in the settings lists provided by Schmidt.

Another element regulated by these settings lists was the ring, marked with the twenty-six letters of the alphabet, which was around the rim of each wheel. The ring could be rotated relative to the inner core of the wheel, and then fixed into position with a catch. The settings at which the rings were fixed were referred to as the Ringstellung by the Germans. If the ring setting on a wheel was, say, A, the ring had to be rotated manually until the A on the ring was opposite the Ringstellung marker, which was a red dot on the catch on some Enigma machines. The letters around the ring – visible through a window above the wheel once the wheel was in its working position inside the Enigma machine – were used by message senders to describe the position of the wheel to message receivers.

The rings also had another function. A notch on each ring ensured that the wheel placed on its left turned one twenty-sixth of a revolution whenever the ring reached a particular position in its cycle.

This position was different for each of the three wheels. So, for example, when wheel 1 was placed on the right, the ring on wheel 1 ensured that the middle wheel turned one twenty-sixth of a revolution anti-clockwise if Q was showing through the window above the right wheel when a keyboard key was tapped. The middle wheel was turned as the right wheel turned so that R rather than Q was showing through the window above the right wheel. (The 'turnover positions' for wheels 2 and 3 were at E and V respectively.) The middle wheel would then remain in the position to which it had turned until the keyboard keys were tapped twenty-five more times, by which time the right wheel would have rotated one complete revolution. At this point Q would once again be showing through the window above the right wheel, and the ring around the right wheel would then ensure that the middle wheel turned another one twenty-sixth of a revolution when the next keyboard key was tapped. Following the same principle, the left wheel would be turned one twenty-sixth of a revolution each time the middle wheel passed its 'turnover position'. After the three wheels were set to a particular position, they would only return to their original position after the keyboard keys had been tapped about 17,000 times.[7]

Rejewski knew that if he was to break the code, he would first have to construct a replica Enigma machine. To do this he worked out a formula which, he hoped, would enable him to discover the wiring inside the wheel which was placed on the right.[8] However, the formula could not be solved unless Rejewski could somehow get his hands on the settings which the Germans had used. It was only at this point that Ciężki gave Rejewski the settings for September and October 1932 which had been supplied by Hans Thilo Schmidt in August 1932.[9] Rejewski believed that these settings would enable him to reconstruct the wiring inside two of the three Enigma wheels. One of these wheels was on the right during September 1932, and the second wheel was on the right during October 1932, according to the settings lists he had been given. But he quickly discovered that the formula was still not giving him the correct answer. He only worked out what he was doing wrong when it suddenly dawned on him that there was one solution to the problem which he had not tried.[10]

When interpreting the algebraic symbols in his formula he had always assumed that the wires inside the stationary entry disk – shown in Diagram 1 – diverted the electric current in the same way as the current was diverted by the entry disk inside the commercial

Enigma machine. The connections in the commercial Enigma were:

Point where current goes into right face of entry disk
Q W E R T Z U I O A S D F G H J K P Y X C V B N M L
Point where current comes out of left face of entry disk
A B C D E F G H I J K L M N O P Q R S T U V W X Y Z

so that if the current went into the right face of the entry disk at 'Q', it came out of the left face at 'A'; if it went into the right face at 'W', it came out of the left face at 'B', and so on.

Rejewski decided to alter his assumption, and guessed that no diversion took place inside the entry disk. In other words, he guessed that the connections were as follows:

Point where current goes into right face of entry disk
A B C D E F G H I J K L M N O P Q R S T U V W X Y Z
Point where current comes out of left face of entry disk
A B C D E F G H I J K L M N O P Q R S T U V W X Y Z

When he tried out this new assumption on paper, it was as if a miracle had occurred and, as he later put it, 'From my pencil, as by magic, began to issue numbers designating the connections' in the right-hand wheel.[11] One of the secrets of the Enigma machine had been cracked open at last.

Once Rejewski had discovered the wiring inside two wheels, he was able to work out the wiring inside the third wheel and the end disk. He received unexpected help in making these mathematical calculations when he discovered that the Germans had inserted an example in the Enigma manuals furnished by Hans Thilo Schmidt which gave a sample message in German and its equivalent cipher text, using given settings.[12]

4

A Terrible Mistake

Poland

1933–9

After Rejewski had worked out the wiring inside the Enigma wheels and disks, orders were given to Antoni Palluth and his partners at AVA to make some replica Enigmas. Because this had to be kept secret, a substantial part of the manufacturing process was carried out in a special workshop which was set up inside the General Staff buildings in Warsaw. Only the stages which required the operation of noisy machinery were dealt with on AVA's premises. The work at AVA was done after normal office hours when everyone except the four AVA partners and a trusted assistant had gone home.[1]

One reason why a replica Enigma could be built quickly was that Palluth and Ludomir Danilewicz, the two engineers who had been called in to examine the intercepted German cipher machine in 1929, had already constructed an Enigma prototype. Working with the other partners at AVA, they had secretly assembled the prototype before the end of 1930; it was based on a cipher machine they had designed for the Poles to use themselves. Of the first thirty Polish cipher machines manufactured, five were set aside so that they could be transformed into Enigma replicas, complete with rotating rotors. The rotors did not of course have the same wiring as the German Army cipher machine, which was not known until Rejewski worked it out, but it contained all the elements which could be used once the German Army rotors' wiring was discovered. The creation of the prototype took around six months; that must have been the approximate amount of time that was saved when the AVA partners were commissioned to reconstruct the German Army Enigma in 1932–3.

As soon as the replicas were ready, Rejewski, together with Różycki and Zygalski, who were called in to help him at this point, attempted to read some German Enigma messages. Here again they were to be helped in their task by the Germans. When designing the procedure which was to be adopted by Enigma operators in the Army, the German code experts had decided that the 'message setting' – the wheels' position when the first letter in the message was enciphered – should be enciphered twice consecutively, and then sent at the beginning of each message. This turned out to be a terrible mistake. Anyone who knows anything about codebreaking knows that you do not repeat anything in a coded message unless you absolutely have to. If you do, there is a risk that the enemy listening in might spot patterns which could allow the code to be broken.

The German sending procedure was as follows. I have assumed that both the message sender and receiver have already set up their Enigma machines in accordance with the settings list, so that the correct wheels are in their Enigmas, the correct plugboard connections have been made etc. The message sender decided what message setting to use. It might be, say, RCM. He would then turn his Enigma wheels to a so called 'initial position' (Grundstellung) which might be, say, ABC, which was specified in the settings list for the day in question, and he would tap the RCM keyboard keys representing the chosen message setting twice. This would cause two enciphered versions of RCM to be lit up, which might be, say, WQR GLT. These six letters were referred to as the 'indicator', since they were used to indicate to the receiver what the message setting was. The sender would then turn his wheels to the message setting, RCM, and would encipher his message before sending the result in morse code.

When the message receiver wanted to read what he had been sent, he first had to find out what was the message setting. To do this, he turned his wheels to the prescribed initial position, in this case ABC, and then he had to tap out the indicator, WQR GLT, on his Enigma keyboard. This would result in the letters RCM RCM being lit up, which was the sender's message setting. One useful characteristic of the Enigma machine was that if a receiver set up his machine in exactly the same way as the sender, he could simply type out the cipher text he had received – in this case WQR GLT – and the letters representing the plain text which had been sent to him would be lit up – in this case RCM RCM. The receiver then turned his wheels to RCM, and deciphered the message by tapping out the cipher text on the Enigma keyboard and writing down the letters which lit up.

It was the instruction to encipher the message setting twice which was to be Enigma's Achilles heel throughout the 1930s, and during the first nine months of the war. Time and again it enabled Rejewski and his colleagues Zygalski and Różycki to find new patterns in the cipher text which had been intercepted. The patterns enabled them to break the code. For the patterns they discovered were like finger-prints. The fingerprints could only be produced if the Enigma machines were set up in a particular way. All the codebreakers had to do was to produce a list of all possible fingerprints, together with the wheel positions which could produce each one, and the Enigma could be broken in a matter of minutes. That was the basic idea behind the 'characteristic' method of breaking Enigma which is sum-marised in Appendix 1(1). The patterns produced by the enciphering of the message setting also helped the Polish codebreakers to work out new methods of breaking the code each time the Germans altered their operating procedure or the Enigma machine itself.

A crucial change in the Enigma enciphering procedure was put into operation on 15 September 1938, in the middle of Hitler's bid to annex Sudetenland from Czechoslovakia.[2] Prior to then, the pre-liminary indicating procedure, mentioned above, had required all German message senders to set their Enigmas to a prescribed initial position before they indicated the message setting they wanted to use for their main message by tapping out their chosen message set-ting twice. From this point on senders had to choose their own initial position, and they sent it to the receiver unenciphered before sending the twice enciphered message setting. That wiped out the 'characteristic' method of breaking Enigma mentioned in Part 1 of Appendix 1, which relied on all message settings used on a particular day being enciphered at the same initial position. But within weeks of the change in the procedure, two new tools, the bomby, described in Part 2 of Appendix 1, and the perforated sheets, were invented which, sooner or later, were to help the codebreakers to read most Enigma messages.[3] Both of these tools would not have worked had it not been for the German practice of enciphering their message set-tings twice.

After the war even Rejewski could not remember how the bomba – 'bomba' being the singular version of 'bomby' – basically a series of Enigmas wired together, came to be so named. One theory was that the bomba was named after the ice cream, bombe glacée, which was being eaten when the machine was invented. Another theory was that the machines dropped weights, just as aircraft drop bombs, when the correct wheel position was identified.[4] Six bomby, one for each of the six possible wheel orders, were quickly manufactured by AVA and were breaking Enigma messages as early as November 1938 according to Rejewski.[5] Once the bomby were up and running, it usually took less than two hours to discover the wheel order on the day in question.[6] By this time speed had become an important factor. When Rejewski first worked out the Enigma wiring, the wheel order lasted for three months before it was changed. In 1936 there was a new wheel order each month and subsequently during the same year the wheel order was changed daily.[7] However the bomby's shelf-life was limited. They only worked if there were a substantial number of plugboard sockets which were not connected to other sockets. This was the case in the autumn of 1938 when only ten to sixteen sockets were connected to other sockets, but it was clear that the Germans only had to instruct their Enigma operators to connect up more of the plugboard sockets, and the bomby would become redundant in their turn.[8]

The second tool, the perforated sheets, which were designed by Zygalski, took much longer to manufacture, but they were destined to be useful for a longer period than the bomby. These low-tech sheets exploited the fact that each day the codebreakers were finding a limited number of indicators – the six-letter groups of cipher produced by the message sender tapping out his message setting twice – with special characteristics. These indicators had either their first and fourth letters, or their second and fifth letters, or their third and sixth letters in common. They came to be referred to as females.[9] The significant point about the females was they could not be produced by German message senders, when they were enciphering their message settings at a substantial number of initial settings. So each time a female indicator was spotted, the codebreakers were able to rule out all of these 'impossible' initial settings. On average around 40 per cent of the total initial settings that could be produced with the wheels at the message senders' disposal could be ruled out for each female indicator spotted.[10] This ruling out did not just happen when the first female indicator was spotted on a particular day. When the second female indicator was spotted on the day in question, the codebreakers would expect that around forty per cent of the remaining initial settings would be ruled out. And so on, until only a few initial settings remained to be tested manually.

The perforated sheets were merely the means whereby the above principle was put into practice. The sheets were large pieces of card which acted as a catalogue. If at a particular initial setting, a female indicator was possible, a hole was punched in the appropriate card in the appropriate place. If no female was possible, no hole was punched. The sheets which were 'perforated' in this way were made up in advance of any codebreaking attempt. Once a complete set was available, the relevant cards relating to a particular day's female indicators were stacked on top of each other on a table with a light shining through its transparent top. There was a separate sheet for each female. Any places where the light shone through all the cards represented the Enigma wheel positions, ring settings and wheel orders which could have produced all of that day's female indicators. These – relatively few – positions could not be ruled out and had to be tested manually to check which was the correct combination. There was one correct combination for each Enigma network. This was specified in the settings list for the day in question.[11]

The method was all the more impressive because the catalogue incorporated in the perforated sheets did not have to include a separate entry for each combination of plugboard socket connections. There were around 8 trillion possible plugboard connection combinations if the Germans chose to connect up all the sockets![12] If the catalogue had had to include perforations for each of these, the perforated sheets would have taken too long to make up. However the beauty of the test which was applied in order to see if a female indicator could be produced with the Enigma wheels set to a particular initial setting was that the same result was achieved whether or not any plugboard sockets were connected. In other words, if a female indicator could be produced with the wheels and rings in a particular position when no plugboard sockets were connected to other sockets, a female could also be produced when the wheels and rings were in the same position even if some or all of the sockets were interconnected; only the letters of the female indicator produced would be different, i.e. if the plugboard socket W was connected to, say, the D socket, the indicator might be, say, DAH DIK rather than WAH WIK, the indicator when no sockets were interconnected. The fact that the letters in the two indicators were different was irrelevant given that the test was merely aiming to discover whether a female indicator comprising any letters could be produced with the wheels at a particular position. So the Polish codebreakers were able to ignore the plugboard when preparing their sheets.

Nevertheless, the task of making up a complete set of perforated sheets was an enormous one. Around 150,000 perforations had to be cut using razor blades.[13] It was here that Rejewski and his team encountered their first insuperable obstacle. They did not have the manpower or the machinery to manufacture the sheets quickly. By 15 December 1938 they had only completed the sheets for two of the six possible wheel orders. On that day their task which was already proving difficult became unachievable after the Germans started to select the wheels to be placed in Enigma machines from the three wheels used throughout the 1930's as well as from two additional wheels made available to all operators.[14] From that moment the Enigma settings lists could specify that any three of the five available Enigma wheels should be used in the machine on any particular day. The provision of the new wheels increased the number of possible wheel orders from six to sixty, a massive ten times increase. This in its turn multiplied by ten the number of perforated sheets which the Polish codebreakers would have had to produce if they were to use the sheets to read Enigma messages. That was clearly impossible in the short term, given the resources made available to the Polish code-breakers.

Another change in the Enigma operating procedure was introduced at the beginning of 1939.[15] The Germans decided that more sockets on the plugboard should be connected: fourteen to twenty now had to be connected.[16] This drastically cut back the effectiveness of the bomby which could only work out Enigma settings from indicators produced without the electric current being diverted inside the Enigma plugboard. Although the connections inside the two new wheels were quickly worked out, by the beginning of 1939, the Enigma messages sent by the German armed forces were only being read on the rare occasions when just the three original wheels were in use. This was partly because there was no time to produce the extra perforated sheets and partly because there was no time to adjust the bomby to allow for the new wheels.[17]

It was presumably this gradual whittling down of the effectiveness of the Polish codebreaking effort which led to the next act in this long saga. Following an unproductive meeting in Paris of the French, Polish and British codebreakers in January 1939, the Polish General Staff finally gave Langer and Ciężki permission to reveal everything they knew about Enigma to the French and British. At the meeting held on 24–25 July 1939 at the Polish codebreakers' hideout in Pyry, just outside Warsaw, Dilly Knox, a senior British cryptographer, Alastair Denniston, acting head of Britain's Government Code and Cipher School, and the French cipher experts Gustave Bertrand and Henri Braquenié were told that the Poles had managed to break the

Enigma code after all. The British and the French were to be given a replica of an Enigma machine. The Enigma allocated for the British would be sent via France to London, along with instructions explaining how to produce the perforated sheets.

When Dilly Knox heard about the breakthrough, the first question he asked related to the connections inside the entry disk. He was mortified when he heard Rejewski's simple solution.[18] But he only gave vent to his frustration when he and Denniston were on their way back to their hotel in a taxi. He was furious with the Poles because they had deceived both him and his French colleagues. He was so angry that he forgot for a moment that one of their Polish hosts, who understood English, was also in the cab with them.[19]

After the meeting, Gustave Bertrand could not fail to notice the sceptical looks and remarks coming from his Deuxième Bureau colleagues in Paris, as they sought to belittle what he had brought back from Warsaw: two Enigma replicas, one of which was to be retained in Paris and the other to be taken by boat and train to London over the next few days. Guy Schlesser, one of the agents who ran Hans Thilo Schmidt, remarked pointedly to Bertrand, 'If I understand what has happened, they have palmed you off with an unusable machine so that we and the British can try to find a way of making it work.'[20] Bertrand did his best to stick up for the Poles in an attempt to preserve his own dignity, but underneath he must have been seething at the way he had been treated. It was bad enough that Langer and Ciężki had deceived him. But allowing Hans Thilo Schmidt to carry on needlessly putting his life at risk for all those years was indefensible; Schmidt had regularly supplied the French Deuxième Bureau with Enigma settings between 1933 and 1936. On at least six occasions since handing over the settings which had enabled Rejewski to work out the Enigma wiring, Schmidt had risked his life in order to hand over further sets of settings to the French.[21]

It was particularly galling now that Schmidt's safety was even more precarious than ever. In March 1938 Rodolphe Lemoine, the man who knew more about Schmidt than anyone, had been arrested by the Gestapo during a visit to Cologne.[22] Although he had been released, and a subsequent enquiry conducted by the Deuxième Bureau had ruled that he had not been turned by the Germans, he was told never to see Hans Thilo Schmidt again. The only fortunate aspect of the affair was that, thanks to the Poles' reticence, Lemoine had been caught before he found out that Enigma messages were being read. For the moment at least, both Schmidt, and the Enigma secret, were safe.

5

Flight

Germany, Poland, France and England

1939–40

During the early hours of 1 September 1939, the scene on the frontier bridge connecting Kehl in southern Germany and Strasbourg in France was like something out of John le Carré's *The Spy Who Came in from the Cold*. At one end of the bridge stood a long line of German soldiers, all armed with rifles. Facing them, at the other end, stood a line of French soldiers, all equipped with equally threatening firearms. Harry Hinsley, a twenty-year-old undergraduate from St John's College, Cambridge was walking slowly between the two lines of soldiers towards France. He was attempting to escape from Nazi Germany, and he was hoping he was not too late to make it across the border.

Even as he crossed the bridge, German soldiers were invading Poland, France's and Britain's ally, and it was only a matter of time before the French and the British declared war on Germany.[1] If the German soldiers had only realised what damage Hinsley would inflict on their country and their comrades during the next two years, they would surely have detained him. Hinsley's grandfather had been the master locksmith who made the locks and keys for the large doors at the front of some of the museums and galleries in Berlin, but young Harry was destined to mastermind the reconstruction of a German key which was infinitely more valuable: the key to the Enigma cipher used by the German Navy. However, the German soldiers knew nothing about that. They merely looked on dispassionately as the German customs office confiscated all of Hinsley's German marks. After he was told that he would not be given any English or French currency in exchange, he was sent, penniless, on his way. He spent the next night on a park bench in France.

At the time of this lucky escape Hinsley had not yet been recruited by the intelligence service in Britain. During the summer of 1939 he was just a student who was attempting to learn some German by spending his vacation in Germany. Although he was aware of the mounting tension between Britain and Germany, he had decided to risk going ahead with his trip. After all, it was not the first time there had been tension between the two countries. He had visited Germany during the Munich Crisis the previous year, and nothing had happened then. When, in August 1939, he had arrived at his girl-friend's house in Koblenz, in south-west Germany, he had been greeted with as much hospitality as ever. The one slight inconvenience was that he was instructed to report to the local police station each day, so that the police could keep an eye on him. But even that was waived after the 23 August announcement of the Nazi-Soviet pact. All of a sudden, everyone whom Hinsley met in Koblenz appeared to be convinced that there would be no war after all. The police told Hinsley that they would get in touch with him if any problems came up.

A week later one of the policeman did get in touch, with the parents of his girlfriend. 'Get him out of the country by tomorrow at the latest, if I were you,' they were told. That explains how Hinsley was tipped off in time, and how he managed to cross the French border before it was closed. He subsequently hitch-hiked to Switzerland, and from there made his way back to England shortly before Prime Minister Neville Chamberlain announced that Britain was at war with Germany.

After war was declared Hinsley found it hard concentrating on his history course at Cambridge University, where he was embarking on his third year as an undergraduate. He had been told that third-year students would be given the option to finish their degrees, rather than being conscripted. But his difficulties were alleviated somewhat by Hugh Gatty, his tutor in modern history. Hinsley found him a delightful companion, but a hopeless teacher. Gatty would ask Hinsley to read him a few lines of his latest essay, and then he would say, 'That's very good. Now would you like to hear me play some music on my harpsichord?' It would have been impolite to have declined to listen, so Hinsley would sit back and try to forget about the war that was raging in Europe, a war which was threatening to destroy his idyllic life in Cambridge.

Unknown to Hinsley, his future was already being mapped out. Alastair Denniston, the de facto head of the Government Code and Cipher School (GC&CS), had asked one of his friends at King's

College, Cambridge to put him in touch with some intelligent graduates and undergraduates. They were needed to man the school's new offices at Bletchley Park in Buckinghamshire. Hinsley, who had achieved a First in part 1 of his history tripos, was deemed at be a suitable candidate, and two weeks after the beginning of his university term, he was summoned by the Foreign Office for an interview in the rooms of Martin Charlesworth, the President of St John's College.

During the interview, Denniston and his colleague failed to explain why they wanted Hinsley. They went through his CV with him, noting that he was good at sifting through old documents such as the Domesday Book. Then they asked if he would be willing to take up a civilian post at the Foreign Office. Hinsley jumped at the opportunity and three days later he received a letter on Foreign Office paper telling him to report to an office in London's Euston station on the next Monday morning. Before he set off for London, Gatty, his history tutor, contacted him, and said that he had heard that Hinsley was being recruited by the Government Code and Cipher School. That was the first time Hinsley knew where he was going to work. 'I'm going there too,' Gatty told him, and offered him a lift down to Bletchley in his car. Hinsley gratefully accepted and, after Hinsley had cleared this with the Foreign Office, they drove down together. As they passed through the black wrought iron gates, Hinsley came face to face with the forbidding Victorian mansion which was to become his place of work for the next six years. It was set in a small park which contained a lake and a few prefabricated huts. Denniston told Hinsley that he would be working under a Mr Birch in the Naval intelligence hut just outside the house. It was referred to as Hut 4.

Frank Birch was head of the German section in Hut 4. He told Hinsley that they were trying to read intercepted German naval messages. The code used by the Germans had not yet been broken. That being the case, Hinsley was to do his best to find out as much as he could from the information they did have about these messages. It was quickly apparent that there was not much evidence to go on. There was the date of the messages, their time of origin and their time of interception, and the radio frequency used by the German morse code operators. Sometimes Hinsley would be told where the messages came from, information which had been gleaned using the Royal Navy's direction finding service.

Using all of the available information, Hinsley worked out that the German Navy only had two radio networks: one for the Baltic and one for outside the Baltic. There did not appear to be a separate network for surface ships and a different network for U-boats. Hinsley could only hope that would change once the Germans began conducting major naval operations. For the moment, he was stuck in a dead end job with no opportunity to make his mark.

*

At the same time as Harry Hinsley was successfully crossing the bridge to Strasbourg, a more frenetic bid for freedom was being made 600 miles away in Warsaw by Poland's codebreakers. As more and more German troops crossed over the border into Poland, Marian Rejewski, who seven years earlier had broken the Enigma code for the first time, prepared to leave the country. By the time war broke out, he was thirty-four years old, and he was married with two young children. He was very worried about his family. It was clear that he would be spirited away before the Germans could enter Warsaw, so as to preserve the Enigma secret. But his wife and children might be left to fend for themselves, unless he took the necessary evasive action.[2]

His first step was to try to withdraw as much money as he could from his bank. But scores of other people had the same idea and at first he merely stood in queues for hours, hoping that the bank would open its doors. Most people in the queue went away disappointed, since the banks were closed to normal customers. However Rejewski, who had a special account, eventually managed to withdraw some money. He returned to his first-floor flat and, in a state of nervous excitement, told his wife, Irena, that he felt they should attempt to leave Warsaw together, even if it was inevitable that they would be separated later. He knew he would have to remain with his fellow codebreakers and the General Staff in case there was an opportunity to carry on reading the German messages. Rejewski's wife replied that it would be better if she remained in the flat in Warsaw with the children. They were not old enough to put up with forced marches and all the deprivations of flight. That especially applied to their daughter Janina who was just seven months old.

On the other side of Warsaw, a similar decision was reached by Basia Różycki, the wife of Jerzy Różycki, Rejewski's codebreaking colleague. The Różyckis also had a four-month-old baby to think about.

None of the Polish codebreakers found out what was to happen to them until 3 September, two days after the start of the German invasion. In the early afternoon, Różycki, accompanied by his colleague Henryk Zygalski, rushed back from their office to tell his wife that their unit was being sent to Brest Litovsk, to the east of Warsaw. It was then that they decided that she would go to stay with his mother in the Polish countryside. The next day Basia Różycki was touched as she watched her husband talking and giving advice to his baby son as if he were an adult, and they wept as they said their goodbyes. A similar scene was being played out at the same time outside Antoni Palluth's flat. His family had said goodbye to him so often in the past as he went off on his missions to Germany. But as he waved from the General Staff saloon, they realised that this was very different, and that it might be a long time before they would see him again.

While the codebreakers were wrenching themselves away from their families, piles of secret documents were being burned outside the General Staff buildings on Gwido Langer's instructions. Any documents which were not burned had to be loaded onto a lorry and taken to the train that had been put aside for the codebreakers and members of the General Staff. Before the codebreakers left their offices for the last time Langer made an emotional speech, begging them to remember that they should keep the Enigma secret at all costs.

Air raids prevented the train leaving the platform, however. So Różycki went back to his flat. There he was surprised to find his wife and child; their train had also been delayed by the bombing. Fearing that Basia and their child would never make it out of Warsaw alone, Różycki insisted that they should accompany him on the General Staff train after all. The train only finally departed during the evening of 6 September, heading east, away from Germany. Every few minutes, it shuddered to a halt again, as the train driver discovered more stretches of track which had been damaged by air raids. Then, as bombs rained down, all the passengers hid under the train until it was possible to climb back in for the next stage of their journey. In the chaos their train crashed into another train, and Zygalski was one of the men who helped to remove the remains of the damaged carriages from the railway track so that they could carry on with their journey.

They arrived in Brest Litovsk three days after setting out. To the shell-shocked codebreakers and their families the peaceful town, untouched by the war, was like an oasis. For a brief moment they wondered if they were now through the worst. During the lull the Różyckis left their baby with a teenage girl whom they had befriended on the train so that they could try to find some milk and some food for their baby. Because they were in such a rush, they failed to register that their train was next to a long line of wagons full of ammunition. The peaceful interlude was soon interrupted however by the sound of German aircraft approaching. As the planes dived down to drop their bombs, the Różyckis jumped into a trench and watched with their hearts in their mouths as they saw one of the bombs demolishing one of the trenches where seconds before they had contemplated taking cover.

Finally, after the aircraft departed, they hurried back to the station which was now just a smoking ruin. To their horror they saw that their train had been hit and was partially destroyed. Zygalski once again joined the rescue party, as it tried to release trapped refugees from the wreckage, while the Różyckis hunted frantically for the young girl who was supposed to be looking after their baby. After a long search, they found the girl and the baby. They were so relieved at finding them safe, they almost forgot about the terrible situation they were still in.

Then Zygalski came and interrupted the happy reunion with what was very bad news. All the codebreakers had to depart immediately. They were to be evacuated to Rumania, leaving their wives and children to muddle through on their own. For the Różyckis this was almost too much to bear. After having just had such a lucky escape together, it seemed unfair that they must part again so quickly. Later, following their separation, Basia Różycki was urged to suffocate her baby, so that she could at least save her own life. But at this stage, although they were tired and had seen the depradations of war at first hand, they were far from even thinking about such extreme measures. That being the case, there was no alternative but to try to be brave. For the second time within the space of five days, they embraced and said their goodbyes once more. Little did they know, as they gazed into each other's eyes, that this time it would be forever.

As the codebreakers were transported east in cars and buses, their valuable Enigma machinery had to be jettisoned. When the lorries carrying the bomby and the replica Enigma machines ran out of petrol near the Russian border, the men escorting them were forced to roll up their sleeves to help the cryptographers bury their codebreaking equipment. Then on the night of 17 September the first group of cryptographers reached Poland's south-eastern border with Rumania.

As soon as they crossed the border, they were told to report to a refugee camp. Rejewski and his fellow codebreakers balked at this and instead went to the local railway station where they caught a train to Bucharest, the Rumanian capital. After explaining to the Army attaché at the Polish Embassy that they were collaborating with the British and French Cipher Offices, they were advised to go to the British or French Embassies.

They arrived at the British Embassy at the same time as the British diplomats from Warsaw. The preoccupied British Ambassador told them that he could do nothing for them until he had spoken to London. Fearing that that meant no action for several hours, or even days, the Polish codebreakers decided to see if they fared any better at the French Embassy. The staff there appeared to be expecting them, and they were quickly furnished with visas and train tickets, which was all that they needed to travel to Paris.

By the beginning of October, the most important Polish codebreakers were safely in France. But all codebreaking was put on hold until their bosses, Langer and Maksymilian Ciężki, were rescued from the Rumanian refugee camps, along with the two Enigma replicas which had been brought with them from Warsaw. The Polish team was then taken to a French château, Château de Vignolles, near the town of Gretz-Armainvilliers, about forty kilometres north-east of Paris. The château's code name was PC [Poste de Commandement, or Command Post] Bruno. But no Enigma messages could be read immediately. Although the French arranged to have more replica Enigmas manufactured, that did not enable the cryptographers to read the Germans' messages again. To do that they needed a set of perforated sheets. However they certainly did not have the resources to make them up for themselves. All they could do was to wait patiently until the sheets were produced for them in Britain.

*

Across the English Channel the codebreakers and administrators at Bletchley Park behaved as if they were scarcely aware of the life and death struggle which had been going on in Poland. On 12 September 1939, Alastair Denniston, the acting head of the Government Code and Cipher School (GC&CS), wrote to his boss, Stewart Menzies, the head of the Secret Intelligence Service, about the difficulties he

52

and his team were experiencing. Denniston was concerned that his team would not operate efficiently if they were to be housed in huts scattered around the large Bletchley Park estate. 'The three weeks we have been here have been remarkably fine,' he wrote, 'and the walking about has been pleasant if wasteful. With dark afternoons, and evenings and cold conditions, people will hesitate to walk out in the open considerable distances to confer with their colleagues. Twenty minutes spent walking backwards and forwards on a dark winter's afternoon is not going to make for efficiency. There is a real spirit of discontent growing among my colleagues. I have congratulated them on the good work that is being done under very trying conditions, and the natural reply is improve our conditions and you will get more good results.'[3]

One of the good results was that a British cryptographer had at last managed to read some Enigma messages. The codebreaker was Peter Twinn, a twenty-three-year-old Oxford graduate with a First in mathematics. He had started his career as a cryptographer in February 1939, working alongside Dilly Knox at Broadway, the codebreaking centre near St James's Park in London, before the GC&CS was moved to Bletchley Park. When he arrived at Broadway, he was given an enciphered Enigma message with the matching plain-language German, and the applicable settings, which unbeknown to Twinn, had been provided by Hans Thilo Schmidt. Twinn could not speak German. But that was not the problem. The obstacle holding up Twinn and Dilly Knox, was their inability to reconstruct the Enigma machine. That changed in July 1939 after Knox came back from Poland with details of the internal wiring. The new information meant that Twinn was able to read a few messages which had been enciphered using the settings he had been given. While he was working out what the messages said, he was tapped on the shoulder by Josh Cooper, the head of the Air Force section at Bletchley Park. Twinn told him what he was doing, whereupon Cooper replied, 'You'll have the satisfaction of knowing that you are the first Englishman to read an Enigma message.' Twinn and Knox still could not read any up-to-date Enigma messages however, since they could not work out any of the new settings. No one could do that until a complete set of perforated sheets was produced.[4]

The perforated sheets were made up as quickly as possible. By the middle of December 1939 the first set had been completed and a start was being made on a second set for the Poles in France. However at the beginning of January 1940, before a complete copy of the perforated sheets had been sent out to the Polish cryptographers waiting anxiously at PC Bruno, a problem was encountered which held up the British attempt to break the code. The problem, and a possible solution, was outlined in the following letter which Stewart Menzies, acting on Denniston's request, wrote to Colonel Rivet, his opposite number in the French Intelligence Service on 10 January 1940:

> As you are doubtless kept 'au courant' by Bertrand regarding our special efforts in attempting to unravel the German 'material', you probably are aware by now that although great progress is being made, it now seems possible that certain changes were introduced at the beginning of the war. If this proves to be the case, further intensive research will become an imperative matter.
>
> In order to assist my experts, it is felt that if it could be arranged for some of the Junior Polish personnel, who have been engaged on this specialised work for many years to come over here, there would be a better chance of obtaining quick results, which are so essential to us both.
>
> If it had been possible for us to transfer certain mechanical devices to you, I would gladly have done so, but this is quite impracticable, and I would therefore appeal to you to consider sending the following three Polish Officers over for a short visit: Jerzy Różycki, Marian Rejewoli [sic], Henryk Zygalski.
>
> Believe me, my dear Rivet,
>
> Yours always,
>
> Chief[5]

This letter seems to have represented an attempt to go over the head of Bertrand, who had already indicated that the three Polish codebreakers would not be allowed to work for the British in England. However, before any transfer of personnel could be negotiated, the log jam was cleared. It was discovered that the Germans had not altered their Enigma procedure again after all. A mistake had been made by the Poles when they passed on information to the British codebreakers about the turnover positions of the two new wheels which had been used by the Germans after 15 December 1938.[6] On 17 January 1940, the first wartime Enigma messages were read. They had been sent by the Germans on 25 and 28 October 1939.[7] But the codebreakers only began reading messages within twenty-four hours of intercepting them after 3 April 1940.

Since the Polish codebreakers were not being allowed to travel to London at the beginning of 1940, their British colleagues had to visit them in France if they wanted to see them. Alan Turing, the codebreaking star at Bletchley Park, spent some time with the Poles in France discussing the Enigma machine and the difficulties he had encountered. During a farewell dinner, which was held at the end of Turing's trip, Zygalski asked him why each little square on the perforated sheets, which the British had given the Poles before the dinner, was such a peculiar measurement – eight and a half millimetres square. Turing explained that the British worked in inches, and that the sides of the squares were one third of an inch long. A jocular argument ensued over whether the British system of measurement was better than the decimal system used in France and Poland. One argument advanced by Turing in defence of the British system was that the pound, which in those days could be divided up into 240 pennies (there were 20 shillings in a pound and 12 pennies in a shilling), permitted three, four, five, six or eight people to split a restaurant bill between them so that no-one paid a penny more than he owed. That did not always happen with the decimal system, he said.[8]

By the time of this visit Turing had already made the groundbreaking invention which was to revolutionise the way in which the Enigma code could be broken. He had invented an electromechanical machine, which came to be known as the bombe, which could work out the wheel settings and plugboard socket connections used by the Germans on any given day. Superficially, the bombe was similar to the Polish bomby. The British bombe consisted of a series of Enigma machines wired together which could be rotated through each wheel setting in turn to test whether the setting in question could be ruled out. However there the similarity to the bomby ended. The Polish bomby could only identify a particular 'fingerprint' if the Germans carried on enciphering their message settings twice at the beginning of each message. Turing's bombe was designed to work even if the Germans stopped using their double enciphering procedure. The need to find a codebreaking machine which would not be made redundant if this happened had immediately been apparent to Dilly Knox, the British codebreaker, when in July 1939 he had been told by the Poles that Enigma could be read using the perforated sheets.[9] He had observed that the German procedure 'may at any moment be cancelled'.

When Turing invented his bombe, he took into account the impracticality of setting up a replica of the Enigma machine at each possible setting combination in turn, and then tapping out on the keyboard some of the cipher text which had been intercepted. That trial and error approach would have identified the correct setting combination when it was eventually tested, since, as has been mentioned before, if you set up an Enigma in exactly the same way as the message sender had set it up, when you typed out the code on the keyboard, the lights representing the German plain text would light up. As soon as the cryptographer conducting this test observed that he had produced plain-language German when he tapped out the code, he would have known that he had set up the Enigma correctly. However because there were literally trillions of possible setting combinations, this method would have taken too long to be a practical proposition. Turing expressed this another way when he was talking to some of the younger cryptographers. 'If I had 10,000 Chinamen at my disposal, there would be no need for the bombe,' he told them.[10]

Turing's bombe was designed to look at the problem facing him from the opposite direction. Since it was difficult to discover the correct setting directly and quickly, Turing concentrated on finding a test which would reveal which settings were incorrect. The idea was that if he could rule out most of the setting combinations, then there would only be a few remaining which could be tested manually. The test he devised is explained in detail in Appendix 2. It could not be carried out unless the codebreakers had access to a crib, which is the guessed plain-language meaning of a given piece of intercepted cipher text. A crib gave the cryptographers a series of pairs of letters which matched up. The bombe's job was to rule out any settings where this matching of pairs of letters was impossible. Finding cribs was simple when the cryptographers were reading the Enigma messages every day, as they were after January 1940 thanks to the perforated sheets. The cryptographers might spot, for example, that at a particular time each day a German in a deserted port would send out a message saying 'I have nothing to report.' While the perforated sheets still worked, there was no need to use the crib. But once the perforated sheets became redundant, the codebreakers would be able to use the crib with the bombe.

The first bombe was installed at Bletchley Park on 18 March 1940.[11] But, as explained in Appendix 2, it failed to make the most of Turing's original idea. Gordon Welchman, another brilliant Cambridge mathematician who was also working at Bletchley Park, explained to Turing how the bombe could be adapted so that it was at least twice as powerful as Turing's prototype. At first Turing was incredulous but, after studying Welchman's drawings, he agreed that the bombe should be redesigned to incorporate Welchman's suggestion.[12] After accepting Welchman's improvement, Turing had another moment of inspiration. At the time, he was working in Hut 8, the hut occupied by the cryptographers dealing with the Naval Enigma. Joan Clarke, who was for a while to become Turing's fiancée, remembered him leaping to his feet during the summer of 1940 and announcing that he had proved that Welchman's improvement permitted 'simultaneous scanning', that is the testing of twenty-six plugboard socket connections during each test. (This is explained in Appendix 2.) Then Turing marched out to Hut 6, where the Air Force and Army Enigma messages were being broken, to tell the codebreakers there what he had discovered.[13]

Turing's and Welchman's improvements were incorporated into an updated version of the original bombe. The codebreakers referred to it as 'the spider', and the British Tabulating Machine Company based at Letchworth was commissioned to manufacture a prototype. The young man who was asked to check whether the spider worked properly was an eighteen-year-old cryptographer named Richard Pendered. Having just left Winchester, he had been about to start as a mathematics undergraduate at Magdalene College, Cambridge when Britain declared war on Nazi Germany. At Winchester, he had been taught mathematics by Hugh Alexander, who had also moved on to become a cryptographer when war broke out; it was probably Alexander who recommended that he should be interviewed at Bletchley Park. Pendered was summoned there at the end of his first year at Cambridge. During his interview, conducted by Gordon Welchman, Pendered discovered that he had only missed a First by a whisker during his first year examinations. Then Welchman said, 'Are you any good at crosswords?' That was the only clue Pendered was given about the job he might be asked to do. A few days later he was asked to report for work. When he arrived, Hugh Alexander took him on one side, and told him, 'We're trying to break a cipher machine', and showed Pendered a replica Enigma before putting him to work in Hut 6, the section dealing with Army and Air Force Enigma messages.

The spider prototype was still being tweaked when Pendered turned up at the Letchworth factory during the summer of 1940. To this day he remembers the thirteen-letter crib which he used to make up the menu for the machine. It was 'Funk Gymnastik' (wireless exercise). Pendered was concerned that the spider would not be able to cope with it. The menu made up from his crib could not have produced a solution if plugged into Turing's original bombe. So he was applying a rigorous test on the new machine. The spider was set up in accordance with the menu Pendered had brought with him and then it was switched on. Pendered watched with bated breath as sparks began to spew out of the machine. Every now and then, factory employees dashed up to tighten a connection here and make an alteration there. Then the machine was started up again. Each time the spider produced a possible solution, the wheels spun on for a while before coming to a halt. To identify the solution, one of the factory employees had to wind the wheels back manually with a crank handle, one position at a time, and at each position, he had to tap the relay switches to see which ones were open and which were shut. Then Pendered took the setting suggested by the spider away with him to a small room on one side of the factory so that he could analyse it without being disturbed or observed.

He was not expecting the machine to come up with the correct solution on such an awkward menu; his main task was merely to check that the results were logical. It was a long job. The spider had to work through sixty possible wheel orders, and only three could run at a time. Once he had seen that the settings were logical, he set the wheels and plugs on the replica Enigma to the positions indicated by the spider, and tapped out the first few letters of the cipher text. He knew that if the correct setting was discovered, German text in addition to the crib would be produced. For days he failed to produce anything but jumbled up letters when he applied this test. But at one of the settings, the X bulb on his replica Enigma lampboard lit up after the letters in the crib, which was encouraging, since the Germans used X's as punctuation marks between words. Then came that exhilarating moment when he realised that the spider had worked. As he tapped out the next few letters in the cipher text, the letters making up the words 'WIRHOFFEN' (we hope) were produced. Pendered did not have to go any further. He knew that the spider had broken the code, and that the new method of codebreaking was up and running.[14] The first spider was installed at Bletchley Park on 8 August 1940.[15]

6

The First Capture

Scotland

1940

The first breakthrough in the British attempt to read the Naval Enigma code took place in February 1940. It had nothing to do with work done by the cryptographers at Bletchley Park. It arose thanks to the alertness of a sailor on a patrolling British warship, and because of a botched raid carried out by an elite force sent over from Germany to Scotland in a U-boat.[1] The U-boat raiders were led by Hans-Wilhelm von Dresky, a tall, handsome thirty-one-year-old captain, who insisted on maintaining his neat goatee beard in spite of the difficulties of shaving at sea. Dresky had been instructed to take his U-boat, the *U-33*, into the Firth of Clyde, off the west coast of Scotland, to lay some mines. It was a particularly dangerous assignment, since Dresky had to sail his U-boat behind enemy lines and operate just five miles off the Scottish beaches.

The fact that the mission was considered so dangerous may have explained why it was that on 4 February 1940, Karl Dönitz, the leader of the U-boat section of the German Navy, appeared in Wilhelmshaven harbour to see the men off. 'Good luck, Hans. Look after yourself,' he had shouted to Dresky. It may also have explained why so much fuss was made of the crew before their departure. They had been invited by some senior Nazi officials in northern Germany to attend a banquet in their honour. It was held in a wooden hut in the middle of a forest, and food, drink and a crowd of giggling girls were laid on, presumably in an attempt to bolster up their spirits. Some of the junior crew members were invited to join their Nazi hosts on the top table, but their table manners left something to be desired. There was a moment of embarrassed silence when one of the less sophisticated members of the crew picked up a chicken leg, and began to tear the succulent flesh off the bone with his teeth, like a ravenous wolf. The silence was only broken when the oldest Nazi official seated at the table picked up his own chicken leg and followed suit. Someone burst out laughing, and soon all the Nazis present were casting aside their knives and forks and gnawing at their chicken bones. Anything to put the U-boat heroes at their ease.

They certainly needed some respite from the rigours and worries of going to war in a U-boat. Before leaving port, they had to put their civilian clothes into a tin box; they knew the box was to be sent back to their parents if they failed to return. It was a potent reminder that, while they might be regarded as heroes today, within the next four weeks, the length of a long patrol, they could all be dead and just another statistic. The men's morale was also sapped by all the discomforts they had to put up with once they were at sea. Their food tasted of the diesel oil which ran the U-boat's motors. The air circulating inside the hull could only be described as revolting. This was partly down to the fact that the men could not wash properly while they were at sea and they rarely if ever changed their clothes before returning to base. But the smell of sweaty damp clothes was nothing compared with the repugnant odour emanating from the one usable toilet. The second toilet was normally out of bounds, since it was commandeered as an extra store room.

Their discomfort was exacerbated by the cramped living space: the forty to forty-five-man crew aboard a 500 ton U-boat, such as the *U-33*, had to sleep, eat and work in an area around 142 foot long by ten foot wide, a space considerably smaller than the U-boat's 210 foot by 19 foot outer shell.[2] Even there, they were not spared some of the discomforts caused by the wet and cold. Seawater often swept down the conning tower into the control room, and if fuel was being conserved so that the U-boat could stay at sea for a long time, the heating was rarely turned up to an acceptable level.

The men eventually became used to the foul atmosphere. More difficult to deal with were the long boring interludes where nothing happened, and the uncomfortable spells on the bridge, as each of the men, not tied to more specialist duties in the machine room, took his turn keeping watch. After being soaked by the Atlantic waves and buffeted by the gales which blew almost continuously during the winter of 1939–40, it was hard to get rid of the feeling that the filthy clothes on their backs were always damp. This would have been bearable, had it not been for crippling bouts of sea sickness, when the U-boat bobbed around on the ocean surface like a cork. Only when they dived was there a temporary respite.

It was not only the U-boat crew's lives which were at stake as the *U-33* set out. The operation represented a major risk as far as cipher security was concerned. The U-boat was going into areas within the Firth of Clyde where the surface waves broke just thirty-five to forty metres over the sea bed. If the *U-33* was spotted, it could not escape by diving down deep, as it could in the open sea. So there was a substantial risk that the cipher machine might be captured.

It was not as if Dönitz was unaware of the risks he was running. During the very first fortnight of the war, there had been a scare during a mine-laying operation carried out by the *U-26* near Portland, the naval base in the south of England. The *U-26* had failed to make contact with Dönitz's headquarters for several days. It eventually reported that it was safe, but not before the German Navy had became concerned that it, and its cipher machine, might have been captured. After that episode, mine-laying U-boats were ordered to leave their Enigma machines behind, even though, as was acknowledged in Dönitz's own War Diary: 'This means they will have to go directly to the mine-laying position and they will have to return back to base immediately the operation has been completed. They will not receive signals made to other boats in Naval Enigma.' A later entry in the War Diary stated that 'the consequent disadvantages and difficulties which will be experienced when working together with other boats have to be accepted, as the risk of confidential books and cipher material falling into the enemy's hands, if the boat is lost in shallow water, is too great.'[3]

But in relation to the *U-33* Dönitz and his staff failed to enforce the rules which had been imposed. Perhaps it was thought that the new regulations should not be applied to ocean-going submarines such as the *U-33*, which was a torpedo-carrying strike boat rather than a dedicated mine-layer. Dönitz only had twenty-seven ocean-going submarines at his disposal at the beginning of the war,[4] and he may have reasoned that these U-boats would have to do more than lay a few mines during each trip if the U-boat force as a whole was to make a real impact. During the first five months of the war, Germany's U-boats had sunk 530,000 tons of merchant shipping (154 ships), a substantial total, but nothing like enough to pose a threat to Britain's ability to carry on fighting.[5] At the beginning of the war the British Commonwealth's merchant fleet was made up of around 3000 ships whose tonnage came to around 17.7 million tons.[6] So it was that the *U-33* was sent out on what almost amounted to a suicide mission with an Enigma machine on board.

The chances of the *U-33* making a success of its mission were reduced by some serious technical problems while in Wilhelmshaven harbour. When supplies were being loaded on 4 February 1940, the bow suddenly slipped under the water. Ice and freezing seawater poured in through a torpedo hatch. Only the prompt action of one of the crew, who quickly blew all the water out of the diving tanks, averted what could have been a disaster. On the way to the naval base in Helgoland, the last German port to be visited before the *U-33* headed out towards its target in Britain, two likely causes of the problem were discovered. There was a hole the size of a thumb in one of the torpedo tubes and there was another hole which appeared to have been caused by a drill breaking through a copper pipe. Both holes were patched up with pieces of rubber and wedges of wood until they could be properly filled in when the U-boat arrived in Helgoland. But no one was absolutely sure the engineers had dealt with the fundamental cause of the problem.

It was not just the U-boat itself which was malfunctioning. Some members of the crew had serious misgivings about the commander and his officers. Although Dresky had a good track record on paper, his shortcomings had been exposed during a previous trip. In October and November 1939 the *U-33* had laid some mines in the Bristol Channel and had sunk several ships on the way back to Germany. It was Dresky's behaviour during one of these sinkings which raised questions about his ability to control his men. Dresky had ordered Hans Heidtmann, an officer on the *U-33*, to instruct the gunners on the upper deck to hold their fire so that he could negotiate with the commander of the ship they had been attacking. The commander of the enemy ship had sent a message asking whether he and the U-boat commander could talk. But Heidtmann decided that this was a trick, and ordered the *U-33*'s gun crew to open fire. Dresky immediately attempted to countermand Heidtmann's order. But Heidtmann, who by this time was past listening to his skipper, continued to shout bloodthirsty insults at the British crew and told the men to carry on firing. The stand-off between Heidtmann and Dresky reached its climax when Dresky drew his pistol, pointed it at Heidtmann's head, and told him once again to give the order to cease fire. This time Heidtmann obeyed. But not before it had become apparent to the rest of the crew that Dresky had lost control for a moment.

Heidtmann did not go out with Dresky on the February 1940 patrol. But this time Dresky's authority was undermined by his less than harmonious relationship with Friedrich Schilling, his leading engineer. The relationship between a commander and his engineer is one of the most important on a U-boat. It is these two men, more than any others, who are responsible for the safety of both the vessel and its crew; the engineer should be the commander's right-hand man. It is the engineer who decides whether the U-boat is in a fit state to go to sea. If the U-boat is in trouble, it is the engineer who will tell his commander when it is no longer safe to remain under the water. When the engineer says the tanks must be blown violently, making use of the last remaining air pressure, so that the U-boat can be propelled to the surface, it is a foolhardy commander who would think of not following his advice. Mutual trust is vital if the U-boat is to operate smoothly. It was that element which was lacking from the relationship between Dresky and Schilling. And as the *U-33*'s engines powered them through the waves taking them deep into enemy territory inside the Firth of Clyde, it was to be this breakdown in human relations which would lead to questions being asked about how the U-boat came to be sunk.

During the early hours of Sunday 11 February Dresky told Schilling his plan. He wanted to be in a good mine-laying position within the estuary before the sun came up. Then he planned to submerge and settle the U-boat on the sea bed until the evening when he hoped it would be safe to come to the surface again. After laying the mines during Sunday night and Monday morning, he hoped to escape to the relative safety of the Atlantic before dawn on Tuesday 13 February. But before any mines could be laid, Dresky's well thought out plan began to go wrong. The *U-33* was chugging along on the surface during the early hours of Monday 12 February, when the four lookouts on the bridge spotted a mysterious silhouette coming towards them out of the darkness. It was a ship travelling in the opposite direction to the U-boat. Fortunately for the Germans, the blacked-out vessel passed the U-boat some distance away. Nevertheless the lookouts on the bridge held their breath as they and Dresky watched it steam past.

Shortly after this Schilling climbed the ladder inside the conning tower to talk to Dresky on the bridge. He could not have arrived at a worse moment. For Schilling was just in time to see what he took to be a British destroyer coming towards them. Seconds later Dresky shouted out, 'Alarm', and he and all the lookouts jumped down the conning tower, as the U-boat lurched forward into an emergency dive. The British ship which Schilling had spotted was not a destroyer. It was HMS *Gleaner*, a converted survey ship in Britain's anti-submarine fleet.[7] It was the same ship which had sailed past the U-boat shortly before. No one on *Gleaner* had seen the *U-33* when the two ships had passed each other for the first time. But at about 2.50 a.m. on 12 February *Gleaner's* hydrophone set operator heard a suspicious noise which sounded to him like a diesel engine. The tonk-tonk-tonk noises were occurring at the rate of two tonks per second. *Gleaner's* commander, Lieutenant-Commander Hugh Price, and the officer on duty on *Gleaner's* bridge swiftly gave the order for the ship to be turned around. As the range between the two vessels lessened, *Gleaner's* searchlights were switched on and the British lookouts caught sight of a white object which, they said, could have been the spray made by a periscope gliding through the water. It quickly disappeared. But by this time, *Gleaner's* Asdic sonar equipment had locked onto the *U-33*. At 3.53 a.m. the British ship dropped its first pattern of depth charges.

At this point everyone inside the U-boat should have been working as a well co-ordinated team. The men in the central control room, the nerve centre of the submarine, where most of the instruments and the periscopes were located, should have been watching the commander and should have been ready to obey his every order. But on the *U-33*, the dissension which had been bubbling beneath the surface quickly made itself known. When Schilling asked how deep they should dive, Dresky had indicated about forty metres. This was not to the helmsman's satisfaction at all. He wanted to dive as deep as possible. 'He's got us,' he said in a voice which made some of the men shiver. Then the first depth charges exploded around them, and within seconds, the calm and orderly U-boat interior was transformed.

The explosion of the depth charges jarred the U-boat. It was as if a giant hammer had been rapped against the U-boat's outer shell, and all the men who were lying in their bunks found themselves pitched unceremoniously onto the floor. At the same time there was a terrifying bang, louder than anything any of the men had ever heard before. It stunned and deafened them, and they found themselves staring up at the U-boat ceiling, as if by doing so they might be able to tell whether more depth charges were about to rain down on top of them. No one panicked. However one of the more experienced officers turned to Max Schiller, who at eighteen was the youngest man on board, and said, 'Come here, Schiller. Can you sit down beside me. I'm a married man. I've got children to think about. It would help me if you could keep me company.' Schiller obliged, grateful that he could calm himself by bringing comfort to someone else. The danger was underlined by the order to put on escape apparatus. All the men had been shown during their training how to escape from a sinking submarine. They had practised in a specially constructed tank. But they found themselves wondering whether they would survive long enough to escape. Or would they just feel one final terrifying explosion before all their faculties were switched off?

Shortly after the first explosions the U-boat hit the sea bed. But that only worsened their situation. The depth meter was showing that they had come to a stop a paltry thirty-six metres beneath the surface. As Dresky took stock in the control room, reports were coming in from fore and aft. One of the motors would not work, the lights were out, so the crew was having to make do with the dimmer emergency lighting, and many of the instruments were broken. Most ominously of all, water was beginning to trickle into the boat.

At first Dresky allowed the U-boat to remain on the sea bed. But between 4 and 5 a.m. two more batches of depth charges exploded around them. At this point Dresky asked Schilling what action they could take. Schilling at first recommended that they should attempt to slip away under the water. But when he attempted to move the U-boat, using subtle applications of pressurised air to remove some of the water inside the diving tanks, he found that it was stuck on the sea bed. He eventually came to the conclusion that the only way out was to blow all the water out of the tanks, a manoeuvre which he hoped would take the *U-33* up to the surface. However he scoffed at the helmsman's view that they should then immediately abandon ship in order to save the crew's lives. Schilling still hoped that they would be able to creep away without being seen by the British warship. Dresky agreed, but it was at this point that their views began to diverge. Dresky's agreement was half-hearted. He was very pessimistic about their chances of escaping, given that they were still in British waters with dawn just hours away.

If only Dresky had been able to track what was happening on *Gleaner*, it might have influenced what happened next. The third pattern of depth charges had put *Gleaner's* Asdic gear out of action. That being the case, the *U-33* could have surfaced, and then submerged again immediately. Once it was moving freely under the water, it could have slipped away without the British being able to seek it out with its probing sonar beams. Such evasive action would only have been sensible, however, if there was enough pressurised air inside the U-boat to bring it to the surface for a second time after it had escaped. Schilling believed that there was enough for this manoeuvre.

At 5.22 a.m. Schilling gave the order for the *U-33*'s tanks to be blown, and it began to ascend towards the surface. As the conning tower appeared above the waves the hatch was thrown open. Before giving the command to abandon ship, Dresky could have consulted with Schilling one more time to see if there was a chance that the U-boat could have carried them out of trouble above or below the water line. Schilling says that he tried to discuss what could be done with Dresky, but he gave up when he realised that the order to abandon ship had already been given. While he was speaking to Dresky, men were already clambering up the conning tower so that they could leap down into the sea.

At the same time as commanding everyone to abandon ship, Dresky also told his engineers to set the fuses for the explosives which had already been placed around the interior of the U-boat. However the fuses were hastily extinguished after one of the engineers realised that they would go off before all the crew were out of the boat. In the struggle to evacuate the U-boat, the fact that the fuses had been extinguished, and new fuses lit, appears not to have been mentioned to Schilling. That would explain why, when the explosives failed to go off quickly, first Schilling and then Dresky climbed back down the conning tower in a desperate, and heroic, attempt to ensure not only that the fuses were lit, but also that as many vents and hatches as possible were opened. They met up once again at the top of the conning tower, whereupon Dresky asked Schilling to go below once again to see if something could be done to make the *U-33* sink more quickly. Schilling was about to refuse, when a wall of flame swept up the conning tower, and he felt a sharp blow on his left shoulder. At first he thought that he had been hit by a shell fired by *Gleaner*. Only later did he discover that it was the conning tower ladder which had struck him as the force of the explosion lifted it bodily out of the tower.

After the explosives went off, the gallant Dresky, who had lost the mouthpiece attached to his life jacket in the explosion, and the equally courageous Schilling jumped into the freezing water to join the other members of the crew who were still waiting to be picked up by the circling British ship. As the U-boat sank, Dresky called out to his men to give three cheers for the *U-33*. For many of the crew who were swimming around him, it was the last time they saw him alive.

But that was not the end of the story. The final act in the drama had yet to be played out, an act which revolved around the Enigma cipher machine wheels. These were put in the pockets of certain members of the *U-33*'s crew who were supposed to drop them into the sea once they were clear of the U-boat. According to one survivor, two of the men did as they were told. Their wheels were lost forever on the Firth of Clyde sea bed. But the third man, Friedrich Kumpf, failed to comply with the instructions. After he was rescued and transferred to *Gleaner,* he is said to have turned to Heinz Rottmann, one of the surviving officers, and said, 'Herr Oberleutnant, I forgot to throw the wheels away.' Whereupon Rottmann walked over to where Kumpf's trousers were hanging and found that the pockets were empty. This was how Rottmann was said to have found out that the British had the wheels.[8]

This story, dramatic as it is, cannot easily be squared with the testimony of Max Schiller who is still living in Scotland. Schiller, as well as being the youngest man on the U-boat, was also one of the fittest. He was a member of the German Navy's water polo team. So he was one of the best swimmers and turned out to be one of the most resilient when it came to surviving for a long time in the icy water. After he was picked up by the *Bohemian Queen*, a passing trawler, he was the only survivor who was able to help the other crew members as they were hauled aboard. Schiller was present when Kumpf was lifted onto the trawler's deck, and it was Schiller who undressed Kumpf, as far as he remembers, before the British had any chance to search Kumpf's pockets. At the time Kumpf was conscious, but he was not in control of himself. The other survivors huddled for warmth around a stove in an attempt to restore the circulation to their freezing bodies. But Kumpf attempted to throw himself onto the stove itself in the mistaken belief that this would enable to him to escape from the appalling cold. Schiller only managed to save him by seizing him, and by bundling him into a cupboard which he then locked. Later all the crew, including a shivering Kumpf, were transferred to *Gleaner.*

Schiller's account calls into question the veracity of the story about Rottmann and Kumpf's trousers. If Schiller really was with Kumpf from the moment Kumpf was pulled out of the sea until he was undressed, and if Schiller is correct in saying that he would have noticed if there was anything heavy in Kumpf's pockets, it is hard to see when the British could have found Kumpf's Enigma wheels. What is clear is that three wheels – including two wheels which were only being used by the Navy – were discovered and brought to the attention of Hugh Price, *Gleaner*'s commander. The person who gave them to Price obviously did not have much experience with ciphering machines, for he later told one of his comrades that what he had handed over 'looked like the gear wheel off a bicycle'.[9]

7

Mission Impossible

Norway and Bletchley Park

1940

The capture of the three wheels from the *U-33* opened up a window of opportunity for Alan Turing and the British cryptographers working on the Naval Enigma at Bletchley Park. It gave them the wiring of two of the three new wheels which were used by the German Navy in an effort to make their signals even more secure than those transmitted by the other armed forces.[1] Whereas the Air Force and Army Enigma operators used three wheels in their cipher machines out of the five wheels given to them, operators in the Navy, during the first two years of the war, used three wheels out of the eight wheels given to them.[2] The final, eighth, wheel used by the German Navy was also captured at sea, in August 1940.[3]

But these captures did not mean that the Naval Enigma could be read immediately. The British cryptographers still had to master the Naval Enigma indicating system which was more complicated than the system used by the German Air Force and Army. (See chapter 4). After 1 May 1937 the German Navy had stopped using an indicating system with the twice enciphered message setting which was still being used by the Army and Air Force Enigma operators at the beginning of 1940. Henceforth, the Naval Enigma system was much more secure. Rather than permitting operators to choose their own message settings (which was what happened in the Army and Air Force), the German Navy required an operator to select a three-letter group out of a book, say 'LXZ', and then it required him to encipher it with his wheels set to the initial setting (Grundstellung) specified in the day's settings list, which might be say 'ABC'. The resulting three letter group, which might be say 'RGL', was the message setting. The operator had to turn his wheels to the message setting before he enciphered the text of his message. The message was then transmitted in morse code. This enciphering method was safer than that used by the Army and Air Force, since it ensured that lazy or rushed operators did not always pick obvious message settings, such as AAA.

But it was the method of indicating to the message receiver what the message setting was which was to be the Naval Enigma's strong point. (It is laid out in detail in Appendix 3.) As well as picking the three-letter group (or trigram), say LXZ, out of a book, as mentioned above, the operators also had to select a second trigram, such as, say, BFA. These trigrams were then written one under the other, after a random letter selected by the Enigma operator was added to the beginning of one, and at the end of the other. At this point the two lines of letters might look like this:

$$C \quad B \quad F \quad A$$
$$L \quad X \quad Z \quad B$$

Each vertical column in the above groups of letters was then converted into the equivalent two-letter group (or bigram) specified in a so-called bigram table. So for example the equivalent bigram for ^C_L might be ^R_E. After all four of the vertical columns were converted, the two lines of letters might look like this:

$$R \quad V \quad M \quad K$$
$$E \quad Y \quad P \quad W$$

The letters then had to be manipulated, so that they were arranged as follows:

$$R \quad E \quad V \quad Y$$
$$M \quad P \quad K \quad W$$

This was the indicator which was sent unenciphered at the beginning and end of each message. It enabled the receiver to work out what message setting had been used.

The receiver merely took the same steps taken by the sender, but in reverse, until he transformed the indicator back to the first two lines of letters selected by the sender:

$$C \quad B \quad F \quad A$$
$$L \quad X \quad Z \quad B$$

He then followed the same procedure as the sender to transform the first three letters in the second line of the above letters, LXZ, into the message setting RGL. In other words, he turned his Enigma wheels to the initial setting given in the settings list for the day, i.e. ABC, and tapped out LXZ on his keyboard, in order to light up the message setting RGL. Lastly, after turning his wheels to the RGL position, he tapped out the cipher text message he had received, in order to light up the letters making up the original plain-language German message which had been sent to him in the first place.

By the end of 1939, without seeing any Naval Enigma manuals, Alan Turing believed that he had worked out the principal characteristics of this indicating system. He did this by drawing inferences from just seven message settings and indicators.[4] These had been passed to him by Rejewski and his Polish colleagues after the historic July 1939 meeting in Poland. The Polish codebreakers had managed to read a limited number of messages in May 1937 after the German Navy changed its indicating system. This was because the Germans made two mistakes when making the change.

Firstly, they carried on using the same wheel order and ring settings, so that the Polish codebreakers did not have to work them out following the change in the system. Secondly, they allowed the telegraphist on a torpedo boat, whose call sign was AFA, to carry on enciphering his signals according to the old system, which could be penetrated by the codebreakers, provided that he utilised the initial position specified for operators using the new system. By exploiting these errors, the Polish codebreakers broke some messages at the beginning of May 1937, and were able to pass on the message settings and indicators to Turing. After analysing them, he was able to guess how a receiver would transform the indicators into the message settings.[5]

But understanding the system did not enable him to apply it to break new messages. To do that, he would have needed the bigram tables mentioned above. So he was stuck. A note signed by Turing, Peter Twinn, Dilly Knox and Gordon Welchman on 1 November 1939 entitled 'Naval Enigma Situation' admitted that this was the case in a roundabout way.[6] They noted that if they had a crib, they would be able to use the 'superbombe machine' which was 'far larger than the bombe of the Poles', being made at Letchworth to break Naval Enigma messages. (They were referring to the bombe designed by Turing and Welchman.) This would enable them to 'solve the indicating system, i.e. to obtain the bigram list,' they wrote, and this would in turn 'enable us to solve all further messages . . . while the bigram list lasts'.

The problem was that when it came to finding cribs, without which no solutions could be made, they had to admit: 'We have at present no information which will be of use ... although when a number of messages have been solved it [the crib and Bombe method] might be applicable.' In other words, they were saying they were in a Catch-22 situation. Without cribs, they could not break any Enigma messages. If they could not break some Enigma messages, they would not be able to identify any cribs. The only other way to read Naval Enigma, as was acknowledged by Turing and his colleagues, was if settings were 'captured from a submarine'.

But capturing a U-boat at sea with its confidential papers was not so easily achieved. The Royal Navy failed to take advantage of one opportunity to do so during the British attempt to expel the Germans from Norway in April 1940. The U-boat in question was the *U-49*. On 15 April 1940 it was stalking a British troop convoy bound for Vågsfjord off the Norwegian coast, when it was picked up on the Asdic sonar sets of two of the destroyers accompanying the convoy. The U-boat was blown to the surface by depth charges. But then any hope of boarding her before she was scuttled was lost. What should have happened was that all available guns should have been directed at the conning tower to stop any of the crew emerging. If the crew had been imprisoned inside the U-boat, they would not have been able to scuttle her without committing suicide. So the U-boat would probably have remained on the surface. A boarding party could then have recovered the all-important codebooks before they could be thrown into the sea.

One crew member on HMS *Brazen*, one of the destroyers involved in the hunt, was all for adopting an approach which might have led to this result. He was an Irishman in his late twenties who a few days earlier had witnessed a German aircraft massacring forty defenceless Norwegian women and children. He wanted to exact an equally bloody revenge. So he seized a Lewis gun and shouting, 'I'm going to shoot them all,' opened fire. As he did so, however, one of his shipmates, fearing that he had taken leave of his senses, knocked him down with a well timed upper cut. When he fell, the opportunity to capture the Enigma codebooks was lost. By the time Brazen's commander had ordered a sharpshooter to take out the men on the *U-49* who were throwing its codebooks into the water, it was too late. They had already completed their task before the sharpshooter had them in his sights.

The tactics followed by the destroyers was subsequently criticised by Admiral Charles Forbes, the Commander-in-Chief of the Home Fleet. On 5 June 1940 he wrote a report setting out how destroyer commanders should behave when faced with a surfaced U-boat.[7] 'Up to date we have not made sufficiently determined efforts to prevent the crews of U-boats from either scuttling their submarines or destroying their papers,' he wrote. 'The action to be taken on seeing a U-boat surfacing must be directed towards gaining control of the conning tower hatch on the bridge of the submarine before the whole crew have made good their escape. To achieve this, the nearest destroyer should proceed at full speed alongside the submarine at the same time opening fire with Lewis or machine gun at the enemy personnel as they appear at the top of the hatch – not at men who have got clear of it and are taking no other steps than to escape and surrender. The object will be most effectively achieved if a body gets jambed [sic] in the mouth of the hatch at an early stage.' He believed that if this ruthless approach was followed boarding party would be able to board and capture the U-boat's codebooks and papers. He recommended an equally robust approach if U-boat crews were seen attempting to throw their papers into the sea. 'The only method of preventing this is to open immediate and effective fire on the personnel concerned,' wrote Admiral Forbes.

Eleven days after the disappointing failure to board *U-49* in Vågsfjord, some Enigma documents were captured from a German trawler further down the Norwegian coast. The capture took place on 26 April 1940, the same day that Churchill, at a meeting of the Military Co-ordination Committee in London, agreed that Britain would have to concede defeat in the south of Norway and withdraw all of its troops from the Trondheim area.[8]

At 10.30 a.m. the lookouts on HMS *Griffin*, a British destroyer, spotted a ship which appeared to be a fishing trawler south of Trondheim, near the town of Andalsnes. The name *Polares* was painted on its side, it was flying a Dutch flag, and had no visible armament. But because *Griffin*'s commander, John Lee-Barber, had just received a report from another British destroyer at which torpedoes had been fired by a similar trawler, Barber set out to head off *Polares* so that he could stop and search it.[9] It turned out to be a correct decision. As *Griffin*'s boarding party rowed over in a whaler, Lieutenant Alec Dennis, the officer in charge, noticed that there was a gun on *Polares*' deck concealed underneath a fake boat made of canvas. Furthermore the trawler's deck was crowded with men, something that he would not have expected to find on a genuine fishing ship.

The huge waves carried the whaler so high in the air as it came alongside *Polares* that Dennis and one of his comrades were able to leap on board without waiting for a ladder to be lowered. They were greeted by a dazed individual who managed to blurt out, 'German ship' in a German accent. Underneath some fishing nets, the incredulous boarders discovered two bow torpedo tubes which could have caused serious damage if they had been fired at *Griffin*. The ship was in fact the German *Schiff 26* which had been on the way to Narvik, to deliver ammunition, guns and mines.

As other members of Dennis's boarding party climbed onto *Polares*'s desk, one man let off the pistol he was holding by mistake. This gave him a terrible shock, but it served the useful purpose of terrifying those members of the German crew who could not see what was happening. They must have thought that an SAS-style raid was in progress in which they were all going to be slaughtered, for they immediately began to co-operate with the British boarders. They were further cowed by the way the other British seamen brandished their pistols. Dennis's statement that the German crew would be left to drown if *Polares* was scuttled must also have played its part in persuading the Germans that it would be best if they helped their British captors. One member of the German crew pointed out the compartment where a booby trap had been set up, and the men who were ordered off the ship queued up so obediently for the whaler which was to ferry them over to the destroyer that Dennis became suspicious. He wondered whether they had set scuttling charges with delayed-action fuses.

During the boarding another drama took place. The Germans had not been prepared to risk drowning by scuttling *Polares*, but they had managed to throw two bags containing some of their most important codebooks into the water. Only one of the bags was weighed down with a shell. Presumably it was the one which sank quickly.[10] The other bag was seen floating in the water by the crew still on *Griffin*. In a last ditch effort to recover it, 'Florrie' Foord, the gunner, dived over the side of the destroyer attached to a line. He caught hold of the bag, but the line broke while he was being hauled on board and he fell back into the rough heaving sea. For one ghastly moment it seemed that no one on *Griffin* would ever see either Foord or the bag again. But then he appeared once more, still gallantly clutching the bag, and thankfully grasped a second line which was thrown down to him. Once again his one-handed grip on the line was not strong enough, and he disappeared under the water, before bobbing up once more. When the line was thrown to him for a third time, he managed to secure a makeshift lasso over his shoulders, and he was hauled up, frozen and dripping wet, along with the all-important bag.[11]

Alec Dennis sailed *Polares* back to Scapa Flow, the British naval base in the Orkneys. The trip was made more hazardous than normal by the fact that all the ship's charts had been thrown overboard, and by Dennis's order that the German flag should be flown below the Royal Navy's white ensign. Two days later the little trawler chugged into Scapa Flow. What happened next was to horrify John Godfrey, head of the Naval Intelligence division, and Forbes, the Admiral of the Fleet. The trawler should have been met by an alert reception committee and placed in a quiet corner, well out of the way of any prying eyes, so that the documents still on board could be inspected in secret. Instead it sailed into the centre of Scapa Flow with its swastika flying provocatively overhead and swept past the Fleet's flagship. Security was so lax that as the German prisoners were escorted off the ship, no one stopped a Universal News film crew filming the occasion.[12] Fortunately, the film was confiscated before it could be shown.

To add insult to injury, when John Godfrey finally sent an officer to inspect the ship, the officer, Lieutenant Pennell, filed an alarming report. He claimed the ship had been 'looted', and it was only with difficulty that he had found 'some cypher tables and also sheets of signal pad on which cyphering had been done. These latter were strewn about all over the ship, one sheet being found underneath a mine on the upper deck.'[13] The report does not specify that these sheets were full of Enigma messages, but it is quite likely that they were, since in the course of this capture, some such sheets were certainly recovered.[14]

When the Navy conducted its own enquiry into what had happened however, Lieutenant Pennell's report was challenged. The Admiral conducting the enquiry felt that Pennell had been so 'overwrought' that it had 'coloured' his report. The Admiral stated that the ship did not appear to him to have been looted, and he was told by members of the boarding party that they had thought that all cipher material had been handed over. Lee-Barber, the commander of *Griffin*, also muddied the water by asserting that the looting must have taken place after his ship's boarders had departed.[15]

Whether or not more cipher documents could have been recovered had it not been for the chaos on *Polares*, the Enigma material handed in to Bletchley Park turned out to be invaluable.[16] Armed with it, the

British cryptographers were able to break the Naval Enigma cipher for 22 to 27 April 1940. The first message in the series to be broken had been transmitted by the Germans on 23 April 1940; it was read at Bletchley Park on 11 May 1940. It was the first Naval Enigma message to have been broken during the war.[17] Part of the delay was caused because several days passed before it was realised that the plugboard socket connections for 23 and 24 April had been captured; the scrap of paper on which the settings were written was overlooked at first. Once these days were broken, so were their paired days, 22 and 25 April; the same wheel order and ring settings were used on pairs of day, which meant that once one day's settings were broken, the settings for the second day in the pair were relatively easy to work out.

The settings for 26 April were subsequently broken on the bombe, which had been installed at Bletchley Park during the previous month.[18] This was achieved through using the cipher text and matching plain-language German messages contained in the Enigma operator's log which amounted to a crib. Nevertheless, delays were experienced again, as the codebreakers struggled to produce a suitable menu from the crib which could work on Turing's rudimentary bombe; the way a menu is built up from the crib is demonstrated in Appendix 2. After about two weeks, the settings for 26 April were finally broken, and the settings for its paired day, 27 April, were also worked out.

The delay in breaking the messages meant that they were too old to be useful in an operational sense. However their message settings, which could be worked out once the wheel and plugboard settings were broken, were to give Alan Turing, and the three cryptographers working with him on Naval Enigma, the opening they needed.[19] This was only because of another document recovered from *Polares*. After reading it, Turing finally understood how the Naval Enigma indicator system worked.[20]

Now at last he was able to work out a way to break some up-to-date Naval Enigma messages. His plan took into account a procedure he had invented after guessing how the indicator system operated. The procedure came to be known as Banburismus, on account of the fact that some of the sheets used were manufactured in Banbury. Banburismus exploited one of the Naval Enigma's weaknesses: message settings for a particular day were all arrived at by tapping out the trigrams, referred to in the description of the Naval Enigma indicating system at the beginning of this chapter, at the same wheel position (the Grundstellung). Banburismus is described in detail in Appendix 3. It was supposed to help the British codebreakers to rule out many of the 336 possible wheel orders which could have been used by the Germans on a particular day. After the Banburismus procedure was completed, the codebreakers were left with a manageable number of wheel orders which could then be tested on the bombe.

To use the Banburismus procedure the codebreakers needed to know the content of the bigram tables. Even after the *Polares* capture, Turing did not have a copy of these tables, but what he did have thanks to the documents seized was a long-winded method of reconstructing them. After the Enigma settings applicable to all messages sent on a particular day were captured or deduced, three gaps in the bigram tables could be filled in each time the message setting for a particular message sent on that day was worked out. Message settings were worked out using a so-called Eins catalogue; the way the Eins catalogue was used, and the way gaps in the bigram tables were filled in are explained in Appendix 3. There were nine bigram tables, one of which was used each day. Typically, message settings for three days had to be worked out when a given bigram table was in use for it to be reconstructed.[21] One bigram table was near enough to completion, after the message settings for the April 1940 series of messages were worked out, to enable the codebreakers to try out Banburismus. But the procedure did not work at first.[22]

It was November 1940 before the Banburismus procedure helped to break a Naval Enigma setting for the first time. Three days were broken: 14 April, 8 May and 26 June 1940. But the 26 June messages broken revealed another unpalatable truth. A new set of bigram tables had been introduced on 1 July. So Banburismus could not be tried out on subsequent messages until the new set of tables was reconstructed.[23] The trouble was that the bigram tables could only be reconstructed if messages could be read, and messages could only be read again if there was either another capture of codebooks, or if the codebreakers managed to find a regular source of cribs. Turing was almost back where he had been before the capture of *Polares*. The only difference was that now he was sure that if the settings were captured, Naval Enigma could be broken.

Once again there was no guarantee that cribs, the settings or the bigram tables would ever be identified or captured again. Nevertheless, the managers at Bletchley Park began to work out the number of bombes which would be needed to break Naval Enigma if these items were to come into their possession. Memoranda flew around the Victorian house as proposals and counter-proposals were laid out in black and white. In one note dated 26 November 1940, which seems to have emanated from the office of Edward Travis, Denniston's deputy, a neat calculation was worked out justifying why as many as twelve new bombes would be necessary. The calculation was based on the premise that there were around 330 wheel orders which would each have to be run four times every other day (the Naval Enigma wheel order was altered every other day), in order to allow for the double turnovers on some wheels, the fact that three of these wheel orders could be run on a bombe at once, and the fact that fifty such jobs could be run on the bombe each day. The calculation assumed that only one in three jobs would produce a positive result.[24]

It was good to think positively, but it did not solve the problem which was fast growing into a crisis: how to capture the Naval Enigma code once and for all.

8

Keeping the Enigma Secret

France and Bletchley Park

MAY—SEPTEMBER 1940

At the beginning of May 1940, as Hitler prepared for his Western Offensive in Europe, the codebreaker's version of a disaster occurred. The German Army and Air Force Enigma operators were told not to encipher their message settings twice at the beginning of their messages. In other words the indicating system described in Chapter 4 was being changed. Henceforth each message setting was only to be enciphered once. There was only one exception. The Enigma operators using the cipher machine in Norway carried on using the old system.[1] In relation to all other Army and Air Force messages, the Germans had, at a stroke, eliminated the Achilles heel of their Enigma message system which had enabled the Allies to read their messages during a substantial part of the previous seven years. Now the Allies were blind again.

The young men who were called on to deal with the crisis were the second wave of Bletchley Park recruits, men such as David Rees, who had been a mathematics pupil of Gordon Welchman at Cambridge University. Welchman had approached Rees in December 1939. At the time Rees was one of the brightest mathematicians at Sidney Sussex, Welchman's own college. Rees had a mathematics First and was starting his own post-graduate research. Welchman and Dennis Babbage, another Cambridge don who was also working at GC&CS, came to Rees's college rooms and told him that they had a job for him to do. Rees naturally asked them what it was, but the two dons would not say. At first they refused even to tell him where the job was to be executed. Eventually the bemused Rees blurted out, 'How will I know where to report to if you won't tell me where to go?' Only then did Welchman deign to tell Rees to meet him a few days later at Bletchley railway station. Rees did what he was told, and was taken to work with Welchman at Elmers School, the former school building on the Bletchley Park estate.

Another of Welchman's recruits was the twenty-one-year-old mathematician John Herivel. He had also been taught by Welchman at Cambridge, and in January 1940 he was called in to work alongside Rees in Elmers School. By the time Herivel arrived the perforated sheets had been manufactured at Bletchley Park and at the end of the his first month Enigma messages were being read, albeit with a substantial delay. Herivel and Rees had to test the various possible solutions produced through using the perforated sheets in order to check which was the correct one. They then worked out the plug-board socket connections for the day in question, a necessary element in the codebreaking procedure.[2] It was a long process, and Herivel wondered if there was some other way which would help the codebreakers to read the Enigma messages more quickly. There was. When he was relaxing one evening, he had the idea which was to revolutionise the way the Enigma cipher would be broken at Bletchley Park.[3]

Instead of thinking about what inferences could be drawn from the cipher texts which had already been intercepted, he found himself thinking about what happened before any messages were sent. What did the German Enigma operators do each day when they were setting up their cipher machines with the prescribed new settings, he wondered. Herivel thought in particular about how the rings around the Enigma wheels were set and how, afterwards, an operator would choose an initial position (Grundstellung) for the first message to be sent that day. Commonsense told Herivel that if the prescribed ring setting (Ringstellung) was, say, ABC, the operator would be likely to placc the correct wheels into the Enigma machine first, and only then would he set the rings to the correct setting for each wheel in turn. To do this for the left wheel, and the procedure would be the same for each wheel, the operator had to line up the correct setting, A, with the red dot on the catch. The catch was used to fix the ring into the correct position relative to the wheel core, and it also served as a marker. The ring was fixed into position most conveniently when both the correct letter on the ring, and the catch, were at the top, or near the top, of the wheel. So Herivel assumed that the fixing would be done with the ring and the catch in this position.

He imagined that the rushed or lazy operator would then close the cover over the wheels without touching them again, and that he would use the letters showing through the windows above the wheels as the initial position (Grundstellung) for his first message. If the operator did this, then the initial position (Grundstellung) for his first message – which was no secret since the initial position, after the change in the indicating system on 1 May 1940, was specified unenciphered at the beginning of the message – would be the same, or approximately the same, as the ring settings for the day. In this way the codebreakers would discover the approximate position of the ring settings for the day in question. If lots of operators using the same network followed the practice Herivel had guessed, then it was likely that the initial positions for all of their first messages of the day would be approximately the same, since they would all be using the same ring settings, and they would all be adopting the same procedure when, and after, fixing their rings into the correct position. All the codebreakers had to do to check whether this was the case was to plot on a graph the first initial position used by each operator on the day in question. If there was a cluster of marks around a particular place on the graph, then the ring settings were likely to be identical to one of the initial positions represented by one of the marks in the cluster.

But as so often happened with great ideas and theories relating to Enigma, this one did not immediately work in practice. For months the codebreakers tried out Herivel's idea without finding any of the tell-tale clusters. After the Germans altered their indicator system on 1 May 1940, which meant that no Enigma messages, other than those in Norway, were being read, Herivel's idea became even more important, since it was one of the few leads the codebreakers had. Then, about three weeks later, a miracle happened. Herivel walked into Hut 6, where the Air Force and Army Enigma codebreakers worked, and found that the night shift had at last discovered a cluster of initial positions. The ring settings for the day were identified, and the Enigma messages could be read once again. It was a very exciting moment. Welchman took Herivel on one side, and said, 'Herivel, this will not be forgotten.' It never was. The technique was referred to thereafter as 'the Herivel Tip'.

The Herivel Tip alone would not have been enough to have enabled Enigma to have been broken quickly. The codebreakers would have had to test the ring settings on all sixty possible wheel orders. Fortunately for the British, the practice spotted by Herivel did not represent the only mistake the Germans were making. There were other equally foolish errors being committed which included the use of obvious message settings; these came to be known as 'cillis', not just because they were silly, but because one of the first obvious set-tings worked out by the Bletchley Park codebreakers was 'CIL'. These cillis helped the codebreakers to identify each day's wheel order. (The way this was done is laid out in Appendix 4.)

Once the codebreakers had identified a day's ring settings, thanks to the Herivel Tip, and the wheel order, thanks to some cillis, the Enigma messages could be broken quickly. On 22 May 1940, the Bletchley Park codebreakers read an Air Force Enigma message for the first time since the beginning of the 1 May black out. The message had been sent on 20 May 1940.[4] The Enigma network broken was referred to as 'Red' by the codebreakers, taking its name from the colour of the pencil used by Welchman to underline the unenciphered characteristics common to all messages transmitted on the network.[5]

The break into the Red Enigma network was a vital step. The code-breakers were already gearing up to break Enigma messages using the bombe. But the bombe could not be used unless the codebreakers had access to cribs, and cribs were usually only identifiable if Enigma messages were being read. The Herivel Tip and the cillis ensured that the Air Force Enigma was being read when the first bombes were installed at Bletchley Park, and so they played an important role in ensuring that the code was broken, and remained broken. The Red Enigma network's messages were broken from 22 May 1940 until the end of the war with few interruptions.[6]

Unfortunately, as in the Norwegian campaign, a combination of factors meant that the Enigma messages broken after 22 May 1940 did not help the Allies to withstand the German onslaught in France and Belgium. Failure to pass the messages to the Commander-in-Chief in the field, failure to tell him that the intelligence contained in the messages was absolutely reliable, and the fact that the Germans out-fought the Allies are just some of the factors which are listed in the official history, *British Intelligence in the Second World War*.[7]

*

The British evacuation of its troops from Dunkirk, beginning on 26 May 1940, and the German attempt to prevent the evacuation, led to the next dramatic episode in the battle for the Naval Enigma code. But the chain of events leading up to it appears to have started three weeks earlier on board a British submarine.[8] On 5 May 1940, the British submarine HMS *Seal* had been hit by a mine while attempt-ing to escape from anti-submarine vessels in the Kattegat, the sea between east Denmark and Sweden. *Seal's* aft section filled with water and the submarine became stuck in the mud on the sea bed. The skipper Rupert Lonsdale did everything he could to free the vessel to no avail. At that moment, as the oxygen supply in the submarine began to run out, Lonsdale called on his men to say a prayer. Fortified by this, he instructed them to make one last effort to climb forward to the front end of the submarine. Shortly after some of the men complied, the bow dipped suddenly, the rear freed itself from the mud, and *Seal*, as if by a miracle, made it up to the surface.

Unfortunately *Seal* never made it back to Britain; the submarine was eventually captured by the Germans. Although every effort was made to destroy codebooks and charts, some documents were discovered after Lonsdale and his crew surrendered.[9] According to one German account, a chart was found amongst these papers which revealed the whereabouts of minefields protecting the east coast of England.[10] According to this report, it was information from this chart which helped the German *U-13* on 30 May 1940 to make its way through one of these minefields.

The *U-13* was one of Dönitz' fleet of 250 ton submarines. These boats, often referred to as 'ducks' because of their duck-like appearance, were half the size of the ocean-going 500 to 750 ton U-boats which were reserved whenever possible for longer patrols. Max Schulte, the twenty-four-year-old commander, had been instructed to go through a gap in the minefield so that he could try to sink ships going to and from Dunkirk. But the U-boat was delayed when it experienced mechanical problems before it reached the minefield. It took a day and a half for the engineers to fix the problem.[11]

At dusk on 30 May, shortly after *U-13* made it through the minefield, the U-boat was spotted off the Suffolk coast between Lowestoft and Aldeburgh by lookouts on HMS *Weston*, a British anti-submarine vessel.[12] The *U-13's* conning tower had been seen silhouetted against the last rays of the setting sun. The U-boat dived after *Weston's* commander ordered a signal to be flashed across asking the submarine to identify itself; another Allied submarine was expected in the area. The evasive action taken by Max Schulte convinced *Weston's* commander that the submarine belonged to the enemy, and battle was joined. For hours *Weston* hunted the U-boat with its Asdic equipment, and many depth charges were dropped overboard. After several of these depth charge attacks, water leaked into the U-boat, and Schulte decided to surface. His watch officer, Rainer Esterer, felt that Schulte was acting prematurely. 'Couldn't we just wait for one more attack?' he asked. 'You never know, it could be the last.' But he could not dissuade Schulte, who was of the opinion that one more set of depth charges might be one too many. Already one of the engines was making a noise which suggested that the propellor had been bent. 'At least we'll take one destroyer with us,' he muttered to Hans Grandjean, his leading engineer. If Schulte had listened to Esterer, the *U-13* might have survived to fight another day. For just as they were having this conference, the commander of *Weston* was receiving instructions to leave the submerged U-boat and to rejoin the convoy it had been escorting.

At 2 a.m. 31 May the *U-13* surfaced. Schulte opened the conning tower hatch and peered out. It was a pitch black night. All he could hear was the sound of small waves lapping against the side of his hull. But his men could not start the U-boat's motors. Then he saw a tell-tale silhouette looming up again about a hundred yards away. He had been seen, and this time they could not escape. Schulte shouted, 'Everybody out.' As the twenty-three men making up the crew clambered out of the U-boat, Schulte heard Grandjean, the leading engineer, shout up that he had opened the vents, and that the tanks were flooding. Although they had left many of their confidential books behind when they had embarked, the Enigma cipher machine and codebooks were still on board, and the U-boat had to be sunk if these items and other secret documents were to be kept out of the enemy's hands. Schulte responded by yelling down to Grandjean that he should also open up a valve in the bow which had been closed during one of the depth charge attacks. But while Grandjean was complying with this order, the *U-13*'s bow suddenly plunged beneath the waves, and the vessel sank with Grandjean inside. Schulte himself was hurled into the sea. For a moment he lost consciousness, but he came to just in time to see the stern of the *U-13* pointing up to the dark sky and the U-boat sliding into the sea like a sharp knife plunging into butter. As Schulte saw her go down, Schulte called out for three cheers, then he struck out towards one of the encircling ships which were waiting to rescue him and, he hoped, all of his crew.

Fortunately for Grandjean, the conning tower hatch slammed shut as the U-boat sank with him inside. So he had time to prepare himself for his attempt to escape to the surface. On the other hand his life jacket had been damaged, so he knew he would have to rely on his own strength to take him out of trouble. As he stood in the conning tower, he was partially blinded by the effects of the chlorine gas given off by the batteries following their immersion in seawater. His eyes smarted, and streamed with tears. The gas also caused stabbing pains in his chest and throat, and he choked uncontrollably. But he found temporary refuge under a hood in the aft section of the U-boat which hung down into the rising water. There was an air pocket inside. He improved the oxygen in the air pocket by using up some of the compressed air in his escape apparatus. Then, when he had recovered some strength, he dashed back to the conning tower.

In order to equalise the water pressure inside the U-boat with that outside, he first opened up a valve. Then, with one hand clinging onto the ladder rungs inside the tower, he opened up the conning tower hatch with the other hand. In this way he managed to hold himself in place as the water flooded in. After the U-boat had filled up with water, he climbed up the conning tower ladder and swam for his life. At first he tried to slow down his ascent, in an attempt to avoid suffering from the bends. But eventually, as he ran out of air, he panicked and swam upwards as fast as he could. Somehow he made it to the surface. Half an hour later, weakened by the sharp pains in his chest and by the overwhelming nausea which threatened to overcome him, he was finally picked up by a passing British ship.

A British attempt to salvage material from the wrecked *U-13* failed to produce any crucial Enigma documents, even though a large haul of books and papers were recovered.[13] However that did not stop Karl Dönitz, head of the U-boat arm of the German Navy, worrying about what the British might have discovered. On 8 June 1940, just a week after the *U-13* had been sunk, he telephoned the Naval Communications Service, which dealt with cipher security questions affecting the German Navy, to ask whether the Enigma procedure followed by his U-boats should be altered.[14] Dönitz was instructed to carry on using Enigma as before. However an analysis of the security measures in place was undertaken to back up the off-the-cuff advice. The resulting report highlighted the fact that Enigma settings were printed in special red print which dissolved when it came into contact with water. But even if the Enigma settings were captured, they would be unintelligible to anyone who did not know the meaning of a special order, codenamed Prokyon, the report stated. The written Prokyon order, which was not allowed to be taken out on patrol, altered the written settings document which was carried by the U-boat.

The assurances given to Dönitz did not completely satisfy him.

On 17 June he called in the Naval Communications Service again to ask about a suspicious move by a British convoy in the Atlantic. Apparently the convoy had unexpectedly altered the location of its planned meeting-up point, and Dönitz had been warned by his staff that his Enigma messages might be being read because of the *U-13* incident. However the Naval Communications Service did its best to convince Dönitz, once again, that the Enigma cipher had not been compromised. It could only have happened, Dönitz was told, if several security measures were overcome. The enemy would have had to seize the Enigma settings list before it was destroyed by the U-boat crew, or before it was immersed in water. The enemy would then have had to work out the Prokyon order, by comparing the written settings with the way the Enigma machine was set up when it was captured, and the enemy would have had to use this information to read about how the German U-boats intended to attack the convoy. 'The existence of any of these conditions and especially the existence of all of them at the same time is most unlikely,' Dönitz was told.

The German Beobachtungs-Dienst Intelligence service (the B-Dienst) which, unknown to the Allies, was reading the British naval codes during the summer of 1940, had not noticed any change in the security provisions taken by the British. This would surely have taken place if the German codes were being read, stated the Naval Communications Service's report. The report also referred to the German attempt to ensure that the *U-13* wreck was destroyed. A bombing raid targetting the place where U-13 was thought to be lying was carried out on 12 June 1940. The crew in one plane which took part in the raid noticed that the target area was marked by a group of buoys. It was unlikely that the buoys would have been left in position if the *U-13* had been towed away before the raid, stated the report. This suggested that salvage operations had not been completed or even started.

It was not the first time that there had been a security scare in relation to the Naval Enigma. Following the loss of the *U-33* in February 1940, Captain Ludwig Stummel, an officer in the Naval Communications Service, had summarised the security measures in place and stated that the Enigma system made it 'better than any other method used even by the enemy'.[15]

It was not just the sinking of the U-boats which had caused concern. The disappearance of two patrol boats off the coast of Norway – including *Polares*, as mentioned in the last chapter – was equally worrying. It was more difficult to scuttle a surface ship, so codebooks on board were more vulnerable.[16] A May 1940 post mortem into the disappearance of these ships analysed the radio messages relating to the trawlers which had been sent out by the German Navy on 26 April, the day when they had gone missing. One message had alerted the master of the harbour at Trondheim that the trawlers were due to arrive on the next day. Another message warned the trawlers to delay their arrival. Crucially it was discovered that the messages had been sent an hour after British destroyers were sighted in the sea off Trondheim, which suggested that the reading of the messages had not led to the destroyers being tipped off about the trawlers' presence. The destroyers' presence was thought to be a coincidence. The loss of any ship carrying an Enigma machine, raised the question of whether the codebooks had been captured. But the report stated that the known duty to destroy the codebooks meant that the capture of the codebooks was no more likely to have resulted in this case than in any other cases where ships were lost. A subsequent report on 21 May 1940 mentioned that it was now clear that the crew of *Schiff 26* – *Polares* – had been captured. The report suggested that *Schiff 26* might have been surprised by a British destroyer, like a German steamer which suddenly found itself sandwiched between two destroyers that had appeared out of the blue. It concluded that since it was most unlikely that the Enigma settings for June 1940 were on the two trawlers, or any other ship sunk during the Norwegian invasion, the security of the Enigma code was assured from the beginning of June.[17]

*

When the Germans invaded France on 13–14 May 1940, the Polish codebreakers and Gustave Bertrand were in their line of fire at the château in Gretz-Armainvilliers. So two days later preparations were made to evacuate them all to Paris.[18] Although they, like the British, could not at first read any of the German Air Force Enigma messages relating to France, after 22 May they decoded messages as if their lives depended on it.[19] Their new offices were at 2 bis Avenue de Tourville, the French Secret Service's headquarters. There they worked night and day, handing the messages to French officers who waited impatiently outside the room where the decoding itself was taking place. They used all the tricks invented by their colleagues at Bletchley Park, which included the Herivel Tip, and they also exploited another error committed by the Germans. The German Air Force was using an uncomplicated code for the weather forecasts it was relaying back to base. The substitutions involved in this code changed every day and the British codebreakers had spotted that they were always the same as the connections for the plugboard sockets on the Air Force Enigma system. So, as soon as the code was broken, the codebreakers knew the plugboard connections for the Air Force Enigma.[20]

It was some time before the Polish codebreakers realised that their codebreaking was not going to make any difference to the final outcome. During the week before Paris was bombed for the first time on 3 June 1940, Rejewski read with some alarm the German messages which explained how the car factories in the French capital were going to be attacked. It was the first knowledge the Allies had about Operation Paula – Paula was the German codeword for Paris. The messages included all the details about the planned bombing raid: the number of planes, the fighter plane escort, the route, the height, the day and the time. In short, everything which the Allies would have needed to intercept it.[21] The information was quickly passed on to the French armed forces. So the Poles were shocked when they saw hordes of German planes attacking on 3 June without any show of resistance from the French or Allied Air Forces. The air raid took place on the very day when Churchill and his War Cabinet, acting on the advice of Air Chief Marshall Sir Hugh Dowding, the Commander-in-Chief of Fighter Command, decided that no more British aircraft squadrons should be sent to France.[22]

Eventually the code breaking by Bertrand's unit had to be interrupted, as the German troops advanced through France. The Poles were evacuated again, this time by bus, ending up in Toulouse by the time the Armistice was signed by Pétain on 22 June 1940. Two days later, Bertrand managed to have all the codebreakers flown to Oran in Algeria.[23] But he quickly took steps to have them returned to unoccupied France. Within weeks of the Armistice, he was looking for a new château which could house the Franco-Polish codebreaking unit. He finally chose Château des Fouzes, situated near Uzès, between Montpellier and Avignon in the south of France. Rejewski and his fellow Polish codebreakers were installed there by 1 October 1940, after being told that its code name was to be Cadix.

It was a move which was not welcomed by the British. The fundamental problem was that while Bertrand wanted his codebreakers to carry on working on Enigma as before, Alastair Denniston rightly feared that they might all end up being captured. The Germans could take over unoccupied France at any minute and, if they did, Denniston did not want them to find anything about Enigma at Château des Fouzes.

At least Denniston knew about the problem posed by the Poles and Bertrand, and it was in his power to do something about it. That was more than can be said in relation to another difficulty in France which was known about by Paul Paillole, the head of the French Counter-Espionage unit. The difficulty related to Rodolphe Lemoine, the French agent who had run the Enigma spy, Hans Thilo Schmidt. The safest solution would have been for Lemoine to have been sent to England immediately after the Armistice. Lemoine knew almost everything about what Enigma settings had been handed over by Schmidt. In addition, it was clear that the Germans would want to find and punish him for failing to help them, in breach of a promise he had made when he was arrested and released in 1938.

However Lemoine's escape had been thwarted, as he explained to Paul Paillole on 23 June 1940 when they met up with Bertrand in Bon Encontre, the town between Bordeaux and Toulouse where Pétain had signed up to the Armistice.[24] On 20 June he had visited the British consul at Saint-Jean-de-Luz, the seaside resort near Biarritz. The consul had advised Lemoine and his wife to go down to the jetty in the harbour at 5 a.m. the next morning, where he would find a British mine-sweeper waiting for him. But when Lemoine arrived, he found that thousands of Polish soldiers were also crowding around the ship in the hope that they too could be taken to Britain. Nevertheless the ship's commander told Lemoine to report back that evening with an overnight bag and a blanket. By the time he returned, the Polish soldiers were already on the ship. Lemoine asked if there was a quiet place where his wife would not feel uncomfortable. This infuriated the officer on duty, who swore at Lemoine and explained to him, in no uncertain terms, why he hated the French. Lemoine replied that he would rather die in France than be insulted in England, and so he declined to take his place on the ship.

It was during his meeting with Paillole and Bertrand that Lemoine did something which made Paillole's blood run cold. After promising to travel to Saint-Raphaël, and agreeing to wait there for further instructions, Lemoine opened his briefcase so that he could give Paillole a file. But it was the remaining contents of the briefcase which took Paillole's breath away. The case was full of codebooks for different countries, blank passports for most of the states in Europe, blank identity cards and everything else that would help

Lemoine to succeed as a fraudster. Bertrand remarked that the code-books had been handed over by Hans Thilo Schmidt in August 1938. Paillole asked Lemoine whether he was sure that nothing of a compromising nature had been left behind in Paris. He was thinking about what would happen to Schmidt if anything was found by the Germans. But Lemoine assured him that he had been very careful, and that he had destroyed everything which was not in his briefcase. Rightly or wrongly, Paillole decided that he had no alternative but to accept Lemoine's word and to allow him to remain in France. So Lemoine, a loose cannon insofar as Enigma was concerned, with minimal restrictions placed on him, was allowed to proceed independently as before.

*

There were also serious difficulties concerning Enigma in England. One of the most pressing related to the intercept stations, which wereplaying such an important, if undervalued, role in the code-breaking process. The codebreakers were astonished to learn in August 1940 that the interception of Germany's morse code signals was no longer going to be carried out by the experienced operators working in Chatham, Kent. A new centre was to be set up at Chicksands, a country house near Bedford, manned by new staff. A letter of protest was written on 26 August 1940 by Hugh Alexander, the British chess champion who would one day take over from Alan Turing as the head of Hut 8, and by Gordon Welchman and Stuart Milner-Barry, two of the senior administrators from Hut 6, the Army and Air Force Enigma codebreaking unit.[25] Its frank description of the day to day problems encountered by the codebreakers is very revealing about the techniques they were using.

The writers claimed that the move would be 'extremely dangerous' and 'may well have disastrous effects on our work'. The problem was that the margin between breaking Enigma and failing to do so was 'already so slender' because 'Enigma traffic is so light that the task of breaking the code is exceptionally difficult.' In spite of their success so far, they made it clear that the question whether they could continue breaking Enigma messages 'hangs by a thread'. A change prior to the expected invasion of Britain was particularly bad timing, they said, given that the codebreakers needed to read the messages continuously if they were to pick up 'advance information of the kind of alteration which they [the Germans] are making in the system' prior to the invasion.

They cited the case which occurred on 5 May 1940 when they could not work out the Enigma settings being used in Norway merely because there was a mistake in relation to one letter in the indicator of one message. It turned out to be the vital link in the chain of evidence which, if taken down correctly, could have made all the difference. They also stated that they had only broken half the days in September 1939, and that the reason must have been that the recording of messages intercepted had been carried out incorrectly.

Their point could best be demonstrated by a recent example when, during one day, there were 267 messages. Only six were needed to break Enigma, yet if any one of the six had been missing, Enigma would not have been broken on that day. 'The actual margin between victory and defeat on a single day is often so small that the slightest reduction in the standards of interception might be fatal,' they stated. After the change in the system of indication in May 1940 there was an even 'narrower margin' than there had been previously. They pointed out that they could only use messages with 'certain peculiarities' and that on some days such messages were 'rare'. They also described how cribs were part of the principal method used to break Enigma. The identification of cribs depends, they explained, on knowing if a message is from the control centre to the sub-station or vice versa. Where it was not possible to work this out by other techniques, such as direction finding, they had to rely on the expertise of the intercept station. But that requires 'a sensibility and delicacy of hearing that can only be gained by long experience'.

According to the letter-writers Chatham was obtaining the right answer four times out of five, whereas the less experienced operators already operating at Shefford, another intercept station, missed out call signs altogether (the call signs identified who was sending the message), and failed to give clear information about where the signals were coming from. Yet without the method which Chatham employed so well, 'the crib method cannot be successfully employed.' In other words, without Chatham's expertise, Enigma could not be broken. One reason for this was that when the German operators moved from one frequency to another, the Chatham operators could hunt them out through knowing the 'peculiarities' of the different operators.

Another administrative difficulty related to the codewords which were to be used in correspondence when referring to the codebreakers and the intelligence secured thanks to their codebreaking. The best idea which John Godfrey, the Head of Naval Intelligence, came up with was that the information in the decoded messages should be referred to as special intelligence, the messages themselves should be special material, and a codebreaker should be called a special intelligence officer.[26] This was generally accepted to be a little less offensive than an idea which Denniston mentioned to Godfrey. Apparently the War Office and Air Ministry had decided to refer to the codebreakers as computers.[27]

9

Deadlock

Bletchley Park

AUGUST—OCTOBER 1940

During the autumn of 1940 Nazi Germany and its U-boats tightened the blockade it was attempting to impose on the British Isles. By October the British government, which had seen the Luftwaffe narrowly defeated in the Battle of Britain, had to face up to the horrific fact that if something was not done soon, Britain might be starved into submission by Germany's Navy. Imports had already fallen by around 25 per cent, from 60 million tons to 45 million tons per year.[1] That was to a large extent the result of having to delay merchant ships, with their cargoes of food, fuel and arms, so that they could cross the Atlantic in convoys guarded by warships.

At first the delays caused by the convoy system seemed a price worth paying. Until the spring of 1940 the amount of merchant shipping sunk by Germany's U-boats had been substantial, though sustainable. Losses of forty ships per month (around 150,000 tons) were considered high. The sinkings had fallen off during March and April 1940, when the U-boats were withdrawn from the Atlantic so that they could patrol off Norway during the invasion there. But following the fall of France in June 1940, there was nothing to stop Dönitz waging war in the Atlantic once again. The U-boats' success this time was frightening. In July 1940, 195,000 tons of shipping (thirty-eight ships) were sunk by the U-boats. In September 1940, the sinkings by U-boats rose to almost 300,000 tons of shipping (fifty-nine ships). In October 1940, no less than sixty-three ships were sunk, representing over 350,000 tons of shipping, the highest number of ships sunk by U-boats during a single month since the beginning of the war.[2]

British estimates of how many U-boats were causing the damage, and the rate at which new U-boats were being built, fluctuated wildly.

At the beginning of the year, John Godfrey, the Director of Naval Intelligence, thought there would be around 109 U-boats by July 1940, compared with fifty-seven when war was declared.[3] By July, he had revised his estimate to around sixty U-boats. In fact, partly because several U-boats were sunk, and partly because Germany failed to build as many as had been anticipated, the U-boat numbers only rose above the pre-war level for the first time in September 1940. Nevertheless, the British government was concerned that the numbers would be increased sooner or later and that merchant shipping losses would increase as well.

Although the number of U-boats had not reached an alarming level by the autumn of 1940, the fall of France had affected the amount of time each German submarine could be in an attacking position while out on patrol. The U-boats were now able to use the naval bases which they set up along the French coast at ports such as Lorient and Saint Nazaire, rather than being forced to make the slow passage in and out of the ports at Kiel and Wilhelmshaven in Germany. This was an important development for Dönitz who, at the beginning of October 1940, still had only eighteen ocean-going U-boats at his disposal. Only seven of these were at sea. But the tactics which Dönitz employed maximised their contribution. During August 1940, he began to deploy his U-boats in groups, or 'wolf packs'. Previously the U-boats had tended to operate independently; if more than one U-boat had attacked the same target, then one of the commanders on the spot often took charge, and the other U-boats reported to him. During August–October 1940, Dönitz changed all that. Instead of reporting to Dönitz once per day, U-boat commanders were expected to report back to him whenever they found a convoy. Then, rather than attacking immediately, the commanders were instructed, wherever possible, to shadow the convoy, and to send out very short beacon signals every half hour so that any other U-boats in the area could home in on the common target. If a U-boat was able to travel to the scene on the surface, it could easily overhaul the relatively slow-moving convoys. A U-boat could travel at between 12–17 knots on the surface, whereas convoys typically moved at between 7–9 knots. It was only if a U-boat was forced to travel submerged that speed was a problem. Under the water, a U-boat's maximum speed was cut down to around 7–8 knots, and even that could only be maintained for about two hours before the submarine's batteries went flat.

Only when Dönitz gave the order were the wolf packs free to

attack. The safest time to do this was at night, when U-boats could safely fire their torpedoes (four in the bow, and one in the stern) while on the surface. Although U-boats had one gun mounted on the deck, this was only used when attacking smaller ships or in an emergency. During a surface attack, the most important person on the U-boat's bridge was the first watch officer. He worked out the bearing of the target ship by lining it up in the large UZO binoculars, which were fixed to a column on the bridge. The information from the binoculars was fed down to the reckoner device inside the U-boat which, in its turn, programmed the relevant data into the torpedoes' mechanism. The first watch officer also had to shout down to the reckoner operator, telling him the target ship's course and speed. After receiving the go ahead signal from the commander, who would usually be on the bridge during a surface attack, the first watch officer would shout, 'Torpedo, los' (Fire), and both he and a man sitting beside the torpedo tubes down below would press a button or pull a lever to fire the torpedo.

If the attack was made from under the water, it was the commander who took control. He was responsible for lining up the target, as he looked through his periscope, for passing the relevant information to the reckoner operator, and for pressing the firing button. Then in order to counter the fact that several 2 ton torpedoes had been shot out of the bow of the U-boat, which meant that the bow was suddenly much lighter, the engineer was expected to order any men who were free to run forward to restore the balance.

In October 1940 the attacks by the wolf packs assumed terrifying proportions. Although changes to Britain's naval codes in August had deprived them of much valuable intelligence about the convoys' routes, the damage caused through the German B-Dienst Intelligence Service reading Britain's messages had already been done. The Germans already knew the convoy schedules, and the area about 350 miles west of the British Isles where the merchant ships met up with their British escorts. So Dönitz had a good idea where to send his U-boats to look for individual convoys. If a convoy was intercepted, the result could be devastating. The convoys were not being escorted by enough well-equipped warships to ward off a determined attack by a pack of U-boats. The nadir of British fortunes at sea during 1940 occurred between 18–20 October. During those three days, two Atlantic convoys, SC7 and HX79, travelling from Nova Scotia to Britain, were set upon by nine U-boats and no less than thirty-two ships (154,000 tons) were sunk.

But although the new U-boat tactics could be very effective, they did expose one crucial weakness. To operate as a wolf pack, the U-boats had to signal their positions to Dönitz's headquarters located in the first place in Paris and, after October 1940, at Kerneval, near Lorient. This gave Britain an opening which had not been available before. If the British codebreakers could only break into the Naval Enigma cipher, they would be able to pin point where the U-boats in the Atlantic were lining up. Then the incoming convoys could be diverted away from the wolf packs.

That was where Alan Turing was expected to step in. By the Autumn of 1940 most of the workers at Bletchley Park knew that Turing was something very special, even if they did not all know exactly what he had done. What was known was that he had become a fellow at King's College, Cambridge at the age of twenty-two and that, although he was still only twenty-six when Britain declared war on Germany, he had quickly established himself as Bletchley Park's star recruit. His assistants referred to him simply as Prof, in spite of his protestations that he had yet to achieve professorial status.[4] But his undisciplined, and disorganised approach to codebreaking did not appeal to Dilly Knox, the veteran codebreaker at Bletchley Park who had masterminded Britain's failed attempt to break the Army and Air Force Enigma before the war. In one surviving letter, which may have been sent to Denniston at the end of 1939, Knox wrote: 'Turing is very difficult to anchor down. He is very clever, but quite irresponsible, and throws out a mass of suggestions of all degrees of merit. I have just, but only just, enough authority and ability to keep him and his ideas in some sort of order and discipline.'[5]

Turing was certainly unlike anybody the Foreign Office civil servants had ever worked with before. For a start, he was a practising homosexual which made him a security risk. If he was ever caught breaking the law, he was liable to be blackmailed. Whether or not Denniston knew his sexual preferences, some of his colleagues did. Peter Twinn, Turing's assistant, found out one night in London. Returning to their shared hotel room after dinner, Turing asked Twinn whether they should go to bed together. When Twinn said he was not like that, Turing matter of factly made his excuses and got into his own bed alone.

Turing was also very eccentric. One of his closest associates suggested that if examined today, he might have been diagnosed to be suffering from a mild form of autism. Perhaps it was Asperger Syndrome, otherwise known as high grade autism, which Isaac

Newton is also thought to have had. People with this disorder frequently come up with brilliant ideas which no normal person could have thought of. At the same time, they have no idea how to relate to other people, and cannot understand what other people will think of their behaviour. Asperger Syndrome sufferers are often obsessive about their work, and like to do it alone.

Whether or not Turing had Asperger Syndrome, he certainly had many of its symptoms. He was an isolated loner at work and at play. In 1934, while still an undergraduate studying mathematics at King's College, Cambridge he had 'discovered' the so-called Central Limit Theorem, only to be told subsequently that his 'discovery' had already been written up twelve years earlier by another mathematician. He had failed to consult the relevant reference books.[6] He admitted that he had only agreed to research Naval Enigma 'because no one else was doing anything about it and I could have it to myself'.[7] His favourite sport was long distance running, since, as he put it, 'it gives me time to think.' He would utter a staccato mind-numbing 'Ah-ah-ah-ah-ah-ah-ah' in a curious high-pitched tone each time he wanted to say something. This had the effect of stopping anyone butting in and interrupting his train of thought. What he said was usually serious. He did not like small talk and rarely made jokes. If someone else made one, he would usually only smile after he saw that everyone else was laughing.

One thing he hated above all else was having to deal with people who were less intelligent than himself. Women were a particular problem, especially the flirtatious socialites who, more due to their family connections than their abilities, had found themselves working in the relative safety and comfort of Bletchley Park. To avoid having to speak to them, he would never look up as he walked over to the canteen in the main house from the Cottage where he worked, and he would scuttle away like a crab if anyone attempted to strike up a conversation. 'I find it so difficult spending time with women,' he would say to his male colleagues. 'I don't know if it's their education, or their background, or what. But they just open their mouths and say things which are so banal, it's as if a frog had popped out.'

The nearest he came to being intimate with a woman was in 1941, when he became engaged to Joan Clarke, one of the cleverest cryptographers working in the Naval Enigma codebreaking section at Bletchley Park. But Turing called off the engagement a few months later and told his colleagues that he did not go through with the wedding because he had a dream that his beloved mother did not like his girlfriend. His mother was far and away his closest woman friend.

Turing reserved his most unusual behaviour for the summer months. He suffered from hay fever, but rather than staying inside when the pollen count was high, he would bicycle around the countryside wearing a gas mask. He refused to repair his bicycle, even though the chain was faulty. Instead, he counted the number of revolutions it took before the chain became unstable, and then backpedalled until it was safe to ride normally again. Anyone could see the state the bicycle was in, he reasoned, so no one would try to steal it. That was not the case with his tea mug. Rather than risk losing it, he chained it to a radiator with a padlock.

The hope that Naval Enigma might succumb to Turing's strange but very inventive mind was buoyed up by the installation of the 'spider' bombe invented by Turing at Bletchley Park in August 1940. It quickly became the main instrument used to break Air Force Enigma, and the Bletchley Park administrators still believed that Turing might be able to break Naval Enigma as well. If he had succeeded, the most immediate beneficiaries would have been Frank Birch and his naval intelligence staff, including Harry Hinsley, in Hut 4. Birch had been told at the beginning of the war that no German codes were breakable.[8] But after the Air Force Enigma was broken, he became frustrated when there was no progress on its naval equivalent. He found Turing's and Peter Twinn's methodology particularly exasperating. 'Turing and Twinn are brilliant,' Birch wrote to Edward Travis, Denniston's deputy, in August 1940, 'but like many brilliant people, they are not practical. They are untidy, they lose things, they can't copy out right, and they dither between theory and cribbing. Nor have they the determination of practical men.'[9]

Birch was concerned that Turing and Twinn were not making the most of the suggested cribs which he and his team were passing on to them. According to Birch, Turing and Twinn were altering the cribs in an attempt to make the solution time quicker. 'Quicker, my foot!' Birch wrote to Travis on 21 August 1940. 'It hasn't produced any result at all so far. The "slower" method might have won the war by now.'[10] Birch felt that Turing and his assistant would have a higher chance of success if his section was consulted before any amendments were made to the cribs, so that all possible variations could be tried out 'systematically'.

Birch was not the only person becoming frustrated about the failure to break the Naval Enigma. The cryptographers in their turn became demoralised by Birch's section's inability to produce correct cribs.

' "Hinsley's certain cribs" became a standing joke,' wrote the author of 'The History of Hut Eight', the official, but unpublished, tale of how the Naval Enigma was broken. Birch's frustration was heightened by his feeling that not enough resources were being committed to the naval problem. At the end of 1940 the codebreakers in Hut 6, who dealt with the Air Force Enigma cipher, were still monopolising the two bombes which had been installed at Bletchley Park.[11] The cryptographers dealing with the Naval Enigma were only being allowed the partial use of one bombe, in spite of the escalating crisis at sea. More bombes had been ordered, but Birch was concerned that they too would be needed to deal with the Air Force Enigma, as more and more networks were broken. 'The long and the short of it is Navy is not getting fair does [sic],' he wrote on 21 December 1940. 'Nor is it likely to.'[12] He continued: 'It has been argued that a large number of bombes would cost a lot of money, a lot of skilled labour to make and a lot of labour to run, as well as more electric power than is at present available here. Well, the issue is a simple one. Tot up the difficulties and balance them against the value to the Nation of being able to read current Enigma.'[13]

Some of Birch's complaints, particularly those about the failure to manufacture enough bombes, were fair. But his concern about the Naval Enigma was encapsulated in the following extract from his 21 August 1940 letter to Travis: 'Turing and Twinn are like people waiting for a miracle, without believing in miracles.'[14] Alan Turing's pessimism about his ability to break into Naval Enigma and about the war in general was highlighted by his decision, in 1940, to transform a substantial proportion of his savings into silver ingots. He wrapped them up in brown paper, put them into a pram and pushed them out into the countryside near Bletchley where he buried them. He was sure that the Germans would liquidate everyone's bank accounts after invading Britain, and the hidden ingots were to be his insurance policy against that happening in his case. Another sign that Turing was not confident about the outcome of the war was his decision to join the Home Guard.

Given that the Naval Enigma could not be decrypted using standard codebreaking techniques, other more creative suggestions had to be considered. One solution, which Birch's Naval Section endorsed, was nicknamed the Wild Cat Scheme. The idea was that a meaningless jumble of letters should be sent out in morse code on one of the frequencies used by the U-boats. It was hoped that this would provoke a predictable reply which could be used as a crib.[15] A variation on this theme was proposed by Dilly Knox. He wanted a bogus signal to be sent out asking for the Enigma settings.[16]

At the same time, the Royal Navy commanders were given instructions on what to do if they came across a cipher machine on an enemy ship. On 29 August 1940, the following order was circulated: 'It is known that many German Naval Signals are cyphered on a machine. A photograph of a cyphering machine is reproduced. [The picture looked like an Enigma machine.] Any machine of this type found on board a German man-of-war should be carefully packed and forwarded to the Director of Naval Intelligence, Admiralty, in charge of an officer, by the quickest possible route. It is important that the machine should not be touched or disturbed in any way, except as necessary for its removal and packing.'[17]

The Director of Naval Intelligence, John Godfrey, also wanted his department to take up a more pro-active role. At the end of October 1940 he reported that he was setting up an organisation to arrange 'pinches', and to think up other 'cunning schemes'.[18] One top secret scheme had already emanated from Godfrey's assistant, Ian Fleming, whose novels about James Bond would later be released to a much wider audience. The essence of Fleming's proposal was contained in the following memorandum which he gave to Godfrey on 12 September 1940:

I suggest we obtain the loot by the following means:
1. Obtain from the Air Ministry an air-worthy German bomber.
2. Pick a tough crew of five, including a pilot, W/T operator and word-perfect German speaker. Dress them in German Air Force uniform, add blood and bandages to suit.
3. Crash plane in the Channel after making S.O.S. to rescue service in P/L [plain language].
4. Once aboard rescue boat, shoot German crew, dump overboard, bring rescue boat back to English port.[19]

Fleming's scheme, which was codenamed Operation Ruthless, included a contingency plan in case it all went wrong:

Since attackers will be wearing enemy uniform, they will be liable to be shot as franc-tireurs if captured, and incident might be fruitful field for propaganda. Attackers' story will therefore be 'that it was done for a lark by a group of young hot-heads who thought the war was too tame and wanted to have a go at the Germans. They had stolen plane and equipment and had expected to get into trouble when they got back.' This will prevent suspicions that party was after more valuable loot than a rescue boat.

Fleming added that the pilot should be a 'tough bachelor able to swim', and a German-speaker, who was also to travel on the bomber, was to be known as 'Fleming'. Operation Ruthless was quickly given the go-ahead, and Fleming travelled down to Dover, once a plane and crew had been procured, with the hope that he could put it into practice. But on 16 October 1940, the Vice-Admiral at Dover wrote to Godfrey: 'Operation Ruthless postponed. Two reconnaissance flights by Coastal Command revealed no suitable craft operating at night and evidence from W/T is also negative. Suggest material and organisation should not be dispersed. Possibly Portsmouth area may be more fruitful. Lieutenant-Commander Fleming returns to Admiralty 1800 today Wednesday.'[20] However, the plan eventually had to be abandoned.

On 20 October 1940, as U-boats in the Atlantic carried out some of the most savage attacks on convoys which had been seen in the war so far, Frank Birch wrote the following desperate note:

Turing and Twinn came to me like undertakers cheated of a nice corpse two days ago, all in a stew about the cancellation of Operation Ruthless. The burden of their song was the importance of a pinch. Did the authorities realise that since the Germans did the dirt on their machine on 1 June there was very little hope if any of their deciphering current, or even approximating current, enigma for months and months and months – if ever?[21] Contrariwise, if they got a pinch – even enough to give a clue to deciphering one day's material, they could be pretty sure, after an initial delay, of keeping going from day to day from then on; nearly up-to-date if not quite, because the level of traffic now is so much higher and because the machinery has been so much improved. The 'initial delay' would be in proportion to the pinch. If the whole bag of tricks was pinched, there'd be no delay at all. They asked me to add – what is self-evident – that they couldn't guarantee that at some future date, near or remote, the Germans mightn't muck their machine about again and necessitate another pinch. There are alternative operations possible. I put up one suggestion myself, and there are probably lots better. Is there anything in the wind? I feel there ought to be.[22]

Fleming, who must have been as disappointed as anyone that his Operation Ruthless plan had not worked, replied that he did not underestimate the value of a pinch. But for once his inventive genius let him down. He just could not come up with another viable plan.

It all added up to one dreadful conclusion. Not only was Naval Enigma not being read, but there was only a faint possibility that it ever would be read. Only the naval equivalent of a miracle could break the deadlock.

The Italian Affair

Bletchley Park and the Mediterranean

MARCH 1941

While Alan Turing was struggling to break the German Naval Enigma cipher, Dilly Knox and his staff, working in a section of Bletchley Park's converted stables known as 'the Cottage', were having more success with the Enigma cipher used by the Italian Navy. Dilly Knox's task was, in some ways, easier than Alan Turing's. Unlike the Enigma used by the German armed forces, the Italian Enigma did not have a plugboard. As a result, Knox and his team had far fewer settings to test than the codebreakers working on the German Navy's cipher machine. On the other hand, the Italian Navy did not use its Enigma as often as its other ciphers and codes, so Knox had to work out a way of breaking the code even when only a few messages were intercepted.

He had a lot to prove. Since July 1939, when the Poles had shown him how to reconstruct the German Air Force and Army Enigma, Knox's reputation as a codebreaker had been tarnished. This made him bitter. Although he could see the results which young mathematicians, such as Alan Turing, were obtaining, he resented the fact that he and his more intuitive style of codebreaking was being sidelined. Knox, who was fifty-five years old at the beginning of the Second World War, was a codebreaker of the old school. He was a classical scholar, who relied more on commonsense than on high-powered mathematical theories. He had served with distinction in Room 40, the First World War equivalent of Bletchley Park. In 1917 he had broken the Naval flag-code used by the German Commander-in-Chief. This was achieved after he realised that a piece of code was the enciphered version of a German poem by Schiller. Knox saw the light when he worked out that the bigram EN appeared five times within the space of seventy letters in the plain-language version of the code; one would not expect to find EN appearing so frequently in German, unless one was looking at rhyming poetry.[1]

However there was something which Knox and Turing had in common, in addition to both being fellows at King's College, Cambridge before becoming cryptographers. They were two of the world's great eccentrics.[2] Knox's eccentricity came to the fore when he was driving. He liked to recite Milton's *Lycidas* as he drove along and, when he came to the climax of the poem, he would take his hands off the wheel so that he could accompany the verse with appropriate gestures. Passengers who were not alarmed by this had to put up with another disturbing trait; whenever he approached crossroads, he would accelerate rather than slow down. He believed there was less chance of hitting anything if he went fast. 'Isn't it funny how people apologise when you nearly knock them down,' he would say to those who, in spite of everything, dared to venture out with him. He was equally dangerous when riding motorbikes, and had to give them up after a bad crash in which one of his legs was broken. That explained why he walked with a pronounced limp. Unfortunately, the game leg was not Knox's only physical disability. Before the war, he had suffered from cancer. Although it appeared to go into remission following treatment, there was always the fear that it might return. Another eccentric habit was his insistence on gardening even when out walking in the countryside; he usually took an axe with him so that he could chop branches off trees as he passed.

Although Knox had turned down an offer of a professorship to pursue his career as a cryptographer, he retained all the stock characteristics of the absentminded professor. Work in his section ground to a halt each time his pipe went missing, so that everyone could look for it. Conversations with him sometimes had to be interrupted to warn him that he was trying to fill it with a piece of bread torn off one of his sandwiches. The sandwiches were rarely eaten. Knox preferred to survive on a diet of tobacco and chocolate bars, to which he was addicted. He was often distracted from menial domestic tasks by his work. On one occasion he spent such an inordinate amount of time in the bathroom, a concerned young man waiting outside finally pushed open the door, only to find that Knox was neither having a bath nor committing suicide, but was standing up lost in thought, with the taps running and the plug out.[3] The fact that his head was in the clouds made him appear disorganised. His attempts to make quick exits from his office in the Cottage were nothing if not farcical. There were two doors in the office. One led into the corridor and the other was the way into a cupboard. Knox would invariably choose the wrong door and end up walking into the cupboard. Sometimes he would be seen walking around the Park in his dressing gown, having forgotten that he had not yet dressed for the day.

Unlike Turing, Knox was very keen on women. It was not that he was a womaniser. It was just that he liked having pretty women around him, and if he saw any beautiful girls wandering around Bletchley Park, he would ask his staff if they could try to recruit them for his department. There was one woman at Bletchley Park whom he found particularly fascinating. Her name was Mavis Lever. When war was declared, Mavis, who was eighteen at the time, had broken off her German studies at London University so that she could apply for a job at the Foreign Office. Her curriculum vitae had a blemish on it however as far as the security services were concerned. While at university, she had supported a scheme which helped Jewish refugees from Germany find jobs in England. Two of her refugees turned out to be German spies who were caught photographing military installations. Nevertheless, a few weeks later, she had been cleared to undertake Foreign Office work. Her first job was at Broadway, the codebreaking centre, near St James's Park tube station. It was only in April 1940 that she was sent to work for Dilly Knox at Bletchley Park.

In spite of the age gap which separated them, they quickly established a rapport. As well as being very pretty, she had similar interests to Knox. They were kindred spirits. He enjoyed her outspoken innocence all the more because it was offset by a shared interest in literature and lyrical poetry. If he quoted *Lycidas* at her, she would respond with an appropriate extract from *Alice In Wonderland*. However when, on her first day, he showed her an Italian coded message, she blurted out, 'It's all Greek to me.'

'A pity it's not,' Knox the classical scholar, retorted drily.

To get to know Mavis better, Knox took her out for a meal at a local hotel. Observers could have been forgiven for thinking that the tall gangly figure was the father of the fresh faced young girl he was accompanying. However she was thrilled to be picked out from all the girls working for him, though embarrassed by not knowing what to order while they were sitting chatting at the bar; well-bred young girls in those days did not venture into pubs. She recovered when he ordered her a gin and tonic, but she never forgot his half-concerned, half-amused expression as he watched her grimace when taking her first sip.

Knox's friendship with Mavis Lever was platonic; there was no question of his ever making a pass at her. But he was fond enough of her to appear jealous when Mavis told him she was engaged to Keith Batey, one of the mathematicians who worked on the Air Force Enigma in Hut 6. At first Knox tried to put her off Batey. 'He's just one of those clever mathematicians from Cambridge,' he would tell her, as if she were expected to share his mistrust for anyone who had anything in common with Alan Turing or Gordon Welchman. Only when he saw how determined she was to go through with it, did he let up. When Mavis and Keith Batey married in November 1942, he gave them a generous wedding present.

That was much later. In 1940, when they were tackling the Italian Naval Enigma together, she learned not to be put off by his messy work sheets whose appearance was not improved by his insistence on writing out all his calculations with a very blunt pencil. She realised that he had a lot to teach her. He taught her, for example, that cipher problems should be looked at from all possible angles. His favourite question for new recruits was: 'Which way do the hands on a clock go round?' If the recruit replied, 'Clockwise,' Knox would say, 'Well that depends on whether you are the clock, or the observer.' That was a very important lesson, as Mavis found out when she had to learn about rodding.

Rodding (which is explained in detail in Appendix 5) was the procedure Knox wanted Mavis Lever to use when she was asked to look at the Italian Naval Enigma. It took its name from the rows in tables, or catalogues, which the codebreakers had produced showing the electric current's path as it passed through the wheels inside the Enigma. The rows of entries in these tables were originally written on long thin strips of cardboard known as 'the rods'; they were still being used when Mavis started working on the Italian Naval Enigma in the summer of 1940. By then, it was known that rodding was the best way to decode a message enciphered on an Enigma without a plugboard, such as the Italian Naval Enigma. Using the rods, a cryptographer could work out the wheel order inside the Enigma on a particular day, as well as the starting position of the wheels for the message being rodded; once this was done, all messages transmitted that day could be broken.

However rodding only worked if the cryptographers either had access to a crib, or if they could somehow guess the meaning of one of the enciphered messages intercepted. Dilly Knox told Mavis his best guess; he thought the Italians might be starting their messages with PERX, PER meaning 'to' and X representing the gap between two words. Mavis tried out Knox's guess for some time before she had her breakthrough. While working alone in the Cottage one night in September 1940, the rods 'suggested' to her that the first four letters of the message she was testing might match up with the Italian plain-language PERS rather than PERX (see Appendix 5, which explains how the rods 'suggested' this to her).[4] This opened the way for her to guess that the first word in the message might be PERSONALE ('Personal'). When this educated guess was in its turn fed back into the rods, they 'suggested' other possible letters. So it went on through the night. First she guessed a few letters. Then the rods kicked in, and 'suggested' some more. That gave her the skeleton of another word, enabling her to guess the missing letters. Sometimes it was like cross ruffing while playing a hand of bridge. At other times, it was like filling in a partially completed entry in a crossword puzzle. By the end of the night shift, which ended at midnight, she had worked out that the message began: PERSONAL-EXPERXSIGNORX, followed by a name, and she had identified the day's wheel order and the message setting for the signal she was rodding. Mavis immediately told another cryptographer what she had achieved, and he promptly rang Dilly Knox. Next morning Knox rushed in and gave Mavis a spontaneous, warm hug. Thanks to Mavis's work, some Italian Naval Enigma messages could be read, and other more regularly used words identified as potential cribs. The cribs were used to break the cipher on subsequent days. Using this procedure, the Italian Naval Enigma was read each day until the summer of 1941 when the Navy stopped using it.[5]

There were hitches however. About three months later one of the Italian Enigma wheels was replaced with a new one. Once again, Mavis identified the clue which led to the break into the cipher. In one unreadable enciphered message, she noticed that there was not one 'L'. Using her knowledge that if a keyboard key marked with a particular letter was tapped, that letter was never lit up on the Enigma lampboard, she guessed that the entire message was made up of L's. It turned out that she had guessed correctly. The Italian operator had evidently been told to send a dummy message. Dummy messages were often sent when nothing was happening. The idea was that if a certain level of message-sending was maintained, even on days when there were no special operations, then when something important was about to happen the enemy would not be alerted merely by spotting an increase in the number of messages transmitted.

At first the break into the Italian Naval Enigma failed to produce any important intelligence. But then, on 25 March 1941, an Italian Enigma operator transmitted a three-line message beginning with one of the words which the Bletchley Park codebreakers had identified as a crib: SUPERMARINA, the Italian for the Naval High Command. Using the rodding procedure, the message was duly broken and passed on to the Admiralty. It was from Supermarina in Rome and was addressed to an Italian commander on the Greek Island of Rhodes. It stated: 'With reference to the message 53148 dated 24. Today 25 March is day X-3.'[6]

If that message had been looked at in isolation, it would have meant nothing. But the Bletchley Park intelligence analysts had already been alerted that something was afoot. It had not gone unnoticed that German air reconnaissance in the eastern Mediterranean had been stepped up, and the German Air Force Enigma messages deciphered in Hut 6 had indicated that the Axis powers might be planning a landing on the Libyan coast at the end of March. It quickly became apparent that these German messages referred to routine coastal supply manoeuvres, but another message on 25 March stated that German fighters in Libya had been ordered to Palermo, in Sicily, 'for special operations'.[7]

Within hours of the Italian message being intercepted and deciphered, the following information was being sent out by the Admiralty to Admiral Sir Andrew Cunningham, the Commander-in-Chief of the Mediterranean Fleet: 'Rome informed Rhodes that today 25 March is day minus three. Comment. Signal refers to a message from Rhodes to Rome on 24 March. Any further information will be forwarded is [sic] possible.'[8]

It was not until the next morning, 26 March, that the 24 March message referred to was deciphered, analysed, and forwarded to Cunningham.[9] It told the Commander in Rhodes, which was under Italian control, that he was to organise reconnaissance over the route between Alexandria, Crete and Piraeus in Greece during the three days commencing 26 March. It also specified that the airport in Crete was to be bombed on the night leading up to 'Day X', and at dawn on 'Day X'.[10]

Unknown to either Bletchley Park or the Admiralty, a third message relating to the special operation had been sent on 23 March from Naval Headquarters in Rome to Admiral Angelo Iachino, the commander of the Italian Fleet. It clearly stated what was intended to happen on 28 March. Three sections of the Italian Fleet were to patrol the area north and south of Crete on 28 March. 'If the enemy is sighted an attack should be made', Iachino was told, but he was only to do so 'if conditions are favourable'.[11] If this order had been seen by Cunningham, he would have known exactly what to expect. The Italian Fleet was being asked to attack British troop convoys which were being sailed from Alexandria to Piraeus, as part of Operation Lustre, in a bid to save Greece from being overrun by the Germans. But the 23 March message, and the messages amending it, which were sent on 25 and 27 March, were not sent by radio, so they could not be intercepted and read by the British codebreakers.[12]

During the late afternoon of 26 March Cunningham summarised the intelligence he had received 'from a most secret source' for Vice-Admiral Pridham-Wippell who commanded the British Fleet's 'Light Forces' in the Mediterranean: 'My appreciation is that operation is either a large-scale air attack on convoys or else a surface raid into Aegean ... My intention ... is to clear area concerned and so endeavour to make enemy strike into thin air whilst taking all action possible damaging him whilst he is doing so.'[13]

Within an hour of this message, Cunningham sent detailed instructions to Pridham-Wippell. On the morning of 28 March he was to be waiting thirty miles south of Gavdo, the island south of Crete, 'standing by for eventualities'.[14] Convoy AG9, which was heading towards Piraeus from Alexandria, would be turned back towards Alexandria after dusk on 27 March, and another convoy, GA9, was to be held back in Piraeus. 'Your action must depend on circumstances,' Cunningham told Pridham-Wippell. 'Your dawn position has been selected to enable you to withdraw in face of an unreasonably superior force or to intercept force as it returns.'[15]

In the early hours of 27 March, however, Cunningham received another message from the Admiralty. It warned him that the special operation might not be an attack on the British convoys after all, but could involve the enemy's army and the landing vessels which were said to be available in the central Mediterranean since 26 March. The Admiralty also could not understand why German aircraft were in Palermo.[16]

From all this it can be seen that neither the Admiralty nor Cunningham had any definite intelligence telling them what was going to happen on 28 March. But they evidently had enough evidence with which to make an educated guess. On 27 March Cunningham summoned his ten most senior staff officers to a final strategy meeting on board HMS *Warspite*, the Fleet flagship, which at the time was in harbour at Alexandria. Most of the staff officers did not know about the breaking of the Enigma. All they were told was that a reliable source had given them the information on the table. Cunningham summed up what he thought could happen the next day. Either the Italian Fleet would go to Tripoli, or to Rhodes, or it might attempt to interfere with the troop convoy bound for Greece.[17] At the end of the meeting, Cunningham told his staff to work out which of the alternatives he had specified was the most likely and then to report back to him. When they reconvened, everyone agreed that the Italians must be after the troop convoys. Cunningham clearly was of the same opinion, since he immediately said: 'That's decided then,' and started handing out the orders he had already prepared. He instructed his escorting destroyers and HMS *Formidable*, the aircraft carrier, to rendezvous outside the harbour at dusk.

He also sent the following message to Pridham-Wippell: 'I have now decided to take 1st B.S. [battle squadron] and HMS *Formidable* to sea after dark to-night Thursday to proceed westward south of Crete.'[18] One minute later, at 12.20 in the afternoon, a British Sunderland aircraft from Malta sighted three enemy cruisers and a destroyer off the south-eastern corner of Sicily, steering south-east towards Crete.[19] The Italian Fleet was coming out as planned. But before the British warships sailed to intercept them, a charade was to be played out in Alexandria, and the principal role in the play-acting was to be taken by the Commander-in-Chief of the Mediterranean Fleet. After the meetings with his staff officers, Cunningham told his flag lieutenant, Lieutenant Hugh Lee, that he wanted Lee to play a round of golf with him. At first Lee was concerned that they might miss a vital message from the Admiralty. But Cunningham quickly put him in the picture. The game of golf would be a good way to relax, but that was not its principal objective. Cunningham wanted anyone watching to be in no doubt that the British Fleet intended to stay at Alexandria that night. Lee was also to make it clear to anyone listening that they intended to throw a dinner party that night at the Ambassador's Residence in Alexandria, where Cunningham and his wife were staying. If any eavesdroppers happened to pass this on to the Italian Navy, it would increase the chances that the Italian Fleet would fall into the ambush which Cunningham was setting up.

The golf match was played at Alexandria's Sporting Club and, as always, Lee made sure that his commander came away the winner. But the important play-acting only took place after the game, as the two men were about to depart from the club house. For skulking in the bushes, Cunningham had spotted the squat shape of the Japanese Consul, who was known to be in touch with the Axis Powers on a regular basis. Noting that the Japanese Consul, dressed in his smartest plus fours, was straining to hear what they were saying, Cunningham shouted to Lee, 'Is everything ready for dinner tonight?' Lee replied, 'Yes, everyone's invited,' and as he walked over to the car, he did his best to make it appear that the empty suitcase he was carrying was, in fact, Cunningham's heavy overnight bag. In order to validate their story, they drove back to the Ambassador's Residence, but shortly after 6 p.m., as the sun went down, they drove off again to HMS *Warspite*. By 7 p.m., they were sailing out of the harbour.

In spite of all the play-acting, Cunningham was not very optimistic about catching the Italian Fleet, and he bet Manley Power, his staff officer, ten shillings that they would not see any of the enemy's ships. At dawn the next morning, 28 March, a reconnaissance aircraft which had taken off from HMS *Formidable* sent its report back to *Warspite*. It was Lee's task to take the message in to Cunningham, who was eating his breakfast. Lee reported that four Italian cruisers and four destroyers had been sighted. But when Cunningham heard where the ships were, he said to Lee, 'Don't be silly. They've just seen our own ships.' The ships which had been spotted were in the area where Pridham-Wippell's force was supposed to be. But Lee said, 'I'll leave the marker on the chart just in case.'

Less than an hour after the first message, another message came through from Pridham-Wippell saying 'Enemy in sight'. So Cunningham had been wrong, and Lee had to tell him. As Lee knocked on Cunningham's cabin door, he was nervous about the reception he would receive. He wondered if Cunningham would put on his much talked about caged tiger act, which involved him marching up and down the bridge as he thought about what to do next. Cunningham was in the bath when Lee walked in. But when he heard what Lee had to say, the caged tiger rose out of the soapy water like some glorious warrior prince and, without bothering to cover up his naked body, began dictating orders: 'Battlefleet to increase to full speed. VALF [Vice Admiral of Light Forces, i.e. Pridham-Wippell] to retire towards us. *Formidable* to prepare torpedo striking force.'

At about 10.20 p.m. that night, Cunningham finally saw some of the Italian ships. They had been sent back by Iachino to rescue *Pola*, an Italian cruiser, which had been crippled by a torpedo fired from an aircraft flown off *Formidable*. Iachino had failed to appreciate that the British Fleet was so close. At first Cunningham could only see silhouettes in the darkness about two miles away as two Italian cruisers and four destroyers sailed peacefully from starboard to port across the bows of the British Fleet.

Then, as the British ships' searchlights were switched on, Cunningham saw the huge ships, now clearly visible as silvery blue shapes, caught with their gun turrets still pointing fore and aft as if on parade at a naval show, and with their crews running around on the decks. Seconds later he heard the calm voice coming from *Warspite*'s gun director: 'Director layer sees the target,' which meant that one of the ships was already in his sights, accompanied by the ting-ting-ting of the firing gongs. Then came the blinding orange flash and the violent shudder *Warspite*'s 15-inch guns fired, and the sight of their huge projectiles flying through the air. Finally he saw the splashes of brilliant flame as the shells obliterated *Fiume*, the third ship in the line, transforming what was a beautiful proud cruiser one moment into a glowing torch on fire from bow to stern just minutes later. The same treatment was handed out to *Zara*, the second cruiser, and to *Alfieri*, the destroyer at the front of the line. Another destroyer was sunk three-quarters of an hour later, and at about 4 in the morning of 29 March, *Pola*, whose plight had caused Iachino to send his ships back into Cunningham's trap, was also sunk.

The stunning British victory, in which 2400 Italian sailors lost their lives, was later summed up by Cunningham as follows: 'Five ships of the enemy fleet were sunk, burned or destroyed . . . Except for the loss of one aircraft in action, our fleet suffered no damage or casualties.' He added, 'There is little doubt that the rough handling given the enemy on this occasion served us in good stead during the subsequent evacuations of Greece and Crete. Much of these later operations may be said to have been conducted under the cover of the Battle of Matapan.'

During the evening of 29 March, John Godfrey, the Director of Naval Intelligence, rang Bletchley Park, and asked to be put through to Dilly Knox. When Edward Clarke, who answered the phone, told him that Knox was unobtainable because he was at home, Godfrey asked him to pass on a message: 'Tell Dilly that we have won a great victory in the Mediterranean, and it is entirely due to him and his girls.'[20]

When Cunningham was next in England, he went down to Bletchley Park to thank the codebreakers for the part they had played. While he was there, Mavis Lever and her young friends could not resist playing a schoolgirlish prank on him. Seeing that he was dressed in a spotless naval uniform, and that there was a freshly whitewashed wall behind him, they crowded around him in such a way that he was forced to lean against the whitewash. When he undressed that night, he was in for an unpleasant surprise.

Knox and 'his girls' may have helped the Royal Navy to win a historic victory at Matapan, but he was to have less success in another battle fought behind the scenes at Bletchley Park. Knox was upset that he was not allowed to circulate the results achieved by his unit in the Cottage. Denniston had arranged for all naval intelligence resulting from codebreaking to be handled by Bletchley Park's Naval Section. In this way, the overall picture derived from all Italian, German and other naval intelligence could be looked at. In October 1940, Knox had complained that Denniston had 'tricked' him into agreeing with this arrangement,[21] and at the end of 1941 he took up the same theme again, referring in the following letter to Denniston's 'monstrous theory' of making the codebreakers collect material for others, which, wrote Knox, was 'impossible for a scholar'.[22]

My dear Denniston, I am almost despairing of making you see reason on the major issues . . . As a scholar, for of all Bletchley Park I am by breeding education profession and general recognition almost the foremost scholar, I naturally set about enlarging the raw material of my research . . . By profession and in all his contacts a scholar is bound to see his research through from the raw material to the final text (with or without translation). From 1920–30 I was always able to proceed as a scholar, and, as a scholar, I simply cannot understand, nor I imagine can the many other scholars at BP your grocer's theories of 'window dressing'. Had those been applied to art scholarship science or philosophy . . . [giving] the inventor no right to the development and publication of his discoveries, we should still be in the Dark Ages.

Denniston started his reply, which was written on 11 November 1941:

My dear Dilly,
Thank you for your letter. I am glad that you are frank and open with me. I know we disagree fundamentally as to how this show should be run but I am still convinced that my way is better than yours and likely to have wider and more effective results.

If you do design a super Rolls-Royce that is no reason why you should yourself drive the thing up to the house of a possible buyer, more especially if you are not a very good driver. I lost any confidence you had in me when I disagreed with you in Dec. 1939 and said that you could not exploit your own success and run huts 6 and 3. I was right – you broke new ground while the building in your foundation was carried on by Travis etc who, I say, were better adapted to this process than you.

The letter ended:

You are Knox, a scholar with a European reputation, who knows more about the inside of a machine than anyone else. The exigencies of war need that latter gift of yours though few people are aware of it.

The exploitation of your results can be left to others so long as there are new fields for you to explore.

I do disagree with you.

Yours ever.

A.G.D.[23]

While the battle between Knox and Denniston continued, Knox's methods enabled Mavis Lever and Margaret Rock, another of Knox's 'girls', to reconstruct the main Abwehr cipher machine. On 8 December 1941, they read an Abwehr message for the first time. Subsequently many Abwehr messages were read. This was another coup for British Intelligence. The British had managed to 'turn' some of the German spies arrested in England, and persuaded them to send bogus messages back to their spymasters in neutral countries such as Spain. These spymasters used the Abwehr Enigma cipher to forward their spies' intelligence to Berlin. When these messages were read, British intelligence officers could monitor the success of their double-cross operation.

After this latest success, Denniston wrote the following note dated 12 December 1941: 'Knox has again justified his reputation as our most original investigator of Enigma problems. He has started on the reconstruction of the machine used by German agents . . . He attributes the success to two young members of his staff, Miss Rock and Miss Lever, and he gives them all the credit. He is of course the leader, but no doubt has selected and trained his staff to assist him in his somewhat unusual methods. You should understand that it will be weeks, possibly months, before there will be a regular stream of these.'[24]

*

There was an interesting post-script to the breaking of the Italian naval cipher. In his 1962 book, *The Quiet Canadian*, about Sir William Stephenson, Montgomery Hyde raised the question of how Cunningham had managed to find the Italian Fleet in March 1941 off Cape Matapan.[25] Hyde's answer was, in substance, as follows.

A beautiful spy – codenamed Cynthia – had offered herself to Admiral Alberto Lais who was working as a naval attaché in the Italian Embassy in Washington. Lais became so enamoured of Cynthia's charms that she was able to persuade him to betray his country. As soon as she had him enthralled, she told him that she absolutely must have the key to Italy's Naval cipher. He did not stop to question her motives, and had the key handed over to her immediately. The codebooks were quickly copied and sent over to Britain. From there they were flown out to Admiral Cunningham, the Commander-in-Chief of the Mediterranean Fleet, who used them to ambush the Italian Fleet. In March 1941 Cunningham won the Battle of Matapan, one of the most important victories at sea during the Second World War. After Matapan, the Italian Fleet was sidelined for the rest of the year.

In 1964, a high-profile Italian libel case was brought to decide whether pillow talk between the love-struck Admiral and his blonde-haired siren really had caused Italy to suffer one of its most shameful defeats. The libel action was brought by the son and the nephew of the dead Admiral to clear the Lais name. In their quest to seek the truth, questions were asked about whether the British had read the Italian ciphers. That was something which was only partially answered in 1970 when the Supreme Court in Milan came to its decision. The court was confused by the conflicting claims presented to it. Was it possible that the British had used their supposed knowledge of the Italian naval cipher – which at the time of the case was always referred to by its serial number SM 16/5 – to listen in to the Italian Fleet's battle plans, the court was asked. Or was it, in fact, true that the plans were sent down a land line and by courier, rather than by radio, so that there was no opportunity for the British to listen in to the messages, let alone to decode them? The point was never proven either way beyond a shadow of a doubt in Milan, although the Supreme Court appeared to believe that the latter position was the true one.[26]

However the court was absolutely sure that Hyde had failed to tell the truth about Cynthia and Lais. The author of *The Quiet Canadian* had made a silly mistake when writing up the story. He wrote that

Lais had told Cynthia where to find the codebook while the two lovers were bidding each other farewell. According to Hyde, they were on the ship which was about to take Lais back to Italy. Lais ignored his wife and children, said Hyde, while he concentrated on saying goodbye to Cynthia. Unfortunately for Hyde, the departure of Lais from America took place on 25 April 1941, almost a month after Cunningham was supposed to have used Lais's codebooks at Matapan. There could be no mistake about it. The departure was written up in the *New York Times* on 26 April 1941. So Hyde's story about how the codebooks were handed over to Cynthia, and then used during the Battle of Matapan, could not have been true. The only woman who had escorted Lais to the ship to say goodbye was his twenty-year-old daughter Ellen. His son was serving on an Italian ship in the Mediterranean, another reason why it was most unlikely that Lais would have wanted to hand over any naval codebooks to the British. Besides, Lais had never had any access to the Italian Fleet's codebooks. The story was a lie from start to finish, said the judges in the Supreme Court.

The End of the Beginning

Norway

MARCH 1941

On the very day when the first British troops were being ferried from Egypt to Greece at the start of Operation Lustre – the operation which had paved the way for the Battle of Matapan – another operation, which was to have important consequences for the German Naval Enigma, was reaching its climax in Norway. At 4.30 in the morning of 4 March 1941 an expeditionary force, consisting of five destroyers and two troop carriers, steamed into Vestfjord, and crept into position off the Norwegian Lofoten Islands. Operation Claymore was about to begin.[1]

As far as the commandos taking part in the operation were concerned, it was merely a diversionary raid, one of the morale-boosting attacks favoured by Winston Churchill who, notwithstanding Britain's stretched resources, wanted to take the fight to the Germans, thereby forcing them to leave extra troops in Norway. Fuel tanks and fish factories were to be hit, German ships were to be sunk and Norwegian collaborators captured. Then the commandos were to withdraw. But there was another top secret mission to be carried out by the Royal Navy during Operation Claymore. German trawlers were operating along the Norwegian coast. There was a possibility that they might be using Enigma cipher machines. If one of the trawlers could be captured during the raid, there might be a simple way to break the Naval Enigma cipher after all.

The command post during the raid was aboard HMS *Somali*, the destroyer. At about 6.20 a.m., while the ship was steering around between the four landing spots on the Lofoten Islands coast, the lookouts spotted the German trawler which was going to make all the difference in the battle for the code. The trawler, *Krebs*, was sailing away from Svolvaer, one of the landing spots. *Somali*'s gunners opened fire when the trawler was just under two miles away, but the first shells missed. *Krebs* fired back and one of its shells whistled over the heads of *Somali*'s crew, ripping apart one of the destroyer's flags. But that was *Krebs'* last chance to cause any damage. One of the next shots from *Somali* hit *Krebs* in the wheelhouse, instantaneously killing her captain and some of the crew. *Krebs'* boiler room and ammunition store were also hit and, within minutes, the trawler was steaming around in circles with smoke billowing out of its engine room.

During this exchange the commandos' guns could be heard firing ashore and the crippled trawler was left behind as *Somali* steamed off to investigate how they were faring. Shortly after 9 a.m., having established that all the landings were proceeding satisfactorily, *Somali* passed by Scråven, the tiny island just opposite Svolvaer, near to the rocky islet where, following the attack, *Krebs* had been beached. The burning trawler had subsequently slipped away, and was floating towards the centre of the fjord. Lieutenant Sir Marshall Warmington, the signal expert on *Somali*, then suggested to the ship's commander, Captain Clifford Caslon, that they should send over a boarding party. At first Caslon was reluctant to do so. On a previous occasion, his ship had been attacked and torpedoed by a U-boat off Norway, and he did not intend to be caught out again. It was only when Warmington said that he was willing to go over on one of the Norwegian fishing boats, which were crowding around the destroyer, in order to save the lives of *Krebs'* crew, that Caslon relented. So Warmington commandeered a fishing boat.

As the three men making up the boarding party clambered aboard *Krebs*, they pulled out their pistols and revolvers. They could have saved themselves the trouble. Five members of the *Krebs'* crew were cowering on deck, one waving a white flag. Another man was bleeding profusely after having a piece of muscle shot out of his arm. In the wheelhouse there was no sign of life at all. The captain of the trawler was lying dead beside the wheel, surrounded by the inert bodies of two other members of the crew. Stuffing his pistol into the pocket of his duffel coat, Warmington marched off to search the captain's cabin. Here he found a pile of papers which he left for the other members of the boarding party to pick up. He was more interested in finding out what was hidden inside a locked drawer. Feeling a little like a cowboy in a western, he carefully aimed his pistol at the lock and pulled the trigger. For one ghastly moment he thought that he was going to be killed by his own bullet, as it ricocheted around the cabin.

But when he pulled the drawer open and took out the wooden box inside, he knew that he was on to something. Inside the box, he found two discs which he immediately realised were for some kind of cipher machine. No one had ever told him anything about Enigma.

Meanwhile, on *Somali*, another drama was brewing. Caslon was cross that Warmington was taking such a long time and eventually, after about forty-five minutes, he told his signalman to instruct Warmington to return to the ship immediately. The order was duly flashed over to *Krebs*, and Warmington was brought back to HMS *Somali* with his booty. By 1.30 in the afternoon, the convoy was setting out for home, after the commandos had all returned to their ships, and forty-eight hours later, the expeditionary force was back at Scapa Flow.

But the columns of smoke rising from the burning fish factories and oil tanks left behind in Norway did not represent the principal benefit of the raid. Nor was the box containing the cipher machine wheels the most important item captured, even though, according to the official report of the raid, they were identified as being similar to the 'wanted' spare wheels for the cipher machine depicted in CAFO Diagram 242/40 (the Diagram with CAFO 1544 which was circulated as mentioned in chapter 9). The prize booty was a document labelled 'Schlüsseltafeln M-Allgemein "Heimische Gewässer" Kennwort HAU. Prufnummer 1566'. Warmington had managed to lay his hands on the Enigma settings for the Home Waters network, the very documents which Alan Turing and Peter Twinn had been crying out for ever since the cancellation of Operation Ruthless in October 1940. In the document, there were headings such as 'Innere Einstellung' (Inner Settings), 'Aussere Einstellung' (Outer Settings), and 'Steckerverbindungen' (Plugboard Connections).

Although Warmington had only found settings for the month of February, which were out of date by the time they were handed to Alan Turing at Bletchley Park on 12 March, the cryptographers in Hut 8 were going to find them very useful. That same day some Enigma messages which had been sent by the Germans on 27 February 1941 were read in Britain.[2] The contents of the messages did not, at first, appear to be very useful. But each message was of assistance when it came to reconstructing the bigram tables (as mentioned in chapter 7). The cryptographers knew that once the bigram tables were reconstructed, Alan Turing's Banburismus procedure could be tried out again. It was hoped that the same bigram tables would remain in use for several months.

But reading the February 1941 messages took longer than antici-pated. This was because at the same time as the bigram tables were being worked out, new staff were being taught how Naval Enigma could be broken.[3] Some of the February messages were still being read for the first time at the beginning of April, more than a month after the capture.[4] Nevertheless the bigram tables were 'more or less complete' by the end of March, according to the official 'History of Hut Eight', and this gave Turing his chance to put his Banburismus technique to the test in relation to new messages intercepted in April 1941.[5] As had happened after the capture of *Polares*, however, the Banburismus procedure did not immediately produce results. One of the problems was that many of the messages being worked on were dummies, consisting of a string of consonants. These messages could not be catered for by the statistics worked out by Turing which were used during the procedure. A way had to be found to identify the dummy messages before applying Banburismus to the remainder.[6] All of these problems meant that no March signals were decrypted at all, and only eight days in April were read by 10 May.[7]

Given these difficulties, Admiral Jack Tovey was correct to rebuke his subordinates for not having thoroughly searched *Hamburg*, one of the German ships sunk during Operation Claymore. 'It was nec-essary to sink the *Hamburg* rather than attempt to steam her down Vestfjord and then some 750 miles to the Faeroes with the resources available, but she should first have been boarded and searched for papers,' he said.[8]

The capture of *Krebs'* wheels and documents once again led to worries that the German Navy might guess that its cipher was being read. Even before the capture, Dönitz was concerned that the British convoys were being diverted around his U-boats. At first he thought that the problem was that the British could take bearings on the radio reports which were being sent out by his U-boats.[9] However by April 1941, he was writing in his diary: 'It seems that the British ships are getting around the locations picked out for [U-boat] attacks. This leads one to suspect that our ambush points are known to the enemy. Although this is only a suspicion one has to exclude the slightest possibility without paying regard to the down side.' So he ordered the number of people who were allowed to know about the ambush points to be drastically restricted in case there was a traitor amongst his own staff. He also demanded that his U-boats should be given a special key which would keep their messages secret from other ships using the Naval Enigma cipher.[10]

But the greatest threat to Britain's Enigma secret appeared not in Germany, but in France. In December 1940 the Germans began to sift through the files at the police headquarters in Paris. One of the documents found was a statement made by an Italian agent in March 1938. According to the agent, hc had in his possession a copy of a note which a German Cipher Office employee had written about a German code. The agent stated that it was Rodolphe Lemoine who had offered to sell the details of the code to him.[11] This was the first time the Germans had found out that someone was leaking documents from the Cipher Office.

During the summer of 1940, the German Secret Service in Paris had made another discovery. Amongst the French General Staff documents, which they found on an abandoned train at Charité-sur-Loire, were a series of documents which appeared to mirror reports produced in Germany by the Air Ministry's Forschungsamt (Research Office). The Forschungsamt was the telephone tapping organisation which Hans Thilo Schmidt had joined in 1938. Questions were asked inside the Abwehr about whether someone inside the Forschungsamt had leaked intelligence to the French. If so, there was a traitor at the Forschungsamt as well as at the Cipher Office. Or perhaps it was one and the same person who had worked at both organisations; such as Hans Thilo Schmidt. At first no one made that connection. He was not the only person to have moved from the Cipher Office to the Forschungsamt. But an order was put out to find Lemoine, the French secret agent, who, it was thought, might be able to reveal who the culprits were.

In April 1941 Lemoine was discovered in Saint-Raphaël by Paul Paillole, the French counter-intelligence officer. Lemoine was making cnds mcct by cxploiting the black market. He had been selling passes to people who wanted to travel across the French border. Paillole ordered him not to carry on with this trade and told him to go into hiding immediately so as to avoid the German agents who were, even then, looking everywhere for him. Lemoine was told to book into a hotel in Marseille which was closely watched by friends of Paillole in the French police. Paillole hoped that Lemoine had enough sense, and money, to see him through the rest of the war. So he allowed him to stay on in unoccupied France. But his liberal attitudc towards Lcmoine turned out to be misplaced. Lemoine was an inveterate wheeler-dealer, always looking for the chance to make another buck. There would come a time when Lemoine would tire of being marginalised and would want to go centre stage one last time, even if it was on the German side. When he did so, all the secrets which he had ever come across in his long career would be up for sale, and no one who had worked as his agent would ever be safe again.

12

Breakthrough

North of Iceland

MAY 1941

The Enigma messages read following the March 1941 capture of *Krebs'* codebooks were passed to the Naval Intelligence section in Bletchley Park's Hut 4. One of the analysts there was the twenty-two-year-old Harry Hinsley. But it was not the long-haired, shabbily dressed Harry Hinsley who had failed to produce any useful intelligence during 1939. The Hinsley who looked at the messages was a revitalised version of the original model. He no longer had to rely on the charity of his fellow workers to pay for a new pair of corduroy trousers. Nor did he have to listen to the patronising reaction to his phone calls by the naval officers in the Admiralty. By 1941 he was swanning around in a bespoke Burberry suit and having his hair cut regularly at a barbers shop in the West End of London. The men at the Admiralty did not wait for him to ring them; they sought his opinion, as did the Admirals of the Fleet whose ships were anchored at Scapa Flow. They nicknamed him 'the Cardinal'.[1]

The extraordinary turnaround in Hinsley's fortunes had nothing to do with Enigma, and everything to do with traffic analysis, the task he had been given in the Naval section when he first arrived at Bletchley Park. Traffic analysis meant looking at all the evidence relating to enciphered messages which could not be read, and reaching a conclusion on what the enemy was doing. Until April 1940, traffic analysis revealed next to nothing. But as the Germans prepared to land in Norway ahead of the British, there was a sudden upsurge in wireless activity, a fact which Hinsley was able to report to the Admiralty on 7 April 1940 before the invasion took place.[2] It was part of the growing body of evidence which suggested that a movement by the German armed forces was about to occur. Unfortunately, none of the generals or government ministers could be persuaded to act on the intelligence they were receiving. Consequently, the German invasion was allowed to take place, unopposed by the British Fleet.

The man at the Admiralty who Hinsley contacted when he came across anything interesting was Pay Commander Ned Denning. He, in his turn, reported to Rear-Admiral Jock Clayton, the head of the Admiralty's Operational Intelligence Centre (the OIC). This was the division which analysed all intelligence having a bearing on where German surface ships and U-boats were to be found. Until Norway was invaded, Hinsley had never met Denning or Clayton. They were just grand voices at the other end of the telephone who were unwilling to take much notice of anything he told them. That was not altogether surprising because, until the Norway invasion, Hinsley had not had much to say.

But at the end of May 1940 Hinsley noticed another unusual phenomenon. Messages which were being transmitted on one frequency in the Baltic area were being repeated on other frequencies which had never been used before. The chain of messages indicated to Hinsley that the Germans were about to move some of their ships from the Baltic Sea to the Skagerrak, the narrow stretch of sea separating Denmark and Norway. He passed this information on to Denning.[3] By 7 June, Hinsley was warning Denning that German ships were in Norwegian waters, and were well placed to take offensive action in the North Sea. He even asked Denning, and Clayton who came to the phone when Hinsley had anything important to say, whether a message could be passed on to the Fleet to warn them that they might at any minute come face to face with German naval forces. He might have been more insistent, if he had been told that, at that very moment, the British forces were being evacuated from Norway. But incredibly, neither he, nor any of the junior staff at the OIC, were told about the evacuation until after the event.[4]

Even as Hinsley was giving the Admiralty notice that the German ships were moving in, the German cryptographers, who, unknown to the British, could read the Royal Navy's codes, were telling the German Navy the whereabouts of Britain's warships.[5] One crucial signal intercepted by the Germans, and read by them on 2 June, revealed the exact position of HMS *Glorious*, the aircraft carrier, off the coast of Norway. It was one of the ships sent to protect the troop ships as they brought home the British Army.[6] Hinsley's warning was noted in the OIC's logbook, but it failed to receive a wider circulation. As a result, *Glorious* and her two accompanying destroyers were allowed to carry on steaming around off Norway. The aircraft carrier's commander was never given the intelligence which might have prompted him to fly off aircraft to see what was approaching over the horizon.

At about 10 p.m. on 5 June, the German battle cruisers *Gneisenau* and *Scharnhorst* were between the Orkneys and Norway, as they steamed north to intercept.[7] But it was not until 5.15 p.m. on 8 June, that a lookout on HMS *Glorious* spotted the large German warships. *Glorious* sent off the following message, which was duly intercepted again by the German codebreakers: 'Two battle cruisers on bearing 308 degrees at 15 miles and course 30 degrees.'[8] But it never reached the British Fleet, or the British headquarters in the Narvik area. Even if it had, it would have been too late to save the aircraft carrier. Minutes later *Scharnhorst* opened fire, hitting *Glorious* with salvo after salvo of shells shot out of her 11-inch guns, until the British aircraft carrier was just a blazing inferno full of mutilated corpses. The outgunned escorting destroyers were also sunk, leaving behind just three survivors. No one in Britain knew about the catastrophe until the Admiralty listened in to a German radio broadcast about the engagement at two o'clock in the afternoon on the next day.[9] It was only then that Hinsley was telephoned by Denning and told that he had been right all along.

Shortly after the sinking of *Glorious*, Hinsley was asked to go up to the Citadel in London, the building in the Mall where the OIC was situated, to explain how his traffic analysis worked. The OIC, which operated in the basement of the Citadel, had its own intelligence team, and Clayton wanted them to be well briefed, so that everyone could react quickly next time Hinsley rang them up. Clayton and Denning must have been surprised when Hinsley was ushered into their office. For standing before them was a man who was young enough to be one of Clayton's grandchildren. Hinsley was acutely aware that his long hair and casual clothing, which no one thought twice about in the laid back dons' common room atmosphere at Bletchley Park, was out of place beside all the spotless naval uniforms and suits worn at the Admiralty. Perhaps that was one reason why Hinsley found that his ideas did not receive a good reception from the junior officers he was supposed to be teaching.

Another reason was that traffic analysis was not as easy as it sounded. Not everyone could cope with hours of searching through incomprehensible enciphered messages in the often vain hope of finding a ray of light hidden amongst the sea of paper. Hinsley on the other hand was well prepared for the job he had been given. His medieval history course at Cambridge had required him to look for the minuscule changes made to the charters he was analysing. His upbringing also helped. He had been brought up to make the most of the little which was available to him. Money had always been in short supply when he was young. His father was an occasional labourer, who spent most of the 1930s out of work. His mother worked as a cleaner, providing just enough to keep the Hinsley family clothed and fed. He was proud of the fact that when he went to Germany in 1939, he managed to survive on a meagre budget of just £5 for the entire summer.

On 21 October 1940, Alec Dakin, one of Hinsley's colleagues in Hut 4, wrote to Frank Birch, describing some of the problems which he and Hinsley had encountered at the OIC's ID8G Division:

> ID8G, its relations with us and its attitude to our staff. Here the prime test is Hinsley and his dope; practically we stand or fall with him. I believe that anyone who reads one or two of Hinsley's best Y serials, (especially the *Glorious* one, of course), and bears in mind that A.C.N.S. has been letting him send signals to the fleets, must conclude that there is something in it, that Hinsley's linkages do give him 'indications' of future activity, which examination of the bulk of the traffic do not give. But ID8G, not least the day and night watchkeepers, who are the people concerned, seem never to have studied a Y . . . and if one discusses the validity of the linkage approach with them one has to start at the very first principle, and say that a non-linked message may be dummy, or weather, or 'I have anchored because of fog', or even 'The captain's wife has had twins', whereas a linked message is pretty certain to mean something. In their present state of ignorance, these people are not able to interpret and pass on any information they receive from Hinsley or the watch. That they should be jealous of his success is understandable, and that they should dislike him personally is a small matter, but that they should be obstructive is ruinous.[10]

Hinsley's own letter, sent two days later, is even more outspoken:

> . . . The only conclusion is that they not only duplicate our work and other people's work, but duplicate it in so aimless and inefficient a manner, that all their time is taken up in groping at the truth, and putting as much of it as is obvious to all on card indexes. If they duplicated in the right spirit, and with some purpose, they would be able to answer questions properly, and also possibly to contribute to general advancement . . . One reason that prevented them from doing this, appeared to be a competitive spirit,

which instead of being of a healthy type, is obviously personal and couched itself in a show of independence and an air of obstruction. It appeared to be based on personal opposition to Bletchley Park. It was increased by the fact that the presence of one person from BP appeared to them to remove all their raison d'etre. They felt themselves cut out . . . Apart from the above, I suspect that another reason for their inadequacy is incapacity, pure and simple. They know facts . . . But they seem to have no general grasp of these facts in association. They lack imagination. They cannot utilise the knowledge they so busily compile.[11]

The hostility from the OIC was not the only difficulty Hinsley had to surmount. A jealous administrator who worked at Bletchley Park for the Secret Intelligence Service complained about the privileges being given to Hinsley, who was still a junior civil servant. One such privilege was Hinsley's use of a special taxi service if he had to work late at night in Hut 4; most of the other workers at Bletchley Park had to use the bus laid on at the end of each shift. The administrator only backed down after Frank Birch told him that it was none of his business.

Hinsley had to acknowledge that his traffic analysis work did not compensate for the failure to break the Naval Enigma itself. He had sat with Clayton and Denning at a Battle of the Atlantic committee meeting chaired by Winston Churchill, and so he knew all about the carnage in the Atlantic. It was not that Britain was likely to be starved into submission during 1941. During the first months of 1941, the U-boats were sinking less ships per month than in the last six months of 1940. Only twenty-one ships (126,000 tons) were sunk by U-boats during January 1941, compared with a minimum of fifty-six ships per month (267,000 tons) during August to October the previous year. But the numbers were creeping up again: thirty-nine ships (196,000 tons) in February 1941, fifty-eight (325,000 tons) in May.[12] Although many of these sinkings occurred in the South Atlantic, each ship lost meant a further reduction in the Allied merchant fleet. The Royal Navy's apparent inability to sink U-boats, let alone to capture them, only exacerbated the growing problem. Only twelve ocean-going U-boats had been sunk during the whole of 1940, and only three were sunk during the six months before Churchill set up his weekly Battle of Atlantic emergency committee in March 1941.[13]

The dreadful fate which afflicted Convoy SC 26 between 2 April and 4 April 1941, as it trundled across the Atlantic from Nova Scotia to Britain, was an example of the nightmare scenario which could be expected to happen to every group of ships making for the United Kingdom if the Royal Navy did not improve its anti-submarine tactics. SC26 had been intercepted by a solitary U-boat in mid-Atlantic, but within hours no less than eight other U-boats had been summoned to the scene. The horrified convoy commander ordered the ships which were not sunk to scatter, which they did, until more escorts arrived to put an end to the rout. But by the time the remains of the convoy arrived in Britain, half of the twenty-two ships had been sunk.[14]

Hinsley was in a position to see that the reading of the Naval Enigma messages decrypted following the capture of *Krebs* was too slow to affect the battles at sea. So he was quick to report another brainwave that came to him while he was reading through the decrypts, piled up on his desk. They revealed that trawlers were being sent to isolated spots north of Iceland and in mid-Atlantic to observe the weather and report what they had seen back to Germany. Hinsley had at first overlooked what these messages implied. Then it suddenly dawned on him that these unprotected weather ships must be carrying Naval Enigma cipher machines and codebooks. They were not using Enigma machines to encipher their weather reports. But they were sent Enigma messages confirming that the weather reports had been received, and they sometimes used the Naval Enigma cipher themselves.

Hinsley's formal report to the Admiralty on 26 April 1941 stated: 'The seizure of one of these ships, if practicable, would . . . offer an opportunity for obtaining cyphers', but in private his advice was much more specific. He said that the Royal Navy should go after a ship such as *München*, which was due to be at sea throughout May and likely to remain on patrol during June. If *München* was captured during May, the ship's crew would doubtless have time to throw the May codebooks into the sea. But they might not have time to do the same for the June codebooks, if they were locked away in a safe. By this time, the Admiralty were looking very carefully at any suggestion coming from Hinsley; his recommendation to capture the Enigma codebooks made sense and within days it was given the green light.

The British ships sent out to round up the little weather trawler included three enormous cruisers, as well as four of the fastest destroyers in the Fleet. The contrast with the escort provided to *Glorious* would have been laughable, had it not been so tragic. The plan for 'Operation EB', as the expedition was called, was for the three cruisers to rendezvous with the destroyers on the morning of 6 May, north of the Faeroes. Then, in order to throw the daily German reconnaissance plane off the scent, the plan was to sail back towards Scotland for three hours from 3 a.m. to 6 a.m. on 7 May, before resuming the race to catch *München* north-east of Iceland.[15] At 3 p.m. on 7 May the British ships were lined up at ten-mile intervals, ready to sweep towards *München*'s expected position. Two hours later, a lookout on *Somali*, the same ship whose boarding party had captured *Krebs* during the Lofoten Islands raid, spotted a plume of smoke on the horizon. The British fleet moved in for the kill.

The sight of the large warships racing through the waves towards them was the last thing the *München*'s crew expected. They had become accustomed to the boring routine of being incarcerated on their trawler for weeks with only themselves for company. Now they had to deal with some very unwelcome guests. The first thing to do was to check whether the battleships were friend or foe, so *München* fired off a recognition signal. On receiving no signal in return, the captain assumed the worst, and began laying a thick white smoke screen.

When *Somali* was about three miles away, it opened fire. It was vital that *München*'s crew was persuaded to panic, or abandon ship, before they dumped all their Enigma codebooks. Shortly afterwards, two lifeboats full of *München*'s crew were seen being lowered into the water and being rowed away. One of them was pulling in an unfortunate sailor who had somehow ended up in the sea. Within minutes, Captain Caslon's *Somali* was coasting alongside the trawler, taking care to steer well clear of the stern in case the crew had laid some mines. But before the boarding party, led by Sir Marshall Warmington, could leap aboard *München*, a desperate message was transmitted to Germany: 'Being chased.' The Enigma cipher machine and the current codebooks were also thrown into the water in a weighted bag. The boarding party found *München*'s radio operator tapping out another message back to base. Presumably it would have said 'Being boarded', if he had been allowed to finish. But he was interrupted in mid-sentence and quickly hauled away from the radio set. As Warmington made a cursory search for documents, he realised that he was not going to be able to act as he had done on *Krebs*. He was under strict instructions to summon the prize crew from the cruiser, HMS *Edinburgh*, which had stopped about 200 yards away.

Twenty minutes after Warmington had leapt aboard *München*, the prize crew from HMS *Edinburgh* set off in another boat. It was led by a man wearing civilian clothes called Captain Jasper Haines. He was the OIC's representative who had been told what to look out for, and where he was likely to find it. It did not take him long to do the job. Within minutes of going down to the captain's cabin, he emerged carrying some codebooks, and asked to be taken back to HMS *Edinburgh*. That night he sailed to Scapa Flow in the destroyer HMS *Nestor*, while the cruisers carried on searching for another weather-ship. Fifteen minutes before Haines left, a signal was sent out from HMS *Edinburgh* to the Admiralty. It was headed 'Hush Most Secret' and stated: 'Operation E.B. Trawler *Muenchen* intercepted at 1730A/7th . . . and is being sent in Thorshaven or if possible to Scapa with prize crew and under escort of H.M.S. *Somali*. German crews are in H.M.S. *Somali* and H.M.S. *Edinburgh* – no casualties. Captain Haines has important document. Trawler made enemy report so it is suggested that it be announced that she scuttled herself before we were able to board.'[16] This report was not entirely accurate since there had been one casualty. After one of the boarding party had returned to *Somali*, he mistakenly fired his rifle as he tried to unload it. The bullet hit one of his shipmates in the sole of his foot.

Three days later the documents which looked so uninteresting in their dull maroon jackets were handed over to Peter Twinn at Bletchley Park.[17] They were exactly what was needed. One sheet labelled 'Innere Einstellung' contained the inner settings for June 1941. Another two sheets contained the outer settings. This was even better than what had been found on *Krebs*, since the captured documents would enable the codebreakers to read the Enigma messages currently during June.

While Haines was racing back to Bletchley Park, Captain Caslon on *Somali* towed *München* back to the Faeroes, where she was to be hidden away from prying eyes. There was to be no repetition of what had happened to *Polares*. Caslon was upset when he found that the trawler could not be pulled as fast as he would have wished. So he instructed the engineer, called Fripp, to attempt to start the trawler's engines. The smile which came over Caslon's face when the engines worked was wonderful to behold. Soon the trawler was being towed along at 10 knots, and Caslon forgot himself sufficiently to ask his signalman to flash out a message of encouragement to the engineer: 'Whack her up, Frippo.'

But Caslon's good humour was quickly forgotten as the trawler was towed into the harbour in the Faeroes. Warmington had thrown away the recognition signal which they needed to be allowed back into Scapa Flow. Consequently, Caslon, who had imagined himself entering Scapa Flow in triumph, was forced to report to the examining trawler. After a lot of quizzing from a lowly reserve lieutenant, *Somali* was only permitted to steam into the harbour on condition that it flew an international flag, which was as good as saying, 'We are a suspicious vessel.'

Before the crew disembarked, Caslon caught sight of a man with a pair of binoculars from *München*. He called the man over, and said, 'You cannot keep those. No one is to see any evidence that this raid ever happened.' Vice-Admiral Lancelot Holland, who had masterminded Operation EB from HMS *Edinburgh*, was also told that his report describing what had happened would need to be treated with the utmost caution. The word 'Secret' was typed in above the report's heading, and instructions were given that on no account were the passages marked with an 'X', which related to the capture, ever to be circulated to anyone.[18] Two of the paragraphs marked in this way stated:

> On an operation of this type, the presence of an Intelligence expert is essential. Without the assistance of Captain J.R.S. Haines, Royal Navy, who took passage in my flagship, the importance of some of the rather undistinguished looking documents might have been overlooked.
>
> I think it is probable that the northern ship was withdrawn to the eastward on receipt of the enemy report which is known to have been made by the *Muenchen*. The disappointment in not securing a second ship is however tempered by the thought that the Germans may not realise that we had these ships as our special objectives, and will not necessarily take steps to make a repetition of the operation more difficult.

Shortly after the completion of the operation, a communiqué was put out which stated: 'One of our patrols operating in northern waters encountered the *München*, a German armed trawler. Fire was opened, and the crew of the *München* then abandoned and scuttled their ship. They were subsequently rescued and made prisoner.'

13

Operation Primrose

The Atlantic

MAY 1941

At midday on 9 May 1941, the day before the Enigma documents captured from the *München* reached Bletchley Park, yet another convoy was being stalked by a U-boat in the Atlantic. One of those life-threatening situations was developing which the seizing of the code-books was designed to avoid. The U-boat was *U-110* and the convoy was OB318, consisting of thirty-five merchant ships, most of which were travelling from Britain to America.[1]

Fritz-Julius Lemp, the twenty-eight-year-old commander of *U-110*, was the U-boat commander who had sunk the *Athenia*, the passenger liner which was the first ship sunk by a German submarine during the war. The sinking turned out to be a mistake; Lemp claimed he mistook *Athenia* for an armed merchant cruiser and he narrowly missed being court-martialled. But after being pardoned, he had gone on to become one of Dönitz's most successful commanders. During the second half of 1940, the so-called 'happy time', when U-boats had picked off Britain's merchant ships almost at will, only thirteen German submarine commanders accounted for more tons of shipping than Lemp. He sank eight ships (38,000 tons) between mid-May and the beginning of December 1940.[2]

However Lemp, for all his success and bravado, was something of a loose cannon. He allowed his men to party into the early hours of the morning and encouraged them to flout the rules which forbad the playing of English music. He even made it clear to Dönitz if he felt that the U-boat chief, or his staff, had overstepped the mark. When during one patrol he was instructed to file weather reports rather than sail back to Lorient for repairs, he became incandescent with rage, and told his radio operators to send the following terse, and insolent, signal to the U-boat headquarters: 'Shit, Lemp.'

His refusal to kow-tow to authority meant that the relationship between the officers on *U-110* was like something out of the classic film, *Das Boot*. Lemp played the part of the rebellious commander to perfection, while the part of the sullen Nazi, who could be expected to complain about his commander to the authorities at any moment, was played by Lemp's second-lieutenant, Ulrich Wehrhöfer. Helmut Ecke, the twenty-three-year-old member of the German armed forces propaganda unit, was like the shocked journalist in *Das Boot*, who cannot believe he is really seeing the hardship endured day in and day out by the U-boat crew.

The atmosphere did not improve after Lemp allowed his fellow officers to hang a piece of bacon over Wehrhöfer's bunk when he was asleep. Lemp roared with laughter when Wehrhöfer, who was often sea sick, woke up, smelt the bacon, and promptly vomited. Wehrhöfer attempted to reassert his authority following the sinking of an Allied steamer in April 1941. He swore at the survivors who were crying out for help from the water, and shouted out, 'Why should we help you? It's your own fault for fighting us.' Then, when Lemp allowed one of the survivors onto the U-boat, and Ecke offered the man a cigarette, Wehrhöfer stepped in, insisting that the cigarette should be put out, and telling Ecke that it was madness to even think of fraternising with the enemy.

Lemp's attitude to discipline rubbed off on the crew. Wehrhöfer was supposed to alter the settings on the Enigma cipher machine every night at midnight, but although he collected them from the safe under Lemp's bed, he rarely set the machine himself, preferring to hand them to the radio operators during the day, and allowing the telegraphists on duty to change the settings unsupervised. It was this failure to act by the book which was to play a critical role in what happened next.

U-110 was not the only U-boat following convoy OB318. Two days earlier two ships in the convoy had been sunk by *U-94* before the escorts and their depth charges had frightened it off. During the early hours of 9 May another U-boat, *U-201*, commanded by Adalbert Schnee, arrived on the scene, reacting to Lemp's sighting report. Lemp and Schnee compared notes on when was the best time to attack. Lemp would have preferred to wait until nightfall, by which time, he hoped, the British warships would be on their way back to Iceland, leaving the merchant ships to carry on to America without an escort. Schnee, however, was all for attacking during the morning, in case they lost contact with the convoy, something which had already happened once during the night. The convoy had abruptly changed its course following an urgent signal from the Admiralty, stating that the merchant ships were being followed by a U-boat. Although the Admiralty was not able to read Lemp's signals, it could work out the approximate location in the Atlantic where they had been transmitted by making a direction-finding fix.

By midday (Greenwich Mean Time) on 9 May U-110 was submerged to periscope depth, and was homing in on the convoy's right flank. The merchant ships were still about 300 miles south-west of Greenland. In spite of the time it took to manoeuvre the U-boat into an attacking position, Heinz Brandle, U-110's helmsman, was caught out of position when Lemp called his men to action stations; Brandle was sitting on the toilet. He rushed back to the control room to hear the familiar duet between the control room and the torpedo room as the final preparations were made before U-110's torpedoes were fired:

Control room: 'Rohr eins fertig?' (Is tube one ready?)

Torpedo room: 'Rohr eins fertig.' (Tube one ready.)

Control room: 'Rohr eins, los.' (Tube one, fire.)

Then Brandl felt a slight tremor as the first torpedo shot out of its flooded tube in the bow. Water was simultaneously pumped to the forward tanks to compensate for the heavy missile which had just been fired. The same procedure was followed three times. Lemp quietly said, 'Well done,' to the man standing next to him, after they heard an explosion. It suggested that at least one of the torpedoes had hit its target. But when the call came for the fourth torpedo to be fired, something went wrong. For some reason, the torpedo never left the tube, and the seawater, which was nevertheless pumped to the tanks in the bow, unbalanced the U-boat to such an extent that for a few vital minutes Lemp lost control. It was while the balance was being restored that Lemp realised that a warship was charging towards him. Only then did he shout out the order 'Dive!'

The men inside U-110 feared that they were not submerging quickly enough, as they listened to the ominous sound of the warship's propellers approaching. The sound grew louder and louder, and when it was overhead, they winced as they heard the tell-tale splash of 'water bombs' being dropped into the sea. Then the depth charges exploded. Ecke, the propaganda man, had never heard such loud bangs, even on the Eastern Front. Each time the depth charges went off, the whole U-boat vibrated, as if it was in a major earthquake, and there was a scraping, creaking sound, as the metal deck plates rubbed together and bent, until it seemed inevitable that the deck itself would be torn in half under their feet. Then the booming sound and the noise made by metal grinding on metal subsided and was replaced by a tense silence, leading some of the men, shivering inside the U-boat, to wonder whether the noise of the bombs was somehow preferable. It was in this disorientated state of mind that they crouched at their action stations waiting for the next attack.

When the extinguished lights came on again, all eyes in the control room were fixed on Lemp. He knew exactly what to do and say to calm his men. It was not the first time he had been pursued by British warships. But he had always managed to escape. Provided that no-one panicked there was a good chance that he would be able to escape again. At least that is what some of U-110's crew believed. They knew that one shout or sob would be enough for the hunting enemy to pinpoint where they were hiding.

Lemp certainly appeared to be relaxed. Leaning nonchalantly against his periscope, with his cap pushed onto the back of his head, he murmured soothing words of reassurance to those around him. 'It's OK. We're all going to be fine,' followed by the odd grim joke: 'You don't think I'm going to let them catch me and shoot me, do you?' His men assumed this was a reference to the punishment he expected the Allies to dish out, if he ever fell into their hands, on account of his having sunk the *Athenia*.

At this point, First-Lieutenant Dietrich Loewe, another of the committed Nazis on the U-boat, turned to Ecke and told him to look carefully at the faces of the terrified crew. It would be something worth recording in one of Ecke's propaganda articles, Loewe said. As the reports specifying the damage came through the intercom from the front and rear of the U-boat, even Lemp's jokes and reassuring words began to wear a little thin. The rudders were not functioning, the batteries were damaged, and were giving off a threatening whiff of chlorine gas, and the wheel which had to be turned to blow water out of the tanks, so that they could stabilise the balance in the U-boat, had fallen off its stem, and was lying on the floor. None of the depth meters were functioning, so it was impossible to tell whether the U-boat was rising or falling. Each broken item closed off another of Lemp's escape options.

Ecke, the journalist, noticed another problem. He heard a loud hissing sound. The pressurised air, used to blow water out of the U-boat's tanks, was escaping from the containers where it was stored. The leak represented a potential disaster, since the U-boat could not reach the surface again unless the tanks were blown, and the tanks could not be blown without the air. It was only then that Lemp admitted they were in serious trouble. There was nothing more he could do for the moment, he announced. 'We must wait and see what happens,' he muttered, and to anyone else who was still listening, he added, 'I want you all now to think of home, or something beautiful.'

Herbert Langsch, one of the four radio operators on board, who imagined that the U-boat might already be sinking down to the depths of the ocean, prepared to die. Although he thought he might only have minutes left, he could not bring himself to believe that his life was about to end. He was confused. He was relieved that the terrifying battle was over, and at the same time he was so sad that it had come to this. As his mind pictured the U-boat tumbling into the abyss, where it would soon be crushed by the growing pressure, he thought of Irmchen, his childhood sweetheart, and tried to imagine what she would feel once she knew he was gone.

Then the U-boat began rocking from side to side. At first the trapped crew thought that *U-201* might be disturbing the water as it passed above them, but the word came back down the chain of men lined up along the length of the U-boat that they had managed to make it to the surface after all. They were saved. Before they had time to celebrate, Lemp coolly announced, 'Last stop, everybody out,' as if he were a bus conductor in Berlin, telling all his passengers that they had reached the end of the line. But the scene which greeted the German crew, as they swarmed up the conning tower ladder, and climbed down onto the deck outside, was like something out of Dante's Inferno. Two large warships were steaming towards the crippled U-boat, as if intent on ramming it. At the same time, guns were firing at U-110 from all sides. They were surrounded. Some of the U-boat crew took their chance and jumped into the water immediately. They were drowned if their life jackets deflated after being pierced by bullets or shell splinters. Others hung around on deck, hypnotised by the sight of the destroyers bearing down on them. One of these men turned to Herbert Langsch, the radio operator, and told him that he could not see out of one of his eyes. Langsch turned to examine him, only to find that he was peering into a bullet hole where one of the man's eyes had been. 'You've just got some blood in your eye from a cut. That's why you can't see,' Langsch told him. This reassured the man sufficiently to persuade him to jump into the ocean. Langsch waited for him to surface, but when he failed to reappear, Langsch jumped in after him.

Helmut Ecke, who was also standing on the U-boat deck, had seen something even more horrific. The man standing next to him was hit in the head by a shell. It was as if a rifle bullet had cracked open a pineapple at a funfair shooting range. The man's brains were sprayed all over the deck, before his decapitated crumpled trunk collapsed into the water. The sight of the decapitation was enough to send Ecke over the side in his turn, even though his life jacket was not inflated. As soon as he emerged from the waves, spluttering and struggling to stay afloat, he began to cry out that he needed help. No one had taught him how to blow up his life jacket. A man swimming near him gasped out, 'I've no time to help,' before swimming away. Ecke only survived because Langsch swam up to him at that moment, and inflated his life jacket with the air from the attached oxygen flask.

Meanwhile, Heinz Wilde, another radio operator, climbed up the conning tower ladder to ask Lemp whether he should destroy the Enigma machine and codebooks. Lemp merely shouted back at him to get out. 'The U-boat is sinking,' he told Wilde dismissively, and so the radio operator followed the other crew members out onto the deck and from there into the sea. Georg Högel, the third radio operator to make it to the top of the conning tower, climbed back down again inside the U-boat when he remembered that he had forgotten his notebook full of the illustrations and poetry which he had written for his girlfriend. Ignoring the Enigma codebooks and the cipher machine, he grabbed the notebook, stuffed it into his pocket, and climbed back up the conning tower.

Hans-Joachim Eichelborn, the engineer, and his assistant opened up the vents so that the tanks would be flooded. They then jumped overboard with Lemp, mistakenly believing the U-boat would disappear beneath the waves in a matter of minutes. It was only when the U-boat failed to sink that Lemp, who by now was swimming in the sea, called out to Lieutenant Dietrich Loewe that they should try to climb back on board to see what could be done. At that moment the U-boat was swept beyond their reach and so Loewe struck out towards the corvette which was waiting to rescue the German survivors. That was the last time either Loewe, or anyone else, saw Lemp.[3]

The sudden attack by the British warships which caught *U-110* just beneath the surface had come about because of a clever ploy. The escort commander, Joe Baker-Cresswell, did not think that the convoy would be attacked on 9 May, since U-boats normally did not venture so far to the west. Nevertheless, he persevered with the tactics he always adopted when U-boats were expected. Five of the eight warships guarding the convoy were spread out in a line about a mile and a half in front of the nine columns of merchant ships. This was calculated to prevent any U-boats following their favourite manoeuvre which was to submerge in front of the convoy, and then to surface amongst the merchant ships after the escorts had passed. If a U-boat tried to pass under Baker-Cresswell's screen of warships, it would, he hoped, be picked up on their Asdic sets. However, tucked in on both flanks of the convoy, in a position where they might not be noticed, were two other warships, which could chase after any U-boat attacking the merchant ships from the side.

The first sign that a merchant ship had been hit was when Baker-Cresswell spotted a tower of water shoot up into the air on the starboard side of *Esmond* which was leading the convoy's right-hand column. Within minutes *Esmond*'s stern was lifted out of the water, rising slowly but surely until it was vertical, while the cargo of vehicles and cartons on its deck fell into the sea like a child pouring toys out of a box. Then the ship slid into the water. A second tower of water which shot up beside another merchant ship two columns to the left told Baker-Cresswell that it had also been torpedoed. The convoy made an emergency turn to port, away from where the torpedoes had been fired, leaving Baker-Cresswell to watch the trap he had set spring shut. HMS *Aubretia*, the tucked-in corvette on the convoy's starboard wing, turned to the right and, after picking up the U-boat on her Asdic, set off in pursuit. *Aubretia* had already dropped her first depth charges by the time Baker-Cresswell's destroyer, *Bulldog*, and another destroyer, HMS *Broadway*, arrived on the scene. Further depth charges were dropped by *Aubretia* and then came the chilling sight which every convoy escort commander prays for, but rarely sees, that of a sinister black submarine breaking the surface.

It was then that Baker-Cresswell's customary reserve temporarily deserted him. As HMS *Bulldog* raced towards the U-boat, about 800 yards away, he felt himself losing control. The 'animals' inside the U-boat had killed some of the defenceless seamen whom Baker-Cresswell was supposed to be protecting. Now he himself was experiencing what it was like to be an animal, with its blood up. As his ship charged in, he wanted to rip the enemy apart. He was about to give the order to ram the U-boat, when his brain cleared, and he was himself again. He ordered the engines to be put into reverse, and *Bulldog* stopped 100 yards away from *U-110*. However, no sooner had his ship come to a halt, than he began to wonder whether he had made a mistake. Perhaps the men gathering around the gun on the U-boat were going to try to fight it out on the surface after all. So he ordered his gun crew to open fire. An officer, behind him on the bridge, asked if he also should fire at the Germans with a stripped Lewis gun, and Baker-Cresswell, who by now wanted to clear the U-boat deck, said, 'All right, let them have it.' But far from firing back with their gun, the German crew were jumping into the water. Baker-Cresswell, realising that they must be trying to surrender, changed his mind again, and ordered his gunners to cease fire. Just as he began to think about capturing *U-110*, he saw to his horror that HMS *Broadway* was still heading straight for it. Baker-Cresswell quickly asked his signalman to flash a 'Keep clear' signal, but *Broadway* kept on steaming in. As a last resort, Baker-Cresswell seized the microphone of the loud-hailer, and bellowed, 'Keep clear! Do not ram.'

Lieutenant-Commander Thomas Taylor on *Broadway* had never intended to ram the U-boat. He wanted to stop *U-110* diving again by steaming up alongside and dropping depth charges under the hull. Unfortunately, the blast caused by the firing of his own guns had cracked the windows on his bridge making it difficult for him to see. So he failed to notice the U-boat's protruding fins as *Broadway* drew up alongside and it was these which ripped a hole in the thin plating of the destroyer's hull. Meanwhile on *Bulldog* Baker-Cresswell was giving orders to Sub-Lieutenant David Balme, the twenty-year-old officer who was to lead the boarding party: 'Get on board as quickly as you can. I think she is completely abandoned, but there may be one or two left behind. Get hold of the signal books first, and then anything useful you can take away. Never mind if you lose the whaler while getting on board. I will send over another boat.' As he spoke, the *U-110*'s crew were being rescued by *Aubretia*, and the convoy was sailing away into the distance.

Balme and his eight-man boarding party rowed quickly across to the U-boat and jumped on board. They were followed by their whaler, which was hurled onto the U-boat deck, and smashed to pieces by a particularly ferocious Atlantic wave. Balme decided that he should be the first to go down the conning tower. He climbed up the ladder from the deck and steeled himself to go inside. It takes a particular kind of courage to venture inside a captured submarine. Balme had no idea whether scuttling charges had been set. For all he knew, they might explode at any minute, and he had no way of defending himself while clambering down the conning tower ladders; he had to place his revolver back into its holster, so that he could hold onto the rungs with both hands. As he stepped into the U-boat's control room, he suddenly felt very lonely and isolated. The interior was tinged with blue by the emergency lighting. Apart from the sound of his own breathing, all Balme could hear was a faint hissing, and the sound of the Atlantic waves lapping against the hull. To his relief, he soon discovered that there was no one else inside it.

Balme ordered the other members of the boarding party to come on down. The U-boat was in a mess. Books, charts and papers were strewn all over the place and Balme immediately ordered his men to form a human chain, so that they could pass all the codebooks and documents out to the members of the boarding party who had remained on deck. Speed was of the essence in case the U-boat sank. While the human chain was being formed, Balme was summoned by his telegraphist. 'Come and look in the radio room,' Balme was told. 'There's something rather interesting I want to show you.' On the table in the radio room was a machine like a typewriter. The telegraphist proceeded to show Balme how when he pressed one letter key on the keyboard, another letter was highlighted on a display panel. Balme instructed the telegraphist to use the screwdriver in his toolbag to undo the four screws securing the machine to the table. Then it too was passed along the human chain up to the deck outside.

It took the men about an hour and a half to clear all the books, papers and machinery out of the U-boat. It was an unnerving experience. They flinched whenever they heard the depth charges going off around them. They were being dropped by the warships in order to scare away other U-boats. At one point, Balme and his team were abandoned by the British warships, when the destroyers and corvette which had been circling the *U-110* steamed away in order to follow up a suspected U-boat contact. While Balme and his men were waiting for them to come back, they could do nothing but pray that *Bulldog*'s navigator would not forget where he had left them. They all breathed a sigh of relief when *Bulldog* returned. Baker-Cresswell sent over some sandwiches to the *U-110*. Balme settled down to eat his, sitting at Lemp's roll top desk. Inside the desk, he found an Iron Cross, some pictures of Lemp's family, and a sealed envelope. Balme carefully put all three items into his pocket.

On HMS *Bulldog* Baker-Cresswell observed the boarding party's progress with his heart in his mouth. He saw one man walking along the deck with an armful of papers. One moment he was there, and the next, he was engulfed by a towering wave. But when the water cleared away, the man was still there, clutching on to the documents as if his life depended on it. Somehow, no papers were lost, although many were dripping wet by the time they, and the boarding party, made it into the whaler. Notwithstanding the drama going on all around him, Baker-Cresswell did not forget the etiquette which he had learned in the many pheasant shoots he had attended back home in Britain. 'This is your bird,' he signalled to Captain Funge Smith, the commander of *Aubretia*, the ship whose depth charges had brought *U-110* to the surface.

Balme and his crew had attached a towing rope to the *U-110* before they left and at around 6.30 that evening, *Bulldog*, escorted by *Broadway*, began the long task of pulling the U-boat back to Iceland. Baker-Cresswell also informed the Admiralty about what had happened. The Admiralty signalled back: 'Your operation is to be referred to as Operation Primrose in all future signals. Reference to it is to be prefaced Top Secret and signals to be made only in cypher.' Another signal addressed to all the ships at the scene of the capture instructed them: 'Operation Primrose is to be treated with greatest secrecy and few people allowed to know as possible.' A third signal from Admiral Sir Percy Noble, the Commander-in-Chief of Western Approaches, stated: 'Am sending submarine expert immediately by Sunderland flying boat.'

However the next morning a strong wind blew up and Baker-Cresswell noticed with dismay that the *U-110's* stern was much lower in the water than before. At about 11 a.m. the submarine's bow suddenly reared up in the water, until the whole body of the submarine was nearly vertical. Then it slowly slipped down, stern first, beneath the waves. Seconds later, there was no evidence that Baker-Cresswell had ever had a U-boat in tow, apart from the tow rope trailing behind *Bulldog*. It was cut as the U-boat began to sink. Baker-Cresswell later wrote: 'It was one of the worst moments in my life. What a triumph it would have been to have sailed into Hvalfjord with *U-110* in tow.' The codebooks stored in his cabin at the back of the ship were very much a consolation prize, as far as he was concerned. That evening, on 10 May, the Admiralty sent out the following signal to Baker-Cresswell and the commanders of the other ships involved in the capture: 'Primrose having sunk makes it no Repeat no less important that fact of having had her in our hands should remain secret. This fact is to be rigorously impressed on all who have any knowledge of facts.'

Baker-Cresswell arrived in Iceland in the early hours of 11 May. By 10.30 a.m. he had refuelled and was sailing, with the prisoners from *U-110*, to Scapa Flow. Before taking the prisoners on board, he assembled his crew and told them that the capture should remain a closely guarded secret. But shortly after setting sail, he came across a boat hook from *U-110*. He quickly ordered one of his men to put it out of sight. He only hoped that none of the German prisoners had seen it.

Shortly after they arrived at Scapa Flow, in the early evening of 12 May, two naval intelligence officers stepped on board. Baker-Cresswell led them to his cabin and showed them the two packing cases full of books and papers. 'Oh surely not this!' one of the intelligence officers said when he saw the cipher machine. 'We have waited the whole war for one of these.' That night, the intelligence officer set about drying the codebooks. Some of them had to be held over the stove in Baker-Cresswell's cabin. Others were hung up to dry, until the commander's quarters looked like a Chinese laundry. By morning everything was dry and the intelligence officers told David Balme and Baker-Cresswell that the most important documents would have to be photographed before being sent back to London in case the originals were caught in an air raid and destroyed on the way.

After a prolonged photographic session, Lieutenant Allon Bacon, one of the intelligence officers, sought out Baker-Cresswell to say goodbye. 'Never mind about losing the *U-110*,' Bacon said. 'From our point of view, it was a good thing, as we can now keep all this quiet. For God's sake never breathe a word about this to anyone.' Baker-Cresswell replied that he would have to tell Admiral Jack Tovey, the Commander-in-Chief of the Home Fleet, and the Rear Admiral of Destroyers, as well as Admiral Noble. 'Yes, of course,' said Bacon, 'but no one else.'

As Bacon started out on his journey south, Baker-Cresswell went to the battleship *King George V* to report to Admiral Tovey. 'You fellows get all the fun,' the admiral said. 'I just stay here and wait for the German fleet to come out. It's a dull job.' Before Baker-Cresswell left Tovey's flagship, Admiral Louis Hamilton was shown in. He told them that he had been flying from Rosyth in a Walrus amphibious plane, when they had run out of petrol and been forced to land in the Pentland Firth. He was furious because a destroyer had sped past him at full speed, without bothering to enquire whether he needed help.

'If I could get hold of that damned fellow, I'd give him a piece of my mind,' was the substance of what he said. Baker-Cresswell was embarrassed. He admitted that he was the 'damned fellow' who had swept past but, because of his promise to Allon Bacon, he could not explain the real reason. As a result, Admiral Hamilton never forgave him.

*

Allon Bacon was down in London by 6 p.m. on 13 May. Three hours later, he was driven through the gates into Bletchley Park. As he walked into Harry Hinsley's office in Hut 4, he triumphantly held his briefcase containing the most important captured papers over his head, like an athlete who had just won a gold medal in the Olympics. Minutes later the teleprinters in the basement of the Citadel in Whitehall sprang into action after having been silent for more than forty-eight hours.[4] The clattering machines were relaying the decrypted Naval Enigma messages for the first half of May to the Admiralty. However, the intelligence in the messages did not necessarily bring immediate security to convoys already at sea. Some of the messages had been sent as long ago as 1 May. The messages for 13 May were only read for the first time seven days later. But those in the know realised that a corner had been turned. At the beginning of June, the codebreakers would be able to use the Enigma settings stolen from the safe in the *München*. This information would enable the OIC in London to route convoys around the U-boat packs.

Later that night, as Baker-Cresswell sailed back to Iceland, he received the following signal from Sir Dudley Pound, the First Sea Lord: 'Following from First Sea Lord. Hearty congratulations. The petals of your flower are of rare beauty.' He and the rest of the crew were to receive further congratulations from King George VI who, when handing out their decorations later that summer, stated that the operation was 'perhaps the most important single event in the whole war at sea'.[5]

King George VI was probably incorrect when he said this, as are many of the books, articles and television documentaries which have focused on the capture since the war. Although the capture of the *U-110* was one of the most heroic and dramatic episodes of the war, and although David Balme's bravery should have earned him a George Cross, the documents recovered were, in some respects, not as important as those found on board the *München* weathership.[6] The documents captured from *U-110* did not include the all-important Naval Enigma settings for May 1941 (still missing after the *München* capture), or for June 1941 (which were captured from *München*). It was the latter settings which subsequently enabled the Bletchley Park codebreakers to read U-boat messages currently for the first time. Before the June settings were captured from *München*, Bletchley Park was taking an average of ten days or more to read Naval Enigma messages. Once the captured June settings became operative, the average decryption time was reduced to just six hours.[7]

That is not to say that the documents captured from *U-110* were unimportant. The documents delivered by Bacon to Bletchley Park on 13 May included the June 1941 special settings and the manual used for so-called 'Offizier' messages, that is, important messages, enciphered on the Enigma machine using the U-boat officer's settings, before being enciphered again using the settings circulated to all Enigma operators. Thanks to these documents, the Bletchley Park codebreakers were eventually able to work out a method for reading Offizier messages, a feat which was to play a vital role in the future breaking of the Naval Enigma.[8] Time and again, when new measures were introduced altering the Naval Enigma procedure, these measures were specified in Offizier messages.

Then there was one set of bigram tables which helped fill in gaps in the reconstructed tables produced by the codebreakers following the capture of *Krebs* during Operation Claymore. A recent television documentary shown in England stated that the capture of these bigram tables from *U-110* was crucial. This appears to be incorrect if the History of Hut Eight compiled by GC&CS after the war is accurate. This states that the bigram tables which were being reconstructed following the capture of *Krebs* 'were more or less complete' by late March 1941, more than a month before the capture of *U-110*. It should also be pointed out that these bigram tables were superseded by a new set, brought into use during June 1941.[9] Another batch of documents retrieved from *U-110* included the short signal codebook used by U-boats, and the short weather report codebook used by U-boats to send weather reports back to base (also captured from *München*). These documents would, one day, help the Bletchley Park's codebreakers produce some of the cribs which were to become indispensable, once the bombe became the main tool used to break the Naval Enigma.[10]

*

Following the capture, the British were worried that some of the prisoners from *U-110* might have seen the boarding party go down into the U-boat, and might report this fact back to their relations in Germany. The methods adopted to deal with Dietrich Loewe, Lemp's first-lieutenant, highlight the subterfuge which was adopted in Britain and in Canada in order to keep the capture of documents a secret. Loewe was rescued, along with thirty-one other *U-110* survivors, and taken to a prison camp in Britain. On the way, he managed to talk to six members of the *U-110*'s crew. None of them could swear that they had actually seen the U-boat sink. A few days later Loewe's suspicion that the U-boat might have been captured increased after the British returned to Hans-Joachim Eichelborn, *U-110*'s leading engineer, his citation for the Iron Cross. Eichelborn told Loewe that he might have had it in his pocket when he was captured, but he could, he said, have left it in a folder in *U-110*'s control room. Loewe realised that, if that was the case, then his suspicions were well founded. He told Otto Kretschmer, one of the captured U-boat aces, what had happened, and it was decided that a report should be sent back to Germany, stating: 'Suspect that UEO [the code name for *U-110*] in enemy hands.' Fortunately, British codebreakers had already broken the code used by German prisoners of war, and they must have intercepted and read Loewe's warning.

If Eichelborn's citation really had been left in the *U-110*, it was highly unlikely that the British would have been so foolish as to hand it back to him, unless they had some ulterior motive for doing so. It is likely, in view of what happened later, that they were playing mind games with their prisoners, and wanted to know whether any of the POWs suspected that the *U-110* had been captured. If this is what was behind the Eichelborn incident, Loewe soon showed Britain's intelligence staff that they were right to be worried.

In April 1942, either by chance or more probably by British design, Loewe met another member of *U-110*'s crew on the way to another prison camp in Canada. This man told Loewe that he had talked to two other members of the crew, who had seen the *U-110* sinking. This prompted Loewe to write another coded letter to his relatives, stating: 'UEO sunk, possibly enemy on board.' However, in February 1944, just four months before the Allied invasion of France, Loewe was allowed to meet up with yet another *U-110* ex-comrade, who told him how he had watched a boarding party go onto the *U-110*'s deck and shut the conning tower hatch. Shortly afterwards, he told Loewe, he had seen the boat sink. Loewe then sent a report back to

Germany stating: 'Boat sank. No enemy inside boat.' After that, the British must have believed that Loewe could only help them convince Dönitz that the Enigma code had not been compromised, and he was allowed to return to Germany in a POW swap.[11]

Above: Hans Thilo Schmidt, the Enigma spy, seen with his wife Charlotte during the 1930s, after he had passed Enigma manuals and settings to the French secret service.

Above and right: Two of the French secret agents who ran the Enigma spy during the 1930s. *Above*: Rodolphe Lemoine, aka 'Rex', who betrayed Schmidt to the Germans after being arrested. *Right*: Guy Schlesser, walking with his father on the Promenade des Anglais in Nice during 1935.

Above: Gustave Bertrand, seen here with his wife, Mary, after the fall of France. In 1931 Bertrand insisted that Hans Thilo Schmidt's Enigma manuals would enable the code to be broken in spite of discouraging comments from British and French cryptographers; Biffy Dunderdale (*right*), a British SIS agent based in Paris, passed the British comments on the manuals to Bertrand.

Top right: Gwido Langer, the head of the Cipher Bureau in Warsaw, told Bertrand in 1931 that Polish cryptographers might be able to use Schmidt's manuals to break the code. After war was declared, Langer was nicknamed 'Monsieur Beaujolais' because he drank so much wine.

Above: Maksymilian Cie̦z̓ki, at the front of the group photographed, the head of the German section of the Polish Cipher Bureau. Cie̦z̓ki asked Marian Rejewski, pictured below right with his wife Irena during the 1930s, if the German cipher machine could be reconstructed. Rejewski duly worked out the internal layout of the Enigma machine in 1932, and proceeded, with assistance from two colleagues, to break the code from 1933 to 1938.

Below: Henryk Zygalski, one of Rejewski's colleagues, who devised a new method of breaking the code in 1938, after the Germans altered their enciphering procedure.

Above: Antoni Palluth (third from right), and Edward Fokczyn´ski (far left), two of the Polish engineers who built the Enigma replicas used by the Poles. Second and third from left: Henryk Paszkowski and his wife; she became pregnant, and had labour contractions while attempting to escape from France. The cryptographer Kazimierz Gaca (second from right) was captured by the Germans along with Langer in 1943.

Left: Jerzy Róz˙ycki, the third Polish cryptographer who broke the Enigma code between 1932 and 1938. He was drowned in 1942 while on his way from Algeria to France.

The Enigma replica used by Polish cryptographers to read Enigma messages in France. Note the keyboard keys and plugboard are in different positions to those on the Enigma made by the Germans.

Left: Alastair Denniston, the head of Bletchley Park until 1942. He told Dilly Knox (*centre*), that he was not up to running Hut 6, the Army and Air Force codebreaking section, but that he was a brilliant cryptographer. Knox proved Denniston's point when his team, spearheaded by Mavis Lever (*right*), broke first the Italian Naval Enigma, and subsequently the Abwehr Enigma.

September 1938 photograph of cryptographers milling around outside Bletchley Park, the Victorian mansion in Buckinghamshire where the Enigma was broken during the war.

Right: Edward Travis, who took over from Denniston as the head of Bletchley Park in 1942. He presided over its golden years, when Enigma was finally mastered.

Above left: Alan Turing, Bletchley Park's star cryptographer, represented a security risk because he was homosexual. He was also very eccentric; he bicycled around the countryside wearing a gas mask, and padlocked his coffee mug to a radiator. But he was a genius. He invented the bombe machine which enabled the British and Americans to master the Enigma.

Above right: Hugh Alexander, the British chess champion and one of the best cryptographers in Hut 8, succeeded Alan Turing as the head of Hut 8 during 1942.

Below: Gordon Welchman was a fast thinker. In 1940, he had the all-important idea which dramatically improved the performance of the bombe machine invented by Turing.

Top: Hitler salutes Hans-Wilhelm von Dresky, the commander of *U-33*, and his crew on 27 September 1939 in the harbour at Wilhelmshaven. Four months later their U-boat (*centre*) was sunk; one of the crew failed to throw the Enigma wheels into the sea, so they were captured by the British. This was the first of the captures which played a part in the breaking of the Naval Enigma.

Right: Dresky is congratulated by Hitler following his successful patrol.

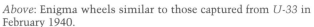

Above: Enigma wheels similar to those captured from *U-33* in February 1940.

Right: If the prescribed wheel ring setting was, say, A, the central core of the Naval Enigma wheel was rotated while the ring was held still until the white dot (marked with an arrow in this photo) was lined up with the letter A on the ring around the wheel.

Below: The German *Schiff 26*, attempting to pass itself off as the Dutch fishing vessel *Polares*, is approached by HMS *Griffin's* whaler on 26 April 1940. The documents seized from *Polares* enabled Alan Turing and his colleagues in Bletchley Park to understand the Naval Enigma indicating system for the first time, a crucial step in their attempt to read up-to-date Naval Enigma messages.

Far left: Frank Birch, the head of the German naval section at Bletchley Park, complained in August 1940 that Alan Turing and Peter Twinn (*left*) were holding up the attempt to break the Naval Enigma by failing to systematically test potential cribs provided by Birch's intelligence section.

Centre: The German trawler *Krebs* before her capture on 4 March 1941 together with the February 1941 Enigma settings. This capture enabled Harry Hinsley (*right*), working in Frank Birch's German naval section, to see that isolated weatherships operating north of Iceland were using Naval Enigma machines. Hinsley recommended that these weatherships should be ambushed.

Above: HMS *Tartar's* boarding party prepares to board the weathership *Lauenburg* north east of Iceland on 28 June 1941. The capture of the *Lauenburg's* copy of the July 1941 Enigma settings enabled Britain's cryptographers to break the Naval Enigma code during the crucial months from August 1941 to January 1942.

Right: The *Lauenburg's* crew are blindfolded so that they do not see the Enigma codebooks being captured.

Right: Fritz-Julius Lemp (on the right of photograph), the commander of *U-110*. It was damaged by depth charges dropped by the British corvette *Aubretia* on 9 May 1941.

The crippled *U-110* photographed shortly after she surfaced from the British corvette HMS *Aubretia*. HMS *Bulldog* is seen lowering the whaler which was to take the boarding party over to the U-boat.

Far right: Sub-Lieutenant David Balme, who boarded the *U-110*, and was the first to climb down the ladder in its conning tower. An Enigma machine and codebooks were seized.

Near right: Allon Bacon, from the Naval Intelligence Division, dried *U-110's* codebooks, including the all-important Offizier Naval Enigma settings for June 1941, over a stove on a British destroyer before delivering them to Bletchley Park.

Top left and right: A four-wheel Naval Enigma similar to the machines issued to the Atlantic and Mediterranean U-boats for use after 1 February 1942. When a four-wheel Enigma machine's inner lid is shut (as shown in the photo top left), four letters can be read through the windows above the wheels (see bottom left photo). When the inner lid is open (*top right*), the wheels can be seen inside.

Right: An Army Enigma cipher machine with three wheels.

Above left: Rolf Noskwith, and Leslie Yoxall (*centre*), unexpectedly showed Alan Turing that Offizier Naval Enigma messages could be read as well as the general Naval Enigma messages; they exploited the knowledge gained from codebooks captured from the *U-110* in May 1941.

Above right: Jack Good infuriated Alan Turing by taking a cat nap in the middle of his first night shift; Good only won Turing's respect after working out how to identify which of the Naval Enigma's nine bigram tables was being used.

Right: Lieutenant Commander Ned Denning, the head of the surface ships section of the Admiralty's OIC, was hampered by the codebreaking blackout at Bletchley Park on 4 July 1942 when he was attempting to work out whether the *Tirpitz* was about to attack convoy PQ17.

Below: The German trawler *Geier* being captured by the British destroyer HMS *Ashanti* at the end of December 1941. Bigram tables needed at Bletchley Park were discovered on board.

Below: Mark Thornton, the commander of the destroyer HMS *Petard*, who masterminded the capture of vital codebooks from the *U-559* on 30 October

Right: William Prendergast, the *Petard's* doctor, recommended that Thornton should be relieved of his command after an incident in December 1942. Thornton ordered his crew to mow down Italian submariners who appeared to be surrendering.

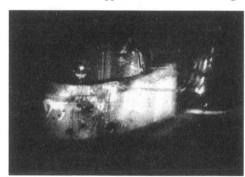

Left: The *U-559's* holed conning tower is lit up by the spotlights from circling British destroyers on 30 October 1942; shortly after she was boarded, she sank with two British seamen on board.

Right: Lieutenant Tony Fasson, retrieved codebooks from the *U-559* which enabled the Bletchley Park cryptographers to break back into Shark, the Atlantic U-boats' Enigma, after a ten-month blackout. However, he failed to react quickly enough to warnings that the U-boat was sinking; he, and his helper Colin Grazier, went down with the U-boat, and drowned.

Far right: Ken Lacroix, the only British seaman to have entered the *U-559*, who has survived to tell the tale.

Above: Friedrich Bürgel (on the right of the photo), the commander of *U-205*, seen here on top of the conning tower of his U-boat, was horrified when, after abandoning ship and being rescued following a depth charge attack on 17 February 1943, he saw that *U-205* had not sunk and had been boarded. Enigma documents were recovered.

Below: Canadian seamen board U-*744* on 6 March 1944. Although Enigma documents were discovered, they fell into the sea after the boarding party's boat sank.

Top and centre: American boarding parties take control of the surfaced *U-505*, on 4 June 1944. Admiral King, the Commander-in-Chief of the American Navy, considered court martialling Daniel Gallery, the commander of the American hunter-killer force which captured *U-505*; Gallery's failure to sink the U-boat immediately could have alerted the Germans that their Enigma cipher was broken during the critical hours leading up to the Allied landings in France.

Right: Colonel Paul Paillole (on the right of the photo), the French counter intelligence chief, correctly concluded in June 1944 that his former colleague Gustave Bertrand had not compromised the Allies' Enigma secret. Here he is being awarded the order of merit by General Lewis in November 1944 at the American Embassy in Paris.

14

The Knock-Out Blow

North of Iceland

JUNE 1941

The codebooks captured from the *München* and the *U-110* did not provide a permanent solution to the Naval Enigma problem. On 15 June 1941, just over a month after Allon Bacon had rushed into Harry Hinsley's office at Bletchley Park with his bulging briefcase, the German Navy started using a new set of bigram tables. A disappointed Alan Turing told Hinsley that the codebreakers dealing with Naval Enigma would need another month's settings to carry on breaking the code after the end of June, when those captured on the *München* ran out.[1] Before finding out about the adoption of the new tables, Turing had been hoping to use the old ones to break into the Naval Enigma traffic for July 1941. The only quick way around the difficulty was either to capture the latest set of tables, or to capture the next month's settings, and then to use them to reconstruct the new tables (as explained in chapter 7). Turing was, yet again, almost back to square one.

Hinsley recommended that the Royal Navy should attempt to capture a second weather ship. He had already identified a potential target, the *Lauenburg*, operating west of Jan Mayen Island, north-east of Iceland. Four days after the bigram tables were changed, Hinsley completed the following report on the weather ship:

She left Drontheim [sic] overnight 27–28/5, to take over from *Sachsen*, and had therefore been 3 weeks at sea (including days on passage) by 17/6 and will have been at sea almost 5 weeks at the end of June . . . Evidence of her predecessor's patrol suggests that *Lauenburg* intends to be out after the end of June, i.e. for more than 5 weeks: *Sachsen* patrolled (exclusive of passage time) from about 13/4 to 28/5, when she was relieved by *Lauenburg*, after being out for more than 6 weeks. Evidence for the patrol-periods of other ships is less complete, but evidence of a tendency to over-stocking with cypher material in addition to the *Sachsen* evidence, suggest that *Lauenburg*, leaving in the last days of May, will be carrying keys both for June and July.[2]

Frantic discussions ensued between Hinsley in Hut 4 and the Admiralty. The question was: would it be safe to capture another weather ship so soon after the *München*? Would it alert the German Navy that something was up? And once the bosses in the German Navy applied their minds to what was up, wouldn't they reach the conclusion that both ships had been captured with their codebooks?[3] That was too awful to contemplate. The result would doubtless be another Naval Enigma black out as the Germans altered their enciphering procedure. Air Force Enigma might be blacked out as well. The latter had already betrayed the German plans leading up to the invasion of Crete in May 1941; the Allies only failed to repel the invaders because they had insufficient soldiers and weapons on the island, and because of misguided tactics pursued by their commander. It was hoped that one day it would also give the British a winning hand in north Africa.[4] Even without another capture, there was the possibility that the cryptographers might find a way of reconstructing the bigram tables for Naval Enigma, using cribs identified in June.

Eventually it was decided to risk it. A raid, codenamed 'Operation EC' and orchestrated by Rear-Admiral Harold Burrough, was to be made. Jack Tovey, the Commander-in-Chief of the Home Fleet, sent Admiral Burrough the following orders on 22 June 1941: 'Operation EC. An enemy weather reporting trawler operates in the vicinity of Jan Mayen Island. She is based in Trondjheim . . . Object – the capture of this trawler and particularly of the codes and cyphers on board.'[5]

The raid was to be carried out by four warships, which set out from Scapa Flow on 25 June 1941. However the men on board were only told what they were looking for two days after they set out. Even then they were only given a garbled version of the true story. On 27 June Commander Lionel 'Kim' Skipwith, on the destroyer HMS *Tartar*, summoned the senior members of his crew to the bridge and told them that they were looking for a meteorological ship which provided weather reports to the German aircraft bombing London. 'If you chaps don't want your homes to be bombed, you'd better find her,' he told them. Another officer on *Tartar* offered £1 to the first man who spotted the ship, a good incentive, given the low rates of pay within the Navy during the war. Then Skipwith turned to Tom Kelly, the chief gunner's mate, and told him that when they found the ship, he would be instructed to open fire. But he must on no account hit the target.

'That'll be very easy,' Kelly retorted impudently.

'I just want to encourage the crew to abandon ship, pronto,' Skipwith explained.

By 2 p.m. on 28 June the line of British warships was sweeping the area where *Lauenburg* was supposed to be operating. The men on the ships had to be very alert. There were banks of fog about and there was always the possibility that they might encounter icebergs. The weather only cleared up during the late afternoon. They searched for almost five hours, and were just about to call it a day, when a lookout on *Tartar* shouted: 'There's something over there, near the ice!' As binoculars were trained on the spot, officers on *Tartar's* bridge could see the enemy ship's silhouette about ten miles away. *Tartar*, and another destroyer in the line, whose commander had been tipped off by Skipwith's signalman, immediately raced towards the weather ship. But they had been seen by the Germans. A lookout had spotted the mast of one of the warships.

A furious row broke out on *Lauenburg*, as it attempted to escape from the much faster warships. Some members of the crew wanted to fire at the destroyers. *Lauenburg's* radio operator sent out a signal warning the British ships not to come any nearer. However, the captain of the weather ship said that they must surrender. 'If we don't, they'll sink us,' he told his crew bluntly. As if to underline what he was saying, a shell from Kelly's guns on *Tartar* whistled over their heads. Admiral Burrough, looking on from the cruiser *Nigeria*, also instructed his gunners to open fire. It was all part of his plan to terrorise *Lauenburg's* crew, until they could think of nothing except abandoning ship.

That is precisely what happened. Shortly after opening fire, Burrough and his crew watched with satisfaction as two lifeboats full of the *Lauenburg's* crew rowed away from the weather ship. Minutes later *Tartar* drew up alongside and the boarding party, led by Tom Kelly, the gunner, leapt on board. Eight feet above them, on the destroyer's upper deck, Hugh 'Spider' Wilson, the twenty-three-year-old lieutenant who had been put in charge of the boarding party, realised that he was being left behind. So he jumped onto *Lauenburg's* deck as well. Unfortunately, he mistimed his leap as the ships rocked beside each other, and landed on a hatch, in the process spraining his ankle. He nevertheless managed to hobble up a ladder to *Lauenburg*'s charthouse so that he could direct operations from there. While the some members of the boarding party checked that the ship was not being scuttled, others searched for her codebooks.

Allon Bacon, the intelligence officer, who had dried and sorted the documents captured from *U-110*, was rowed across from the destroyer, HMS *Jupiter*. When he reported to the charthouse, Wilson said, 'There's nothing much here. You don't want this rubbish do you?', nodding dismissively at the disorganised piles of papers lying all over the charthouse and the deck. Wilson had been disappointed not to find a pile of codebooks, and presumed that most of them had been thrown overboard or burned. A heap of ashes had been found inside the boiler. Bacon replied that he wanted all of the papers, and only declared himself satisfied when they were all placed in bags and transported over to *Tartar*.

Before they left *Lauenburg*, some members of the boarding party asked whether they could stay behind to set up an ambush for the relief ship. Wilson thought that this was a good idea, but his orders were to return to *Tartar* as soon as Bacon was finished. After Bacon and the rest of the boarding party were safely back on *Tartar*, the destroyer's gunners were told to sink the weather ship. It took just four shells. Shortly after 9 p.m. the warships turned around, and began their long trek back to Scapa Flow.

An hour later the commander of the destroyer HMS *Bedouin*, who had been responsible for rescuing and interrogating *Lauenburg*'s crew, sent this message to Admiral Burrough: 'Wireless Operator states that he reported to Wilhelmshaven that "Langenburg" was being attacked without stating type of enemy but got no receipt.'[6] Admiral Burrough responded by sending the following message to all the ships involved with the raid: 'The utmost secrecy must be observed with regard to the operation we have completed. If questioned, ratings should not commit themselves beyond saying that an armed German trawler was met and sunk, the crew being taken prisoner.'[7]

The next morning, Burrough signalled to the Admiralty: 'Operation EC. Object not repetition not completely achieved as most important item was missing. Trawler sunk 22 prisoners. W/T operator states he reported being attacked but did not specify nature and received no acknowledgement.'[8] The 'important item' missing was, presumably, the Enigma cipher machine itself, which had been thrown into the sea long before the warships came alongside the weather ship. Burrough appears not to have been told that a cipher machine was already in Bletchley Park's hands.

On the journey back to Scapa Flow, Allon Bacon closeted himself in the captain's day cabin in order to sort out the documents he had seized. Wilson looked in from time to time to offer him a glass of gin, but Bacon refused to be distracted. When Tom Kelly popped his head around the day cabin door and asked Bacon if he had found what he was looking for, Bacon said, 'No, I've found something a damned sight more important.' Amongst the mass of charts and signal forms, he had come across three loose sheets which Hinsley had hoped he would find. Two of the sheets were headed: 'Steckerverbindungen' (plug connections), and one sheet was a list of the 'Innere Einstellung' (inner settings), i.e. the wheel order, and the settings for the rings around the wheels.[9]

The warships finally made it back to Scapa Flow at 5.15 p.m. on 30 June, and by 11 a.m. on 2 July Bacon was delivering his haul to Hut 4 at Bletchley Park. Bacon proudly wrote up the raid, and at the bottom, stated: 'Overall time from north of Jan Mayen Island to Bletchley Park – 3 days 14 hours.'[10] The following inaccurate write-up headed: 'Depression Off Iceland for 22 Germans' was issued as a press release for the benefit of any spies who scanned the British newspapers: 'In the course of a periodical sweep to the northward of Iceland our forces sank a German weather reporting trawler, capturing her crew of 22, said the Admiralty last night.'[11]

Hinsley and the men in the Admiralty held their breath after the raid, as they waited to see how the Germans reacted. It soon became apparent that they had got away with it. The codebreakers in Hut 8 carried on reading Naval Enigma signals within hours rather than days, throughout the rest of July. The pinch turned out to be such a success that, in August and September 1941, more plans were made to cut out German vessels. The targets this time were to be patrol ships in convoys passing through the English Channel. Unfortunately, all these attempts failed, one case even ending in farce. On Monday 15 September 1941, Bacon was taken out to sea in HMS *Berkeley* with five other warships to intercept a German convoy. But when the British ships raced into action they found that 'the convoy' seen on the radar screen was an escaped barrage balloon, trailing about 100 feet of wire cable.[12] After that anti climax, all planned pinch operations were suspended. But by then, the British codebreakers had won the first bout in the battle to break the Naval Enigma code.

After the first week in August 1941, when the Banburismus procedure invented by Alan Turing failed to work, 18 and 19 September 1941 were the only pair of days whose Home Waters settings could not be broken until the end of the war. That is not to say that the codebreakers could immediately break every day's settings. However if a day's messages could not be read at first, its paired day – when Enigma operators used an identical wheel order and ring settings – was broken.[13] Thus Bletchley Park managed to break the code without any prolonged interruptions; the average time to read Naval Enigma signals, after *Lauenburg*'s settings ran out at the end of July 1941, rose to around 50 hours.[14]

The codebreakers were helped by being able to pursue two lines of attack. The preferred option involved the use of the Banburismus procedure and the bombe. Banburismus limited the number of wheel orders, and then either a menu derived from a crib, or from the information gleaned in the course of carrying out Banburismus, could be tested by setting up the relatively few wheel orders not ruled out on the bombe. If Banburismus did not succeed, the codebreakers could always switch over to the crib and bombe method, which involved running the menu produced from a crib on all possible wheel orders. This ate into the bombe time required by the codebreakers in Hut 6, the section responsible for breaking the Army and Air Force Enigma settings, but the position would have been much worse if the Germans had not made a basic error.

The German section which had compiled the list of wheel orders to be used by Enigma operators appeared to be complying with certain rules which were to be of great assistance to the British. Rule one was that one of the three newest wheels, 6, 7 and 8, was usually included in the wheel order; this meant that out of the 336 possible wheel orders, the sixty which did not include a wheel 6, 7 or 8 were never used. Rule two was that if a wheel was used in a particular position inside the Enigma on one day, it was never used in that position the next day. This meant that if, say, the wheel order on Days one and two was 2, 6 and 7, and on Days five and six it was 8, 7 and 4, the codebreakers were sure that on Days three and four, neither 2 or 8 would have been used as the left wheel, neither 6 or 7 would have been used as the middle wheel, and neither 7 or 4 would have been be used as the right wheel. In these circumstances, the number of wheel orders to be tested on the bombe would be 105, a substantial number compared with the ten or so which were not ruled out if Banburismus was being used, but less than a third of 336, the total number of wheel orders.[15] Notwithstanding these wheel order rules, the Naval Enigma could not be read currently using the crib and bombe method given the limited number of bombes available; the average time to test a menu on a particular wheel order took around twenty minutes.[16] If 105 wheel orders had to be tested, that would take around thirty-five bombe hours.

The first cribs used at Bletchley Park to break Naval Enigma were mostly included in messages about the weather. After the fall of France, German weather stations along the French coast broadcast regular stereotypical weather reports at particular times, and on particular frequencies. They also inserted a particular call sign, usually including three letters, at the beginning of their signals. Once this was known, it was easy to identify which pieces of intercepted cipher text incorporated these signals, and what was being said; the-signals usually began with words such as 'VON-VONWEWABOULOGNE', (From weather station Boulogne), or 'VVVWEWACHERBOURG'. 'WEWA', which was included in these weather cribs, was short for Wetter Warte, meaning weather station. When such stereotypical words were placed at the beginning of the messages, it was easy to match up the cipher text letters with the correct crib letters. The cribster merely wrote the appropriate cipher text under the crib, so that the first letter of the cipher text was level with the first letter of the crib.

Unfortunately, security conscious Germans sometimes inserted dummy letters in front of the main message in order to throw anyone attempting to break the code off the scent. So instead of merely encyphering 'WEWA Boulogne', the crib known about by the British, the Germans in Boulogne might encipher 'ABCDWEWA Boulogne'. The cribsters then had to work out how to line up the cipher text and the crib. They did this by exploiting one of the great weaknesses of the Enigma cipher machine: if a German tapped a key representing a letter on the Enigma keyboard, say, L, that letter would never be lit up on the lampboard. Armed with this knowledge, the cribsters knew that if they wrote the crib above the cipher text, and if a pair of identical letters in the crib and cipher text were aligned, the alignment must be incorrect, i.e. if the crib and cipher text were aligned as follows:

Crib   W E W A B O U L O G N E . . . . . .
Cipher text   X T R W E F B L Y D P G A C Q S . . . . .

it was obvious that the L in 'Boulogne' was aligned with the L in the cipher text, and that the alignment was wrong. A 'crash' would have been said to have occurred. To discover the correct alignment, the cribsters had to slide the crib against the stationary cipher text, until a position was found where there were no crashes. This is the case in the example given above after the crib was slid four places to the right, so that the alignment was:

Crib   W E W A B O U L O G N E
Cipher text   X T R W E F B L Y D P G A C Q S

That was likely to be the correct position.

Only after the correct alignment was worked out, could the code-breakers produce the menu from the aligned crib and cipher text which would enable the bombe to reveal the wheel and plugboard socket settings. Even then there were pitfalls. The bombe would not work if the right wheel had turned over the middle wheel in the course of producing the portion of the cipher text used to draw up the menu. To avoid such a situation, the cribsters often split their cribs in two, in the hope that if the middle wheel had been turned over in the course of one half of the cipher text being produced, it would not have turned over in the course of producing the second half.

One of the Bletchley Park cribsters, who became adept at lining up cribs with stretches of cipher text was Rolf Noskwith, a German jew, who had emigrated with his parents to England in 1932. This was not so much because they feared they would be persecuted in Germany, but more because a tariff had been imposed on the stockings Rolf Noskwith's father was exporting to England; the tariff made the business uneconomic.[17] Noskwith was first looked over by a panel of Bletchley Park recruiters during 1940. At the time Noskwith, then aged twenty, was a mathcmatics student at Trinity College, Cambridge. He had registered with the recruiting office in Cambridge, and had indicated that he would be interested in working on codes. However, although he and his family had become British subjects, his foreign roots were at first an obstacle to his being hired to work as a codebreaker. After being interviewed by Gordon Welchman, he received a letter telling him that he would not be hired after all. But by May 1941, the security rules appeared to have been relaxed somewhat, and Noskwith was interviewed again, by Hugh Alexander. He was asked to go to Bletchley Station on his birthday on 19 June 1941. There he was greeted by Alexander, who escorted him to Hut 8 in Bletchley Park.

Noskwith quickly made his mark after being asked to find a way of breaking the Naval Enigma Offizier settings. These were the settings used for enciphering special messages sent to or by officers; the messages were doubly enciphered, as explained in chapter 13 and Appendix 6. The Offizier system had been exposed for the first time during June 1941 after the settings were seized from the *U-110*.[18] But after new settings were introduced in July 1941, the Offizier messages became a mystery once again. Although they utilised the same wheel order as was used for general Enigma traffic, the plugboard socket connections were different. The codebreakers all agreed that the only way to break these settings was to find a crib which would enable a menu to be drawn up and tested on the bombe. However it was feared that the traffic might never be broken regularly, because there were unlikely to be any stereotypical Offizier messages which could serve as cribs.

Noskwith nevertheless, after combing through the traffic broken in June 1941, managed to identify a possible crib. It started with the letters: 'EEESSSPATRONE' (Patrone means a cartridge). Messages starting in this form had been seen in previous signals; they referred to the colour of the recognition flares which were fired by German vessels so that other German ships would know that they were not part of the enemy's fleet. However Noskwith was so uncertain about whether this crib would lead to positive results, that after the menu from the crib was drawn up, and handed to the bombe operators to test, he left Bletchley Park while the bombes were still running to take a couple of days' leave. Before going, he took the precaution of telling Shaun Wylie, the head of Hut 8's crib section, to send him a telegram mentioning a fish if the crib turned out to be correct.

A telegram duly arrived at Noskwith's home in Nottingham. Charles Noskwith, his father, who had written down the contents of the telegram when it was read to him over the telephone, was flummoxed by the reference in it to a 'pompano'. Rolf Noskwith, realising that the mysterious word in the telegram began with a P, which corresponded with the first letter of the code word 'Paula' mentioned at the beginning of the Offizier message, quickly consulted a dictionary. After satisfying himself that a pompano was indeed a fish, he sighed with relief. The Offizier Naval Enigma settings were broken.

15

Suspicion

Bletchley Park, the Atlantic and Berlin

MAY—OCTOBER 1941

Just days before the June 1941 Enigma settings captured from *München* came into effect, a battle highlighting the Allies' need to read the German Naval cipher was reaching a climax in the Atlantic. On 21 May 1941, the German battleship *Bismarck*, accompanied by the heavy cruiser *Prinz Eugen*, had sailed from Bergen in Norway to the Denmark Strait, north-west of Iceland. The threat to Allied shipping was underlined on 24 May when the German ships sank the British battle-cruiser HMS *Hood* in the process killing Vice-Admiral Lancelot Holland, the man who had masterminded the capture of the Enigma settings from *München* just over a fortnight earlier. *Hood* blew up after being hit by a German shell, but *Bismarck* was also damaged in the encounter.

Having shaken off her British pursuers, *Bismarck* steamed for home after *Prinz Eugen* peeled off to attack British shipping alone. But the question facing Jack Tovey, the Commander-in-Chief of the Home Fleet, on 25 May, was which home would she make for, France or Norway? Tovey, who flew his flag from the battleship *King George V*, one of the ships out looking for *Bismarck*, had to answer the question using ambiguous direction-finding fixes sent to him from the Admiralty. At 6.10 p.m. on 25 May, Tovey finally guessed that *Bismarck*'s destination was France.[1] He was right. Aircraft flown off the aircraft carrier *Ark Royal* spotted and torpedoed *Bismarck* on 26 May. She was finally sunk the next day by one of Tovey's cruisers.

The *Bismarck* episode showed what could and could not be achieved if Naval Enigma was read after a delay. Alan Turing and his colleagues at Bletchley Park had no current settings during the chase, so they had to work them out. Turing's Banburismus procedure helped, but it took too long. Messages were only being read three to seven days after they were sent, which was too late to affect the outcome of the hunt.[2] The out of date messages were not all useless however. On 21 May some April 1941 Enigma messages were decrypted, disclosing that *Bismarck* had taken on prize crews and charts. This led the Admiralty to conclude that the battleship intended to carry out a raid on the Allies' trade routes.[3] But that was the Naval Enigma's sole contribution to the sinking.

Nevertheless, there was jubilation in Bletchley Park's Hut 6, the Air Force Enigma codebreaking unit, when the news of the sinking came through. The codebreakers there believed that without their contribution Germany's giant battleship would never have been found. Codebreakers did not normally read messages once they had worked out the Enigma settings for the day. But on 25 May, Keith Batey, the man who was to marry Mavis Lever, (Dilly Knox's helper during the Battle of Matapan), happened to pay a visit to the machine room. That was where secretaries, using British Typex cipher machines, set up so as to act like replica Enigmas with the correct settings for the day in question, typed out the coded messages to produce the true plain-language texts. One of the typists turned to Batey and, pointing to a piece of paper containing the message she had just deciphered, said, 'This one looks interesting.' A German Air Force officer in Athens in connection with the invasion of Crete, had wanted to find out *Bismarck's* whereabouts, since a close relation was on the ship. A signal was sent requesting this information. The reply stated that *Bismarck* was making for the west coast of France.[4] This information appears to have reached Admiral Tovey on his flagship shortly after he had already decided that *Bismarck's* destination must be Brest. So unknown to the celebrating Batey, and the codebreakers in Hut 6, their work, which could, in different circumstances, have been decisive, may not in fact have influenced the search for *Bismarck* after all.[5]

But Bletchley Park may nevertheless have played an important role in finding the battleship. After the British Fleet lost touch with *Bismarck* in the Atlantic during the early hours of 25 May, Harry Hinsley in Hut 4 noticed that something very strange had occurred. Until midday on 24 May 1941, the unreadable Enigma messages sent to *Bismarck* had been sent from the German controlling transmitter at Wilhelmshaven. Hinsley noticed that subsequent messages were being sent from France. Hinsley immediately telephoned Ned Denning at the OIC, and told him, 'All this uncertainty about the

D/F. I think it's over. This chap is going to France.' He then pointed out the evidence.[6]

After 1 June 1941 the codebreaking picture changed overnight. All of a sudden Bletchley Park's codebreakers could read Naval Enigma messages almost as quickly as the Germans. This enabled the British Admiralty to set up ambushes for the German supply ships which had made their way out to the Atlantic. They were supposed to replenish *Bismarck* and *Prinz Eugen*, as well as the U-boats, when they ran out of food, torpedoes, or fuel on their long patrols. Eight of these ships were sunk between 3 June and 21 June 1941, six of them as a direct result of using Enigma information.[7] Another seven supply ships and weather ships were sunk during the next three weeks. But after 21 June, the Admiralty decided that it should stop acting on Enigma intelligence, even when it was available, in case the British successes alerted the Germans to the fact that their Naval cipher was compromised.

Ironically, it was the capture of the supply ship *Gedania*, without using Enigma intelligence, which led to greatest anxiety in Germany. The Admiralty had requested that *Gedania* should be spared in order to avoid that very result. But on 4 June 1941 the British destroyer HMS *Marsdale* blundered into the supply ship. After stripping her of her codebooks, *Marsdale* escorted *Gedania* back to Scotland. The German Navy might have been none the wiser about the precise circumstances in which *Gedania*'s patrol was interrupted, had it not been for the 1 July 1941 attack by a German bomber on the *Malvernian*, an Ellerman Line passenger liner which had been converted into an armed ocean boarding vessel. Amongst the survivors were Lieutenant Keats and Able Seaman Blackburn, who had witnessed *Gedania*'s capture while serving on *Marsdale*. After being picked up by the Germans, they told their captors what they had seen.

Marsdale's crew had originally thought *Gedania* was a suspicious neutral ship. They attempted to flag it down. At first, that had no effect, and *Marsdale* pursued the German ship for two hours before it finally stopped. *Gedania*'s crew abandoned ship and manned its lifeboats. One of these was apprehended by a small boat launched from *Marsdale*. *Gedania*'s captain, who was in the German lifeboat, and some of the lifeboat's crew were then instructed to return to their ship. But before the Germans could comply with the order, three explosions were heard as scuttling charges went off in *Gedania*'s bow and in the engine room. This did not put off the boarding party. They climbed on board and filled in the large hole beneath *Gedania*'s waterline which would have sunk the ship had it not been dealt with promptly. At the same time, other members of the boarding party, fearing that there might be more scuttling charges on the ship, quickly gathered up all the documents they could find in the captain's cabin, the chart house and the radio office, stuffed them into bags and sent them over to *Marsdale*. Neither Blackburn nor Keats could specify what documents were captured. But the Abwehr, when examining the evidence in October 1941, stated: 'the rules concerning the destruction of secret documents were not properly complied with . . . It is worrying that codes . . . and sea maps as well as secret messages have been seen by the enemy.'[8]

Winston Churchill, the British prime minister, had for some time been worried that Britain's penetration of the Enigma cipher would be revealed. Long before the capture of *München*'s settings, he had insisted that the number of people outside Bletchley Park who were allowed to see decrypts should be rigorously pruned.[9] He was always chivying his Naval and Army commanders only to use Enigma information when they also had other sources which could have given them the same intelligence. Senior officers who knew about Enigma were often forbidden to go into combat. That being the case, it was unfortunate that something was not done to ensure that the postings of junior seamen, such as Blackburn and Keats who knew about sensitive captures, were not equally constrained.

Churchill might have been even more security conscious than he already was had he known about a document containing Air Force Enigma intelligence which was captured by the Germans during the May 1941 battle for Crete. The document dated 24 May 1941 was a telegram from London marked 'Personal for General Freyberg', who was the commander of the Allied forces on the island. The telegram began with the incriminating words: 'According to most reliable source', and then proceeded to give details not only of where the German troops were on the previous day, which presumably could have been worked out by normal reconnaissance, but also specified what the Germans were going to do next: 'attack Suda Bay'. The document was subsequently translated into German, and sent back to Berlin.[10]

When Churchill travelled down to Bletchley Park, on 6 September 1941, to see for himself how the Enigma information was produced, he had no idea that the continued supply of both Naval and Air Force Enigma decrypts was under serious threat. During his visit he tried to walk into Hut 8, where the daily struggle to break the Naval

Enigma took place, only to find his way barred by Shaun Wylie, one of the senior cryptographers, who was sitting on the floor in front of the door reading a document. Then Churchill tried the next door in the corridor and burst in to find Hugh Alexander, the man who was to take over the administration of the hut from Alan Turing, also sitting on the floor, sorting through piles of papers. Of course, everyone got up when they saw it was the prime minister, but it was clear that Churchill was a little nonplussed by the apparent chaos he had encountered.[11] This was reflected in the speech which he gave to the Bletchley Park workers gathered in front of the house. It began with the words: 'To look at you, one would not think you knew anything secret . . .'[12]

It was not what happened during his visit, but what happened afterwards, which was important. The prime minister's visit prompted some of Bletchley Park's senior codebreakers, including Alan Turing and Hugh Alexander from Hut 8, to write to Churchill to complain about the obstacles impeding their work. Their letter dated 21 October 1941 began with the following words:

> Dear Prime Minister,
>
> Some weeks ago you paid us the honour of a visit, and we believe that you regard our work as important. You will have seen that, thanks largely to the energy and foresight of Commander Travis, we have been well supplied with the 'bombes' for the breaking of the German Enigma codes. We think, however, that you ought to know that this work is being held up, and in some cases is not being done at all, principally because we cannot get sufficient staff to deal with it. Our reason for writing to you direct is that for months we have done everything that we possibly can through the normal channels, and that we despair of any early improvement without your intervention.

Included amongst the complaints was the following disturbing statement of fact which, if made public, would have horrified the merchant sailors who were having to face up to murderous attacks from Nazi Germany's U-boats day in and day out miles out in the Atlantic: 'The effect of this is that the finding of the naval keys is being delayed at least twelve hours every day.' The codebreakers added:

> We have written this letter entirely on our own initiative. We do not know who or what is responsible for our difficulties, and most emphatically we do not want to be taken as criticising Commander Travis who has all

along done his utmost to help us in every possible way. But if we are to do our job as well as it could and should be done it is absolutely vital that our wants, small as they are, should be promptly attended to. We have felt that we should be failing in our duty if we did not draw your attention to the facts and to the effects which they are having and must continue to have on our work, unless immediate action is taken.[13]

It was hardly surprising that when Churchill saw the complaints on 22 October, he immediately issued the following note to General Ismay which was to become one of his most famous 'Action this Day' memoranda: 'Make sure they have all they want on extreme priority and report to me that this has been done.'[14]

Even before Churchill's visit, the breaking of the Naval Enigma was one of the principal factors which had completely transformed the course of the Battle of the Atlantic. Between 1 and 23 June 1941 the U-boats were not able to intercept any convoys in the North Atlantic, as the OIC used the information taken from Naval Enigma messages to route Allied merchant ships clear of the wolf packs. In July 1941 no convoys were sighted on the transatlantic routes for three weeks. In August 1941 the U-boats again patrolled fruitlessly for ten days.[15] During July and August 1941 the monthly shipping tonnage sunk by the U-boats fell beneath 100,000 tons for the first time since June 1940. During November 1941 just 62,000 tons of shipping was sunk, in spite of the fact that the number of operational U-boats had increased by more than 50 per cent since the beginning of the war.[16]

The reading of the Enigma messages was only one of several reasons for this turnaround in Britain's fortunes. The dramatic fall in the tonnage sunk by U-boats in November 1941 occurred at a time when Hitler was insisting that many of the submarines previously set aside for use in the Atlantic had to be redeployed in the Mediterranean to support the Axis forces in Africa, or had to abandon their attacking role altogether so that they could escort German surface ships on their patrols. During the summer of 1941 the U-boats were forbidden to attack American convoy escorts during the early stages of the invasion of Russia, so that America would not be provoked into declaring war on Germany as well. Although this diversion of U-boat resources made more available to attack shipping between west Africa and Gibraltar and Britain, these vessels were in many cases smaller than the oceangoing ships to be found in the Atlantic. Consequently, the tonnage sunk during each successful attack fell. On the other hand convoys in this area were often spotted by German aircraft, thereby lessening the effect of the Admiralty's attempt to route them around the U-boats thanks to Naval Enigma. Another factor which contributed to the reduction of the U-boats' strike rate was increased air patrols north-west of England and south of Iceland which persuaded Dönitz to shift his U-boats even further west towards Greenland at various times during the summer and autumn of 1941; the fuel used up travelling so far west limited the amount of time the U-boats could spend searching for convoys. The larger areas which had to be searched around Greenland also diminished the number of convoys which were discovered.

Although there is no definitive study stating how many ships Naval Enigma saved, the following figures suggest that many convoys were routed around the wolf packs in the North Atlantic as a result of the breaking of the code; this was the case especially when the capture of Enigma settings enabled U-boat messages to be read within hours of their interception: the percentage of North Atlantic convoys seen and reported by U-boats during August–December 1940 was 36 per cent and 23 per cent during January–May 1941. After Naval Enigma was broken currently, the figure fell to just 4 per cent between June–August 1941, although it rose again to 18 per cent during September–December 1941, by which time Bletchley Park was often taking as long as forty-eight hours to break the code each time all the Enigma settings were changed.[17] The Naval Enigma settings were all changed every second day. During the same months the percentage of convoys which lost at least three merchant ships to a wolf pack attack was 16 per cent during August–December 1940, and 10 per cent during January–May to 1941. After Naval Enigma was broken currently, the figure fell to just 4 per cent during June–August 1941, although it rose again to 9 per cent during September–December 1941.[18]

*

Paradoxically it was fortunate that the British ability to read Naval Enigma messages was masked, in part, by Bletchley Park's and the Admiralty's inability to understand a new code-within-a-code introduced by the Germans in June 1941. This prevented the Admiralty having one hundred per cent success when attempting to route its convoys clear of U-boat lines, which would surely have disclosed to the Germans that their cipher was compromised. Prior to 16 June

1941, Bletchley Park had been able to understand the positions of U-boats indicated in Enigma messages. The German grid map covering the North Atlantic had been captured from *U-110*. But on 16 June a new system was introduced, apparently designed to prevent unauthorised people from knowing where the U-boats were going, rather than representing an attempt to prevent enemy codebreakers from reading Enigma messages. Under the new system positions at sea were indicated by relating them to arbitrarily chosen fixed points, referred to by code names such as 'Franz' and 'Herbert'. This code-within-a-code was not solved until July 1941. The alteration of this system in September 1941 led to more carnage at sea, until that was solved in its turn.[19] During the last three weeks of October 1941, none of the U-boat patrol lines in the mid-Atlantic succeeded in finding and attacking a convoy.[20]

The German Secret Service was not the only organisation concerned about the U-boats' failure to find convoys. On 7 June 1941, just days after Naval Enigma was read currently by the British for the first time, Dönitz wrote in his War Diary that there were 'other known or suspected causes' revealing his U-boats's positions, in addition to the enemy's intercept and D/F service. On 20 July, he complained again: 'The lack of traffic in July is significant,' he wrote. 'The bad visibility which exists at present in all areas of the North Atlantic may have a lot to do with this. However I am under the impression that the number of single vessels has again become considerably less.'

Shortly before two o'clock in the afternoon on 27 August, Dönitz received a desperate message which was to have far more worrying implications for Enigma's security than anything he had seen or heard before. The message from *U-570*, stationed in the Atlantic, stated: 'Am not able to dive, and am being attacked by aircraft.' The message came from Hans Rahmlow, one of the new wave of inexperienced U-boat commanders who had been rushed into the front line. Dönitz noted in his War Diary: 'the boat has interference in its reception and it is therefore impossible to communicate with her. Boats in the vicinity were ordered to help her.'[21] As he wrote up his notes, an armada of British ships was steaming towards the spot south of Iceland where *U-570* was floating under the threatening shadow of a British aircraft circling overhead.[22]

Rahmlow should have scuttled *U-570* when, later that night, the first ship, a British trawler, approached; the trawler's commander would have had to rescue the crew from the water. But once the trawler, and other British and Canadian ships which arrived during the night, had made contact with Rahmlow, it was too late. When Rahmlow's crew finally did make an attempt to scuttle the U-boat, a signal was flashed across threatening to sink *U-570*'s life raft and floats if the U-boat were to sink. This threat was reinforced by a barrage of shells from the British destroyer, HMS *Burwell*, after a gunner misheard *Burwell*'s commander's order to fire warning shots across the *U-570*'s bows. In the process five of the German crew were wounded. After that *U-570*'s crew were convinced that any further attempts to scuttle the boat was as good as committing suicide. Eventually, the U-boat was boarded, Rahmlow and his crew were evacuated, and the *U-570* towed to Iceland where it was beached.

Bill Arnold, the officer from *Burwell*, who had recommended opening fire to prevent the scuttling, then climbed into the U-boat. He found a scene as unsavoury as an unprocessed sewer. He had to wade through vast quantities of flour, dried peas, soft fruit and the remains of scores of loaves of black bread which had combined with oil, water and spilt buckets of excrement to create what was described in an official report as a 'revolting muck'. As he searched, he could hear the sinister ticking of several clocks which reminded him that he might come across a booby trap at any minute. Rahmlow's men had destroyed most of the Enigma codebooks. But some documents had been overlooked. They included papers containing matching plain-language German and enciphered text for at least three days, and some Enigma settings.[23]

After the *U-570*'s crew were interned, other POWs, including the captured U-boat ace Otto Kretschmer, convened a Council of Honour to try Rahmlow and his first watch officer Bernhard Berndt for dereliction of duty. Both men were found guilty of cowardice. The verdict, and the prospect of being ostracised in the POW camp where they were being held, persuaded Berndt to try to redeem himself. He escaped with the professed aim of destroying *U-570*, which had been brought to England, only to be shot while running away from the Home Guard who had rearrested him.

Dönitz heard some details about the capture of the *U-570* from reports in English newspapers. In his War Diary he referred to it as a 'depressing event', which might be explained in part by the fact that the commander was at the time incapacitated by gas. That would mean that 'the decision to surrender was taken and carried out by the First Watch Officer . . . Berndt,' Dönitz concluded. He had also heard Bernhard Berndt's fate. 'He probably did not appreciate the full significance of what he had done until he was a prisoner, whereupon he preferred to die while trying to escape rather than anything else,'[24] Dönitz commented. But a more important question for Dönitz to answer was whether the British were able to read his and his U-boats' Enigma messages as a result of the capture. He asked Vice-Admiral Erhard Maertens, the head of the German Navy's Communications Service, to tell him whether he thought the Naval Enigma cipher was compromised. Maertens reported back to Dönitz on 18 October 1941, and repeated his conclusions in another report two days later.[25] His verdict included some very worrying conclusions:

> We have to accept that the *U-570* might have been captured by the enemy without anything having been destroyed. In these circumstances it cannot be ruled out that . . . a large amount of cipher documents are in the enemy's hands. If this is true, the security of our enciphering procedure has been weakened . . . Our cipher will have been compromised if, as well as the enemy capturing the codebooks, our officers, who are now POWs, have told the enemy the keyword, which since June 1941, has been given verbally to the U-boat commander so that he could alter the printed list of Enigma settings. If that has occurred, then we have to accept that our radio messages are being read by the enemy . . . The same would be true if the keyword has been written down in breach of the regulations, and the codebooks and the keyword have fallen into enemy hands, or if, for example, the settings arrived at by using the keyword order were written on the original settings list. If this happened, the enemy could work out the meaning of the keyword.

In spite of this bleak picture, he was not saying that the British were reading Enigma messages. 'Everything suggests that the crew had the chance to destroy at least one of the secret cipher documents.' If this had occurred, 'it would be impossible for the enemy to read our messages.'

Maertens thought that the U-boat's message transmitted at 13.58 on 27 August, stating that the boat was having difficulties understanding incoming messages, was significant. 'It is possible that the boat, in sending this message, wanted to indicate that the codebooks had been destroyed, and for that reason coded messages could not be read any more,' he said. 'It would be hard to believe that no one in the crew had the courage to destroy any of the documents, such as documents with red print on them . . . by throwing them into the sea.' Maertens also did not believe that the British had cracked the keyword procedure which made the reading of their messages 'nearly impossible'. He concluded by pointing out that, even if he was wrong about the keyword, and it had been captured, new settings would come into force on 1 November 1941, which had not been given to the commander of the U-570. So from that date, security would be restored once more.

The keyword (Stichwort) procedure which Maertens hoped would defeat British cryptographers if Enigma settings lists were captured, worked as follows: if the key word was say DANZIG, that told the German Enigma operators that 4 had to be added to each of the wheel numbers making up the wheel order; the 4 was gleaned from the D in DANZIG, which was the fourth letter in the alphabet. When carrying out the aforementioned addition, the total returned to '1' if the counting exceeded '8', (8 being the largest number inscribed on any of the Naval Enigma wheels) just as the hands on a clock return to '1' after passing the '12'. So if the wheel order in the settings list was 2, 7, 5, it became 6, 3, 1[26] after being modified by the keyword procedure. Similarly the next letters in DANZIG: A, N and Z, the first, fourteenth and twenty-sixth letters in the alphabet, told the Enigma operators to add on one, fourteen and twenty-six onto the letters making up the ring settings in the settings list; if the ring settings in the settings list were BYL, they became CML after being modified. In the same way, the I in DANZIG, the ninth letter in the alphabet, told the Enigma operators to add nine to the plugboard connections; if one of the plugboard connections in the settings list had the A connected to the F, the J had to be connected to the O, after being modified.

While this could have been a useful emergency measure if the British cryptographers had been attempting to use trial and error methods to break the code, it was no defence against the bombe if the British identified a correct crib. Even without the bombe, the Stichwort system was not watertight once British cryptographers knew about the procedure. If the Bletchley Park cryptographers had been attempting to read Enigma signals using trial and error methods, and if they had captured the Enigma settings for a particular day, they would not have had to test all 336 wheel orders, and the trillions of possible plugboard connection combinations; they would merely have had to test eight wheel orders and twenty-six plugboard connection combinations. Given the procedure, the original settings in the settings list could not be altered by more than eight in the case of the wheel orders, and twenty-six in the case of the plugboard connections. That gave it a 'nuisance value', according to the history of Hut 8 written by Hugh Alexander, but as he wrote after the War, it was 'clearly not equivalent to a new key'.[27] So Maertens' reliance on it to ward off Dönitz's anxiety about whether the Naval Enigma was compromised was a misjudgment.

At the same time as analysing the Enigma security implications of *U-570*'s capture Maertens also gave his verdict about the capture of *Gedania*. He felt that there were 'no worrying circumstances'. Not only did the radio operators have time to destroy the codebooks before the ship was boarded, but since then, the keyword procedure had been introduced. Maertens' verdicts about what had been captured on *U-570* and *Gedania* turned out to be correct. Isolated Enigma documents were picked up from both *U-570* and from *Gedania*. Some settings were discovered on the *U-570*, and a set of bigram tables was found on *Gedania*.[28] Neither of these documents would have been enough on their own to have enabled the British to break the code on an ongoing basis. However Maertens' reports were prepared in a strange way. The Germanic mind, with its love of order and attention to detail, had concentrated on individual captures, without stopping to stand back and look at the wider picture. Had Maertens done this, he could not have failed to notice how the ability of the wolf packs to contact convoys had suddenly fallen off in July and August 1941, shortly after the capture and sinking of the supply ships and *Lauenburg*. Because he did not view the question of compromise in this way, Britain was let off the hook. But how long would it be before the penny dropped?

16

A Two-Edged Sword

The Atlantic and the Cape Verde Islands

SEPTEMBER 1941

The progress of convoys as they lumbered across the Atlantic were recorded on the giant green cork wall plot in the Operations Room in Derby House, Liverpool. That was the headquarters of the Western Approaches Command. The convoys' routes were represented on the plot by pieces of coloured tape; a different colour was allocated to each convoy. If Naval Enigma decrypts, passed by Bletchley Park to the Admiralty's Operational Intelligence Centre (the OIC), revealed that a line of U-boats lay in a convoy's path, the Wrens keeping up the plots climbed their tall ladders and placed a line of submarine symbols in the appropriate place. The submarines were white if there was any doubt about their position, and black if their positions marked on the plot were certain. Each time a U-boat sank a merchant ship, the Wrens placed a red symbol showing a merchant ship at an angle on the plot.[1] Similar plots were to found in the OIC in London and in the Operations Room at St John's Newfoundland, the Canadian naval base. After May 1941 the Canadian Navy was expected to protect convoys in the western Atlantic.

Observing the U-boats and merchant ships being moved around one of these plots was like watching a giant game of chess. In the operations rooms there were no screams, or sounds of ships sinking, no revelations about the emotions of those involved in the battle; there were only expressionless symbols. That could not be said of the Enigma decrypts made available to Rodger Winn, the head of the OIC's Submarine Tracking Room. The Enigma messages were sometimes happy and sometimes sad; one moment Dönitz would be ticking off a commander for not attacking robustly enough. The next he would be congratulating another man effusively for a job well done. These messages enabled Winn to look into the very minds of

Karl Dönitz, and the commanders in his U-boats, but they were particularly painful to read for anyone who knew men on the Allies' ships that had been sunk. When Winn failed to divert a convoy clear of a line of waiting U-boats, he could 'see' the inevitable wolf pack attack building up by listening in to their messages. The fact that he received the intelligence several days late merely highlighted his impotence.

Winn would have liked to have diverted convoy Sydney-Cape Breton (SC) 42 south of where he thought the U-boats were lining up at the beginning of September 1941. He thought the line was somewhere in the North Atlantic south-east of Greenland, but he could not be sure because the position was disguised by a code even after the Naval Enigma message was decrypted, a code-within-a-code. His uncertainty did not stop him diverting four convoys south of where he thought the U-boats were lying in wait. However the sixty-five-ship eastbound SC42 could not be diverted such a long way south because its escorts were short of fuel.[2] The only alternative, short of turning the merchant ships back to Sydney in Cape Breton Island, Nova Scotia, was to try to squeeze them between the south-east tip of Greenland, and the northernmost U-boat in the line he had guesstimated. When this attempt failed, Winn could only watch as the wolf pack attack unfolded step by step; he could not send out a warning to the Allies' ships, because he received the decrypts between two to three days late; that was the time it took for Bletchley Park's Hut 8 to unbutton the Naval Enigma cipher in September 1941.

The tale of woe started during the early afternoon of 9 September with the following short message from *U-85*:

'ENEMY CONVOY IN SIGHT IN SQUARE 9259. STEERING NORTHERLY COURSE, SPEED 7 KNOTS.' (Bletchley Park only sent this message to the OIC at 9.32 a.m. on 12 September.) Shortly after receiving *U-85*'s sighting report, Dönitz, 'Admiral Commanding U Boats', passed information to the other U-boats in the area:

'U 85 REPORTS CONVOY IN SQUARE . . .' Then, some time later, he ordered all the U-boats to attack:

'THE MARKGRAF GROUP IS TO OPERATE ON U 85'S CONVOY.'

A day later Dönitz sent the following rousing message:

'TO MARKGRAF GROUP. THIS CONVOY MUST NOT PASS. AT THEM – ATTACK THEM – SINK THEM!'

As more and more U-boats moved in for the kill, the ether was full of sighting reports enabling as many U-boats as possible to stay in touch with the convoy. Later, Winn was able to read the sinking reports revealing that a major disaster was developing:

'THREE SHIPS OUT OF CONVOY, 20,000 TONS (SUNK)' from *U-652*.

'31,000 TONS . . . 4 SHIPS OUT OF CONVOY' from *U-81*.

'5 SHIPS OF 25,000 TONS OUT OF CONVOY' from *U-432*.

These reports were followed by congratulations from Dönitz:

'TO U 85. GOOD WORK! YOU WERE THE FIRST TO SIGHT THE CONVOY.'

'TO U 81. WELL DONE! WELL DONE!'

'TO U 82. BRAVO!'

By the time the convoy made it across the Atlantic, it had lost no less than nineteen ships, almost one third of the merchant ships which had set out.[3]

The first Allied seaman to die during the boarding of a U-boat, in an attempt to grab its codebooks, followed the first wave of attacks on SC42. The incident happened shortly after midnight on 10–11 September 1941 as a newly formed Canadian troubleshooter escort group, consisting of two corvettes, HMCS *Chambly* and *Moose Jaw*, came to the convoy's rescue. Eight of the nineteen ships in the convoy which were eventually sunk had already disappeared beneath the waves before the troubleshooting unit caught up with the convoy. Lookouts on *Chambly* had only just spotted the convoy's distress signals as it was attacked yet again, when, at about 12.30 a.m. on 11 September, the asdic operator on *Chambly* heard a suspicious echo. Douglas Prentice, the commander, immediately ordered depth charges to be dropped. The resulting explosions brought *U-501* to the surface.

As Chambly's sister ship *Moose Jaw* steamed in to ram the U-boat, the German vessel changed course at the last minute so that the submarine and the corvette were running alongside each other for a time. Hugo Forster, *U-501*'s commander, took advantage of this and jumped onto *Moose Jaw*'s deck. This upset *Moose Jaw*'s commander, and fearing that his ship would be hijacked if other members of the German crew followed their leader, he ordered his own men to sail *Moose Jaw* away from the U-boat. *U-501* only came to a halt after shouts through *Chambly*'s loud-hailer warned the Germans that they would be sunk unless they stopped their engines. They were quickly stopped, and *U-501*'s engineer, Gerhard Schiemann, saw that a boarding party was setting out from *Chambly* in a small boat. He immediately rushed down to the radio room and smashed the Enigma machine with a hammer. He shouted to his assistant, Fritz Weinrich, to warn him when the Canadians were about to climb on board so that he could take the necessary steps to sink the U-boat. As the skiff full of Canadian seamen arrived, the vents were opened.[4]

Lieutenant Ted Simmons and his men were carrying machine guns and pistols when they boarded *U-501*. They frisked the eleven Germans on the deck and Simmons asked one man, who spoke English, to accompany him inside the U-boat. His request was met with a violent protest from the Germans, which was only quelled when Simmons pushed one of the *U-501*'s crew into the sea. The U-boat engineer's assistant, Fritz Weinrich, tried to intervene, shouting out, 'Kaput, kaput!' in an effort to dissuade the Canadians from going down below. Simmons was then told that the U-boat was about to explode, and that the seacocks had been opened. He responded by pointing his loaded pistol at two of the Germans, and he proceeded to push them over to the conning tower. However they refused to go any further, even when Simmons threatened to shoot them.

In a last attempt to capture the U-boat's codebooks, Simmons climbed into the conning tower alone. His first attempt to descend had to be aborted after his gas mask became entangled in the conning tower ladder. Taking it off, he started to climb down again, in spite of the fact that he was almost overwhelmed by the smell of chlorine gas. As he reached the bottom of the ladder, he saw a wall of water coming towards him, presumably because one of the internal hatches had given way. So he hastily climbed back out and ordered the rest of his boarding party to swim for their lives.

The U-boat sank beneath his feet and he was dragged down with it by the resulting suction. Fortunately, he managed to claw his way to the surface again. But when he made it back to the lifeboat, he found another battle was raging. *U-501*'s crew were attempting to climb into it and the Canadians were throwing them back into the water. Adolf Natzheim, one of the U-boat's machine room crew, was punched in the face when he grabbed hold of the rope which had been used to attach the skiff to the U-boat. The blow knocked Natzheim unconscious, but paradoxically, it probably saved his life. When he came to, he was lying in the bottom of the skiff, the Canadians realising that he would drown if he were not rescued immediately.

Bill Brown, the stoker who had tied the skiff to the U-boat as the Canadians climbed on board, was not so lucky. He had been standing at the base of the conning tower, covering the prisoners with a Lewis gun, while Simmons attempted to climb inside. He had stoically remained at his post until the water level on the U-boat's deck was up to his knees. At that point, he had handed his gun to Eugene Tobin, another member of the boarding party, so that he could blow up his life jacket. But at that very moment, the U-boat began to sink, and both Brown and Tobin were forced to swim for it along with their prisoners.

Brown's progress was observed by Weinrich, the engineer's assistant, who was partly responsible for the U-boat's sudden plunge to the bottom of the ocean. Weinrich had grabbed one of the oars being wielded by a Canadian seaman on the skiff, and had carried on clinging on to it when a wave tore it out of the Canadian's hands. For a while Brown and Weinrich swam side by side. To this day Weinrich is not certain what happened to Brown next. Perhaps Brown never managed to fully inflate his life jacket. All Weinrich knows is that one minute Brown was there and the next he had disappeared under the water. No one ever saw him again.

*

In spite of all the U-boats in the area, none of their crews saw *U-501* being boarded. This was fortunate for the Allies since, although no Enigma documents were captured, the sight of Simmons going down the conning tower could have been enough to lead a German observer to assume the worst. Another incident which took place about two weeks later demonstrated how close the Germans were to realising that their naval cipher had been broken. The incident took place as the Admiralty decided once again to use its ability to read Naval Enigma to help it mount offensive operations against attractive targets.

On 23 September 1941 *U-111* sent a message confirming that it was to meet up with the *U-68* and the *U-67* in Tarrafal Bay in Santo AntaÄo, one of the Cape Verde Islands off the coast of West Africa. The meeting had been arranged so that the *U-111* could pass its unused torpedoes to *U-68* before returning to France. At the same time *U-67*'s commander wanted to ship a member of his crew, suffering from VD, back to Germany on *U-111*, if *U-68*'s doctor could not sort out the problem on the spot. Bletchley Park read *U-111*'s message, and the Admiralty acting on the tip off, instructed HMS *Clyde*, one of the British submarines in the area, to go to the bay in order to sink the U-boats.[5]

Clyde's commander, David Ingram, first heard about the planned meeting on 25 September 1941 while he and his men were lying in wait for a German tanker which was in the port of Santa Cruz in Tenerife. The tanker was expected to leave harbour at any minute, but Ingram was told to abandon this assignment in the Canary Islands immediately so that he could ambush the U-boats while they were exchanging supplies and personnel at the rendezvous. It had been hoped that *Clyde* would arrive at the meeting point before the Germans. But at dawn on 27 September, when *U-111* made it to the sea outside Tarrafal Bay, *Clyde* was still some distance away.

U-111's crew had been out on patrol for about six weeks when they saw their first Cape Verde island. They could not stop themselves thinking about what a gorgeous holiday they would have had in this heavenly spot had there not been a war to fight. As the dawn watch looked out for any sign of *U-68*, the lookouts could barely see the dividing line between the contours of the mountains and the haze over the sea. The sea was as smooth as a mirror. Then, at last, a flare shot up into the sky and through the morning mist *U-111's* lookouts spotted the other U-boat. 'It's the *U-68*. Well done,' said *U-111's* commander, and ordered a flare to be fired in response.

U-111 slowly followed *U-68* into Tarrafal Bay. As the two U-boats moved closer to Santo Antão the men on the bridge stared transfixed at the palm trees and the people going about their daily tasks on the beach. It was as if a veil had been lifted, revealing a tropical world which they could never have dreamed of while they were sweating inside the dark confines of their U-boat. 'Welcome to Tarrafal,' said Karl-Friedrich Merten, the commander of *U-68*, as the two U-boats came to a halt side by side inside the bay. 'The same to you,' said Kleinschmidt crossing over to *U-68* to shake Merten by the hand. He then asked Merten whether he was ready to take the four torpedoes on the *U-111's* upper deck. Merton was ready and he suggested that Kleinshmidt should have a meal with him on *U-68* while the torpedoes were transferred. Kleinschmidt replied: 'There is something about this place I don't like,' and added 'I can't explain what it is, but I'd rather get on, and get away quickly.'

While the two commanders were talking, a small boat was rowed out to the U-boats carrying a dark skinned man wearing a smart uniform. His chest was covered with medals. The man asked whether the U-boat crew were Americans. When they said no, he rowed back to the island and returned waving a sealed envelope. But because he was not allowed to row up to the U-boats, the content of his message remained a mystery. As soon as the torpedoes had been passed on to *U-68*, the two U-boats began to make their way out of the bay. Both commanders intended to spend the night out of sight of any prying eyes which might be observing them from the beach. They both intended to return the next day for the meeting with *U-67*. Just before *U-68* left the bay, the first watch officer turned to Merten and remarked that it was dangerous to go out to sea because they could not see where they were going. Merten replied that it would be even more dangerous to remain where they were. It was midnight before the two U-boats made it out of the bay, and it was then that they came across *Clyde*.

Before arriving at the meeting point, the officers in *Clyde* had been drawing up their plans for the attack. David Ingram, the commander, had agreed that George Gay, the engineer officer, should swim ashore to see whether he could learn anything about the U-boats' where- abouts. But when Ingram peered through his periscope outside the bay, he saw sharks around the submarine. Gay's swim was swiftly cancelled. Ingram eventually decided to approach the island under water, and then to surface as night fell. He hoped to go near the bay to see what was happening inside under the cover of darkness. How- ever when he did surface about seven miles away from the island, he could not see anything in the bay because of the mist. On the other hand, he realised that any lookouts on ships in the bay would be able to see *Clyde*, standing out against the horizon in the bright moon- light. The fact that *Clyde* had been painted light grey only served to make the submarine more visible. Ingram therefore changed his plan yet again. He told his officers they would wait outside the bay until the moon set.

The moon set shortly before 12.30 a.m. on 28 September and a few minutes later *Clyde* was stationed on the surface about three miles outside the bay. Faint flickering lights could be observed all along the shore, but *Clyde*'s lookouts presumed they were coming from fishing boats. There was nothing which looked like U-boats signalling to each other. The first sign which told Ingram a U-boat was approach- ing was the sound of a motor picked up on *Clyde*'s hydrophone appa- ratus. Then a lookout shouted that he could see a U-boat. It was *U- 68*. An alarm bell rang inside the British submarine to indicate that a night attack was about to be made. Ingram ordered his helmsman to turn *Clyde*'s nose toward *U-68* so as to be ready to fire. Hedley Kett, the navigating officer, told one of the lookouts to carry on look- ing around for the other U-boats, and not to bother about the attack which was at that very moment being lined up. Within seconds, the lookout shouted again. He had seen *U-111* coming in on *Clyde*'s left flank.

Clyde's torpedo crew were told to hold their fire, while the submarine was swung around with a view to ramming the second U-boat. But *U-111* somehow managed to submerge seconds before *Clyde* could make contact, and Hedley Kett found himself staring at the U-boat's propellers on their port side at the same time as Ingram was looking at the wash from the U-boat's conning tower to starboard. *U-111* had passed directly underneath *Clyde* and escaped without a scratch. Ingram quickly had *Clyde* turned again so that the British submarine was in position to fire its torpedoes at *U-68*. Minutes later *U-68* was seen about a mile away, attempting to send a signal, and Ingram gave the order to fire six torpedoes. But once again, *Clyde*'s attack was frustrated, when *U-68* turned away just as one of the torpedoes appeared to be homing in on target. The exploding torpedoes prompted Merten to turn to his fellow officers on *U-68*'s bridge and say, 'I think we've just been lucky.' He then gave the order to dive. At the same time Kleinschmidt on *U-111* muttered to one of his men, 'I hope Merten's not been hit.'

Ingram also gave the order to submerge so that his crew could safely reload their torpedo tubes before resuming the hunt. The British submarine only surfaced two hours later. Ingram was not even on the bridge when the third U-boat, *U-67*, was sighted. George Gay, who had just deciphered another message from the Admiralty, had called Ingram down to read it. Worse still, one of the *Clyde*'s two propellers had been disconnected so that one of the engines could charge the submarine's batteries. Because of this Hedley Kett, who saw *U-67* moving through the water towards *Clyde*, was not able to turn the submarine quickly enough to sink the U-boat by ramming it. As the two submarines converged, there was frenetic activity on both bridges. Hedley Kett heard an officer on *U-67*'s bridge yelling out, 'Achtung!' Kett shouted to the men in *Clyde*'s conning tower to pass him a Lewis gun. However before the gun arrived, *U-67* crashed into *Clyde*'s stern. Its bow rode up onto *Clyde*'s hull, then it fell back into the water, dived and disappeared. The third and last U-boat had got away.

But the nightmare was not yet over for the British submariners. As *Clyde* submerged in its turn, two of her crew were shocked to see water leaking into the compartment in the stern where they were sitting. Panic-stricken, they quickly left the compartment, slamming shut the watertight hatch which isolated it from the rest of the submarine. For one ghastly moment, *Clyde*'s crew wondered whether their submarine was going to sink. If the back compartment really was filling up with water, the submarine's balance might be upset, and it might never be regained. However Gay had the presence of mind to pull the hatch open quickly so that he could assess the damage before the chamber filled up with seawater. To his relief, he saw that the leaks were not as bad as the two men had described, and he soon had them patched up with pieces of rubber and wedges of wood. After the submarine was watertight once again, *Clyde* sailed back to Gibraltar to have her hull repaired.

Restoring the Germans' confidence in their Enigma cipher was a much more difficult task. The failed attack could easily have convinced the Germans that their Naval Enigma cipher was being read. Even before the three U-boats moved away from the Cape Verde Islands there was talk amongst the officers about how they had been discovered. Most of them agreed that the location and time of their meeting point must have been leaked to the enemy. Only the method of betrayal was in dispute. Kleinschmidt and his officers on *U-111* remembered how two destroyers had appeared out of the blue after they had sunk a Dutch ship earlier in the month, and had pursued their U-boat until they had dived. They were sure that their messages had somehow been intercepted and read by the enemy. Dönitz obviously suspected that Kleinschmidt was right. In his War Diary for 28 September 1941, he wrote: 'The most likely explanation is that our cipher has been compromised, or that there has been some other breach of security. It is highly unlikely that an English submarine would just happen to turn up in such an isolated area.'

Dönitz's concern about the Tarrafal Bay ambush was another reason for the investigation into cipher security undertaken by Erhard Maertens, the head of the German Navy's Communications Service. Maertens noted that *U-111* had mentioned the meeting point in a message transmitted on 23 September 1941, four days before the ambush. 'If *U-111*'s message was read, then there could have been an attempt to disturb the meeting,' Maertens said. But he once again shied away from the suggestion that the British had broken the Naval Enigma cipher. He could not believe that the British could make such a mess of the attack in such favourable circumstances if the cipher really was being read.

Perhaps he was swayed by his cipher experts' report stating that the Naval Enigma was 'one of the most secure systems for enciphering messages in the world'. On 24 October 1941 Maertens' overall conclusion was contained in a letter to Dönitz. It stated: 'The acute disquiet about the compromise of our Secret Operation cannot be justified. Our cipher does not appear to have been broken.'[6]

Living Dangerously

The South Atlantic and Norway

NOVEMBER 1941–MARCH 1942

After the failed attempt to sink the three German U-boats at Tarrafal Bay, one might have expected Sir Dudley Pound, the First Sea Lord, to have exploited Enigma intelligence more cautiously in future. He should have realised that the Germans would question whether their cipher was compromised. But Pound and the staff at the Admiralty do not appear to have learned their lesson. They carried on instructing British commanders at sea to use the intelligence gleaned from Enigma messages as a sword and a shield.

The Enigma decrypts were very tempting. They gave the Royal Navy the chance to sink a second series of supply ships in the Atlantic, thereby depriving U-boats of the fuel, torpedoes and food which enabled them to prolong their patrols. On 4 October 1941 the supply ship *Kota Pinang* was sunk by a British warship 750 miles west of Spain. Another more controversial ambush was sprung on 22 November 1941. An Enigma message had instructed a U-boat, *U-126*, to meet up with *Atlantis*, the German armed merchant raider vessel, 350 miles north-west of Ascension Island (south-west of Freetown, west Africa).[1] *U-126* needed extra supplies if it was to continue its patrol off the west African coast. When the meeting took place during the early morning of 22 November, *Atlantis*'s Captain Bernhard Rogge was so certain that there were no British ships in the area that he invited the *U-126*'s commander and some of his crew to breakfast on the supply ship. During the meal *U-126* was towed by *Atlantis*, while a motor boat chugged to and fro taking supplies over to the U-boat. But just as the submariners were finishing their first cups of coffee, *Atlantis*'s lookout shouted, 'Two mast ahead!' It was HMS *Devonshire*, a British cruiser, whose commander, Captain Oliver, had been tipped off by the Admiralty.

But Oliver could not be sure he had discovered the right ship. His difficulties were exacerbated after *Atlantis* sent out a message stating that she was *Polyphemus*, a Dutch ship. The problem facing Oliver was that, although he wanted to take a closer look at *Atlantis*, he had to stay more than five miles away, in case either the supply ship, or her accompanying U-boats, tried to shoot at his cruiser. So at about 9 a.m. he signalled to the Admiralty: 'Is *Polyphemus* genuine?' The Admiralty replied, 'No repetition No.' Meanwhile evidence began to come in from *Devonshire's* Walrus aeroplane which had been circling *Atlantis*. Oliver asked its crew: 'What type of stern has she got?' and the reply came back: 'Hull similar to *Atlantis*.' That was enough to convince Oliver that he had the right ship in his sights, and at 9.35 a.m., he gave the order to open fire. By 10.15 the merchant raider had been sunk and the survivors had taken to the ship's lifeboats. They were subsequently rescued by *U-126*, after Captain Oliver, correctly assuming there were U-boats in the area, had ordered his crew to take *Devonshire* to Freetown.

However shortly after *Devonshire* opened fire, another message was transmitted to Captain Oliver, referring to the earlier message, which had stated that the sighted ship was not *Polyphemus*. The message said: 'Cancel my . . . [previous signal]. Ship may possibly be genuine.' Oliver's 10.05 signal confirming that *Atlantis* was now out of action caused more than a little alarm at the Admiralty as concerned officials frantically sought to discover whether *Devonshire* had attacked the wrong ship. *Atlantis's* true identity was only confirmed later after *Polyphemus* was eventually discovered in New York harbour.

Even more worrying was the potential fall out from the attack as far as Enigma was concerned. As had happened with the ambush at Tarrafal Bay, the operation was badly thought out on the part of the British. It should have been obvious that it would be impossible to kill or capture all *Atlantis's* crew, or the crew on the U-boat being supplied by *Atlantis*, if Captain Oliver complied with international law, unless Oliver was prepared to order that no surrendering German seamen were to be spared. The officers in the German High Command were likely to receive eye-witness accounts telling them what had happened. The German survivors were not presented with any evidence to suggest that the British cruiser had stumbled upon the meeting place by chance. *Atlantis's* crew had not even seen *Devonshire's* aeroplane when it first spotted the German ship. All they knew was that a British cruiser had steamed straight up to their rendezvous with a U-boat in a deserted part of the ocean. It was just the kind of incident which was likely to persuade the German Navy that its Enigma code was compromised.

For a time it seemed possible that many of the survivors would not make it back to Germany. *U-126* could not take all *Atlantis's* 305 survivors on board. Most of them were towed behind the U-boat in motor launches and iron-cutters, rendering both the U-boat and the lifeboats vulnerable to attack from the air. To make matters worse from the German point of view, *U-126*, whose commander wanted to tow the survivors all the way to South America, was running out of fuel. The German Navy's concern was only allayed on 24 November, when *Python*, another supply ship, arrived on the scene, and rescued all the survivors.[2] This gave the Royal Navy the opportunity to finish off the job it had started. More intelligence extracted from Enigma decrypts revealed *Python's* next rendezvous with U-boats. The Admiralty promptly authorised another ambush.

The first U-boat to meet up with *Python*, 750 miles south of St Helena Island (south-west of Ascension Island) was *U-68*. Its commander, Karl-Friedrich Merten, was so alarmed by what had happened to *Atlantis* and at Tarrafal Bay two months earlier, that he arrived at the rendezvous on 30 November 1941, the day before the date specified in Dönitz's orders. If the British knew about the meeting, he intended to be ready to take them on.

The next morning saw the arrival of *U-A*, a U-boat originally built for Turkey, which was taken over by the Germans at the beginning of the war. Hans Eckermann, its commander, was equally worried, and even talked about being prepared to move to another location before refuelling. He did not insist, however, because he did not want to inconvenience Merten, whose U-boat was already being refuelled when *U-A* appeared. Both men were so keen to complete the transfer of supplies and fuel, that they both refused lunch with *Python's* Captain Lüders on the supply ship. Nevertheless, loading was still continuing, when at about 5 o'clock in the afternoon, a lookout on *Python* shouted out, 'Enemy cruiser in sight!' He had sighted three funnels on the horizon. It was *Devonshire's* sister ship, HMS *Dorsetshire*, whose commander, Captain Augustus Agar, had been told where to look for *Python*.

On the cruiser, a game of deck hockey was being played when *Python* was spotted by *Dorsetshire's* lookout. The men swiftly went to their action stations. But it was not a good start to the operation; once again the circumstances were bound to suggest to the Germans that the cruiser knew exactly where to find them, which would lead them to call into question Enigma's security. However, Captain Agar was so keen to catch up with his quarry, that he not only failed to withdraw out of sight so that he could send in his aeroplane to 'find' *Python*, but he made the potentially fatal mistake of passing within two miles of where *Python* and the U-boats had left the boats which had been used to ferry supplies to and from the supply ship. For all he knew, there could have been a U-boat waiting concealed beneath the waves near these boats, and Agar was very fortunate that he was not punished for his recklessness with a torpedo fired at his hull.

The sight of the cruiser bearing down on them horrified some of *Atlantis*'s crew, who stood transfixed, as if caught up in a recurring nightmare. It was only nine days since they had been attacked in almost identical circumstances. Another group of *Atlantis* survivors reacted in a different way, racing around the ship like a plague of locusts, grabbing any food and water containers they could find, and throwing them into the lifeboats. Some of them were more successful than others. When a crowd of men ran down to the storeroom, intending to pick up a pile of leather jackets, they were sent packing by the storeman, who refused to release anything unless an officer signed a chit authorising him to do so.

Two warning shots from *Dorsetshire* convinced them that they should abandon ship as quickly as possible. Although *Python*'s captain had at first hoped that the cruiser might be sunk by the U-boats which he had so recently supplied, he soon realised that this was most unlikely. *Dorsetshire*'s Captain Agar had been warned that there would be U-boats about, and was taking care to stay at least eight miles clear of the ship he was attacking. This, combined with the fact that the cruiser never stopped zig-zagging around *Python* throughout the attack, ensured that the torpedoes which were eventually fired by *U-A* missed their target.

Python's lifeboats, brimming with supplies, were almost ready to be lowered, when the sailors on deck saw thick white smoke begin to rise up into the sky from their own ship. A seaman had accidentally activated the valve controlling *Python*'s smoke screen and everyone held their breath and waited to see if this would prompt the cruiser to finish them off. Agar thought the smoke might be intended to warn another ship and he ordered his crew to sail *Dorsetshire* around *Python* in an attempt to spot it. By the time that he had satisfied himself that there was no such ship, he saw that *Python* was on fire and was being scuttled by her own crew. At about 6.30 p.m. the supply ship rolled over and sank to the bottom of the ocean.

The sinking of *Python* was a major setback for Dönitz. On 1 December 1941 he wrote in his Diary: 'After the sinking of *Python*, it is now impossible to refuel in the Atlantic. It will be impossible to resume refuelling on the surface – the time for such operations is now passed.'

'It is the third time a supply ship has been caught by the enemy at a meeting point,' wrote Heinz Bonatz, the head of the B-Dienst code-breaking unit, on 2 December 1941. Since September 1941 the Germans had been reading a substantial number of Britain's messages sent in its naval code after having difficulties with it for just over a year.[3] 'It is still not possible to tell from the British radio messages whether they knew about the meeting points, but the fact that there have been three interceptions is remarkable,' Bonatz concluded. He proposed that all the most recent German and British messages should be analysed to see if there was any indication that German messages had been read.[4]

There was no shortage of witnesses who could describe what had occurred. Over 400 survivors from *Atlantis* and *Python* made it back to France by the end of December 1941, following a heroic rescue operation mounted by German and Italian U-boats. None of the survivors had seen any evidence which suggested that they had been discovered as a result of a chance sighting from a passing aeroplane. They could all attest to the fact that they had simply been spotted by the British cruisers which appeared to know exactly where to find them.

The enquiry into what had happened was only completed more than two months later. On 18 March 1942, Admiral Kurt Fricke stated that 'both the officers in charge [of *Atlantis* and *Python*] and the Naval Staff were suspicious that the loss of the two boats could only have happened because of treason or through the cipher used by the radio service not being kept secret enough.'[5] However he felt that neither treason, nor the compromise of the cipher was to blame. No one had broken any rules when enciphering messages about the meetings, an important consideration, given Fricke's belief that 'the system of sending radio messages . . . is superior to that used by any other country.' Secondly, he said that 'none of the numerous messages sent by the enemy and read by Germany since the beginning of the war showed any evidence that our Key M [Naval Enigma] has been decoded.'

Fricke stated that his conclusions were backed up by events which had occurred since the sinking of *Atlantis* and *Python*. One such event related to the movements of *Tirpitz*, Germany's giant battleship. *Tirpitz* had finally made its first move out of the Baltic, where for a year its crew had been involved in training exercises, on 12 January 1942. For months, Naval Enigma traffic had been telling the British about *Tirpitz*'s state of readiness. Knowing where *Tirpitz* was going was crucial since, wherever it was, it could totally alter the balance of power at sea unless counter-measures were taken swiftly. Although British battleships could just about match *Tirpitz* when it came to fire power, and the ability to carry on floating after being hit by shells, *Tirpitz* was two knots faster. As a result it had the capacity to steam in, destroy a convoy, and then race away before the British Fleet could bring its own considerable fire power to bear. That was why the Naval Enigma messages concerning *Tirpitz* were watched so closely. They told the British that *Tirpitz* had had torpedo tubes installed, that she had taken part in war games, and that she would be ready to leave the Baltic by 10 January 1942. But it was then that Enigma let the British down. Naval Enigma messages were still being broken after *Tirpitz* left the German port of Wilhelmshaven on 14 January 1942. But at the time, there was an average delay of thirty-two hours.[6] Enigma decrypts only told the British that *Tirpitz* had reached Trondheim in Norway a day after the battleship's arrival on 16 January. As a result, it was not attacked during its journey.

The German admiral conducting the enquiry into Enigma's security made no allowance for the possibility of delayed decryption. Admiral Fricke felt that if *Tirpitz*'s move had not been noticed by the British, then its codebreakers could not be reading their Enigma messages. A similar argument was used by Fricke in relation to the break out by the German battle-cruisers, *Scharnhorst* and *Gneisenau*, from Brest, exactly one month after *Tirpitz*'s departure from the Baltic.[7] Enigma intelligence had alerted Ned Denning in the Admiralty that the German cruisers might attempt their break out between 10–15 February 1942. It was thought that they would pass through the Dover Straits on their way to Germany or Norway. They could not stay at Brest indefinitely; ever since arriving there in March 1941, they had been sitting targets for British bombs. Although a French spy, working in the docks at Brest, reckoned that they might leave at night and pass through the Dover Straits in daylight the British admirals and Air Force commanders proceeded on the presumption that the Germans would prefer to leave during the day, so that they passed Dover at night. It was this mistaken assumption which was behind a series of errors committed by the British.

The German battle-cruisers, along with the cruiser *Prinz Eugen*, left Brest at 22.45 on 11 February.[8] Because the Naval Enigma for 10–12 February 1942 could not be deciphered until 15 February, the Royal Navy were not forewarned. The German ships missed a British submarine which had been on patrol in the area earlier that evening. The submarine might have been expected to spot the ships, had the Germans not delayed their original time of departure, scheduled for earlier in the evening, because of a British air raid. Subsequently, when two of the British aircraft flying over the area during the night had to return to base because their radar sets were not working, none of the other commanders concerned were notified, so they were not alerted that additional precautions might be necessary.

During the early morning of 12 February alarm bells failed to ring at first when Britain's coastal radar was jammed, and when German aircraft were seen to be circling over the sea in the area north of Le Havre, the radar operators, who had not been warned that there might well be a break out that night, failed to report promptly what they had observed. Even the aircraft sent to investigate were not told they could break radio silence if they spotted the ships. As a result it was 11 a.m. on 12 February before a report was made that the ships were at sea and were already in the area of Boulogne. Worsening weather frustrated the later attempt to bomb the German ships. Bombing raids were delayed because Air Marshal Arthur Harris had used some of the waiting aircraft so that they could take part in raids on Germany and had placed the remainder at four hours' rather than at two hours' notice.

The Times, whose correspondents knew nothing about the breaking of Enigma, was moved to describe the break out in these terms on 14 February 1942: 'Nothing more mortifying to the pride of sea-power has happened in home waters since the Seventeenth Century.'[9] This harsh judgement might have been tempered somewhat if it had been known that both battle-cruisers had been damaged by mines laid by the British along the German ships' likely route between Brest and Germany. This route had been betrayed by earlier Enigma intelligence. But the fact that *Scharnhorst* and *Gneisenau* had been damaged had to remain a secret; the Admiralty only knew about it because it was revealed in further Enigma messages. Nevertheless

Fricke, who was looking at what had happened with a view to monitoring cipher security, stated that the 'breakthrough' had worked 'surprisingly well', and he used this to back up his judgement that Naval Enigma had not been broken by the British.

Given the almost cavalier way in which intelligence derived from Naval Enigma was exploited on occasions, it is interesting to contrast the care that was taken when collecting the Enigma intelligence in the first place. At the beginning of 1942, Gordon Welchman, whose prime responsibility was the Army and Air Force Enigma cipher broken by Hut 6, wrote to Edward Travis, shortly before Travis took over from Denniston as the head of Bletchley Park, about the danger which could arise from not telling the people at the intercept stations that Enigma was being broken. 'Any intelligent operator must know that we break Enigma traffic,' he wrote. The danger arose 'because if he was never told about it he may feel at liberty to discuss it.'[10]

Welchman was also very anxious about the conclusions which the Germans might draw from Britain's expansion of her interception facilities:

> If the enemy should ever suspect that we are breaking 'E' traffic our chances of ever breaking it again would vanish completely. Worse than that, the chances of success with the naval enigma traffic would vanish with ours, and the implications of such a disaster need not be stressed. The German wireless security measures are so good that I doubt if we should have been able to make any important deductions from pure W.T.I. applied to 'E' traffic without the use of decodes. The Germans know this and if they ever know that
> a) we attach great importance to the interception of 'E' traffic.
> b) we know a great deal about the wireless system that passes 'E' traffic they are bound to guess that we have succeeded in breaking, and a guess will be quite enough to induce effective countermeasures.[11]

The concern about safeguarding the Army and Air Force Enigma was presumably increased by the knowledge that these ciphers were, by this time, playing an important role in the British Army's success in north Africa. The contribution of Army Enigma was particularly treasured. Although the Army used the same Enigma procedure as the Air Force, its operators used their cipher more securely. As a result it was only broken intermittently at the beginning of the war. It was, however, being broken regularly before Britain's Operation Crusader offensive was launched in north Africa on 18 November

1941, and it played a valuable role in monitoring the German armour and movements in the desert. It was used in conjunction with the decrypts of the Italian Navy's C38m cipher, which enabled the Royal Navy to reduce the amount of cargo getting through to the Germans in north Africa by more than 60 per cent in November 1941.[12] By the time the offensive petered out in January 1942, the Germans had been pushed back to El Agheila on the Tripolitanian border.[13]

The fear that the Enigma secret would be compromised was not shared by Britain's Allies in France. From June to December 1941 a war of attrition was fought between Denniston at Bletchley Park and Gustave Bertrand in the south of France over whether Bertrand's Cadix station should have access to the Air Force and Army Enigma settings worked out by the British codebreakers. On 15 June 1941 Denniston wrote a somewhat devious letter to one of his subordinates suggesting how to fob Bertrand off:

> If he wishes to have the decoded texts of these telegrams we should not consider this on account of the ultimate risk of compromise. We send him the keys and he can decode such material as he has intercepted. It is true we have sent him no keys since the 23rd May and it is obviously objectionable that the current keys should be sent to him. I would suggest replying that we are meeting increased difficulties in obtaining solution for the following reasons:
> 1. The German habit of multiplying the discriminants has greatly reduced the traffic on any one discriminant and our only method of solution is now to use the Bombe . . .
> I hardly think we can reply to his suggestion . . . which apparently means that he insists on having everything from us in order to be ready to dash to our assistance in the event of a successful invasion . . .[14]

In December 1941 Bertrand wrote back to Denniston: 'Are you really having no success with Enigma or don't you want to give it to us? . . . We are working in complete safety here, trust me.'[15]

It has to be said that Denniston's attempt to deprive Bertrand of current Enigma settings was unlikely to protect Britain's Enigma secret. Denniston could argue that his stand would mean that the Germans were less likely to discover evidence that Enigma messages had been broken if the Cadix centre ever had to be evacuated in a hurry. But his willingness to supply old Enigma settings to the French was inconsistent with this reasoning. Also, whether or not any Enigma settings were supplied, the biggest danger was represented by what the Polish codebreakers in France knew already. If Bertrand, or his team, were captured and interrogated by the Germans, it was likely that someone would reveal something about their acquaintance with the Enigma. Once it was mentioned, it would be hard to stop the Germans discovering everything. The French and Polish codebreakers knew enough about the British ability to break Enigma to persuade their German captors never to use an Enigma cipher machine again.

The Hunt for the Bigram Tables

Bletchley Park and Norway

DECEMBER 1941

Alan Turing and Dilly Knox were not the only eccentric geniuses at Bletchley Park. The park was full of men who were abnormal for one reason or another, men such as Alan Ross, for example: Ross was famous within his section for having sedated his young son, Padmint, with laudanum and for having laid him out on the train's luggage rack when travelling together. He went on to invent the concept of 'non-U' speech which was subsequently popularised by Nancy Mitford in *Noblesse Oblige*. At Bletchley Park he worked in the section dealing with the German Navy's hand cipher, Reservehandfahren (RHV) which was used by small German ships sailing up and down the Norwegian coast and by other vessels, including U-boats, which were not carrying an Enigma. The section was run by John Plumb (later Sir John Plumb, the historian).

Another eccentric working on RHV was Bentley Bridgewater (later the Secretary of the British Museum). He became a legend at Bletchley Park after he chased his homosexual lover Angus Wilson (who later became a well known novelist), into the lake in front of the house following an argument. Angus Wilson, another RHV man, was also very strange. He had uncontrollable tantrums; on one occasion he kicked in his landlady's front door, and codebreakers who passed by his digs the next day saw him sheepishly helping with the repairs.

Although the colourful characters working on RHV had domestic lives which left a lot to be desired, their work played an important role in relation to the Naval Enigma. RHV was broken for the first time in June 1941; some RHV codebooks were captured in May 1941 from *U-110*.[1] But the cipher would not have been read thereafter had the Germans not committed another error. To encipher plain-language text into RHV, a telegraphist first had to fit the German message into a 'cage', a shape drawn on a piece of paper. The cage's shape changed each month. The function of the cage was to ensure that each letter in the plain-language text became part of a vertical bigram (a two-letter group). These bigrams were then transformed into other bigrams by the telegraphist looking them up in the special bigram tables produced for RHV operators. Rather than altering the bigram tables and the shape of the cage at the same time each month, the Germans, for some reason, staggered the changes. Because of this John Plumb and his codebreakers always knew one of the principal elements of the enciphering process, and this helped them to break the cipher regularly.

The content of RHV messages was not often useful from the Royal Navy's point of view. However RHV messages were very important as far as the Naval Enigma was concerned. Messages sent using the Naval Enigma cipher were often repeated on RHV. If the RHV cipher was broken, the codebreakers could read the RHV message, and then they could use the plain text as a crib for the Naval Enigma.

The same trick was played with 'Werftschlüssel' (the dockyard key), the code used by small ships in dockyards and harbours. It was also used by large German warships when communicating with these smaller vessels. Bletchley Park's codebreakers first broke Werftschlüssel in 1940, but it made its most important contribution to the battle to break Naval Enigma at the beginning of October 1941.[2] On 3–5 October 1941, the codebreakers in Hut 8 were mystified by their inability to break messages transmitted by the U-boats, even though the surface ships' signals were read. The lives of thousands of Allied seamen hung in the balance as Bletchley Park battled to overcome the problem. They did so by using a Werftschlüssel message as a crib. It turned out that a new net had been set up for the U-boats; the U-boats' settings lists included a different initial setting (Grundstellung) to that utilised by surface ships. It was one of the security measures introduced by Dönitz and the head of the German Navy's Communications section after they became concerned that the U-boats' positions were being betrayed.

The creation of the new net for the U-boats led to some anxious correspondence between Stewart Menzies, also known as C, the head of the Secret Intelligence Service, and Winston Churchill. On 7 October 1941 Menzies wrote to tell Churchill: 'From the beginning of October, our difficulties have been increased by the Germans separating the U. Boat cyphers from the Main Fleet traffic. The latter should present no increased difficulties, but the U. boats present a separate problem which will have to be solved by our machines. Actually, we succeeded today in reading the U. Boat cypher for the 5th October. C.' In reply, Churchill scribbled the following note on the bottom of Menzies' memorandum: 'Give my compliments to those concerned. WSC. 7.X.' Later that same day, Churchill received another note from Menzies: 'The difficulties regarding the U. Boat cyphers have been resolved. C.' Menzies received the following short reply, again scribbled on the bottom of his memorandum, 'Good, WSC.'³

The repetition of Werftschlüssel messages in Naval Enigma traffic opened the way for the British codebreakers to orchestrate the design of the cribs which suited them best. In a process known to the codebreakers as 'gardening', they would instruct the Royal Air Force or Navy to lay mines in places which were likely to provoke the Germans to send out predictable signals in response. It was obviously better, from Bletchley Park's point of view, if the resulting mine warnings and all-clears could not be expressed in many different forms. So, for example, the laying of mines in a location which could be expected to lead to the Germans transmitting: 'Weg fünf ziffer sieben' (lane five number seven), in Werftschlüssel, and to their sending the same signal in Naval Enigma to the Baltic U-boats, was not ideal, since 'fünf' could also be written as 'fuenf', 'ziffer' could be written as 'ziffx' or 'ziff', and 'sieben' could become 'siben'. If the laying of mines could provoke the more complicated: 'Kriegsansteuerungstonne Swinemuende', on the other hand, this was preferable, since the codebreakers discovered that the Germans only utilised one form of this signal.⁴

Another German security measure related to the Naval Enigma's bigram tables. Each day one bigram table out of the current set of nine was used; the German telegraphists were given a monthly list telling them which table to use each day. Because the codebreakers did not have the list, they had to work it out for themselves. This was a simple matter at first. After the bigram tables, and the Kenngruppenbuch (the book of trigrams used during the indicating procedure, as explained in chapter 7), were captured in May 1941 from *U-110*, Joan Clarke and her colleagues in Hut 8 noticed that German telegraphists were not acting in a random way, as they were supposed to, when making up their message indicators. Rather than selecting any trigram out of the Kenngruppenbuch, they had a tendency to choose ones at the top, or near the top, of the columns. There were 733 columns in the book but the telegraphists tended to prefer those on the pages in the middle of the book. This discovery enabled Joan Clarke to work back from the indicators given at the top of each message to the trigrams which resulted from the application of each of the nine bigram tables. The bigram table which transformed the indicator letters at the top of several messages into one of the favourite trigrams at the top of a column in the centre of the Kenngruppenbuch, was normally the table being used that day.[5]

However, as so often happened, the Germans must have realised that their telegraphists' habits risked compromising the security of the system. New rules were enforced. Henceforth telegraphists were not allowed to use trigrams from the Kenngruppenbuch which they had chosen before. This put an end to Joan Clarke's way of identifying the correct table; another method had to be discovered. Fortunately, during 1941 new recruits were still being employed in Hut 8 and their fresh eyes were able to spot flaws in the German system not noticed by the codebreakers who had been looking at the cipher for some time.

Jack Good was one such recruit. He was another Cambridge mathematics scholar with a First class degree who was working on his Ph.D. at the beginning of the war. He was also an accomplished chess player, which was how he knew Hugh Alexander and Stuart Milner-Barry, one of the senior codebreakers in Hut 6. When war was declared, Good, then aged twenty three, was put on the reserve list of bright young men and women, who could, it was felt, be best employed using their brains to help the war effort. In 1941 he was finally called in to an interviewing centre in Cambridge, where he was interviewed by Gordon Welchman and Alexander. As usual, nothing was said about what job had to be done, but a friend of Jack Good, who was also called in, somehow guessed that it must be something to do with ciphers. The next time Good saw Milner-Barry, Good asked him whether he was working on codes. Milner-Barry discreetly shook his head, and said, 'I'm working at the Foreign Office.' He told Good he could be contacted in Room 47.

A few days later Good was asked to report to Bletchley Park. Alexander met him at the station and, as they walked across the fields to the house, Alexander informed Good that they were just beginning to break the German Naval cipher. Good was to help out in Hut 8. It was 27 May 1941, the day when the battle with the *Bismarck* was reaching its climax. As Good was being shown to his desk, a man rushed in and gave the thumbs down signal, thereby indicating, not failure, but that *Bismarck* had finally been sunk.

Good was naturally very impressed. He, like the other codebreakers, assumed that the sinking had only happened because of work carried out at Bletchley Park.

Good was glad to be working alongside Hugh Alexander, but he initially found it much harder striking up a relationship with Alan Turing. Turing had caught Good sleeping on the floor while on duty during his first night shift. At first, Turing thought Good was ill, but he was cross when Good explained that he was just taking a short nap because he was tired. For a few days afterwards, Turing would not deign to speak to Good, and he left the room if Good walked in. The relationship between the two men was only put onto a more harmonious footing after Turing reiterated that Good was a brilliant statistician; a few days after Turing had found Good sleeping on duty, Good suggested that by simplifying the statistics used during the Banburismus procedure the amount of time taken by the procedure could be drastically reduced without lessening its efficacy. Good's suggestion was quickly adopted and his reputation, in Turing's eyes, was salvaged. Good also won Turing's respect for making another, relatively simple, observation which everyone else had missed. It enabled Hut 8 to solve the bigram tables problem. During a subsequent night shift, when there was no more work to be done, it dawned on Good that there might be another chink in the German indicating system. The German telegraphists had to add dummy letters to the trigrams which they selected out of the Kenngruppenbuch (see chapter 7). Good wondered if their choice of dummy letters was random, or whether there was a bias towards particular letters. After inspecting some messages which had been broken, he discovered that there was a tendency to use some letters more than others. That being the case, all the codebreakers had to do, was to work back from the indicators given at the beginning of each message, and apply each bigram table in turn in the same way as Joan Clarke had done before. The bigram table which produced lots of the popular dummy letters was probably the correct one. When Good mentioned his discovery to Alan Turing, Turing was embarrassed, and said, 'I thought that I had tried that.' It quickly became an important part of the Banburismus procedure.

Jack Good's decision not to go on working when tired was vindicated by a subsequent incident. During another long night shift, he had been baffled by his failure to break a doubly enciphered Offizier message. This was one of the messages which was supposed to be enciphered initially with the Enigma set up in accordance with the

Offizier settings, and subsequently with the general Enigma settings in place. However, while he was sleeping before returning for another shift, he dreamed that the order had been reversed; the general settings had been applied before the Offizier settings. Next day he found that the message had yet to be read, so he applied the theory which had come to him during the night. It worked; he had broken the code in his sleep.

On 29 November 1941 the Germans replaced the bigram tables with a new set.[6] It was the first time this security measure had been adopted since the middle of June 1941. At a stroke the codebreakers were deprived of the information they needed to carry out the Banburismus procedure. That did not mean that Naval Enigma was insoluble. By this time the codebreakers had identified numerous cribs, which once fed into the bombe, would yield up the wheel order for the day under consideration. Using cribs and the bombe immediately, rather than waiting for the Banburismus procedure to be completed, was even in some ways preferable. Banburismus could not commence until enough messages were intercepted and sorted; around three hundred messages were needed if the procedure was to work. The crib and bombe method, on the other hand, could be started as soon as the cipher text linked with the crib was identified; only one message was necessary, as long as it was matched up with the crib.[7] However, up to 336 wheel orders had to be tested rather than the number of wheel orders between 3 and 90 which were normally left outstanding after the Banburismus technique had been applied.[8] As a result the time taken by the bombes to work out the correct wheel order escalated, just when they were needed to deal with the growing number of Army and Air Force Enigma nets. Fortunately, by this time Bletchley Park possessed fifteen bombes, which alleviated the problem.[9]

The fourteen cryptographers working on the Naval Enigma in Hut 8 – new staff, having been hired during the summer and winter of 1941 – decided to reconstruct the new set of tables, using the same methods adopted after the capture of *Krebs* in March 1941.[10] However, before this could be completed, the Royal Navy, whose reckless escapades had created the problem for the codebreakers in the first place, came up with a means of sorting it out more quickly. In December 1941 plans were made to mount two raids on the coast of Norway. Capturing codebooks was only a subsidiary reason for the raids, but officers in the Naval Intelligence Division were instructed to go with the task forces and do anything they could to help the codebreakers at Bletchley Park.

'Operation Anklet' was supposed to be the more important of the two raids. It required the Royal Navy to transport commandos to four landing positions in the Lofoten Islands. The troops were supposed to rush ashore and dig themselves in for a couple of months, in a bid to cut off the line of communication between the Lofoten Islands and German forces in the north of Norway. But it was the subsidiary raid, code-named 'Operation Archery', an attack on German bases on two islands off the coast of south-west Norway, which was expected to give the Navy its best chance of capturing Enigma documents. This judgement was made by Allon Bacon, the Naval Intelligence officer who, in May 1941, had dried out the Enigma documents seized from the *U-110*, and who, in June 1941, had seized the Enigma settings from the weather ship *Lauenburg*.

Bacon helped to plan the December 1941 raids. Rather than waiting to be told what to do, he made his own recommendations to John Godfrey, the Director of Naval Intelligence. On 18 December 1941, just one week before the task force for Operation Archery was due to sail, Bacon identified four potential targets. These targets were mentioned in an intelligence report made on the basis of information taken from a Norwegian fisherman, John Sigurdson, who had arrived in the Shetland Islands nine days earlier. Sigurdson was said in the report to be 'reliable'. He was the brother of a member of Britain's Special Operations Executive, the organisation set up to carry out acts of sabotage in countries occupied by the Germans. The targets chosen by Bacon included German patrol boats which escorted convoys of cargo vessels up and down the coast, and ten naval personnel staying in a hotel on Måloy, a small island situated between Bergen and Trondheim on the stretch of Norwegian coast which was to be raided in the course of Operation Archery. Bacon scrawled the following note onto the intelligence report: 'In view of this report which provides 4 possible Z targets and greater speed than the Northern Anklet party, I have decided that this party i.e. Archery offers best chances.'[11] On the strength of what he wrote, he was ordered to accompany the troops taking part in Operation Archery, which later came to be known as the Vågsoy raid.[12]

The Operation Archery task force was scheduled to leave Scapa Flow on 24 December 1941. Before they left, 'Beaky' Armstrong, the commander of HMS *Onslow*, the destroyer which was to transport Allon Bacon to Norway, called his officers together to explain what to do if their ship came under fire. 'If you see anyone panicking, shoot him,' he ordered. One of his officers remonstrated at this, saying, 'That's a bit steep, sir.' Whereupon Armstrong replied, 'You're right. Bring him to the bridge, and I'll shoot him.' He had no time for cowards.

On the night before *Onslow* left Scapa Flow, a play was performed on the ship. After the play, the men had a last drink. While struggling to open up a can of tomato juice, a Norwegian sailor tried to puncture the lid with his knife. Unfortunately, his hand slipped and the knife plunged into an officer's hand. For a moment everyone thought that it was covered with tomato juice. Then they realised it was the lieutenant's blood. It was an inauspicious start to the raid.

There were more problems on the way from Scapa Flow to Sullom Voe in the Shetlands, as the ferries carrying the commandos developed leaks on account of the bad weather. Because of this Admiral Harold Burrough regretfully delayed the departure of his task force by twenty-four hours to allow the ferries to be repaired. The ferries, protected by one cruiser and four destroyers, only set out during the afternoon of 26 December 1941, too late to distract the German Luftwaffe from dealing with Operation Anklet, one of the main reasons for carrying out Operation Archery in the first place.

It was still dark as the five warships and their charges sailed silently into Vågsfjord at about 7.30 a.m. on 27 December. The men on *Onslow* waited tensely at action stations, expecting their presence to be discovered at any minute. The warships passed through the narrow channel between the surrounding snow-covered mountains. At one point, they saw a light go on in the window of a seaside cottage, but they relaxed a little when no one looked out. Then one of *Onslow*'s crew mistakenly switched on a radio and the voice of a British newscaster echoed around the fjord. Once again the men froze, while the radio was hastily switched off. The ships carried on gliding silently through the icy water, homing in on their targets.

But unbeknown to the British sailors on their warships, they had been spotted. At about 8 a.m., while the ferries full of commandos were still being manoeuvred into position in the fjord, before moving in to land the troops on Norwegian soil, a telephone rang on Måloy Island in the German commander's quarters. The ringing telephone was not heard by the commander, who was still asleep, but his batman listened to it, unmoved, while polishing his master's boots.[13] On receiving no answer, the lookout rang another base on the island, where his frantic message was noted down by the soldier on duty.

This soldier was so alarmed, he ran in the wrong direction. Rather than alerting the sleeping battery commander on Måloy Island, where the commandos were about to land, he decided instead that he should warn the commander on Vågsoy Island, which separated Måloy Island from the North Sea. He jumped into a rowing boat and rowed across Måloy Sund, the stretch of water separating the two islands. The commander on Vågsoy Island decided they must go straight back to wake up the battery commander on Måloy Island.

They were too late. When they were halfway across Måloy Sund, the cruiser HMS *Kenya* opened fire in order to protect the British Hampden bombers flying overhead. Ten minutes later, the commandos moved in; the battle had begun. Any hopes that the British would get away with no casualties were quickly dashed. The men on *Onslow* watched helplessly when one of the smoke bombs dropped by a British bomber fell into a landing barge and almost fried the occupants alive. As the fighting intensified in the streets of South Vågsoy, *Onslow* and another destroyer sailed between the two islands and on up the Ulvesund, the channel between Vågsoy Island and the mainland.[14]

It was there that Beaky Armstrong and his crew came across one of the small convoys of ships which Bacon had read about in the Norwegian fisherman's report. All three ships in the convoy quickly beached themselves on Vågsoy Island, and it was then up to Bacon and his boarding party to see whether they could capture their secret documents before they were destroyed. As a motorboat set off from *Onslow* with Bacon aboard, he slipped a pair of thick socks over his boots to enable him to move silently around the beached ships. He was carrying a large rucksack, which he referred to as his 'pinch pack', with all the equipment he needed: a double-skinned waterproof bag, a burglar's jemmy, a large supply of blotting paper and six canvas bags. The rucksack also held a supply of 'Top Secret' labels addressed to the Director of Naval Intelligence, along with sealing wax and a seal which would enable him to send the documents he captured back to the Admiralty in London as soon as the task force returned to base. If he ever made it back to Scapa Flow. It was a dangerous moment. One man who had been standing beside the motorboat just before it was lowered into the sea, fell to the deck dead, shot in the throat and, as they sped through the water towards the beached German ships, bullets whistled past. They all held their breath when a line of bullets from a machine gun punctured the wooden canopy over their heads. A few inches lower, and there would have been a bloodbath.

Föhn, the armed trawler which had been escorting the merchant ships, was to be their first target. As they approached, they saw that her captain was throwing the ship's secret documents into the sea. When Beaky Armstrong observed this from *Onslow*'s bridge, he picked up a Lewis gun, took careful aim and shot him dead. At first it seemed that Armstrong had not acted in time. When Bacon and the rest of the boarding party clambered over the captain's corpse into his cabin and the radio room they could not see any codebooks. The boarding party rushed off, through a hail of bullets, to search the other beached ships, leaving Bacon behind to search the captain's cabin more carefully. It was here that his jemmy came in useful. He used it to lever open the captain's desk drawer. Inside he found a piece of pink paper covered with Enigma settings.[15] He found another treasure in the wardrobe, concealed amongst the captain's immaculately laundered shirts: a set of bigram tables, the very documents the codebreakers at Bletchley Park were crying out for. By the time he was ready to go up on deck, he had filled two sacks with books and papers. The sacks also contained five Enigma wheels. But when Bacon reappeared on deck, he was horrified by what he saw. The lookout, left behind to guard him, was juggling with three grenades. He did not appear to notice that a German sniper was trying to shoot him. He only came to his senses when he heard Bacon shouting at him; mercifully, he put the grenades down before there was an accident.

Bacon finally made it back to *Onslow* at around 11.30 a.m. It turned out that he and his boarding party had been lucky. Another whaler sent to search for documents had two casualties; one man killed, another shot in the buttocks. When Bacon was asked whether he had found anything useful, he nonchalantly replied that he had picked up a few charts. No one stopped to press him for more information. They guessed that he was an intelligence officer; he and a colleague who had travelled with him had already been nicknamed 'Cloak' and 'Dagger'. Or perhaps it was because they were all more interested by a signal which came in from another ship in the task force, which was finding space for Norwegian refugees. The signal said simply: 'I've got a blonde.'

The commandos were still caught up in street to street fighting in South Vågsoy when another opportunity to capture Enigma documents was presented to Alastair Ewing, the commander of the destroyer, HMS *Offa*.[16] Ewing sighted *Donner*, a second armed trawler, escorting another German ship down Vågsoy Island's North Sea coast. When the German lookouts saw the destroyer, the merchant ship was quickly beached, but *Donner* steamed out to sea in an attempt to escape. The chase did not last long. After *Offa* opened fire and blew up the depth charges on *Donner*, killing her captain in the process, the trawler's crew quickly abandoned ship. However, it took another two hours before Ewing was able to bring *Offa* alongside the ducking and weaving trawler, as it carried on steaming through the North Sea waves. One of *Offa*'s officers eventually leaped aboard the trawler, stepping over the pitiful remains of the helmsman, who had been in the wheelhouse when it was hit by a shell. He eventually mastered his revulsion and threw the mutilated and contorted limbs and trunk over the side. The dead man's sheepskin coat had already been commandeered by one of the other members of the boarding party.

Finding the Enigma codebooks and cipher machine did not require as much perseverance as had been the case on *Föhn*, but taking them back to *Offa* turned out to be much harder. The officer leading the boarding party attached a bag holding some of the documents to a line, and then attempted to have the bag pulled across the gap separating the two ships. But just as the bag was being sent across, a strap broke, and the bag tipped its valuable contents into the sea. An officer from the Naval Intelligence Division who had accompanied the boarding party nearly followed suit, as he tried to catch the bag with his one free hand. It was lost, but he made it back to *Offa* with the rest of his booty which included an Enigma cipher machine, along with five wheels and another set of the all-important bigram tables.[17]

After sinking *Donner*, *Offa* turned away to pick up the crew; there were only five survivors, all sitting on a raft. Four of them were pulled aboard the destroyer. But the fifth man was so shocked, he appeared to have gone stark raving mad. He waved his hands in the air and gabbled senselessly, all the time staring suspiciously at *Offa*'s crew as they stretched out their hands to him, while hanging like bats from the scrambling nets over the side of their ship. The attempt to rescue him was broken off when a German bomber broke through the clouds above the British warship. Alastair Ewing shouted to his men that he could not wait any longer and was getting under way. Nevertheless the would-be rescuers carried on reaching out their hands, still hoping that the madman would come to his senses. They only gave up as the destroyer finally steamed away from the raft, leaving the man to what they knew would be a cold and lonely death. It was a scene which marred the excitement they felt at sinking the trawler and for days afterwards *Offa's* crew were haunted by the memory of those staring eyes, the waving arms and the blabbering mouth.

Their thoughts were further disturbed by the death of a young man who they had rescued from the raft. After he stopped breathing, *Onslow's* crew gathered round to watch him being buried. He was sewn up in a hammock by a retired sailmaker, who had elected to join the Navy, and a stitch was sewn through his nose, to make absolutely sure he was really dead. Then the sailmaker nudged one of the officers, and said, 'Come on, sir. Say a prayer over 'im. 'E's some mother's son.' So a prayer was said and the young lad was slipped over the side just as the next line of enemy aircraft appeared over the horizon.[18]

By the time *Offa* made contact with Admiral Burrough again, the commandos were climbing back onto their ferries, having finally wiped out the German resistance and destroyed factories, wireless stations, fuel tanks and ammunition dumps, as planned. At 3 p.m., the task force sailed back out of the fjord and set off towards Scapa Flow.

Twenty-four hours before the beginning of the Vågsoy Raid, Operation Anklet had commenced further up the Norwegian coast.[19] Although the main objective of the raid, to dig in on the Norwegian coast for two to three months, was to be frustrated, the task force did manage to capture some Enigma documents. As the cruiser HMS *Arethusa*, flanked by no less than twelve destroyers, corvettes and minesweepers, steamed with their charges into Vestfjord near the Lofoten Islands, *Geier*, a German trawler, was sighted in the distance. Because the destroyer *Ashanti* was flying a German flag at the time, the crew on the *Geier* did not at first realise they were about to be attacked by the enemy. They soon understood what was happening, however, after *Ashanti* opened fire. A Norwegian officer on *Ashanti*, using his loud-hailer, instructed *Geier's* crew to surrender. He ordered them to line up on the deck with their hands above their heads, which most of them did at first. The officers on *Ashanti* could only hope that there was no one setting scuttling charges out of their sight.

A fortuitous mistake was to relieve the growing tension on the British destroyer. *Ashanti's* gun crew had become so interested by what was happening that they forgot to train the destroyer's guns onto their target. This was only picked up by the responsible officers as *Ashanti* drew up near *Geier*. All of a sudden the destroyer's powerful guns began to swivel round towards the Germans standing on deck. The movement terrified them, and first one, and then others, and finally all the men on deck, fearing that they were about to be massacred, ran to the side of their ship and jumped into the water. The evacuation proceeded all the faster because Dickie Onslow, *Ashanti*'s commander, had not seen the late movement of his ship's guns; he came to the conclusion that *Geier*'s crew were rushing off to scuttle their ship, and he gave the order to open fire. He only gave the cease fire order once he realised what had happened. Fortunately for the British, one of *Ashanti*'s shells, which flew in through one side of the radio room and out the other side, so terrified the telegraphist that he abandoned ship without first attempting to send out a distress signal revealing that the ship was being captured.

The cipher material captured during Operation Anklet matched what was recovered during the Vågsoy raid the following day: an Enigma machine, both sets of bigram tables, as well as copies of some of the same code manuals which had been captured over the past seven months on weather ships, supply ships and the *U-110*.[20] Although attempts were made to tow *Geier* back to the anchorage which had been established for the night, the order was given to sink the trawler after the first German aircraft were seen approaching the task force.

That was not quite the end of the story, as far as the documents were concerned. As the officers settled down for the night, a member of *Ashanti*'s crew drank a bottle of brandy, and then proceeded to pick a fight with the sentry who was supposed to be making sure that the prisoners from *Geier* did not escape. After seizing the sentry's rifle, the drunken man pulled the trigger, wounding one of his comrades in the hand. For an hour no one dared to approach him. He was only overpowered when the ship's doctor rushed up to him with a syringe in his hand and jabbed it into the unsuspecting man's backside. The man immediately keeled over and order, and the security of the Enigma secret, was restored.

Geier's documents and the cipher machine were subsequently transported back to Britain, as Operation Anklet was called off on 28 December when Rear-Admiral Hamilton, who was in charge of the naval task force, decided that his ships might be sunk by the Luftwaffe if they remained where they were without air cover. *Geier*'s documents and the cipher machine reached Bletchley Park on 1 January 1942. That was just one day after the documents, the Enigma machine and the Enigma wheels captured during the Vågsoy raid were handed in. The first documents were handed to Alan Turing, and he and his colleagues swiftly began to break the code again, using the Banburismus procedure.

The day before the first Enigma documents arrived at Bletchley Park, a report about the Vågsoy raid appeared in *The Times*. Headed 'Brilliant Combined Raid On Norwegian Coast', it described how 'a convoy of five merchant ships had been surprised lying off South Vågsoy. They ran themselves ashore, and were destroyed on the beaches by the Navy. In addition, armed trawlers . . . were sunk.' There was, of course, no description of what had happened on board the armed trawlers before they were sunk.

19

Black Out

The Barents Sea, Bletchley Park and the Admiralty

FEBRUARY–JULY 1942

The captures made during Operations Archery and Anklet helped to usher in a golden period for the Bletchley Park codebreakers. The Home Waters Naval Enigma settings used by Germany's surface ships, and by the U-boats in the Arctic, were broken every day for the rest of the war. The Germans referred to this net as 'Heimisch' (or 'Hydra' after 1942), while the British codebreakers knew it as 'Dolphin'.[1]

It was a codebreaking feat which was to save countless lives, especially in the Arctic. After October 1941 the Allies were sending regular convoys of merchant ships to north Russia via the Arctic route. The convoys formed up in Iceland, a convenient meeting point for the merchant ships from America and Britain. From there the ships sailed to Murmansk and Archangel, escorted by British and American warships. The convoys carried tanks, aircraft and weapons, all badly needed by the Russians, as they fought to halt the German invasion.

The high point for Naval Enigma came in March 1942 when, but for the reading of German messages, convoy PQ12, an eighteen-ship convoy protected by just one cruiser, two destroyers and some anti-submarine whalers, would almost certainly have been set upon by the German battleship, *Tirpitz*. Thanks to the breaking of the Enigma, the convoy was diverted out of harm's way.[2] Such diversions were a matter of life or death in the Arctic. Seamen who fell into the water after their ships were torpedoed could freeze to death in a matter of minutes. Enigma intelligence also gave aircraft, launched from *Illustrious*, the Home Fleet's aircraft carrier, the opportunity to torpedo *Tirpitz* after it abandoned its search for PQ12, and made for home. As it turned out, *Tirpitz* escaped unscathed, but one torpedo narrowly missed her stern.

During the PQ12 adventure, Naval Enigma messages were being read within two to three hours of their being transmitted by the Germans.[3] Unfortunately for the British, that was an exception. The Royal Navy often had to operate without receiving any Enigma intelligence for many hours or even days. The Enigma's so-called inner settings (the wheel order and ring settings, which could only be altered if the cipher machine's inner lid was opened) could take forty-eight hours, or even longer, to break. Once they were broken, the Enigma messages were read quickly for a while. This was because the inner settings were used for two consecutive days at a time; as soon as the inner settings had been identified, the outer settings, (the external connections, linking up pairs of sockets on the plugboard), for the second of the two consecutive days could be mastered relatively quickly, often within an hour or two.[4] But then the inner settings would be changed at midday on the third day, Bletchley Park would be blacked out, and the battle to break the code would commence again.

Banburismus was being used to break the Enigma's inner settings; that was the procedure which reduced the number of wheel orders to be tried out on the bombe to a manageable number. It was an ingenious method, but long-winded. It could take the Bletchley Park code breakers around twenty-eight hours just to produce the statistics needed to carry out the rest of the Banburismus procedure. Then the procedure had to be completed, a crib broken on the bombe, and the paired day had to be broken within the next twenty hours, if at least some Naval Enigma messages were to be read currently during the forty-eight-hour period under consideration.[5] Naval Enigma messages were often only read currently for around two hours out of each forty-eight-hour period.[6] Codebreaking black outs were a fact of life in 1942.

One of these black outs provided the backdrop to the terrible losses experienced during the passage to Russia of Arctic convoy PQ17 in June–July 1942. (All eastbound Russian convoys during 1941–2 were referred to as 'PQ', followed by a number; they were named after Peter Quennell Russell, a planning officer in the Admiralty.)[7] The wisdom of allowing PQ17 to sail was called into question after a disturbing message was sent to London by Henry Denham, the British naval attaché in Stockholm. On 18 June 1942 he warned the Admiralty that *Tirpitz*, backed up by a cruiser, pocket battleships and six destroyers, intended to attack the 'next Russian convoy'. The message was followed by the words: 'Graded A3', which meant that Denham thought that the person giving him the information was absolutely reliable, and that the information was probably true. The Admiralty subsequently graded it A2,[8] to indicate it believed the information itself was almost as likely to be true as Enigma intelligence, which was normally graded A1. Denham's information came from a friend in Swedish intelligence, who had previously warned him when *Bismarck* was about to break out into the Atlantic. The Swedes had secretly tapped the land lines connecting Berlin to the German Naval commands in Norway,[9] although this was not disclosed to the British Admiralty in 1942.[10]

With the almost certain prospect that the convoy would be annihilated if *Tirpitz* caught up with it in favourable conditions, Admiral Jack Tovey, the Home Fleet's Commander-in-Chief, talked to the 64-year-old First Sea Lord, Sir Dudley Pound, about what tactics should be followed while the convoy was at sea. Tovey wanted permission to turn PQ17 around and sail it back towards the protective umbrella provided by the Home Fleet if the threat from *Tirpitz* materialised; the Home Fleet could not, safely, follow the convoy all the way to Russia. Except in an emergency, Britain's Fleet was required to stay out of range of the Luftwaffe. However, Pound instructed Tovey not even to contemplate such a defeatist move, and instead informed him that he was thinking in terms of scattering the convoy if *Tirpitz* went after it. This horrified Tovey. He told Pound that this was tantamount to 'sheer bloody murder'. But his comments failed to move Pound to reconsider his strategy.[11]

The thirty-five-ship convoy was to have a strong escort.[12] For half its journey, it was to be shadowed by a group of four cruisers and three destroyers, as well as being accompanied all the way to Russia by a large escorting force which included six destroyers, four corvettes and nine other anti-submarine trawlers, mine-sweepers and anti-aircraft ships. However, it was recognised that *Tirpitz*'s superior fire power gave it the capacity to sink the British warships before their guns could be brought to bear.

The convoy set out from Iceland on 27 June 1942. On 1 July it was sighted by a German aircraft.[13] From that moment tension began to mount in the Admiralty's Operational Intelligence Centre (the OIC) in London each time there was a code-breaking black out, as the staff sat waiting anxiously for the Naval and Air Force Enigma decrypts to come through from Bletchley Park.

The OIC man responsible for tracking what *Tirpitz* was doing was the thirty-seven-year-old Commander Ned Denning; it was the same Denning who had been in touch with Harry Hinsley in Bletchley Park's Hut 4 concerning the sinkings of *Glorious* and *Bismarck*. Denning had done more than anyone to make the OIC an effective source of intelligence for British warships. In 1937 he had been the first officer to be appointed to the new unit, which was to handle all intelligence relating to ships at sea. Denning got on well with Winston Churchill. At the beginning of the war the two men occasionally had a drink together when the prime minister in waiting was the First Lord of the Admiralty. Churchill would drop into the OIC from time to time in order to see if there was any up-to-date intelligence which he ought to know about. They would have a drink in the small bar in the duty captain's room. On one occasion, after learning that a German bombing raid had caused many civilian casualties, Churchill had mused to himself, 'Unrestricted submarine warfare, unrestricted air bombing – this is total war.' Denning responded that total war required total intelligence, a statement which Churchill was still talking about at the end of the war.[14] Denning was a man whom it was difficult to ignore.

But when it came to dealing with Sir Dudley Pound, Denning was on less sure ground. The two men had completely different ways of operating. Denning believed that the best results were achieved through delegating responsibility to subordinates. When setting up the OIC, he had insisted it should be manned by specialists with the time and resources to find out everything there was to know about their subject. So, for example, he handled the intelligence relating to surface ships, but another man was brought in to deal with intelligence relating to the U-boats. Each section was to have a large amount of autonomy. Their authority was further extended after Denning won the OIC the right to transmit messages directly to the fleet at sea, something which had been anathema during the First World War. In those days all intelligence was fed to the warships via other officials within the Admiralty. At the beginning of the Second World War all OIC messages had to be signed off by John Godfrey, the Director of Naval Intelligence, but by 1942 even that requirement had been dropped, and Denning and Jock Clayton, the Admiral who came out of retirement to head up the OIC, were allowed to communicate with ships at sea without asking anyone's permission.

It was this belief in the benefits of delegation which was to put Denning on a collision course with the First Sea Lord. Sir Dudley

Pound was an autocrat, who had no time for the democratic style of leadership favoured within the OIC. By 1942 Pound was one of the old guard in the Navy. It was not just his age which set him apart. He would sit through meetings with his eyes closed so that no one around the table knew whether he was awake or asleep. Whichever was the case, his subsequent orders sometimes led participants to believe that he had made his mind up about what to do before anyone else had a chance to air their views. The brain tumour which eventually forced him to retire in 1943 may have been one of the reasons for his failing powers of concentration. Another likely cause was his insistence on doing everything himself; he had an enormous work load. He was famous for requiring his subordinates to attend meetings which he had convened long after most people had retired to their beds. These came to be known as 'the First Sea Lord's Midnight Follies'.[15] He would justify his refusal to delegate by stating that it was wrong for the man at the top to pass the buck to junior officers, a point of view which went against everything Denning and the OIC stood for.

The temperature began to rise sharply in Denning's OIC section on 3 July 1942 after the interception of a message from Group North (General-Admiral Carls in Kiel) to the Admiral Commanding Battleships (Admiral Schniewind) indicated that *Tirpitz* had left Trondheim during the previous night; although the body of the message had not been deciphered, (the message was enciphered with the Offizier Enigma settings, as well as the general settings, and so took longer to decrypt), it was clear to the Admiralty that a message would not have been sent to the Admiral Commanding Battleships unless he was at sea. The crew in a British aircraft flying over Trondheim had failed to sight the battleship.[16] There was no evidence to indicate where *Tirpitz* had gone.

If Bletchley Park's codebreakers had been reading Naval Enigma currently, the intelligence gap would have been bridged during the early morning of 4 July. An Enigma message originated at 7.40 a.m. on 4 July mentioned that *Tirpitz* was approaching Altenfjord in the north of Norway. But at the time when the message was composed, Bletchley Park had already been blinded by one of the recurring Enigma black outs for more than nineteen hours, and there was no immediate prospect of the black out being terminated in the foreseeable future.

The situation at Bletchley Park had not changed for the better when, during the early evening of 4 July, Pound visited Denning in the OIC to discuss what should be done. After the war, Denning wrote down his version of what happened at the meeting:

> Pound sat down on a stool in front of the main plotting table. The plot showed the planned convoy route, the position of the convoy, our own forces and as far as was known or estimated the position of U-Boats and German surface forces . . . Almost immediately Pound asked what would be the farthest on position of *Tirpitz* assuming she had sailed direct from Trondheim to attack the convoy . . . Someone . . . estimated that she could by then be within striking distance of the convoy. I interjected that it was unlikely in any event that she would have taken a direct course from Trondheim Fjord as she would almost certainly have made as much use as she could of the Inner Leads and proceed via Vest Fjord. I also considered that she would put into Narvik or Tromso to refuel her escorting destroyers before setting out on a sortie. Pound gazed at the plot for some time but said very little. I broke into his apparent reverie to inform him that more definite information was possible within three or four hours when Bletchley would most likely have broken into the Enigma keys for the previous twenty four hours.[17]

No Enigma messages transmitted after midday on 3 July had been read by the codebreakers. Pound then left the OIC.

The reason Denning was so sure that Enigma intelligence would arrive soon was that he was keeping in touch with Harry Hinsley at Bletchley Park; Hinsley had told him that the codebreakers were taking emergency measures, which were calculated to produce the break in more quickly than normal. Rather than waiting for the codebreakers to complete the long-winded Banburismus procedure, bombes normally allocated to the Air Force and Army Enigma were being 'borrowed' by the Naval Enigma hut to allow menus derived from cribs to be run against all possible wheel orders.[18] Because it took about twenty minutes to test one wheel order on the bombe, including the time to set the machine up correctly, if all 336 wheel orders had to be tested, it would take 112 bombe hours, or around twenty-two hours if five bombes were dedicated to the job.[19] This was only permitted during crises, known as 'flaps' by codebreakers at Bletchley Park: on this occasion it starved the Army and Air Force Enigma huts of bombes at a particularly difficult time. After a long gap, Army Enigma was being read quickly once more, and was playing an important role again in second guessing Rommel's offensive moves against the British Eighth Army in north Africa.

Shortly after the meeting with Pound, Hinsley rang Denning on the scrambler telephone to tell him that the Naval Enigma messages for the twenty-four-hour period commencing at midday on 3 July would be available soon. Up until this point, Denning and Pound had had no serious differences of opinion over the intelligence about PQ17 coming into the OIC. But two of the first Enigma signals to be sent over from Bletchley Park following the end of the black out were to lead to serious cracks in what had until then been a united front. One of these signals was the message originated by the Commander-in-Chief of the German Fleet to the Admiral Commanding Cruisers at 7.40 that morning. The wording sent over to Denning in the OIC at 6.59 p.m. on 4 July, read as follows: 'Arriving Alta 0900. You are to allot anchorages *Tirpitz* outer Vagfjord (as received).[20] Newly arriving destroyers and torpedo boats to complete with fuel at once.'[21] The other signal which had been originated by Fliegerführer, Lofotens at 12.40 a.m. on 4 July, about seven hours before the message mentioned above, read: 'Own Shadower 'C' 3/406, [which Denning identified as the German aircraft shadowing the convoy], reports at 0015: am in contact with one battleship, one heavy cruiser, 2 light cruisers, 3 destroyers . . .'[22]

The latter message, which reached the OIC at 6.51 p.m. on 4 July, led Denning to believe that the aircraft shadowing the convoy had spotted Rear-Admiral Hamilton's covering force, consisting of four cruisers and three destroyers; the aircraft crew had incorrectly claimed that it had seen a battleship. The mistake was understandable, because the Luftwaffe ship recognition book, which had been captured by the British earlier in the war, classified warships by the number of funnels they possessed. The recognition book took no account of the fact that the cruiser HMS *London*, Hamilton's flagship, had been modified so that it was left with just two funnels; it was usually reported as being a battleship, presumably because the ship it most resembled was the two-funnel battleship, *Duke of York*.

The question which Denning had to take on board, as he decided what he should tell Hamilton and Tovey was, would the German Naval Staff believe that a battleship had really been sighted near the convoy? And would they believe that it was either a unit within the Home Fleet, which had last been sighted by the Germans on 1 July, or part of another formidable force which might be supported by an aircraft carrier? Denning felt that if the report was believed, the German Naval Command would not allow *Tirpitz* to go anywhere near the convoy. He reached this conclusion because of evidence he had seen in Enigma intelligence following the attack carried out by

British aircraft on *Tirpitz* during its sortie against PQ12. The Germans clearly did not want their battleship to be pursued by British aircraft again.

As Denning began to draft a message to send out to Hamilton and Tovey, Pound and some of his staff walked into the OIC. When they asked Denning what he intended to transmit to the British fleets, he replied that he wanted to comment that all indications pointed to *Tirpitz* still being in the harbour at Alta. Pound did not agree with this; he did not think the messages received necessarily supported Denning's conclusion. So the message sent to Hamilton and Tovey at 7.18 p.m., 4 July, stated: 'C-in-C Fleet in *Tirpitz* arrived Altenfjord 0900/4th July. Destroyers and torpedo boats ordered to complete with fuel at once.' Pound refused to sanction the sending of a comment stating that *Tirpitz* was still at Alta.

Denning later described what else happened at this meeting:

Pound resumed his seat on the stool at the head of the plotting table, and enquired how long it would take for the destroyers to top up with fuel. I had already mentally calculated this as about three hours. Then he asked what was likely to be the speed of *Tirpitz*. I replied probably 25 or 26 knots provided the weather was favourable for the destroyers, but two or three knots less if the pocket battleships were also in company. Taking up the dividers, and using a smaller chart of the area for plotting, Pound remarked that if *Tirpitz* had sailed from Alta that morning, she could be up with the convoy about midnight. He then asked me why I thought *Tirpitz* had not yet left Alta. I expounded what had happened during *Tirpitz'* sortie against PQ12. I pointed out that up to noon that day, no decrypt had been received ordering U-boats to keep clear of the convoy, and even now direction finding of U-boat transmission showed that they were still very much in contact with the convoy. Despite intensive air reconnaissance, the Luftwaffe had not yet relocated Tovey's force. They had indeed located the cruiser covering force early that morning, but the formation was reported as including a battleship, and the Luftwaffe had now reported sighting an aircraft in its vicinity. Therefore the German Naval Staff could not disregard the possibility that this might be a major force, maybe supporting an aircraft carrier. I continued that although Bletchley had not yet broken the 'Enigma' from noon that day, 4 July, nevertheless the nature of the radio transmissions intercepted during the afternoon revealed none of the characteristics normally associated with surface ships being at sea. Moreover there had been no sighting report from our own, or Russian, submarines patrolling off the North Cape . . . After a time Pound got up to proceed to the U-boat tracking room, but before leaving, he turned to me, and asked: 'Can you assure me that *Tirpitz* is still in Alten Fjord?' My reply was to the effect that although I was confident she was, I could not give an absolute assurance. But I fully expected to receive confirmation in the fairly near future when Bletchley had unbuttoned the new traffic.[23]

Before the new traffic was unbuttoned, the Admiralty sent the following message to Rear-Admiral Hamilton, the commander of the cruiser force shadowing the convoy: 'Further information may be available shortly. Remain with the convoy pending further instructions.'[24] At about 8 p.m. on 4 July the first decrypts of the messages sent after midday (when the new Enigma settings had become operative) began to come through on the OIC's teleprinter. They included some worrying signs. Although a U-boat was still referring to a battleship being in the area, one message originated by Fliegerführer Lofotens, at 2.55 p.m. on 4 July, stated that another shadowing aircraft codenamed 'K' had reported that Hamilton's covering force consisted of four cruisers and three destroyers. For the first time a report had been made which did not state that a battleship was included amongst the convoy's escorts.[25] Denning might have been even more concerned by this, if he had had access to a message sent around one and a half hours earlier from the same aircraft. It stated that a group of warships had been seen, including a battleship and three cruisers;[26] taken together, the two messages contained the implication that the aircraft crew were intentionally correcting their first report that a battleship had been sighted. But Denning only received the decrypt of the earlier message at around 9.25 p.m., ninety minutes after he had received the second message, and by then it was too late to influence Pound's decision.

There are conflicting accounts about what happened next. There is Denning's version and a version which was included in *The Destruction of PQ17* by David Irving.[27] Denning's account is as follows. Deprived of the evidence which might have undermined his theory about *Tirpitz* still being in Alta, Denning remembers looking at a message which appeared, to him, to support the theory. The message, which arrived on Denning's desk shortly after 8.30 p.m. on 4 July had been originated at 11.30 that morning by the Admiral Commanding Northern Waters and transmitted to Eisteufel (Ice Devil), the codename for the group of U-boats operating around the convoy. It stated: 'No own Naval Forces in the operational area. Position of

Heavy enemy group not known at present, but is the major target for U-boats when encountered. Boats in contact with the convoy are to keep at it . . .'[28] This told Denning that *Tirpitz* had still been in Altenfjord shortly before noon, and Denning assumed that she would not depart until the Germans satisfied themselves about there being no battleship or aircraft carrier with the convoy. Denning says that he immediately passed the decrypt to Clayton, his boss, who was on his way to another urgent meeting called by Pound. He then remembers drafting a message to be sent to Tovey and Hamilton confirming that *Tirpitz* was thought to be still in Altenfjord at midday, and commenting that there were indications she was still there. However he decided that he should not send it without first showing it to Clayton, given what had been discussed with Pound earlier that evening.

In the meantime, Rodger Winn, who was in charge of the U-boat tracking section of the OIC, came into Denning's room and looked at his proposed message. What Winn said astounded Denning. Winn, who had just spoken to Pound, was under the impression that *Tirpitz* was thought to be at sea, and he stated there was talk of scattering the convoy. Denning also spoke to Harry Hinsley. Denning and Hinsley, who was still on duty in Bletchley Park's Hut 4, had been speaking on the telephone every few minutes. Hinsley now urged Denning not to let the convoy be scattered and advocated a compromise approach which would have involved sailing PQ17 back towards the Home Fleet until the Naval Enigma messages clarified the situation about *Tirpitz*'s whereabouts.[29] Unfortunately for the merchant seamen in the convoy, Hinsley's views were once again ignored.

There is no official record of what happened at the meeting attended by Clayton. According to the account in David Irving's book, Pound asked each of the officers around the conference table in his room what line of action he preferred. None of the officers wanted to see the convoy dispersed, apart from Admiral Henry Moore, the Vice-Chief of the Naval Staff, who, using the chart in the conference room and a pair of dividers, worked out that *Tirpitz* could attack the convoy in a matter of hours. Because of the lack of documentary evidence, it is uncertain what intelligence information was given to the officers at the meeting. However Admiral Moore subsequently stated that he had only agreed to the dispersal because he had been led to believe that *Tirpitz* was already at sea.[30] After everyone had spoken, Pound leaned back in his leather-backed chair and closed his eyes. A few moments of silence was broken when one of the young staff officers whispered irreverently, 'Look, Father's fallen asleep.' Then Pound opened his eyes again, reached for a message pad and announced dramatically: 'The convoy is to be dispersed.'[31]

At 9.11 p.m. the following signal was sent out to Admiral Hamilton: 'Cruiser force withdraw westward at high speed.' Twelve minutes later, Pound's signal to Jackie Broome, the commander of the convoy's close escort, was sent: 'Owing to threat from surface ships convoy is to disperse and proceed to Russian ports.' But then Admiral Moore realised that the order did not make it clear that the ships were to scatter, so after consulting with Pound, he drafted the final order which was to be the death warrant for so many ships and their crews: 'Most Immediate. Admiralty to Escorts of PQ 17 . . . Convoy is to scatter.'

After the meeting in Pound's office Denning suggested that Clayton should take the message he had drafted and try one more time to convince Pound that he should change his mind. Clayton agreed to try. He was not away very long. When he came back he said, 'Father says he's made his decision and he is not going to change it now.'

An ambiguity hidden within Pound's and Moore's signals to Admiral Hamilton was only noticed some time later. Denning's assistant, Lieutenant Archie Hutchinson, who had recently come on duty, was reading through the messages to bring himself up to speed, when it suddenly dawned on him that nothing had been said about what the destroyers, corvettes and anti-submarine vessels, which had been accompanying the convoy, should be doing.

'I wonder what Turtle [Hamilton] will make of that,' he said. 'He'll think *Tirpitz* is on his tail. I wonder what will happen to the escort?'

Hutchinson was right to be concerned. Hundreds of miles away, in the Barents Sea, the ambiguous orders were being misunderstood by Captain Jackie Broome, the commander of the convoy's escorting warships. Pound had intended that Broome's destroyer, HMS *Keppel*, and its five sister ships, should remain with the merchant ships as they scattered. They obviously would not have been able to protect all the merchant ships from the circling U-boats, but they would have been able to screen at least some of them. In the absence of clear instructions, Broome took it upon himself to reach a different conclusion. He believed that if, as the signals seemed to suggest, *Tirpitz* was about to appear over the horizon at any minute, it would be better if he and his destroyers steamed to the south, so that his force would be between *Tirpitz* and the convoy while the merchant ships scattered.[32]

Broome gave the order to scatter by raising a white flag bearing a red St George's cross. Some of the merchant ships acknowledged they had understood by raising a similar flag on their masts, but just to make sure no one would miss the signal, Broome also sent out the same signal to the convoy's commodore by searchlight and radio. Commodore John Dowding, the man in charge of the convoy, dipped his flag to indicate that he did not understand the signal he had seen. So Broome took his ship through the merchant ships alongside Dowding's flagship, *River Afton*, to explain what had happened. As the two vessels eventually parted, Broome signalled: 'To Commodore: Sorry to leave you like this. Goodbye and good luck. It looks a bloody business.' Dowding signalled back: 'Thank you. Goodbye and good hunting.'

At that moment Broome saw Admiral Hamilton's cruiser force approaching from the north. He decided to join them. Together they would be a more effective unit than if they opposed Germany's battleship independently. So the warships steamed away together leaving the merchant ships, and the remaining escorts, to defend themselves.

It was only then that the consequences of Pound's order began to be played out, as U-boats and German aircraft picked off the unprotected merchant ships almost at will. The slaughter started early the next morning when a U-boat torpedoed *Empire Byron*, a 6000 ton merchant ship carrying tanks. A young radio officer from Manchester quickly asked the ship's captain, John Wharton, whether to put an emergency radio into one of the lifeboats. The Captain demurred. While they were talking they could hear the shouts and screams of the twelve gunners trapped below deck as the water rushed in. There was no way of getting them out. Eventually Wharton dived over the side of his ship into the sea, and was picked up by a lifeboat. Floating past him in the sea, he saw the body of the young radio officer from Manchester to whom he had spoken just minutes earlier, one of the eighteen men from the crew of sixty who died as a result of the sinking. After the ship sank, *U-703*'s telegraphist transmitted the following signal back to Admiral Schmund in Narvik, Norway: 'HAVE SUNK 9000 GRT EMPIRE BYRON . . . CARGO A.F.V.'S PORT OF DESTINATION ARCHANGEL. HER CAPTAIN ON BOARD AS PRISONER . . . CONVOY TOTALLY DISPERSED . . . AM PUR-

SUING.'³³ A copy of the message was delivered to the OIC in London at 2.40 p.m. on 5 July.

The ether was full of such signals. First came the desperate SOS from the merchant ship, often specifying it was being attacked by a U-boat. Then came the U-boat's ominous sinking report, enciphered with the Enigma, mentioning the ship, its tonnage and its cargo. To those listening in, it was like a giant game of naval monopoly being played out over the airwaves. At sea, it was like visiting hell. In some cases the merchant ships' lifeboats were damaged by the torpedoes fired into the ships' hulls. When *Hartlebury*, the 5000 ton merchant ship, was torpedoed on 7 July, some members of the crew had to make do with a lifeboat which was half full of water; when there was no more room inside it, the rope attaching it to the ship was cut leaving one man who had been holding onto it hanging over the water. He had to climb on board the ship again. As the lifeboat floated away from the sinking ship, the men inside watched transfixed as this soli-tary figure climbed the ladder to *Hartlebury's* bridge, and began to strip off his life jacket, his coat and finally his cap. He had given up the fight and was preparing to die with dignity. The last they saw of him he was waving at them from the bridge as the ship began its last plunge into the sea.

For the twenty survivors in the lifeboat their ordeal was just begin-ning. During the next two hours many of the men sitting up to their waists in freezing water found themselves becoming drowsy, then their eyes just glazed over. They had been frozen to death. The dead men were heaved overboard one by one until there were only five left in the boat. At that point the lifeboat began to rise up out of the water at last. One of the remaining five, either a hero, or driven insane by the cold, suddenly leapt overboard and swam away into the fog. He was never seen again. Some hours later the last four men finally made it to land. The ship had been torpedoed just three miles from Novaya Zemlya, an island off the north coast of Russia. Only twenty of the fifty-six-man crew survived.³⁴

Back at the OIC, the Admiralty's staff could only imagine the tor-ment being suffered at sea. After the scatter order had been sent, Denning settled down to sleep on a camp bed in an adjoining office. He was woken at about 2 in the morning on 5 July so that he could be shown a message which Clayton wanted to send out to the war-ships still at sea. The signal read:

'1. It is not repeat not known if German heavy forces have sailed from

Altenfjord, but they are unlikely to have done so before 1200B/4th.
2. It appears that Germans may be in some confusion whether a battle-ship is in company with CS1 [Hamilton's force].
3. Germans do not repeat not appear to be aware of position of C-in-C Home Fleet.'[35]

The message was similar to the one which Denning had wanted to send more than six hours earlier in almost identical circumstances. The only difference was the time that had elapsed without *Tirpitz* having been referred to in any Naval Enigma messages; this had hardened the men at the Admiralty's view that *Tirpitz* was not at sea yet.[36] The signal was sent out to the British ships at 2.38 a.m. on 5 July.

When the signal was received, the following exchange of signals took place between Captain Broome and Admiral Hamilton in the Barents Sea. 'From CS One [Hamilton's force] to *Keppel*. Had you any instructions concerning the conduct of the escort when the convoy scattered which led you to assume that the destroyers should con-centrate and act under orders of senior officer . . .?' Broome replied: 'No instructions. The suggestion to join your force was my own. The decision to leave remaining escorts was most unpleasant and I am always ready to go back and collect them.' But Broome never received an order to go back. So the scattered merchant ships were not rescued in their hour of need.

German aircraft only sighted Tovey's Home Fleet at 6.55 a.m. on 5 July.[37] It was retreating to the south-west, and was already around 800 miles from the area where the convoy had scattered. That cleared the way at last for *Tirpitz* to go out. The order was given shortly before midday on 5 July, and by 3 p.m. that afternoon *Tirpitz*, the cruiser *Admiral Hipper*, the pocket battleship *Admiral Scheer*, and seven destroyers were steaming out to sea. Unfortunately for the Germans, the German Fleet was quickly sighted by Allied aircraft and by British and Russian submarines. The sighting signals were inter-cepted by the German B-Dienst, and it was then a question for the Germans whether the British Fleet could catch up with them if their 'Knight's Move' operation went ahead. The Germans eventually decided that the risk was not worth taking and that same night *Tirpitz* and its escorts returned to base. That did not affect the out-come of PQ17 as far as the Allies were concerned. The convoy turned out to be one of the most disastrous of the war; only eleven merchant ships made it to Russian ports out of the thirty-six which had sailed from Iceland at the end of June.

The PQ17 story is shocking. But there was another codebreaking black out in 1942 which was to have even more serious consequences for the Allies' merchant seamen. On 1 February 1942 a new Enigma wheel and a new reflector were introduced for cipher machines being used on the Atlantic U-boats' net. (The new wheel and reflector and the remaining three wheels fitted into the same space which were taken up by the reflector and the three wheels on the three-wheel Enigma). The Germans referred to this net as 'Triton' to distinguish it from the 'Heimisch' Naval Enigma net used by surface ships and by U-boats in the Arctic. Bletchley Park called the Triton net 'Shark', a name which aptly reflected the blood spilled as a result of its use. The new Enigma wheel was placed inside the cipher machine alongside the other three wheels; U-boats using Shark were issued with a four-wheel machine. The new wheel could be set to any one of its twenty-six possible positions. This had to be done manually by the telegraphists; unlike the other wheels, the new wheel was not turned by the movement of the wheels on its right. Nor was it interchangeable with them. That was fortunate for the British. If interchangeable, the number of wheel orders would have increased from 336 to 3024. Even so, the introduction of the new wheel meant there were twenty-six times as many settings to be tried out for each wheel order. That made it impossible to break the code regularly on the existing three wheel bombes. The Bletchley Park codebreakers calculated it would take around six hours to test one wheel order in a four wheel Enigma on a three wheel bombe; in other words if the settings were to be worked out within twenty-four hours, eighty-five bombes would have been necessary.[38] At the end of 1941 there were just twelve bombes at Bletchley Park, and they had to be shared with the Army and Air Force Enigma cryptographers.

The wiring for the new wheel and reflector were not a problem. In December 1941 some German operators were already using the four-wheel machine. Until they were given the order that the whole net was changing over to the four-wheel Enigma, they were supposed to use it as if it were a three-wheel machine; they could do this if the ring setting on the fourth wheel was Z, and if A was showing through the window above the wheel. However, some operators made mistakes. One telegraphist had B showing through the window above the wheel when he sent a message. He then compounded his error by sending another message stating: 'E bar 551 [a message] decyphers with setting B.'[39] Such errors enabled the wiring of the new wheel and reflector to be worked out.

The extra number of settings might also have been surmounted if more bombes and cribs had been available. Cribs were available until 20 January 1942, as a result of the way the British exploited the German U-boats' short weather reports. Whenever a U-boat sent a weather report, its telegraphist first encoded the report into a condensed version, using the short weather codebook. The resulting code was enciphered using the normal Enigma settings before being transmitted back to France or Germany. The cipher text was then deciphered by the Germans. The information derived from the deciphered text was subsequently transformed by a German meteorological station using its own codebook, and transmitted. The British codebreakers at Bletchley Park managed to decode the meteorological station's code. As long as they could transform the information arrived at back to the condensed short weather report using the U-boats' short weather codebook, they would have a crib to match up with the cipher text they had intercepted when the U-boat transmitted its short weather report. The problem was that on 20 January 1942 the short weather codebook captured from both *München* and *U-110* in May 1941 was replaced by a new version. So just when the codebook was needed, it was not available. Unless the Royal Navy captured it, there would be no regular cribs, apart from the odd exceptional case.

There were a few isolated days when cribs were discovered because an important event was referred to in a message, or because Enigma messages were re-encipherments of messages sent by German signalmen using other readable codes. One such crib was created on 14 March 1942 when Dönitz announced to the Fleet that he had been made an Admiral. But it took six three-wheel bombe machines seventeen days to break the setting for the day.[40]

Bletchley Park's failure to identify cribs and to manufacture four wheel bombes quickly might not have mattered if Banburismus could have been used to break the cipher produced on the four wheel Enigma. But although in theory Banburismus could be used in connection with the traffic enciphered on the four wheel Enigma, in practice it was impossible to use the procedure. As is explained in Appendix 3, Banburismus could only be carried out if there were several pairs of messages with similar message settings. Because there were so many extra ways of setting up the four wheel Enigma machine, without there being a sufficient increase in the number of messages transmitted, the message settings proved to be too spread out;[41] as a result there were not enough messages with similar message settings to enable the codebreakers to use Banburismus on messages enciphered on the four wheel Enigma.

The dramatic turnaround in the fortunes of the OIC, revealing its inability to divert convoys away from lines of U-boats, is reflected in the following note from its weekly U-boat situation report for 9 February 1942: 'Since the end of January no Special Information has been available about any U-boats other than those controlled by Admiral Norway. Inevitably the picture of the Atlantic dispositions is by now out of focus and little can be said with any confidence in estimating the present and future movements of the U-boats.[42]

The loss of the Enigma intelligence coincided with a dramatic increase in the tons of Allied shipping sunk by the U-boats. After Germany had declared war on America on 11 December 1941, following the Japanese attack on Pearl Harbor four days earlier, the U-boats had managed to institute a reign of terror off the US coast. Acting independently rather than in wolf packs, the U-boats exploited America's failure to form up the ships running along its east coast into convoys protected by warships. The result was that the amount of shipping sunk made the losses during convoy PQ17 pale by comparison. During PQ17 137,000 tons of shipping, (twenty-three ships), were sunk.[43] During the first eight months of 1942, over 4 million tons of shipping were sunk by U-boats at the rate of more than 500,000 tons per month. Between sixty and 108 ships were sunk during each month during this period.[44]

At the same time, imports into Britain during the first eight months of the year dropped by more than 5 million tons, compared with imports during the equivalent period of the previous year, a reduction of almost 18 per cent.[45] The Allies' plight was made worse because in February 1942 the German Intelligence Service mastered the Naval Cipher Number 3 which was being used by the British, American and Canadian Navies to communicate with each other in the Atlantic.[46] This helped Dönitz to work out where to find convoys and Allied ships. On the other hand, this turned out to be a blessing in disguise. German analysts came to the conclusion that their side's ability to read the Allies' codes accounted for the U-boats' growing success. This masked the fact that the Allies' sudden change of fortunes had only occurred after the German cipher department had altered the Enigma cipher machine. So the Enigma secret was retained for a while longer.

Breaking the Deadlock

The Mediterranean and Bletchley Park

OCTOBER–DECEMBER 1942

As the German U-boats sank more and more ships off the east coast of America during the first half of 1942, another battle was being fought, between Britain and America, across the Atlantic. The Americans wanted to know why they were no longer receiving Naval Enigma intelligence from their new allies. The British did not want to tell them in case the information leaked out to the Germans. It was a reprise of an old row which had been bubbling away under the surface ever since the beginning of 1941.

The seeds of the row had been sown at the end of 1940 after discussions had taken place about the possibility of an Anglo-American exchange of cryptographic secrets. On 15 November 1940 Alastair Denniston, the head of Bletchley Park, wrote to Stewart Menzies, the head of the Secret Intelligence Service: 'As regards German and Italian [ciphers], any we may have is of such vital importance to us that we cannot agree at once to hand it over unreservedly. We should require to be informed in detail as to the security of such information after it left our hands.'[1]

Notwithstanding Denniston's objections, the first American code-breaking liaison team arrived in Britain two and a half months later. They had instructions to reveal to their counterparts at Bletchley Park how the Americans had broken the Japanese code known as 'Purple'. In return, they were hoping that they would be told all about British progress on German ciphers. However, while they were being greeted with glasses of sherry and tales of derring-do by Alastair Denniston at Bletchley Park and by Stewart Menzies, the head of the Secret Intelligence Service, these same men were conspiring behind the Americans' backs to reveal as little as possible to them.

Even when Menzies mentioned to Churchill at the end of February

1941 that the chiefs of staff were willing to share the British cryptographers' knowledge concerning the Enigma cipher with the Americans, there was a sting in the tail; Menzies stated that any discussions would not extend to 'the results', that is the intelligence gathered through reading Enigma messages. Churchill wrote the following note at the bottom of Menzies' memo to signify his approval:– 'As proposed. WSC.27.2'.[2] The Americans were quickly sworn to secrecy, one of the naval representatives in the US liaison team signing a note agreeing to inform 'by word of mouth only the head of our section, Commander L. F. Safford, USN'. The US Army representatives gave equivalent undertakings.[3] The Americans were eventually given a 'paper' Enigma to take home with them.[4]

During the summer of 1941 Churchill went back on his agreement with Menzies; Churchill suggested that the Americans should be given Enigma intelligence to help the US deal with the growing threat to their ships posed by the U-boats. However Menzies refused to give way completely, writing back:–

> I find myself unable to devise any safe means of wrapping up the information in a manner which would not imperil this source . . . it [is] well nigh impossible that the information could have been secured by an agent, and however much we insist that it came from a highly placed source, I greatly doubt the enemy being for a moment deceived should there be any indiscretion in the USA. That this might occur cannot be ruled out as the Americans are not in any sense as security minded as one would wish . . .[5]

In the end after the Naval Enigma was finally broken on an ongoing basis at the beginning of August 1941, Denniston decided to go to Washington in an attempt to sort out once and for all the Anglo-American dispute concerning British codebreaking. He intended to explain that the shortage of bombes made it hard to contemplate releasing one of them to the US, as had been requested, but he would have liked to have placated the Americans by inviting some of their young mathematicians to work at Bletchley Park. Menzies objected to both of Denniston's initiatives. He told Denniston not to mention the bombe situation in case the Americans latched onto that as a reason why the bombes should be built in the US. He also wrote: 'I am a little uneasy about the proposal for young mathematicians.' So Denniston was only permitted to offer the Americans the opportunity to work on Enigma research and development; he was not at liberty to allow them to deal with the Enigma intercepts on a day-to-day basis.[6]

That was the situation until the Shark Enigma was blacked out on 1 February 1942.

Denniston, who remained the head of Bletchley Park until February 1942, was telling the Americans that the Government Code and Cipher School (GC&CS) would pass on anything they wanted to know about Enigma, but then British cryptographers, rather than explaining everything, were only giving the Americans information they specifically requested. As a result, the American codebreakers began to make noises about breaking the Enigma code themselves, a prospect which the British did not relish.

In April 1942, at the height of the U-boat blitz on American shipping, John Tiltman, a senior cryptanalyst from Bletchley Park, appeared to have resolved the differences between the two sides. He persuaded his opposite number in America to permit the British to carry on breaking the Enigma exclusively, as long as certain conditions were met. Tiltman referred to the most important condition in the following note which he sent to Commander Edward Travis, the man who had taken over from Denniston as the head of GC&CS: '. . . b. In view of the fact that they [the Americans] are now at war and have a vital interest in submarine traffic, they are entitled to results or a detailed statement as to why this traffic cannot be read at present and what are the prospects for the future. c. Unless a rapid and satisfactory solution is found to (b), the high command will insist on their Naval cryptanalysts attempting to duplicate our work on "E".'[7]

Travis wrote back to the Americans admitting that the four-wheel Enigma messages being transmitted by the U-boats were unreadable. In the same letter he refused to set up a skeleton team in the US which could be told everything about Enigma until he was persuaded that this was absolutely necessary. 'If real danger arose of present facilities being lost, we would certainly send experts to the other side,' he wrote.[8]

However on 13 May 1942 Travis wrote another letter indicating that the British would have no objection to the Americans carrying out their own research on machinery which could break the Enigma. At the same time Travis promised to send a British bombe machine over to the US within four months along with a mechanic to maintain it.[9] It is possible that this was intended to pacify the Americans in the short term. Whether or not this promise was ever intended to be honoured, the bombe was never delivered to America. In September 1942 after the due date for its delivery had passed, William Friedman, the American cryptographer dealing with the Army and Air Force Enigma, wrote the following internal memorandum confirming that he and the Navy's cryptographic team had decided not to force Travis to keep his word:

> The British now have so limited a number of these machines and the volume required of them is so great that, while we could press them and they would undoubtedly make good their promise, they would probably do so with reluctance because it would deprive them of that much capacity for current solution . . . If they did furnish a machine it would be one of the very earliest and most inefficient models – of little use as a model for replication. . . . We now have all the blue prints and drawings . . . and do not need a physical embodiment thereof in order to proceed with our construction.

The American determination to set up what Friedman referred to as 'an Enigma solution unit of our own' was spurred on by the knowledge that new British bombes capable of dealing with four wheel Enigma traffic would not be available for at least six months. The Americans were also worried that Bletchley Park, and its annexes, its staff and all of its secrets might be wiped out by a series of bombing raids, as is evidenced by the following excerpt from a memorandum Friedman wrote to support his conclusion that the Americans should produce their own bombe to break Army and Air Force Enigma: 'should a few well-placed bombs destroy the present three buildings in which the Enigma-solving machinery is housed, all Enigma solution will stop, and with it all the high-grade German communications will become unreadable.'[10]

A showdown meeting was arranged with Edward Hastings, GC&CS's representative in Washington, at the end of August 1942. At the meeting Commander Joseph Wenger, the head of 'Op-20-G', the American Navy's Washington-based equivalent of Bletchley Park's Hut 8, told Hastings that the Americans could not wait any longer and wanted to produce their own codebreaking machine. Hastings protested that this was unfair. The British had complied with the condition mentioned in Tiltman's April 1942 letter; they had explained why the code could not be broken. But his objections were of no avail.[11]

On 3 September 1942 Wenger applied for funds to initiate an independent bombe programme. In his application for permission to spend 'about two million dollars' on machine construction he wrote:

In undertaking this project, it must be understood that it is a gamble . . . By stating that it is a gamble, I mean that, while it appears workable on the present system employed by the Germans, it is quite possible that they may change things entirely, which might, of course, nullify our planned attack.[12]

Also he could not guarantee that the high-speed bombe he and his staff were developing would work. However, using words which were to haunt him later on when the American engineers could not at first make the machinery they had produced work, Wenger added: 'Our investigations have proved to our satisfaction that the proposed methods are theoretically sound. They have, moreover, been demonstrated to be practical, *provided we effect the necessary speed-up, which now looks feasible.*' [Author's choice of italics]. In spite of the reservations, the American bombe project was given the green light on the very next day.

This move was quickly followed by concessions from Britain. On 2 October 1942 Travis signed up to an agreement which meant that British codebreakers would collaborate fully with the Americans in relation to Naval Enigma. The agreement was refined during a subsequent meeting between Wenger and Harry Hinsley, who had flown to Washington for that very purpose. Although the British would retain overall control of the interception of messages, and the breaking of them, they would, if asked, help the Americans to produce their own bombes, and they would make available intercepted traffic, as well as cribs and menus which would enable Op-20-G to attempt to break Shark.

Just three days before Travis made the concession which was to break the deadlock between the Naval Enigma cryptographers in Britain and America, another transatlantic storm was brewing concerning the Army and Air Force Enigmas. On 30 September 1942 the US Army Signal Corps had entered into a contract with Bell Laboratories with a view to another American bombe being constructed. A sample of the machine was demonstrated in November 1942, and promises were made that the production model would be delivered in April 1943.

However, notwithstanding the agreement concerning Naval Enigma, the US Army Signal Corps was for some time unable to reach an agreement with the British in relation to the Army and Air Force Enigma. The British were frightened that the American Army would not be able to keep the Enigma secret even if the American naval cryptographers could. Because of this the atmosphere between the two sides became so acrimonious at the end of 1942 that Alan Turing, who had travelled all the way to America to advise Bell Laboratories in New Jersey on the design of a new scrambler telephone, was denied access to Bell's buildings. Turing was only allowed in after the British confirmed that the Americans would be shown everything they needed to see relating to the Army and Air Force Enigma cipher as long as they were prepared to come to England to see it.

This did not stop the Americans making further requests that they should be allowed to break Enigma settings themselves, and these provoked more furious responses from the codebreakers at Bletchley Park. From the British perspective the Americans were attempting to 'participate in an already proven success, so that they may not appear to lag behind the British either in acumen or knowledge.' Such reactions convinced Telford Taylor, the American liaison officer working at Bletchley Park in April 1943, that a diplomatic approach to the problem might yield unexpected dividends through the back door. His advice is included in the following note:–

> we should not phrase [our solution to the problem] so broadly that it seems to envision a duplicate operation at Arlington Hall [the American centre dealing with Army and Air Force Enigma] or to impose undue burdens on the British in supplying us with traffic . . . What we really want at this time is to gain a foothold in 'Enigma' and develop technical competence, and gradually develop a supplementary operation so as to improve joint coverage. What we ultimately want is independence, but if we get the foothold and develop our technique, independence will come anyhow. As our position in Europe gets better established, we will be less dependent on the British for intercept assistance; as our skill in dealing with traffic grows, we will need less help in securing 'cribs'.[12]

The final Anglo-American agreement relating to the Army and Air Force Enigma which was eventually signed just over a month later gave the Americans the foothold they needed; it provided for American cryptographers to be sent to England, and to be equipped with British bombes so that they could help directly in the decrypting of Enigma messages. A liaison officer in England was to be allowed to send to Washington any intelligence gleaned from the intercepts. The Americans were even to be allowed to set up their own intercept stations in England.[13]

It was the Op-20-G bombe designed to deal with Naval Enigma

which was supposed to be ready first. But Lieutenant Commander Ralph Meader, the US Navy's representative in Dayton, Ohio, where the machinery was to be produced, was to discover how hard it was to meet any of the scheduled targets on time given the need for absolute secrecy and the scarcity of the necessary materials.

Even if Wenger's new high-speed bombe worked when it was designed and manufactured, the British and Americans had to decide what to do in the mean time; Wenger had admitted in his application for funds that the bombes would only become available in 'about five months'. In other words there would be no answer to the U-boat menace until February 1943 at the earliest. By the end of the summer of 1942 the Americans had introduced effective anti-submarine measures off their eastern shores. But this merely transferred the U-boat peril back into the Atlantic. The U-boats sank 700,000 tons of shipping in June 1942, almost 550,000 tons in August, and about 620,000 tons in October.[14] The losses could be expected to rise as the number of operational U-boats grew. By the beginning of September 1942, Dönitz had 126 U-boats available for operations.[15] At the same time, the planned Allied invasion of North Africa could be expected to reduce still further the number of warships available to escort the transatlantic convoys. It looked like a recipe for disaster.

The solution to the Allies' growing problems was sitting inside a U-boat in the eastern Mediterranean. On 30 October 1942, a radar-equipped Sunderland aircraft discovered *U-559* lurking on the convoy route between Port Said and the British naval base in Haifa. Five destroyers were summoned to the scene, including HMS *Petard*, commanded by Lieutenant-Commander Mark Thornton.[16]

Like many destroyer commanders Thornton could not wait to get at the enemy, but he also had an extra obsession. He wanted to capture a U-boat, and its codebooks. For months he discussed how this could be achieved with his twenty-nine-year-old first-lieutenant, Tony Fasson. The first-lieutenant was used to Thornton's demands, even if he did not always agree with them. He knew that Thornton believed that the only way to survive the war was to terrorise his crew into being super-efficient. This management style did not appeal to Fasson, who was always having to smooth over the ruffled feathers which Thornton's bullying inevitably left in its wake. Thornton was famous amongst his own crew for insisting that his men kept a constant lookout for submarines, whether they were on duty or not. He would climb up into the *Petard*'s crow's nest and strap himself to the mast in order to lead by example. Heaven help anyone who did not meet his exacting standards; they would be peppered with stones, pieces of chalk, and sometimes even tea cups if Thornton from his vantage point ever felt they were slacking.

On one occasion Thornton had a fire cracker let off in the middle of the night, and then turned a hose on his men as they rushed to their action stations. On another occasion he ordered his officers to jump into the sea and swim around the ship, even though a gale was blowing. His men were only spared this ordeal after a senior officer persuaded Thornton they could all die if the exercise was not called off. Such behaviour made some of the crew suspect that Thornton was going mad. He was certainly very eccentric. When he was spotted firing a machine gun at a flock of gannets, he shouted to his men that he could not bear the sight of the murderous birds since they were robbing the sea of its fish. Whether or not Thornton was a little crazy, his regime certainly kept his men on their toes. Many of them were prepared to go that extra mile if he asked them to. They were even prepared to put their own lives on the line if it kept Thornton off their backs.

The destroyers arrived at the spot indicated by the Sunderland aircraft at 12.20 p.m. on 30 October.[17] Within fifteen minutes, the U-boat's periscope was sighted by another aircraft which had joined the hunt; from the aircraft the U-boat's outline was clearly visible under the water. For the next ten hours, a deadly game of cat and mouse was played out. The destroyers probed and searched the depths with the invisible fingers of their Asdic sets, while the U-boat commander did everything he could to evade his pursuers. Each time depth charges were dropped, the U-boat would attempt to escape while the Asdic sets were blinded by the churned up water. At one point U-559 dived so dccp that the echo on the hunting ships' Asdic sets became faint. Then one of Thornton's crew had the bright idea of putting soap into the holes on the depth charge pistol, the regulator on a depth charge which determined the depth at which it would explode; this enabled the depth charges to sink deeper before going off. It was an effective ploy. After that the echo became stronger again and the hunt proceeded as before.

As the bright day turned to night, the repeated buffeting from the depth charge explosions took their toll on the men inside the U-boat. Two of the younger members of the crew panicked and cried out after each bang. Even the more experienced men could feel their strength ebbing away. The carbon dioxide in the air made them all feel lightheaded and breathless. A deadly chill began to creep up their limbs.

They listened grimly to an ominous hissing sound which warned them that their vital pressurised air was leaking from its containers. Their morale was further dented by a report that water was coming in and the U-boat began to float at an angle with its stern lower than its bow. Hans Heidtmann, the commander, tried in vain to rectify this by ordering as many men as possible to the front of the boat. At about 10 p.m., the engineer, Günther Gräser, told Heidtmann that he could not maintain the balance of the boat for much longer. Then *Petard* dropped yet another pattern of depth charges. They convinced Heidtmann that he could not wait any longer; he ordered the water to be blown out of the diving tanks and the U-boat rose to the surface.

It was then that Günther Gräser, or one of his men, made a fatal mistake. While the U-boat was being evacuated, they were supposed to be opening up a series of vents so that seawater could flood the diving tanks. Once the tanks were full of water, the U-boat would sink. But in the rush to pull the levers operating the vents, someone forgot to remove the metal pins which were holding them in place. By the time Gräser noticed what had happened, the damage had been done, and the lever mechanism had been bent.

At the same time as this mix up was going on inside the U-boat, equally frantic scenes were being enacted on *Petard*. Thornton shouted down from the bridge to Gordon Connell, the officer who was supposed to lead the boarding party, to dive into the sea immediately so that he could swim over to the U-boat. Connell obediently stripped off his clothes, but before he was ready, he was tapped on the shoulder by Tony Fasson. 'You're not going. You're married,' Fasson told Connell, and stripped off his own clothes.

In the excitement memories of what happened next have clouded over. Some of *Petard*'s crew have claimed subsequently that Fasson and Colin Grazier, an able seaman, jumped into the water and swam over to the U-boat. However none of the survivors actually saw them swimming. Thornton's official report states, more prosaically, that Fasson and Grazier 'jumped over from the bows' as *Petard*'s port bow floated alongside the U-boat's stern. This is backed up by the testimony of Ken Lacroix, the only surviving Englishman to have ventured inside *U-559*. Lacroix had been part of the team manning the Asdic set when *U-559*'s echo was first picked up earlier in the day. When the destroyer steamed up beside *U-559*, Fasson shouted, 'Come on, Lacroix, it's your sub!' Lacroix jumped onto *U-559* after Fasson and Grazier. As Lacroix leapt onto the U-boat, he heard Thornton bellowing at him through the loud-hailer to be sure to search the pockets of anyone he found. Fasson climbed down into the conning tower first, followed by Grazier. Lacroix was the third man to go down.

The three men were joined on the U-boat by Tommy Brown, a sixteen-year-old canteen assistant. Brown was also thought to have swum across to the U-boat. However at a subsequent enquiry, he stated: 'I got on board just forward of the whaler on the port side when the deck was level with the conning tower.' Tommy Brown went on to describe what was happening inside the U-boat:

> The lights were out. The First Lieutenant had a torch. The water was not very high but rising gradually all the time . . . First Lieutenant was down there with a machine gun . . . which he was using to smash open cabinets in the Commanding Officer's cabin. He then tried some keys which were hanging behind the door and opened a drawer, taking out some confidential books which he gave me. I placed them at the bottom of the hatch. After finding more books in cabinets and drawers I took another lot up . . .
>
> [Brown then climbed down into the U-boat again.]
>
> There was a hole just forward of the conning tower through which the water was pouring. As one went down through the conning tower compartment, one felt it pour down one's back. There was not enough coming through this hole to make what was on the deck . . . I went down below to the bottom of the ladder . . . First Lieutenant was trying to break some apparatus from the bulkhead in the control room. This apparatus was a small box about 18 inches long by one foot and nine inches deep. We got it away from the bulkhead but it was held fast by a number of wires which led into the bulkhead. We could not get it free so we gave up. The water was getting deeper and I told First Lieutenant that they were all shouting on deck. He gave me some more books from the cabin. I took these up on deck. This was my third trip . . .

Meanwhile, Connell and his boarding party had set off from *Petard* in a whaler. On the way two Germans were picked up. At first they were taken back onto the U-boat, but subsequently, they were forced to return to the whaler. One of them, Hermann Dethlefs is still alive. He remembers how as a nineteen-year-old he sat in the whaler with a wounded comrade cradled in his arms. He was horrified at seeing the codebooks being dumped into the boat, and considered making a do or die attempt to throw them into the sea. But he thought the better of it when he looked around and saw that he was being guarded by one of the boarding party with his gun at the ready.

From the top of the conning tower, Brown yelled over to Connell, who was still in the whaler, to tell him that there were two bodies lying by the hatch in the conning tower. One of the bodies appeared to be the commander of the U-boat, Brown said. He then told Connell that he was going down again to help Grazier and Fasson; they were trying to pass up what looked like a piece of radar equipment. But Connell, who had seen that the U-boat appeared to be sinking, shouted back that no-one was to go inside the U-boat again, and that Brown should call down to Fasson and Grazier to tell them to come up immediately.

Ken Lacroix was the last man to make it out of the conning tower. He had been trying to pass a box to the men outside when he felt some liquid trickling out of it onto his face. At first he feared that it was acid, then the moment of panic passed; it was only water. But as he climbed the ladder, a wave broke over the top of the conning tower, and he had to cling on to the ladder rungs to stop himself being washed down into the control room again. To get out he had to push his way through what felt like a wall of water. Brown was still waiting at the top. 'I saw Grazier, and then the First Lieutenant appeared at the bottom of the hatch,' Brown told the enquiry later. 'I shouted, "You had better come up" twice, and they had just started up when the submarine started to sink very quickly.'

Connell subsequently wrote a report describing the awful moment just before, and just after, the U-boat went down.

> The seas were breaking continuously over the remaining portion of the hull that remained visible, the conning tower, and water was pouring out through the shell holes. It was a crazy scene, brilliantly illuminated by the slowly circling destroyer that continued to try to give a lee to the stricken and now obviously sinking submarine. There were cries from drowning crew members, and a number still clung to the side of the whaler as we struggled to hold the sea-boat alongside the conning tower and at the same time keep afloat. As I was about to jump into the sea and clamber onto the tower, it quite suddenly disappeared, leaving nothing to be seen above the breaking waves. We yelled and called the names of our shipmates. Only Tommy responded, his head bobbing up almost alongside the sea-boat.

When Thornton saw the U-boat slipping under the waves, stern first, he instinctively gave the order to his crew to steam ahead, in a vain attempt to hold up the stern of the U-boat with the attached tow line, and give the men inside a last chance to get out. But he quickly realised that he was going to capsize the whaler, so he ordered his men to let the line go.

After Tommy Brown was hauled onto the whaler, the shocked boarding party crew asked him, 'What about the others?'

'There's no chance,' he gasped back. 'They were still down below when I dived off.'

Nevertheless the men in the whaler carried on calling their names, desperately hoping the two men would miraculously reappear. The search was only called off after *Petard* steamed up to the whaler, and hoisted the little boat on the run. *Petard* and HMS *Dulverton*, another destroyer, then set off for Haifa together.

On the way, Thornton warned his men not to breathe a word to anyone about the capture. Curiously, the message was not passed on to all the sailors on *Dulverton*. This led to a potentially dangerous incident in Haifa, where the German prisoners were landed. Two members of *Dulverton*'s crew went for a drink in a café where they were overheard talking about the capture by the police. The next day two officers came on board *Dulverton* to take the two crew members away to Cairo where the riot act was read to them.

The German prisoners who had watched the Enigma codebooks being captured presented another security risk. Dethlefs attempted to mention the boarding in a letter to his parents in Germany. 'The British came on board our U-boat, but all's going well,' he wrote, but the correspondence was intercepted and confiscated.

Ironically Hans Heidtmann, *U-559*'s commander, whose failure to destroy the U-boat's secret books had led to their capture, was awarded a Knight's Cross in April 1943, whereas Thornton, whose obsessive striving for perfection had led to the capture of the documents, was to be rewarded by having his command taken away from him within three months of *U-559*'s sinking.[18] William Prendergast, *Petard*'s surgeon, became increasingly alarmed at the way Thornton treated his men. Prendergast was also upset by Thornton's behaviour when another submarine, the Italian *Uarscieck*, was captured by *Petard* in December 1942. Thornton had seized a machine gun and mowed down a row of Italian submariners standing on the submarine's deck, even though the rest of *Petard*'s crew believed they were surrendering. A fine line had to be drawn between ruthlessly, but properly, shooting at submariners to stop them throwing confidential codebooks into the sea and cold bloodedly murdering defenceless men who were trying to surrender. Although there was always a risk that such men might make a run for the deck gun, Prendergast thought that Thornton had gone too far. So he notified the authorities that Thornton needed a rest.[19]

That is one possible reason for Thornton's sudden departure from *Petard*. A rumour going round the ship was that Thornton had broken down after he thought he could see rats running around on the floor in his cabin. Whatever the real reason, Thornton himself, when thanking his men for their help, blamed deteriorating eyesight for his having to abandon his ship prematurely.

The documents recovered from *U-559* turned out to be very important. They included the new version of the weather report codebook, referred to in chapter 19, which the codebreakers needed in order to create cribs. It is surprising, therefore, to discover that this book only reached Bletchley Park on 24 November, over three weeks after it was captured. The short weather codebook did not immediately lead to the four-wheel Naval Enigma being broken. It helped to produce cribs, but that was not sufficient for messages created on a four-wheel Enigma, unless there were lots of three-wheel bombes, or some of the faster four-wheel models.

The breakthrough only happened on 13 December 1942, thanks to another blunder by the Germans. When a message was finally broken, the codebreakers discovered that instead of using four-wheel settings for short signals, the Germans were still using three-wheel settings. The fourth wheel was always set to A, and its ring setting to Z, which meant that the four-wheel Enigma was being used as a three-wheel cipher machine; because of this, the cribs derived from short weather reports could be used to break the code on Bletchley Park's existing three-wheel bombes. The setting of the fourth wheel for messages other than short signals was then relatively simple to work out.[20]

The Bletchley Park codebreakers, who had to match up cipher text including a short weather report sent by a U-boat with a German meteorological broadcast, were helped by the procedure used by the Germans for requesting weather reports, and acknowledging their receipt. A typical request might state: 'Witzendorf to report weather between 0300 and 0600 tomorrow morning.' After the report was sent in by the U-boat commanded by Witzendorf, the acknowledgement might state: 'Short weather signal has been received from Witzendorf at 04.16 hours.' Armed with this information, it was relatively straightforward for the British cryptographers to identify the cipher text which included the weather report; it could then be used as the matching cipher text to be used in conjunction with the crib. Making sure that the correct weather report, broadcast in Germany, had been identified, was achieved by making sure that the longitude and latitude information broadcast matched up with the position of the U-boat in question, worked out with the aid of the Allies' direction finding equipment.[21]

When informed of the break, Sir Dudley Pound, the First Sea Lord, quickly sent Admiral Ernest King, the Commander-in-Chief of the American Atlantic Fleet, the following message on the evening of 13 December 1942: 'As the result of months of the most strenuous endeavour, a few days' U-boat traffic will be readable in the immediate future and this may lead to better results in the near future. You will, I am sure, appreciate the care necessary in making use of this information to prevent suspicion being aroused as to its source. We have found this especially difficult when action by routing authorities outside the Admiralty is required. It would be a tragedy if we had to start all over again on what would undoubtedly be a still more difficult problem.'[22]

Seven months after the *U-559*'s codebooks were handed in to Bletchley Park, King George VI handed out decorations to some of the seamen taking part in the capture. 'We're still not allowed to discuss this, are we?' the King said to Ken Lacroix, who was mentioned in despatches. 'No, it's still a secret,' Lacroix replied. 'Well, congratulations,' said the King, and shook Lacroix's hand.

The Turning Point

South of France, the Mediterranean and the Atlantic

NOVEMBER 1942–SEPTEMBER 1943

Seven days after the capture of the Enigma codebooks from *U-559*, an event occurred at Château des Fouzes in the south of France which threatened to reveal to the Germans that their cipher was compromised. On 6 November 1942 Gustave Bertrand's ablutions were interrupted by the sound of someone banging on the bathroom door. It was Gwido Langer, who had rushed to tell him that the château was about to be raided.[1] Bertrand ran to the window and looked out. A dark blue van and a black Citroën were moving slowly towards the château. On the van's roof there was a circular aerial; they were being checked out by German intelligence.

Although the French decryption centre was inside what was supposed to be unoccupied France, the codebreakers still had to hide what they were up to, since the German intelligence service was being allowed to operate inside the free zone. As the codebreakers inside the château scurried about frantically hiding all their radio equipment, lookouts watched three men get out of the car and walk to one of the two neighbouring farms. The men then walked over to the other farm. After that, they departed, but not before they had beaten the farmers with rubber truncheons. Bertrand, writing after the war, described what happened next: 'We waited, watching the horizon from behind the slats of the shutters – more dead than alive.'[2] Subsequently the van returned three times over the next twenty-four hours, but each time it departed without anyone attempting to enter the château.

Even before this lucky escape, Bertrand had decided that he and his team of codebreakers would have to leave Château des Fouzes. On 4 November he had returned from a trip to the Côte d'Azur, where he had been discussing evacuation plans with a member of the French Resistance, to find a message from London containing the words: 'The harvest is good'; it was the prearranged signal that the Allied invasion of North Africa was imminent. As he read it, Bertrand realised he had to evacuate the château even more quickly than he had anticipated; once the invasion took place, it was almost certain that the Germans would move into unoccupied France, thereby jeopardising the security of his Cadix codebreaking centre. Bertrand signalled back to London stating that he wanted to consult with the French Resistance in Paris, but before he set out, another message arrived, saying: 'The harvest is very good and now is not the time to go travelling.' On 8 November, Bertrand and his team of code-breakers heard on the radio the news that the Allies had landed in North Africa. By the morning of 9 November Château des Fouzes was empty; all the codebreakers had been evacuated. They departed just in time. On the morning of 12 November the Germans entered and occupied it.

Meanwhile, other problems, affecting the security of the Allies' Enigma secret, had to be dealt with in the south of France. The knowledge that the Germans might be moving into the free zone also raised the question: what should be done about Rodolphe Lemoine, the former French agent, who had run the Enigma spy, Hans Thilo Schmidt? Lemoine had been living in the Hôtel Splendid in Marseille since May 1941, as instructed by Paul Paillole, the head of French counter-espionage.[3] In June 1942 Lemoine informed the chief of the police in Marseille that he had been approached by a German agent and invited to work for the Germans in Paris. He wanted to ask Pail-lole whether he should comply with the request, so that he could work as a double agent. Paillole visited Marseilles to talk to Lemoine in person. But when Lemoine refused to help catch the German agent, Paillole became suspicious; he believed that Lemoine was keeping his options open so that he could later work for the Ger-mans. Paillole suggested that Lemoine should go to North Africa, but when Lemoine protested that he was too old to run away and that he did not want to abandon his children in France, Paillole relented. A compromise was reached eventually: Lemoine could go to Sail-lagousse, a small French village in the Pyrenees, as long as he agreed to slip over the nearby border into neutral Spain if the Germans took over the south of France. Lemoine duly packed his bags and moved with his wife to Saillagousse.

At the end of September 1942 Lemoine received a message from the porter at the Hôtel Splendid. An old friend, a Monsieur de Ry, wanted to see him. The two men met at the Hôtel Splendid the next day. De Ry explained that he had been offered an Italian codebook which might be of interest to the Germans. He wanted to know if Lemoine would help him conduct the sale. Lemoine agreed to do what he could. But the transaction enabled the Germans to find out where Lemoine was living. When he failed to leave France after the Germans moved into the free zone, he was as good as surrendering himself into their custody. His wife later claimed that they were about to flee across the border, but changed their minds after receiving a disturbing phone call from their son, Guy. From the way Guy spoke to them on the phone, it was obvious that he had been arrested by the Germans. They could not leave while he was in trouble.

On 15 November a German agent was told to tail Lemoine; he was to be arrested if he attempted to leave the country. From that moment the Germans watched Lemoine like hawks. He was presumably only allowed to carry on living in Saillagousse because it was hoped that he would lead them to other French intelligence agents. On 25 February 1943 Admiral Canaris, the head of the Abwehr, decided that he could not wait any longer. He gave the order that Lemoine was to be arrested immediately. Two days later Lemoine was surprised in his Saillagousse villa and sent to Paris to be interrogated.

Lemoine's arrest cast a long shadow over the Allies' Enigma secret. There was a serious risk he would tell the Germans everything he knew about Hans Thilo Schmidt. But at the time even Paillole was kept in the dark; he only found out about the arrest later. As a result, no special instructions could be circulated to ensure that Enigma was used carefully for a while.

*

The British and Americans were still pursuing a risky strategy at sea, insofar as the security of their Enigma secret was concerned. The next capture of Enigma codebooks highlighted the risks they were running. It happened on the morning of 17 February 1943, just days before Lemoine's arrest. At about 9 a.m. Friedrich Bürgel, the commander of *U-205*, spotted a small convoy off Derna, on the Libyan coast.[4] The convoy, just three merchant ships escorted by four destroyers, was on its way from Tripoli to Alexandria in Egypt. When Bürgel saw the convoy approaching, he decided to dive down to about fifty metres on its port side. He planned to let the destroyer nearest to him steam past; then he intended to come up to periscope depth so that he could torpedo the merchant ships. But rather than zig-zagging away from *U-205*, HMS *Paladin*, the destroyer in front of the convoy, steamed over to where the German submarine was lurking after a promising echo appeared on her Asdic set. Bürgel only realised that he had miscalculated when he heard the rumble of the destroyer's screws passing overhead. Then at about 10.40 a.m. (according to Double Summer Time, i.e. GMT + 2 hours) depth charges exploded in the water above him and the lights in the U-boat were extinguished. In the darkness, Bürgel experienced a most unpleasant sensation. It was as if he was stuck in a lift which was descending too fast. His discomfort and sense of disorientation were exacerbated by a whiff of chlorine which went up his nose and made his eyes stream. All around him men were choking on the toxic fumes.

It was only when the emergency lights came on that he collected his thoughts and understood what was happening. A report from the stern told him water was leaking into the engine room; the extra weight in the stern was unbalancing the boat. He and Horst Georgy, his twenty-one-year-old leading engineer, huddled over the specially designed depth meter which he had insisted on having installed in *U-205*; it was made to withstand the vibrations caused by the heavy machinery in power plants and did not break like the standard depth meters fitted into Germany's U-boats, when depth charges went off nearby. The two men watched transfixed as the hand on the depth meter dial crept up. When it indicated that they had fallen to about 200 metres, Bürgel quietly asked Georgy, 'Can you stabilise the boat?' 'I can't,' Georgy replied, 'and we're still falling.' Then a moment later, he added, 'You must take us up to the surface now, or it'll be too late.' Bürgel told Georgy to blow the water out of the U-boat's tanks. But the depth meter dial kept on going round – 230 metres, 240 metres and still it went round. When it reached 250, Bürgel knew it could not go any further, however far the U-boat fell.

As the needle went round, both men began to come to terms with the idea that they were going to die. Even today Georgy remembers imagining that he was in his mother's bedroom in Berlin looking at the photo of himself which she kept on her dressing table. He wondered what she would say when she learned that she would never see him again. However, just as both men were beginning to give up hope, they saw that the hand on the depth meter was beginning to rotate in the opposite direction. They were going up to the surface after all. At first the hand moved very slowly, then it went a little faster, and finally, as they approached the surface, it whizzed around as the U-boat popped up out of the water like a cork.

Bürgel quickly unfastened the conning tower hatch and looked out. It was a hopeless situation. HMS *Paladin* and another ship were shooting at the U-boat's conning tower, and an aircraft was swooping down towards him overhead. He decided to abandon ship. But as *U-205*'s crew climbed out of the conning tower, the escape procedure began to go badly wrong. Without telling Bürgel, a member of his engine room crew had pushed back the throttle, a move which may have been intended to make the U-boat harder to shoot at as the men escaped. Unfortunately for Bürgel, it may also have sabotaged his attempt to sink *U-205*.

Bürgel and Georgy remember opening up the diving tank vents, an act which should have sunk the U-boat within minutes. They then followed their men into the sea. While Bürgel was struggling to stay afloat, he took his eye off the U-boat for a while. He and his men were buffeted by high waves, and were terrorised by the depth charges dropped by the aircraft amongst the submariners swimming in the water; all the men swimming near the U-boat, where the depth charges were dropped, were killed instantaneously. Bürgel breathed a sigh of relief when he was picked up by one of the warships, but what he saw as he stepped on deck horrified him. The U-boat was still afloat.

While the Germans were jumping off the U-boat, *Paladin*'s twenty-seven foot motorboat was being lowered into the sea. After rescuing the submariners in the water, it chased after *U-205* which was still motoring along at about 7 knots. That made it very difficult to board. However Ron Maflin, the officer in charge of the boarding party, eventually solved the problem by placing his boat in front of the U-boat and allowing it to run gently into them. Then while the *U-205* was pushing the motorboat along two of Maflin's crew simply stepped on board.

One of the boarders, a man named Sidney Constable, immediately climbed down inside the U-boat to retrieve the codebooks. It was a brave act since he knew what had happened to Fasson and Grazier inside *U-559* three months earlier. 'On descending he found the "Boat" in almost complete darkness,' wrote *Paladin*'s commander, Lawrence Rich, in his official report. Constable made for the captain's cabin where he hoped to find some codebooks. He found them in a small cupboard. Other books were discovered in the control room. 'A very large number of books were recovered,' wrote Commander

Rich. Afterwards another ship, HMS *Gloxinia*, attempted to tow the U-boat into a nearby bay at Ras el Hillal, a risky act insofar as the security of Enigma intelligence was concerned, given that other U-boats could have been watching. However, shortly before 5 p.m. *U-205* sank in the bay before it could be beached.

The Enigma documents recovered by the boarding party included a set of the Naval Enigma bigram tables, and the U-boat's short signal book. Both documents had already been captured; the bigram tables during Operations Archery and Anklet in December 1941, and the short signal codebook from *U-559*.[5] If the British codebreakers had been breaking the Shark Naval Enigma cipher without interruptions, this might have prompted the Admiralty to consider calling off any more attempted captures until more codebooks were needed. However by the time the codebooks were delivered to Bletchley Park on 21 March 1943, GC&CS was just recovering from yet another codebreaking black out, which had come less than three months after Shark was broken.

The black out had started on 10 March 1943. It was the result of the Germans bringing in a new short weather report codebook. At a stroke, this starved the Bletchley Park codebreakers of the cribs they had been using since mid-December 1942 to break Shark. John Edelsten, the Admiralty's Assistant Chief of Staff for Trade, passed the bad news to Sir Dudley Pound, the First Sea Lord: 'The foreseen has come to pass,' wrote Edelsten, 'DNI [the Director of Naval Intelligence] reported on March 8th that the Tracking Room will be "blinded" in regard to U-boat movements, for some considerable period, perhaps extending to months.' Pound, in his turn, informed Admiral Henry Moore, the Vice-Chief of Staff, who was in Washington: 'U-boat Special Intelligence has received a severe setback. After 10th March it is unlikely that we shall obtain . . . more than 2 to 3 pairs of days per month and these will not be current . . . After 2 to 3 months the situation should improve considerably.'[6]

Within days of the black out commencing, another disaster, similar in scale to the PQ17 catastrophe, developed at sea, this time in the Atlantic. Deprived of the intelligence which had helped the Admiralty to divert convoys away from the wolf packs, the OIC's U-boat tracking room was all of a sudden unable to pinpoint the positions taken up by Dönitz's lines of U-boats. SC122, a fifty-ship eastbound convoy bound for Iceland and the British Isles, was nevertheless diverted around a line of U-boats south of Greenland on 12 March; a message transmitted by one of the U-boats gave away its position. Direction-finding, rather than Enigma intelligence was used to guesstimate the danger area. However, helped by reading the Allied Cipher Number 3, used by the convoy escorts, the German U-boats discovered another convoy, the thirty-eight-ship Halifax (HX)229, which was sailing about 100 miles behind SC122. A terrifying wolf pack attack ensued, as Dönitz ordered the thirty-eight U-boats in the North Atlantic to converge on the routes taken by the two convoys.

The human suffering caused by these attacks was terrible, as merchant ship after merchant ship was sunk by the pursuing U-boats' torpedoes. This was especially the case on board the British refrigerator ship *Canadian Star*, sailing in convoy HX229; she had civilian passengers on board when she was torpedoed. The women and children were ushered into the lifeboats first. A Royal Artillery colonel watched patiently as his wife and young son were seated in one lifeboat. Then, to his horror, he saw a seaman, who was supposed to be holding onto the lifeboat as it swung above the sea, lose his grip after a sudden lurch. The lifeboat tipped up and fell into the sea; all its occupants were swept away.[7]

After that most of the other survivors had to make do with wooden life rafts. Twenty men made it to one raft designed for ten men. Some of them had to cling onto the side. One of the nine survivors described what happened to them: 'We lost six of these fairly quickly; you would see them getting cold, a certain look came into their eyes and then they just gave up. The army officer who had seen his wife and child drown was the first to go . . . Only nine of us were eventually picked up.'[8]

Some of the men still on board *Canadian Star* preferred to die without a struggle. One man, the fifty-eight-year-old ship's carpenter, called out to an officer, 'Goodbye, sir. It was a good life while it lasted.' Then, according to one witness, he waved and calmly 'walked right into the path of a wave pounding across the after deck. It was like a minnow being swallowed by a whale.'[9]

All over the ocean similar tragedies were unfolding. One man picked up by a passing escort ship was discovered holding onto a raft with one hand, and onto another man with the other. 'As they drifted alongside we could see the one he was holding was dead,' said an observer. 'His head was leaning back . . . his mouth and eyes were open and, as each wave broke over him, his eyes and mouth would not move.'[10]

Finding a raft to hold onto or to sit on was no guarantee you would survive. The sea was very rough when the U-boats struck. The rafts teetered perilously on the crest of the towering waves. Each wave threatened to hurl more of the petrified passengers into the foamy sea. Nevertheless, even amidst all the terror and the discomfort, some survivors managed to keep each other's spirits up with a mixture of British stiff upper lip and bravado. One observer on a rescue ship who was astonished at the courage shown wrote the following description: 'As the raft got closer we thought we could hear these poor, soaked U-boat victims shouting or crying for help until we could hear, borne down to us on the howling gale, the voices were lustily singing, "She's a lassie from Lancashire, just a lassie from Lancashire." We didn't know whether to laugh or cry.'[11]

Survivors found by the convoy escorts were often too weak to make it up the scrambling nets flung over the ships' sides. One witness on the corvette *Anemone* remembers seeing 'a very pretty girl with long hair; she grabbed the net but slipped back. A sailor, with split-second timing, leant over, grabbed her hair and swung her right up and onto *Anemone*'s deck.'[12]

Some of the men who could not make it onto one of the rafts had to make do with waterlogged lifeboats. One boat had capsized, but those men who were not drowned managed to turn it over again. Third-Officer Keyworth described the hellish circumstances as he sat in the boat: 'It was useless to bale; the sea just swept through the boat from end to end. I could see the men, one by one, their eyes glazing and eventually losing their grip and being washed up and down the boat and eventually out of it altogether. Then I started to get a feeling of cosiness, ready to relax just as though I had come in and sat by a warm fire and just couldn't keep awake.' As his mind wandered, he saw a postman walking down the path leading to his mother's house in Wellington, New Zealand. In the postman's hand was a letter telling her he had been lost at sea. The thought so distressed him that he woke up. When he was eventually rescued by the corvette *Anemone*, he heard someone shout, 'Stretcher! His legs have gone.' His legs were so numb, he thought they really had fallen off. It was only when he looked down and saw his sea boots were still there, that he knew he was still in one piece.[13]

Thirty of the eighty-seven passengers on *Canadian Star* perished. It was just one of the thirteen ships from HX229 which were sunk between 15–18 March 1943. More murderous attacks on SC122 between 16–18 March accounted for another nine ships. Three hundred and sixty men, women and children lost their lives during the U-boat attacks out of 1494 crew and passengers being carried on the lost ships.[14] The U-boats were only beaten off after very long-range aircraft flew out from Iceland to provide anti-submarine cover.

Although a series of factors, which could be rectified for future convoys, exacerbated the scale of the disaster – for example, the two convoys had been routed too close together and had been very thinly escorted – these and other losses during March 1943 terrified the Admiralty. During March 627,000 tons of merchant shipping were sunk by U-boats.[15] An Admiralty report made at the end of 1943 included the admission that:

> Up to the 20th March, 1943, there seemed real danger that the enemy would achieve his aim of severing the routes which united Great Britain with the North American continent . . . up to the 20th March . . . it appeared possible that we should not be able to continue convoy as an effective system of defence against the enemy's pack tactics . . . In the first twenty days of March over 500,000 tons of shipping were lost, and for the month the proportion of tonnage sunk in convoy rose to 68 per cent, the highest point in the war. The enemy had by this time over 100 U-Boats at sea, and made his effort at a time when we had so many escort vessels under repair as a result of damage by storm, that the group system, laboriously built up over so long a period, was in some danger of complete disorganization. Evasive routeing was becoming more and more ineffective in face of the great increase in the numbers of U-Boats kept at sea . . . The import programme for the United Kingdom was cut as low as it could be, and even then seemed hardly likely to be fulfilled.[16]

On 19 March, however, the codebreakers in Bletchley Park's Naval Enigma section, which by this time consisted of ten senior cryptographers and their 115 support staff, broke back into Shark again.[17] They did so by exploiting their possession of the U-boats' short signal codebook, captured from *U-559* and *U-205*. This permitted them to utilise a new method of creating cribs which could be used in conjunction with the bombes. It worked as follows: typically a U-boat commander might want to report a convoy's position, its course and might wish to name his U-boat. In order to shorten his message, and therefore make it harder for the Allies to use their direction-finding techniques which might give away his position, he would use the short signal codebook. The message 'Convoy sighted, in Grid square BE4131, going south, signed U-276' would be reduced to:

'CKSA': Convoy sighted
'KBXO MBGV': the position mentioned above

'QQYY': going south
'OJ': U-276.[18]

This code would in its turn be enciphered on the Enigma, and the resulting cipher text was what would be placed in front of the Bletchley Park codebreakers.

When a short message was intercepted, the Naval Section at Bletchley Park would collate all the evidence available in order to guess what the U-boat commander was trying to say. Direction-finding and reports from the convoy itself helped to identify the position, course and speed of the convoy. For example, if another message had been decoded the previous day, and if it asked for particular information, that also gave a clue as to what the short message the next day was saying. Because the codebreakers also had the short signal codebook, they could translate the information about where the convoy was sighted and its course into the short code. This would be the crib, with the letters in the short code matched up with the cipher text. It was cribs such as these which enabled Shark to be broken on the bombes, a task which along with the creation of the bombe menu, typically took between twenty-four and seventy-two hours during the first half of 1943.[19]

On 19 March 1943 Sir Stewart Menzies wrote to Winston Churchill: 'We have been successful in reading the U-Boat Keys for the 16th, 17th and 18th instants. The code which I use for the U-Boat Keys is "Shark".' Churchill scrawled the following note at the bottom of Menzies' letter: 'Congratulate yr splendid hens', and sent it back to Menzies.[20]

Shortly before the 10 March black out on Shark, Bletchley Park's codebreakers also suffered a reverse in connection with the Dolphin net. On 1 March 1943, the bigram tables were changed again, thereby rendering Banburismus impossible. However, by this time, Bletchley Park had access to seventy bombes, more than enough to break the Dolphin settings using the crib and bombe method. In the process of reading the Dolphin messages in this way, the new bigram tables were reconstructed within about three weeks.[21]

Ironically just as the Bletchley Park codebreakers succeeded in mastering a new way into Shark, the Enigma decrypts were found to be less useful than they had been two months previously. Until March 1943 Enigma decrypts were primarily used defensively, so that convoys could be diverted away from the waiting wolf packs. By the end of March there were so many U-boats in the North Atlantic that, even when Enigma decrypts revealed the whereabouts of one line of U-boats, there was often another waiting in the wings ready to stand in on any diverted route. So the convoys had to fight their way through the wolf packs, using the large number of extra warships and aircraft which were made available for the purpose.

It was in these circumstances that Admiral King, by now the Commander-in-Chief of the US Navy, tried to convince the British that it was time to use Enigma offensively, particularly against German U-tankers, which could extend the length of the U-boats' patrols by refuelling them at sea. King's proposals were strongly opposed by Sir Dudley Pound, the First Sea Lord, on the grounds that the aggressive use of Enigma would compromise its source. He sent a cable back to America saying: 'We should not risk what is so invaluable to us.' In another cable he continued on the same theme: 'If our Z [Enigma] information failed us at the present time it would, I am sure, result in our shipping losses going up by anything from 50 to 100%.'[22] King's response was equally persuasive: 'While I am equally concerned with you as to security of Zebra information it is my belief that we are not deriving from it fullest value. The refueling submarine is the key to high speed, long range U-boat operations. To deprive the enemy of refuelers would at once decrease the effectiveness and radius of entire U-boat deployment. With careful preparations it seems not unlikely that their destruction might be accomplished without trace. While there is a risk of compromise it would be a matter of lasting regret if Zebra security were jeopardised in some less worthy cause.'[23]

The reason why Pound was anxious not to compromise the Naval Enigma was that it still had an important tactical role to play. It gave Pound information about improvements being made to the U-boats and their torpedoes, and it revealed their attacking strategies.[24] When the time came for the Allies to invade Europe, it would also help them to transport their troops to France safely without having to be afraid they would be attacked by U-boats. There was also the additional point that if the Germans realised that Naval Enigma was compromised, the Air Force and Army Enigma intelligence might be jeopardised as well. That was to be avoided at all costs. While the benefits of using Naval Enigma may have diminished, Army and Air Force Enigma had recently proved to be an important asset. In March 1943, solely thanks to Enigma decrypts, Montgomery was able to reinforce a poorly defended area at Medinine, in Tunisia, in time to ward off a fierce assault by Rommel.[25] The German Army was defeated so comprehensively that their Enigma messages revealed that they were suspicious their ciphers had been compromised. Montgomery was rebuked for not making more effort to disguise the source of his intelligence.

In the short term the Allies' ability to obtain Enigma intelligence about the U-boats, combined with the new forces which were thrown into the fray against the wolf packs, proved too much for the Germans. After March 1943 all the improvements made by the Allies to their anti-submarine capabilities came to fruition simultaneously. Not only were surface escorts made available which had been previously tied up with the invasion of Tunisia, but they were now equipped with mobile direction-finding equipment and more effective centimetric radar which could not be identified by the U-boats' existing search receivers. With this equipment the Allied warships might have been able to stand up to the U-boats on their own. But they were supported by aircraft, also equipped with the new radar, some flying from the escort aircraft carriers which were beginning to accompany the convoys, and some, with very long ranges, being based on land. Thus convoys had constant support from the air; no longer was there a so-called 'air gap' south of Greenland, on the transatlantic routes.

In May 1943 the U-boats were checked comprehensively for the first time. The tonnage sunk by U-boats dropped to 264,000 tons, compared with over 600,000 tons in March 1943. But it was Dönitz's estimate that thirty-one U-boats had been sunk which convinced him that the Battle of the Atlantic had to be suspended.[26] 'Radar, and particularly radar location by aircraft, had to all practical purposes robbed the U-boats of their power to fight on the surface,' Dönitz wrote after the war. 'Wolf-pack operations against convoys in the North Atlantic, the main theatre of operations and at the same time the theatre in which air cover was the strongest, were no longer possible. They could only be resumed if we succeeded in radically increasing the fighting power of the U-boats ... I accordingly withdrew the boats from the North Atlantic. On May 24 I ordered them to proceed, using the utmost caution, to the area south-west of the Azores. We had lost the Battle of the Atlantic.[27]

The decision which was broadcast to all the U-boat commanders on 24 May represented a dramatic reversal of fortune compared with the situation which had prevailed just two months earlier. The victory was underlined on 21 September 1943 when Churchill revealed to loud cheers in the House of Commons that: 'for the four months which ended on 18th September no merchant vessel was sunk by enemy action in the North Atlantic'. The Allies at last were on the road to victory.

Trapped

South of France

NOVEMBER 1942—MARCH 1943

After Gustave Bertrand and his codebreakers' narrow escape from Château des Fouzes in November 1942, it was important that they were all evacuated from France immediately. But four months after the Germans moved in, men such as Gwido Langer and Maksymilian Ciężki, who knew everything about the Allies' Enigma secret, were still there. One factor which may have contributed to this long delay was a growing rift between Bertrand and the Poles; the delay certainly exacerbated the rift.

The main problem was that Bertrand did not get on with Gwido Langer. The enmity went back to what had occurred before the war; Langer had undermined Bertrand's authority within the Deuxième Bureau by not disclosing that Rejewski had broken the Enigma cipher for more than six years. After the war commenced, Langer and Ciężki further blotted their copybooks in Bertrand's eyes by setting up a radio link with the Polish authorities in exile behind his back. Swiss Enigma messages intercepted in France, and decoded at the Château des Fouzes were passed down this line, once again without Bertrand's consent. Bertrand also objected to Langer and Ciężki's heavy drinking habits. After leaving the Château des Fouzes, Langer went on a drunken binge once too often. The police began to ask questions about who he was, until Bertrand used his influence within the French Resistance to smooth things over.[1] Langer for his part was upset when Bertrand, after becoming frustrated at the British failure to supply him with Enigma settings, talked about handing the Enigma secret on to another, more appreciative, country. As Langer pointed out, it was not Bertrand's secret to give away; the break into Enigma had been produced by Rejewski, a Pole. Bertrand only backed down after Langer dissuaded him from acting rashly.[2]

Their growing irritation with each other was brought to a head by Bertrand and his friends' chaotic attempts to evacuate the Poles from France.[3] The first bone of contention materialised even before the Poles were spirited away from the Château des Fouzes. In October 1942 Langer had wanted to flee, with his Polish codebreakers, to North Africa. However Bertrand had refused to let them go, citing the likelihood that the people in North Africa would turn on the Allies when they attempted to land there, thereby making it a dangerous place for the codebreakers to be. It turned out that Bertrand was incorrect and later, after the Allies' Operation Torch landings were a success, Langer could not resist rubbing in the fact that Bertrand had misread the situation. Subsequently Langer also blamed Bertrand for missing another golden opportunity to evacuate the Poles safely. In November 1942 the Poles were offered the chance to be picked up from one of the tiny islands off the south of France coast. However Bertrand refused to help until he had checked with his superiors. By the time he had their consent it was too late; the occupying forces had already banned the movement of motorboats between the mainland and the islands.

This was to be the first in a long line of missed opportunities and abortive evacuation plans. Langer accused Bertrand of being slapdash and reckless about the way these plans were hatched. Langer's feeling that he and his men were not being treated properly was heightened by the announcement that Bertrand was not going to take part in the evacuation himself. Consequently, there was no incentive for him to make sure that the escape plans were viable. Bertrand for his part complained about Langer's failure to support the plans; because of this it was not surprising they never came to fruition, Bertrand said.

One such plan, codenamed 'Cricket', envisaged the thirteen men and one pregnant woman in Bertrand's team being picked up by a boat on 3 or 4 December 1942 from a deserted spot near Le Trayas which is close to Cannes on the French coast. The password from the boat was to be 'Where is the fish?' and the Poles were supposed to reply, 'In the frying pan.' However the plan had to be abandoned by the French Resistance, because of the changing conditions on the ground; when a recce was carried out on the day before Operation Cricket, it was found that the narrow bay where the Poles were supposed to be picked up was already being guarded by Italian forces. Langer understandably refused to revive the plan in the same place for Christmas Day 1942. This, presumably, was one of the acts which led Bertrand to accuse him of being obstructive.

With the pressure building up from the Polish government in exile to set up the evacuation by sea from another spot on the coast, Langer and his Polish codebreakers and intelligence officers had the first of many close shaves. Another spot on the French coast, at Cros-de-Cagnes, near Nice, was chosen because it was not guarded by Italian troops at various times each day. But the Resistance agent who was supposed to orchestrate the plan was arrested on 26 December, thereby preventing the codebreakers making it to Cros-de-Cagnes on the night for which the evacuation was scheduled. That saved the Poles; one man who did turn up at Cros-de-Cagnes that night was ambushed and arrested. After this débâcle, Bertrand suggested the Poles should be taken out of France through Switzerland. But just before the expedition, scheduled to take place at the end of December, was due to start, it too was aborted because the Swiss officials, who were supposed to help them surmount the strict immigration rules, did not receive the tip off that their assistance was required in time.

The failure of this plan prompted Bertrand to try to evacuate the Poles through Spain, even though Biffy Dunderdale, his contact in London, had advised against it. On 29 December 1942 Bertrand sent the following desperate message to Dunderdale: '. . . We cannot carry on with the Swiss project, because it is apparently impossible to get out of Switzerland afterwards . . . All we have left is the Spanish option which we are going to try. Can you tell your representative in Barcelona to help Langer and his team as soon as they get to him . . . The danger here is growing every day and we must act quickly . . .'

The plan Bertrand and his contacts came up with was very simple, in theory. All the Polish codebreakers would go to Toulouse where they would make contact with a member of the French Resistance. The agent would take them to Perpignan, where they would be introduced to the organisation which would handle their evacuation. Langer, Ciężki and Edward Fokczyński (one of the AVA partners) would be in the first group to go over the mountains to Spain. Rejewski, Zygalski and Kazimierz Gaca, another codebreaker, would follow two days later. Henryk Paszkowski, another member of Langer's team, and his pregnant wife, had decided at the last minute that it would be too dangerous for her to attempt to accompany them; on the night before they left the Côte d'Azur, she had experienced such terrible contractions that a doctor had to give her medicine to delay her baby's birth.

Unfortunately, the plan was poorly executed from the start. The Poles' hearts fell when, after being installed in the attics of some dilapidated cottages in Toulouse on 12 January 1943, they were not given any food; no one had thought to organise it for them. When Langer's group was taken to Perpignan on 13 January, they were told that they would set off for Spain immediately after arriving at Perpignan, following a second breakfast. However, the head of the evacuation organisation at Perpignan, subsequently told them that they would have to hang around until the second group arrived from Toulouse. Next day the second group arrived. But instead of consisting of Rejewski, Zygalski and Gaca, as planned, Rejewski and Zygalski had remained in Toulouse and they had been replaced by Paszkowski and his wife. Langer asked how they could contemplate risking the life of a woman who had been in such distress the night before. He was only silenced when Paszkowski's wife said she should be allowed to take whatever risks she wanted.

The two groups set off together at 8 a.m. on 15 January. They were to take the bus to Arles-sur-Tech, before walking to the Spanish border over the mountains. However, shortly after setting out, a French policeman stopped the bus and, after looking at Langer's identity card, asked him to get out and wait for him on the roadside. Four of the other Poles were told to follow suit, and only Paszkowski and his wife were allowed to remain on the bus. The guide accompanying them also escaped. It was while talking to the gendarmes back at the police station that Langer was told that the evacuating organisation had not bothered to warn the police that they were taking important clients over the border; when such warnings were given, the police were only too willing to look the other way. By the time the arrest had taken place, and the court was informed, it was too late to sidestep the rules. So Langer and his three colleagues were sentenced to spend one month in prison in Perpignan for having attempted to cross the border with false identity cards.

While Langer and his men languished in prison, Rejewski and Zygalski made their first attempt to escape from Perpignan to Spain. However the precautions which had been made for them were even worse than those for Langer's group. Their guide did not even turn up on the day scheduled for their departure, so they were forced to go back into hiding again in Toulouse.[4] A few days later, assisted by the French Resistance, Rejewski and Zygalski made their second attempt to leave the country. They were told to travel by train to Aix-les-Thermes, several kilometres west of Perpignan. As they stepped out onto the platform, they were greeted by two young women, who ran up and kissed them as if they were old friends; this was an act designed to fool the Germans who had instructions to arrest any refugees trying to cross the border a few kilometres away. After a few days, the two codebreakers met up with the smuggler who was supposed to escort them across the border. He told them to take the train to the last stop before the border at Latour de Carol, where they were to get out and hide in the bushes until he arrived.

It was dusk before he found them, but after supper, and a few hours sleep, they began their assault on the Pyrenees; it was 29 January 1943. Their long walk through the inhospitable mountain terrain began well enough, but by midnight, their guide had begun to complain that he had not been paid for what he was doing. Eventually he asked the codebreakers for money and, when they at first demurred, he brandished his pistol and began playing with the trigger. He had timed his request perfectly. Rejewski and Zygalski had no idea where they were, so if they had attacked their blackmailer, they would have been lost. They reluctantly handed over the rest of their money. They eventually made it to Spain and relative safety; once there, they were thrown into jail where they stayed until they were allowed out on 4 May 1943. Two months later they travelled via Portugal to England.

Antoni Palluth, the Polish codebreaker and engineer who had, with Fokczyński, made the Enigma replicas which were used to break the code before the war, was less fortunate. On 12 February 1943, Bertrand received the following message signed by 'Lenoir', Palluth's codename. It stated: 'Je suis malade apres avoir manger des conserves des haricots verts.' (I am ill after having eaten some tinned green beans.) This coded message, written in invisible ink, told Bertrand that Palluth had been captured by the Germans, who were commonly known as 'haricots verts'.[5]

Langer and his group, cut off as they were from Bertrand, never heard about Rejewski's and Zygalski's success, or Palluth's capture. They had to press on independently with their own attempt to escape without knowing where to turn for reliable advice. It was an appalling situation, given what they knew about Enigma, one of the Allies' most important secrets. They decided to have nothing more to do with Monsieur Perez, the head of the evacuation organisation which had botched their first abortive expedition to Spain. Nor did they want to rely on Perez' agent, a Monsieur Gomez, who, according to the friendly police superintendent in Perpignan, was suspected of collaborating with the Nazis; when he was stopped by the police, he was seen to have in his possession a document giving him the right to go into the frontier zone, an area which was out of bounds to people who had not received special permission from the Nazis.

On 12 March 1943 Langer and his group made their next attempt to cross the border. This time, they were accompanied by another man recommended by the police superintendent. However, no sooner had they entered the train at Toulouse, which was to take them to Port-Vendres, the first leg of their journey to the Spanish border, than one of the guide's helpers came running through the train to warn them that the Gestapo were about to check everyone's identity cards. They were moving along the train in an effort to escape when Langer was tapped on the elbow; it was Ciężki telling him to get off the train quickly. He had seen two Gestapo agents inspecting identity cards in the next carriage. As they left the platform, they saw one of the men who worked with Gomez, and this led them to wonder whether the search by the Gestapo had something to do with the fact that they were not using Gomez as their guide.

It was easy to see why Langer and his colleagues began to grow desperate, clutching at straws which, even a few days earlier, they would not have looked at twice. In spite of what had happened, they decided to use the same guide the next day to take them to the border; this time they planned to take a taxi to Port-Vendres, rather than the train. But at about 10 a.m., before they were due to depart, they were visited by the agent who had first taken them from Toulouse to Perpignan to meet Perez. Although they had decided against using the organisation he had recommended, they were grateful when he himself offered to help. He promised to lay on a lorry belonging to the police which would enable them, and the guide they had chosen, to avoid being searched by German soldiers at the border. Then he asked Langer to sign a twenty franc note which he tore in half; he took one half, and told Langer to give the second piece to the guide once they reached the border. The idea was that the guide would only be paid if he presented Langer's half of the note to Bertrand.

But the simple plan quickly began to go wrong. After going off to fix up the police lorry, the agent who had first introduced Langer's group to Perez, returned at around 2.30 p.m. and told them that Gomez would have to act as their guide after all. Also their route was to be changed. They must go via Elne, rather than Port-Vendres. Langer protested that he did not trust Gomez. But somehow the agent succeeded in persuading him that there was nothing to fear. So it was that Langer reluctantly, and against his better judgement, perhaps fearing a repetition of the drama on the train if he chose another guide, and certainly fearing that Bertrand would blame him if the arrangement was cancelled, agreed to accept Gomez.

However even Langer had his limits. At 4 p.m. that same day, Perez appeared on the scene again, supposedly to introduce Langer to the two other men who were to be escorted over the border with them. Perez announced that there was to be no police lorry, and the other two men would not be going with them. At this, Langer put his foot down. He told Perez that if, when he returned at 6 p.m. that night, it was not agreed that the lorry would be laid on and that the other two men were going with them, the deal would be off, and they would make other arrangements. This ultimatum appeared to do the trick, for when at 6 p.m. they returned to meet up with Perez again, Langer's demands had been met. Langer was told to be ready to depart in one hour's time.

They set out at 7 p.m., and met up with Gomez at Elne. He introduced them to his guide, and then kissed all of them goodbye. However the expedition which had started so inauspiciously was to end in disaster. They had only gone about three kilometres when they were surprised by a group of Germans riding motorbikes. The Germans surrounded them, shooting their guns into the air. There was no opportunity to make a run for it; their last chance to escape was gone.

For some time after Langer and his team's capture, neither Bertrand nor Paul Paillole, the head of French Counter-Intelligence, knew what had become of them. Bertrand at first thought they had made it to Spain; when he was handed Langer's half of the twenty franc note, he immediately handed over the amount of money which had been agreed for the evacuation. The news that Langer's group and Palluth had been captured only filtered through to Paillole and to Sir Stewart Menzies, the head of the British Secret Intelligence Service, a month later.[6] At the same time, Bertrand confirmed that Lemoine had also been arrested.

23

The Arrest

Berlin

MARCH–SEPTEMBER 1943

Just four days after Langer and his group of codebreakers were arrested in the Pyrenees, the security of the Allies' Enigma secret was further jeopardised by events taking place in Paris. Although Rodolphe Lemoine, who was under house arrest at the Hôtel Continental in Paris, had at first said nothing about the Enigma, on 17 March 1943 he decided at last to speak out.[1] For four days, he explained how he had met up with Hans Thilo Schmidt, how the Enigma manuals had been handed over, and how Schmidt had also passed other valuable information to the Deuxième Bureau: reports about Germany's rearmament plans, documents which his brother, General Rudolf Schmidt, had shown him and details about enquiries inside the Abwehr. Nothing was hidden.

Included in Lemoine's confession, which he signed on 20 March 1943, was the following statement about Hans Thilo Schmidt: 'His work for the Deuxième Bureau lasted for about ten years. He left the Cipher Office two years before the war . . . I tried to get him to convert his brother to our cause. He said that was impossible. If his brother had had the slightest suspicion about what he was doing, he would have had him shot immediately . . . His wife did not know about him working for the Deuxième Bureau. Schmidt was always short of money. I have the impression that our payments to him were not enough during the last few years. He must have got in touch with another country. That is why I believe this man is very dangerous.'[2] It was this statement which persuaded Admiral Canaris, head of the Abwehr, that Schmidt had to be arrested.

While Lemoine was making his confession, Schmidt was moving into a new flat in Berlin. Although he and his wife's main residence was in Templin, north of Berlin, where he was in charge of one of the regional branches of the Air Ministry's Forschungsamt, he wanted to have a base in Berlin where he could stay when he was in town. Gisela, his twenty-one-year-old daughter, had told him about the flat. She was studying in Berlin, and her boyfriend Bruno, a medical student, had just vacated it on being called up to serve in the Army.

Gisela had arranged to meet her father at the flat on 1 April 1943. But when she arrived, she was accosted by the landlady with tears running down her cheeks. Gisela's father had been arrested, she said. The Gestapo had ransacked the flat. Even the mattress had been cut open.[3] Gisela hurried across Berlin to the Gestapo's headquarters to see if there was anything she could do to help her father. The officials there told her that Hans Thilo Schmidt had no daughter. But when she produced her identity card, she was taken into an office and asked to sit down. Herr Langemach, a Gestapo employee dressed in civilian clothes, advised her what she should do before taking her to see the uniformed Gestapo officers dealing with her father's case. 'Be careful,' he said kindly. 'Don't talk too much about what has happened. You should know that if you go to see your father, it could be very dangerous for you, too.' After she had talked to the men in uniform, she was shown out into the street. They had not told her much; only that some documents implicating her father had been found in France. She immediately thought of the little black envelope which she and her brother had found on her father's desk when they were young. Perhaps that had had something to do with it.

With nowhere else to turn, she telephoned her brother. They agreed she should come to his home in Halle, near Leipzig, so that they could console each other, and so they could discuss what should be done. When she arrived, she could see he was mortified. He had only enrolled as a Nazi because his father had encouraged him to do so; now he could not bear to think that his own father had betrayed the cause he had espoused. Hans-Thilo the younger's confusion was exacerbated by the fact that he was very depressed; his left arm had been amputated after he had been wounded on the Russian front, and he had not yet come to terms with his loss. While he and Gisela were talking, he suddenly pulled out his pistol and held it to his right temple, as if he was about to blow his brains out. However before he could pull the trigger, Gisela grabbed his right hand and, after a fierce struggle, somehow managed to overpower him and to take the gun away.

When he had calmed down, she told him that they should go to their mother's house in Templin. She would have gone alone, but she knew she could not leave her brother in such an unbalanced state. When they arrived and rang the doorbell no one answered, so they let themselves in and walked into Charlotte Schmidt's bedroom. What they saw horrified them; their mother was lying groaning on the bed in a pool of blood. She had cut the veins on her arm and had taken morphine to ease the pain. Fortunately, Gisela knew what to do in an emergency, as she had been trained by the Red Cross. She was able to staunch the flow of blood and to bandage up her mother's wounds herself.

The Schmidt family were never told exactly what crime Hans Thilo Schmidt had committed. They tried to seek help from a friend of a friend who was a member of the local council. At one point they were told that Hermann Göring, whose ministry was in charge of the Forschungsamt, would see if he could help. But then later they were told that Heinrich Himmler had not allowed Göring to interfere. Nothing could be done.

Eventually, Gisela was allowed to visit her father in the Gestapo prison in Berlin. She noticed he was thinner than normal, but otherwise he seemed perfectly healthy. Neither of them wanted to say anything which could be used against them by the watching guards. So she handed him a note that she had written out for him in advance telling him that she still loved him whatever he had done. Seeing that she was about to cry, he mouthed the words, 'Be brave, my darling, be brave.' Before lapsing into silence again, he asked her whether she would mind taking home his heavy winter coat and bringing in a lighter jacket which she could get from her mother. Then, when he noticed that the guards were looking away, he quickly whispered to her, 'Cut the arm off the coat. There's something inside for you.'

As soon as she had returned to the safety of her flat, she cut open the lining of the coat with a pair of scissors. Inside the padding on the shoulder, she found what her father had been referring to. It was a brief note instructing her to bring him some potassium cyanide. No explanation was given, or was necessary. He wanted to kill himself. Gisela's first port of call when she wanted some advice was her chemistry teacher, Dr Wacholz. She knew that one of his wife's grandparents was Jewish, and she hoped that this would make him sympathetic to someone who had defied the Nazis. She was right. He quickly procured some potassium cyanide pills for her and assured her they were strong enough to kill her father.

Unfortunately, she was not allowed in to see her father again, so she sewed the box of pills Dr Wacholz had given her inside his summer jacket and gave it to Herr Langemach, the man who had taken pity on her on the day she had heard about the arrest. He later warned her that the poison had been found and advised her not to go to the prison again. It was only later, after her father had managed to poison himself, that she heard her brother had also been given pills by Dr Wacholz which he had tried to smuggle into the prison. She never found out whether his attempt was more successful than hers, or whether at some point the authorities had allowed the pills to be handed to her father to save them the embarrassment of having to put him on trial. All she knew was that in the middle of September 1943 she was summoned to the prison to identify her father's corpse. He was laid out naked in a box, and she pulled back the blanket covering his torso to check whether he had been tortured. His body was not marked. The only change she could see was that he had become terribly thin during his six months in captivity.

Gisela and her family were handed her father's personal effects. Alongside the bandage which he had used to relieve the pain he was experiencing from an untreated hernia were three touching notes. One was addressed to her and her brother. At the top, her father in a shaky hand had written: '19.9.1943 6.20 a.m.', which was just before he was found dead. It read:

> My dear Bubi and Gieselmaus,
> It's difficult for a father to say good-bye when he would have liked to carry on giving advice about how life should be lived. It is comforting to know that you have both learned a profession which enables you to stand on your own feet. Be strong and enjoy your lives. Stick together and support each other as well as your Mother. You must allow each other to be independent but carry on loving each other and be understanding. Forget everything bad about me and remember me well. Farewell in a peaceful and free Germany.
> Your Daddy

There was another note for Gisela which had been written on the back of a photo of her which she had given to him in prison:

> My dear child Giesel,
> Don't brood or think so much. Always keep your head up and be proud. Fight for life. May you bring sunshine into other people's lives, and may they bring it into yours.
> Your Daddy

There was also the following a note for Charlotte, his wife, which was written on the back of a photograph taken on 19 October 1941 to commemorate their twenty-fifth wedding anniversary:

Dear Mutz,

Twenty-six years of marriage is a good time. Remember me well. I promise you I always loved you more than anything although we sometimes went through difficult times. Be a kind and understanding mother to your children as you've always been so far. With greetings and kisses.

Your Hans

Because neither the State, nor the Church would bury Hans Thilo Schmidt, General Rudolf Schmidt, who had always taken care of his brother financially, paid a private contractor to bury the corpse in a graveyard outside Berlin. It was a brave act, given that his own loyalty to Hitler had been called into question; letters from him criticising Hitler had been discovered in his brother's house. As a result, he had been sacked from the Army.

On 21 September 1943, Hans Thilo Schmidt was buried beside his mother and father in an unmarked grave. No one, apart from his and Lemoine's interrogators, and Hitler's inner circle, were told what he had done; only they and Hans Thilo's family knew where he had been laid to rest. As far as the Nazis were concerned, all traces that the Enigma spy had ever existed were wiped off the face of the earth. But if they believed that was the end of the affair, they were mistaken. The stable door had been slammed shut after the horse had bolted.

Sinking the *Scharnhorst*

The Barents Sea

DECEMBER 1943

Enigma's diminishing importance in combating the U-boat threat in the Atlantic during the latter part of 1943 was counterbalanced by the vital assistance it gave to the Royal Navy in the Arctic. During the spring and summer of 1943 all Russian convoys were suspended; after the PQ17 disaster, the Admiralty realised that the long summer hours made it impossible to protect the merchant ships as they passed so close to the north of Norway. But when, with the arrival of winter, the convoys to Murmansk and Archangel were started again in November 1943, the Enigma decrypts provided the best intelligence about any threatening movements by the German surface ships.

Given that *Tirpitz* was out of action, after being damaged by British midget submarines in September 1943, and given that the pocket battleship *Lützow* had steamed back to Germany, the most potent threat still menacing the convoys was provided by the presence of the battle-cruiser *Scharnhorst*. Although *Scharnhorst*'s 11-inch guns were outclassed by the 14-inch guns on the Home Fleet's battleship HMS *Duke of York*, *Scharnhorst* was 4 knots faster than her British opponent in the right conditions. Unless the Admiralty was tipped off in advance that *Scharnhorst* was going out on a sortie against a Russian convoy, the German battle-cruiser could nip out from her anchorage in Altenfjord, in northern Norway, attack the convoy, and steam back home before the Home Fleet could bring her guns to bear. It was like the threat facing convoy PQ17 all over again.

After the cancellation of the Russian convoys for so many months, Admiral Bruce Fraser, the Commander-in-Chief of the Home Fleet since May 1943, surprised Admiral Golokov, his Russian counterpart, by personally guarding the December 1943 convoy JW55A in his battleship; he arrived in Kola on 16 December 1943, four days ahead of the convoy. In the course of a meeting with Golokov, the British Commander-in-Chief happened to admire a beautiful onyx-topped desk he caught sight of in Golokov's rooms. Golokov immediately ordered his staff to carry the desk to *Duke of York*. Fraser demurred, choosing something less valuable instead. But at a dinner held in his honour, he asked Golokov what he should bring for him next time the Home Fleet came to Russia. Golokov immediately replied that he would like Fraser to bring him the *Scharnhorst*. Everyone laughed, and for a moment the cold relations between the British and Russian Navies thawed.[1]

But Fraser did not stay long in Russia. He wanted to be back in position ready to protect the next eastbound convoy, JW55B, which was scheduled to leave Loch Ewe in north-west Scotland on 20 December 1943. Even before *Duke of York* steamed into Akureyri fjord in Iceland, he was receiving Enigma intelligence from the Admiralty about *Scharnhorst*'s state of readiness. On 20 December, as JW55B set out, the Enigma intelligence alerted Fraser to the fact that the German battle group had been brought to three hours notice two days earlier.[2] By 21 December, *Scharnhorst* had reverted to six hours notice, only for Fraser to be told on 23 December that *Scharnhorst* had been at three hours notice the previous day; although more bombes were available to break the code than had existed during the PQ17 disaster, there was still a delay in reading Enigma messages, often lasting many hours, each time the settings were changed.

An additional problem which the codebreakers had to face up to was the extra delay caused by the German habit of using the Offizier Enigma procedure for especially important, one-off, messages. Because Offizier messages were enciphered twice, they were more difficult to break. The Offizier procedure involved an officer setting up the Enigma with the same wheel order and ring settings as specified for regular Enigma operators. However, as mentioned in Chapter 14, the officer would use different plugboard settings. Offizier message settings were then selected from a list of twenty-six; the list changed each month. Each setting in the list had a letter of the alphabet printed beside it. The message setting and the letter was passed on to the recipient of the message by the sender mentioning a name, whose first letter was the same as the letter beside the message setting in the list. So if the setting chosen was ABC, and it had the letter P beside it, the sender might start his message with the words: 'Offizier Paula'. After enciphering his message, the officer handed the cipher text, with the unenciphered Offizier Paula indicator, to the telegraphist, who, after setting the Enigma up with the regular settings for the day in question, enciphered it again. Only then was the resulting cipher text transmitted.

Although the capture of the June 1941 Offizier settings from U-110 in May 1941 had shown the Hut 8 codebreakers how the system worked, they still had to work out a regular way of breaking Offizier settings once the June settings ran out. As described in chapter 14, the Hut 8 cribster Rolf Noskwith had shown that cribs could be discovered which would enable Offizier settings to be worked out on the bombe. After the first break of the September 1941 Offizier settings, further cribs were identified for multi-part Offizier messages. The cribs often consisted of the word 'Fort' (the abbreviated form of Fortsetzung, meaning continuation) being included in the second part of a two part message, together with the time of origin of the first message. Working out the alignment of such cribs with the cipher text was often a very long-winded process; the Germans would conceal the cipher text representing these words within the text of the second part of the message.[3] So sometimes as many as one hundred different menus were drawn up and tested on a bombe before the correct alignment of crib and cipher text, and the correct menu were discovered. This was not fatal, given that the wheel order was already known before work began on the Offizier, but it was expensive in terms of bombe time, a major disadvantage in 1941–2, when bombes were in short supply.

The man who was to exploit a chink in the Offizier armour was the twenty-six-year-old Leslie Yoxall, another mathematician with a First class Cambridge degree. Although he had attended Sidney Sussex, Gordon Welchman's college, he had not been one of the first wave of students called in to man the Bletchley Park huts. Instead he had taken a job in Manchester Grammar School, where he was next in line to become head of the mathematics department. But in April 1941 Gordon Welchman wrote to him, warning that he would be receiving a letter in the near future asking him to help with some 'war work'. The letter duly arrived, and Yoxall was summoned to be interviewed at Bletchley Park, along with another candidate, Bill Tutte. Hugh Alexander interviewed them first. After he had finished, Yoxall overheard Alexander saying to an assistant, 'They'd better go and see Turing. He's the head of the hut.' Before they left, Alexander gave Yoxall a sealed envelope which Yoxall later discovered contained a note recommending that Turing should select Yoxall out of the two candidates. They were then driven to the pub in Shenley Brook End, a neighbouring village, where Turing was billeted. Unfortunately, he was out cycling and was much put out when the driver of the car tracked him down and asked him whether he could interview Yoxall and Bill Tutte in the pub. When he arrived, he told the two young men that all the theoretical work involved had been done; the successful candidate would merely have to apply the theory. Yoxall was duly selected after Turing read Alexander's note.

He quickly made his mark when he looked into the Offizier problem. The opening he exploited was the result of another German oversight. The Offizier system was constructed in such a way that if you worked out the Offizier plugboard socket settings on just one day in a month, by using a crib and the bombe, the rest of the month became vulnerable. As is explained in Appendix 6, if the Offizier plugboard settings were worked out on a particular day, some of the message settings on that month's Offizier message setting list could also be discovered. If one such setting, say the one referred to as 'Paula', was worked out on day one, then when it was mentioned at the top of a message on day three, the codebreakers would only have one element to work out, the plugboard connections. Turing thought they could only be worked out if there were at least 200 letters in the message being analysed.[4] The other codebreakers in the hut assumed he was correct, until Yoxall, by following the procedure mentioned in Appendix 6, a procedure which had been used at Bletchley Park before but not in connection with the Offizier problem, managed to break a message consisting of just eighty letters. However Yoxall could not get round one difficulty. Offizier messages took even longer to break than ordinary messages, for the simple reason that codebreakers had to break the regular cipher first before going on to work on the Offizier settings. This time constraint was to lead to serious difficulties on the Arctic convoy run.

Although Fraser took the Home Fleet to sea on 23 December 1943 to protect Russian Convoy JW55B, during the next two days he had no firm evidence that *Scharnhorst* was definitely going to make a sortie. Before leaving Iceland he knew from Enigma intelligence that the convoy had been sighted by aircraft on 22 December, but that was not decisive. It was 24 December before he learned that two days earlier the Admiral Northern Waters had requested Admiral Polar Coast to 'make preparations for departure of battle group'. That, and the Enigma intelligence which told him that reconnaissance by aircraft was to be undertaken on 24 December, led him to believe that something might be about to happen. This was very worrying. As Fraser wrote later in his official report: 'the convoy . . . was entirely unsupported, and I was uneasy lest a surface attack should be made.'[5] During the afternoon of 24 December he therefore took the unorthodox step of breaking radio silence to instruct the convoy to reverse its course for three hours. He admitted later however: 'If the enemy surface forces had searched to the westward, this step would have had little effect in bringing the convoy closer, but it would have prevented the convoy being located by them before dark.'

It was then that the slowness in breaking the Offizier messages came into play. If they had been read currently, Fraser would have received some vital intelligence about *Scharnhorst's* plans on Christmas Day 1943. An Offizier message initiated at 10.56 a.m. stated: 'Battle Group is to be at 1 hours readiness from 1300/25/12. Scharnhorst . . . to acknowledge.'[6] However that message was not broken for around thirty-one hours after it was sent, by which time it was too late to influence what was to happen next. The same was true of another Offizier message initiated at 3.16 p.m. that afternoon: 'Battle Group ready for sea at 16.20.' Eleven minutes later an even more momentous message from Admiral Northern Waters to Battle Group and Admiral Polar Coast was initiated. It stated: 'Most Immediate. "Ostfront" 1700/25/12.' Although this message was not sent in Offizier, it was to remain unread for more than eight crucial hours as the Hut 8 codebreakers battled to break the new Enigma settings which had come into force at midday on December 25.[7]

The last important Enigma message initiated by the Germans – at 11.58 a.m. on 25 December – before the new Enigma settings came into effect was from Battle Group. It was transmitted to another vessel and stated: 'Emergency Proceed to "Scharnhorst" in Langfjord. Further orders there.' The decrypt for this message was sent to the OIC at 8.50 p.m. on 25 December and Fraser received this intelligence at 9.42 p.m. that night. An even clearer indication would have been provided by another Offizier message initiated at 12.43 a.m. on 26 December: it contained the following order which was sent out to the U-boats in the Arctic: 'Own battle group consisting of "Scharnhorst" and 5 new destroyers left Lopphavet 2300/25 with the intention of attacking the convoy at about 0900/26.' But once again it was not decrypted at Bletchley Park until it was too late.

Shortly before 12.30 a.m. on 26 December, the Enigma settings used with effect from midday on Christmas Day were broken. One of the first messages to be sent through to Norman Denning in the

OIC was the one referring to 'Ostfront 1700/25/12'. After the message was sent, Harry Hinsley telephoned Denning and told him that he would in future refer to Ostfront by its British codename, 'Epilepsy'.[8] At 1.30 a.m. 26 December, the following message was transmitted from the Admiralty to Fraser on *Duke of York*: 'At 1530A 25 December Admiral Commanding Northern Waters informed Battle Group and Admiral Polar Coast "Codeword EPILEPSY 1700A/25 December". Comment. Meaning not yet evident. ULTRA [i.e. Enigma] information will be available with a delay of some hours until 1200A/26 December but will not necessarily be complete for the North Norway area.' But within minutes of sending this message to Fraser, Denning received another decrypt of a message sent from *Scharnhorst* to another vessel, which stated: ' "Scharnhorst" will pass outward bound as from 1800. Act in accordance with t-days [sic] written instructions.' This decrypt was sent from Bletchley Park to the OIC at 1.33 a.m. on 26 December. At 2.17 a.m. the Admiralty sent the following message to Fraser: 'EMERGENCY. SCHARNHORST probably sailed 1800A/25th December.' One minute later, Fraser received a fuller explanation from the Admiralty: 'A patrol vessel presumably in the Altenfjord area was informed at 1715 that SCHARNHORST would pass outward bound from 1800A/25th December.'

Richard Pendered, the young codebreaker who had tested Turing and Welchman's spider bombe in the summer of 1940, was on duty during the 26 December nightshift. He recalls unbuttoning an Offizier message after 'doing a Dottery', the technique developed by Yoxall, at about 3 a.m. Addressed to the German Naval Command 'Von Kampfgruppe' (from Battle Group), it read: 'JSCHARNHORSTJ MIT FUENF NEUE ZERSTOERER ZWO DREI NULL NULL UHR LOPPHAVET AUS' (Scharnhorst with five destroyers 2300 hours out of Lopphavet).[9] If Pendered has remembered this incident correctly, it was the first confirmation that *Scharnhorst* was at sea. It has to be said however that neither this message nor the decrypt translating it appear in the Public Record Office in London. It is also similar in content to the message initiated at 12.43 a.m. on 26 December and sent out to the U-boats in the Arctic, as mentioned above. So Pendered could have mixed up the message he remembers with the U-boat message. On the other hand, Pendered's clear recollection is consistent with a note in Fraser's report which stated: 'At 3.39 [26 December] Admiralty message 260319 was received in which Admiralty appreciated that "Scharnhorst" was at sea.'

Pendered's version of events is also consistent with the recollection of a telegraphist who was serving on the destroyer *HMS Onslow*, the leader of the close escort accompanying convoy JW 5 5B. During the early morning watch on 26 December Derek Wellman, the telegraphist, was listening in to the U-boat frequencies when he heard some mysterious clicks on his headphones. Prompted by this to retune his radio set, he picked up a morse code message on a different frequency which was definitely not coming from a U-boat. Wellman knew that the sound of a morse code message transmitted from a U-boat was very different to what he was hearing. In the case of U-boat message, the pitch of the signal received on telegraphists' headphones was far higher than the pitch for signals sent from surface ships or from shore stations. The signal ringing in his ears had a normal pitch. After working out the bearing of the transmitter using his direction finding apparatus Wellman could see that it was coming from a source between the convoy and the Norwegian coast, and its unusual beginning led Wellman to believe that it was being given a high priority by the transmitter. All of this suggested to Wellman, who had been told that the *Scharnhorst* might make a sortie at any minute, that it might be the crucial message announcing that the German battle cruiser was at sea. He immediately reported what he had heard to the officers on duty on *Onslow*'s bridge. It is quite possible that the message which he was reporting was the same message which Pendered subsequently deciphered at Bletchley Park.

The news that *Scharnhorst* was at sea left Fraser in a quandary. 'If "Scharnhorst" attacked at daylight and immediately retired, I was not yet sufficiently close to cut her off,' Fraser subsequently wrote in his report. As he considered his options, he must have thought about the situation Sir Dudley Pound had faced up to during the passage of the PQ17 convoy when he thought it was about to be decimated by *Tirpitz*. Fraser, however, decided to break radio silence again and ordered the convoy to steer north away from *Scharnhorst* 'in the hope that the change of course would make it more difficult for the "Scharnhorst" to find it'.

As it turned out, Fraser was lucky. Although his messages were picked up by the Germans, they failed to recall *Scharnhorst*. Even when a German aircraft spotted 'five warships, one apparently a big one' at about 10 a.m. on 26 December, this did not alert the Germans to the fact that the Home Fleet was approaching.[10] By then *Scharnhorst* had had her first engagement with Vice-Admiral Burnett's cruiser force which had also steamed to the convoy's rescue. At this point all the ships were converging on an area between Bear Island and North Cape. One of the cruisers, approaching from the northeast, had picked up *Scharnhorst*, which was coming from the south, on its radar screen. At 9.21 a.m. *Scharnhorst* was sighted by the cruisers, and one of them opened fire. *Scharnhorst* turned away without firing her own guns and disappeared to the south. She had been hit at least once.

Scharnhorst then attempted to make her way around to the north, so that she could attack the convoy from the other side. On the way she was spotted by the cruisers again and shortly afterwards the ships exchanged fire. *Scharnhorst* once again took flight. At 4.17 p.m. *Duke of York*'s radar picked *Scharnhorst* up at about twenty-five miles. An eye witness on the destroyer HMS *Scorpion* recalled what happened when the flagships and the cruiser *Belfast* fired a starshell: 'when the starshell first illuminated *Scharnhorst*, I could see her so clearly that I could see her turrets were fore-and-aft (and what a lovely sight she was at full speed). She was almost at once obliterated by a wall of water from the *Duke*'s salvo . . . When she re-appeared her turrets wore a different aspect.'[11] When a gunner on one of the cruisers observed that *Scharnhorst* was burning, he cheered, and above the sound of the gunfire, he heard most of the watching crew following suit.[12] At 18.50 two destroyers at last managed to catch up with *Scharnhorst*. The German ship's captain instinctively put his wheel over. It was a fatal mistake. In the words of the witness on HMS *Scorpion* 'an onrushing target at a fine inclination became a sitting bird', and the gathering destroyers moved in with their torpedoes at the ready.

While she was being attacked, *Scharnhorst* transmitted messages back to base. A message initiated at 4.56 p.m. stated: 'Heavy Battleship. Am in action.' Just over an hour later, a message from *Scharnhorst* to Gruppe Nord Flotte stated: 'Opponent is firing by radar. Location is more than 1800 (range) . . . Speed 26 knots.' At 6.25 p.m. a message from Admiral Northern Waters stated that *Scharnhorst* was 'surrounded by heavy units'. Then a message initiated by Admiral Northern Waters at 7.45 p.m. reported *Scharnhorst*'s brave message for the Führer: 'We shall fight to the last shell.'

Scharnhorst was eventually sunk by a mixture of gunfire and torpedoes. No one on the British ships saw her go down. Afterwards Fraser wrote: 'All that could be seen of the "Scharnhorst" was a dull glow through a dense cloud of smoke, which the starshell and searchlights of the surrounding ships could not penetrate . . . it seems fairly certain that she sank after a heavy underwater explosion which was heard and felt in several ships at about 19.45.' As she sank the officer manning the radar set on *Duke of York* reported seeing the echo fading on his screen; Fraser, who did not believe the battle-cruiser was sinking, told him to retune his radar set. In an attempt to find out what had really happened Fraser asked the Fleet Signal Officer to call up Admiral Burnett. The Signal Officer did as he was told, but as he did so he dutifully reminded Fraser that he was to address Burnett by his code name, 'Curly'; Burnett was in his turn supposed to use Fraser's code name, 'Wigly'. However when Burnett came on the line Fraser was so excited that he forgot everything he had been told, and started the conversation: 'Bob, this is Bruce. . . .' Fortunately there were no similar slip ups in relation to Enigma signals; Fraser was watched like a hawk by his Enigma minder, Commander Edward Thomas, who was known to everyone on Fraser's flagship as 'Black Beard,' not because he had a beard, but because, like the infamous pirate, he was liable to fight his battles in an unconventional way.[13] It was only half an hour later however, after Admiral Burnett had steamed through the pathetic debris of oil and a raft of frozen survivors, that he signalled to Fraser: 'Satisfied "Scharnhorst" sunk.' All but thirty-six of her 2000-strong crew perished in the freezing Arctic waters. The captain and the commander of *Scharnhorst* were both seen in the water, wrote Fraser. 'The Captain was dead before he could be reached; the Commander grasped a life-line, but succumbed before he could be hauled in.' Fraser, in his turn, signalled to the Admiralty: ' "Scharnhorst" sunk.' The Admiralty replied: 'Grand. Well done.'

Later that night, Richard Pendered, on duty again in Bletchley Park's Hut 8, read *Scharnhorst's* penultimate message which had just been decrypted. The Enigma message had been initiated at 6.19 p.m. It was sent on to the OIC at 11.47 p.m. By that time it was obvious that *Scharnhorst's* last stand must be over and Pendered wondered if any of the messages which he had deciphered had made a difference.

Operation Covered

Paris, the Indian Ocean and the Atlantic

AUGUST 1943–MARCH 1944

Had it not been for the assistance given by the French Deuxième Bureau, the Enigma cipher would probably not have been mastered by the Allies for at least two years after war was declared. (See analysis in notes to the Introduction.) However in 1943 and 1944, errors by the French very nearly gave away the Allies' Enigma secret which they had helped to procure.

By allowing Rodolphe Lemoine to remain in Saillagousse after the Germans occupied the south of France in November 1942, which resulted in his arrest and interrogation, the French gave the Germans the opportunity to find out about Hans Thilo Schmidt and the Enigma manuals. The French failure to evacuate all the Polish code-breakers, cipher experts and engineers, after they fled from Château des Fouzes, and the arrest of some of them in February and March 1943, could have enabled the Germans to discover that Enigma had been broken after the war started in September 1939. Permitting Gustave Bertrand to stay on in France was equally risky insofar as the Allies' Enigma secret was concerned; like the arrested Poles, he knew about the breaking of the Enigma during as well as before the war. However, his presence in occupied France was particularly dangerous after he took on an active role in the French Resistance, becoming the head of the Kléber section of the Resistance in July 1943. Fortunately for the Allies, Bertrand had numerous code names, which provided some protection against his ever being identified, if he was caught. Bertrand himself once saw a German list of wanted people and one of his aliases was on it rather than his real name. But it was obvious that it would only take one agent to talk out of turn, and then, even that security device would be blown away.

The risks taken by the French in relation to the Allies' Enigma secret were highlighted by what happened when he was eventually caught.[1] On 3 January 1944, he had set out on his 101st mission since the fall of France. He was to pick up some radio equipment from a British agent in Paris so that he could keep in contact with London and Algiers during the coming invasion of Europe. The meeting was scheduled to take place that very day, between 9–9.30 a.m. inside the church of Sacré-Coeur de Montmartre in front of the statue of Saint Anthony of Padua. Bertrand was told that the man he was to meet would be carrying a copy of a magazine called *Signal*. To make absolutely sure he had the right man, Bertrand was supposed to say the password 'Salve'; the reply was supposed to be 'Amen'.

He arrived at the meeting early, but when, at about 9.20 a.m., he saw a man come into the church and kneel down in front of the statue he was put off by the fact that the man was not carrying a copy of *Signal*. However Bertrand eventually went up to him and said the password. Rather than replying with the password 'Amen', the man beckoned him to come and talk outside the church. There Bertrand discovered the man's name was Paul. He had just decoded a message from London, asking him to meet a friend of the boss, but only the first part of the message had come through. Presumably the password and the reference to the magazine had been mentioned in the missing second part. The two men arranged to meet up again two days later at the same place. Paul said that by then he would have time to collect the materials Bertrand wanted. However Bertrand was upset when he saw Paul write down the appointment in a little red notebook. In Bertrand's experience, agents in the Resistance normally managed to do without such risky *aides-mémoire*.

That was one reason why, when Bertrand made it back to the same church on 5 January 1944, he had a premonition that something would go wrong. That feeling was strengthened when Paul did not appear at 8 a.m., the agreed time. Bertrand's worst fears were realised when, watching from his place behind a pillar, he saw three men walk up to the statue of Saint Anthony of Padua. Bertrand was sure they were German policemen who must have been tipped off about the rendezvous. A fourth man hurried up to them and then rushed out the way he had come. Bertrand was just about to beat a hasty retreat when he felt a hand on his shoulder, and heard a voice telling him that it would be better for him if he remained seated. It was the fourth man, who had crept up behind him, unnoticed. He was under arrest.

Bertrand's arrest did not represent the Germans' only opportunity to take on board the fact that their Enigma ciphers were being read. On 10 August 1943, shortly after Bertrand was promoted to be the head of the Kléber Resistance cell, the German Intelligence Service in Switzerland filed a disturbing report about the Naval Enigma. The report, which was sent to Dönitz, stated: 'Over the last few months, Germany's naval ciphers, which are used to give operational orders to the U-boats, have been successfully broken. All orders are being read currently. The source is a Swiss American in an important secretarial position in the US Navy Department.'[2]

Not surprisingly this allegation created something of a panic at the U-boat headquarters. However the Naval Communications Department still maintained that the report could not be true; the 'continuous current reading of our W/T traffic by the enemy is out of the question', Dönitz was told. Dönitz nevertheless felt there was strong evidence to suggest that Enigma had been read for a limited period at the beginning of August 1943. The evidence cited in his War Diary was that, whereas between 12 June–1 August 1943, thirteen out of twenty-one meetings between U-boats at sea had been undisturbed, between 3–11 August, all ten meetings had been interrupted. This led him to believe that the Naval Enigma had somehow been compromised between 23 July, when a new 'Stichwort order' – which altered the wheel and plug settings given in the printed settings list – had come into operation, and 11 August, when the then existing Stichwort order was replaced. 'In view of this, it would appear to be reasonable to assume that at the end of July, after the key change of 23 July, the enemy took possession of the keys and read the orders currently for the U-boat rendez-vous,' wrote Dönitz in his War Diary.

The concern about the mysterious Swiss American's intelligence became more acute when on 18 August more details about him were filed. One report compiled by the Germans stated he was 'related to our Military Attaché, and often travelled to London with the US Navy delegation, so he should be well informed'. The same report stated: 'The British Naval Intelligence Office are giving a lot of help [to the Royal Navy] in the fight against the U-boats. A special office has specialised in dealing with codebreaking since war broke out. For several months it has been very successful. They can now read German Admiralty orders to the U-boat commanders. This is a great help when it comes to hunting for U-boats.'

This might have caused even more alarm than it did, if the readers of the report had not had access to a confident rebuttal of Dönitz's conclusion that the Naval Enigma cipher had been compromised. The rebuttal, as well as accentuating the security of the Enigma system caused by the use of the Stichwort order, claimed that the enormous number of plugboard connection possibilities made it most unlikely that the British could find the right ones by trial and error. It was a deduction which must have made the men working in the British Naval Intelligence Division smile when it eventually came into their hands. For the plug connections could be worked out relatively quickly once the other settings were known; it was the wheel order and message settings which taxed the British codebreakers' ingenuity most of all.

It is not clear whether the Naval Communications Department kept in touch with a special cipher security unit attached to the intelligence division for all the armed forces. Working for that organisation was a brilliant mathematician called Karl Stein. In 1942, he had been rushed back to Berlin from the front at Stalingrad so that he could check whether the Enigma, and Germany's other codes, were secure. His verdict was a mixed one. He believed that the Army Enigma could be broken, but only if a special machine was constructed. The Navy Enigma on the other hand was secure in his opinion. Although a machine could break the code in theory, he believed it would take too long in practice.

Ironically, Dönitz's anxiety that his and his U-boats' messages were being read occurred at a time when Bletchley Park was encountering serious difficulties with the Naval Enigma. These difficulties had arisen because the Allies had become the victims of their own success. After the U-boats' defeat in the North Atlantic and their withdrawal from that area of operations for three months with effect from the end of May 1943, the number of short signals, the main source of cribs after 10 March 1943, had fallen off drastically. This prompted Bletchley Park's senior administrator Nigel de Grey to write the following note to Commander Wenger at Op-20-G on 3 June 1943: 'Chances of breaking Shark on short signals are much less favourable than before . . . in view of this four wheel bombes become more than ever important . . . How does your bombe production stand?'[3]

Before Wenger could reply with positive news on the bombes, Bletchley Park had made another important discovery. During June to July 1943 Bletchley Park's cryptographers had identified a different source of cribs which were useable in conjunction with the new four-wheel bombes being tested in England and in the US, as well as with three-wheel bombes which were adapted to deal with so-called 'four-wheel jobs'.[4] Messages sent on the Home Waters (Dolphin) net used by U-boats in the Arctic were being repeated on the Triton (Shark) net used by U-boats in the Atlantic. So as soon as the Dolphin messages were unbuttoned, they were available to be used as cribs for the Shark net. The codebreakers referred to these cribs as 'reencodements'. There was a delay built into this procedure; the Shark messages could not be read until Dolphin was broken. But it was nothing compared to the delay which had been occurring in relation to messages transmitted at the end of May 1943 and during the first half of June 1943, when some messages were being read up to a month after they were sent.[5]

Because the breaking of Shark was now dependent on Dolphin messages being read, efforts were made to break Dolphin more quickly. The codebreakers consequently decided at the end of June 1943 to abandon the long-winded Banburismus procedure whenever there were available cribs; thereafter Dolphin was to be broken solely by using cribs and bombes, which were to become more and more plentiful as the months passed.[6]

That was the situation at the end of June 1943. However, just as the codebreakers in Washington and Bletchley Park were beginning to break the backlog of messages, they had to face up to yet another reverse. On 1 July 1943 a new fourth wheel and a new reflector, called respectively 'Gamma' and 'Caesar', were introduced for users of Shark. Either or both of these new elements could be inserted into the four-wheel Enigma machine instead of the existing fourth wheel, 'Beta', and the existing reflector, 'Bruno'. As a result, messages transmitted on the Shark network could not be deciphered by the Bletchley Park codebreakers. During the short period when the Shark decrypts dried up, the U-boats were not operating offensively in the North Atlantic, and the Allied submarine tracking rooms still managed to use the fixes made by direction-finding equipment to work out some U-boat positions in other areas, in spite of being suddenly starved of Enigma intelligence. So although the shipping sunk by the U-boats shot up from just 95,000 tons of shipping (twenty ships) in June 1943 to 252,000 tons (forty-six ships) in July, the losses were only half as bad as those suffered during March 1943.[7]

The codebreaker who paved the way for the code to be broken again was Richard Pendered. At the beginning of June 1943 he had broken the 27 May 1943 Shark settings manually, using a very long crib; he had exploited a refined version of the rodding procedure which had enabled Bletchley Park codebreakers to read the Italian Naval Enigma cipher prior to the Battle of Matapan.[8] Having proved this was possible, the task of working out the wiring for the new fourth wheel and reflector could be carried out using the same technique. The work was split between the Americans and the British codebreakers, each team applying Pendered's procedure to the wheels allocated to them.[9]

If the Germans had exploited the full potential of the new fourth wheel and reflector, the Bletchley Park codebreakers would have had to deal with four times as many wheel orders each time they attempted to break the code; to achieve this, the Germans would have merely had to vary the combination of fourth wheels and reflectors used each time the Enigma settings were changed, i.e. Caesar and Beta could have been used one day, Bruno and Beta the next, and so on. However not for the first time, the German cipher experts failed to make the most of their opportunities. Even before the end of July 1943, the British codebreakers could see that the same combination – Gamma and Caesar – was being used each day. It turned out that the combination only changed once per month; this meant that the breaking of Shark was delayed once per month until the new combination was worked out. Thereafter, things were just as they had always been.[10]

In spite of this breakthrough, the Allied cryptographers continued to have difficulties. The situation was not helped by what was happening in America. The US Navy's Op-20-G cryptographers in Washington, had initially been hoping to have the fast new American bombes at their disposal by February 1943, as mentioned by Joseph Wenger in his original September 1942 application for funds. However on 17 March 1943 a disappointing conference was held at the bombe manufacturing plant in Dayton, Ohio owned by the National Cash Register, the company which had been commissioned to produce the American bombes. What was said at the conference dashed any hopes of a speedy resolution to the mounting crisis. The men masterminding the US Navy bombe project, and the team running the independent US Army and Air Force bombe project, were told that the first Navy 'test models' would only become available in mid-April 1943. That meant that the production line being set up by the National Cash Register would not be able to deliver the first of the 96 bombes ordered until June 1943.[11]

This was unwelcome news. Even as the ups and downs experienced by the engineers and production teams were being aired in Dayton, Allied ships from convoys HX229 and SC122 were being hunted down by Nazi wolf packs in mid-Atlantic, as mentioned in chapter 21. Unfortunately there was no way of avoiding the delay; it was the almost inevitable consequence of the logistical difficulties inherent in attempting to pioneer a new kind of machine in a very short time.

Professor Colin Burke, the first American historian who obtained access to the relevant files has described what was going wrong. According to Burke, the first bombe prototypes, named 'Adam' and 'Eve', were full of bugs. The main problem appears to have been the rotors which were expected to rotate at the fast speed of 1750 rotations per minute. That was the speed which was necessary on the so-called 'high-speed wheel' if a wheel order and a set of assumptions were to be tested within 22 minutes. The rotors were becoming overheated, and were losing their shape; as a result faulty electrical contacts were appearing after the bombe prototypes had been run for just a few hours. Another problem to be solved was that the electrical current running through the bombes was 'shorting', and was linking up pairs of contact points incorrectly. This appears to have been caused by the current passing through trails of metal particles which had been placed between the contact points in question by the oil that was to be seen spurting out of the machines.

A heated debate ensued as two members of the Navy project team vied to have the last word on how the bombes should be altered. Joe Desch, the hands-on engineer working in Dayton, would have preferred to slow down the movement of the wheels inside the American bombe by substituting each of the large wheels which had to spin around most quickly with two smaller wheels. That was the device he used for the two experimental models of the machine. But Desch's solution did not appeal to Howard Engstrom, the mathematician who was head of Op-20-G's research and development unit based in Washington. He feared that the smaller wheels would be hard to maintain, and that twice as much work would be involved if the Germans ever decided to alter the wiring inside the wheels and disks used inside the Enigma cipher machine itself. Eventually Engstrom's wishes prevailed, but the National Cash Register was ordered to start setting up the production line for the bombes even before it was certain that Desch could accomplish what was being demanded.

There was another blip of a different kind when on 18 June 1943, after Desch had finished writing the specification for the factory

including all the modifications that had had to be made to the prototypes, Engstrom had second thoughts about the bombe that had
been designed. He wanted Desch to make alterations that would
allow the wiring inside the wheels to be changed without having to
remove the wheels manually from the machine. Engstrom's demands
stunned Desch and Ralph Meader. Engstrom had stated that he
wanted the changes to be made without delaying the production of
the bombes, and he only backed down when both Meader and Desch
said that what he was asking for was impossible given the time con-
straints. But Desch still had to try to make the prototype bombes
work consistently, they kept breaking down. Nevertheless on 23 June
1943 an American bombe worked out the 31 May 1943 Shark settings. Meanwhile clearance was given for the so-so-called 'Model
530' to be manufactured. In addition to the larger wheels, it incorporated an ingenious digital electronic tracking system devised by
Desch to identify the setting selected by the bombe during its runs,
notwithstanding that the wheels went on spinning even after the correct solution was identified.

Desch's tinkering did not prevent there being another crisis in July
1943 when the first of the US bombes manufactured were tried out.
Burke says that none of the machines worked initially, and there were
many more misshapen wheels, and despairing cables and telephone
calls to Washington, before Desch finally worked out how the
machines could be operated reliably.[12]

The Allied codebreakers' mastery of Shark had to wait until two-
thirds of the way through August 1943, that is, after the compromised period mentioned by Dönitz had come to an end. The weekly
report of 20 August, which was compiled at Bletchley Park and
which summarised the progress made on Naval Enigma during the
past week revealed that: 'We have had a record week on Shark, the
whole month clearing up. Every day from August 1st to 18th is now
out. As a result we have been hard put to it to use the fast bombes,
and handed them over for a time to Hut 6 [the Hut handling Air Force
and Army Enigma], to run 3 wheel jobs. We have given the first half
of July to the Americans to get out on their own; this should give
them more practice in cribbing and bombe management than they
get under the normal arrangement whereby we decide what to run
and who shall run it.'[13] The History of Hut Eight comments with
respect to this entry: 'It indicates the end of the great Shark battle.
From now onwards, there were always enough cribs and enough
bombes to keep the situation under control.' Most of the new four

wheel bombes were produced by the Americans; they produced seventy-five four-wheel machines during the second half of 1943, more than the British produced during the rest of the war.[14]

The ease with which the Shark settings were broken in September 1943, after the new four wheel bombes had been shipped from Dayton to the refurbished Mount Vernon school in Washington's Nebraska Avenue, led the Americans to question whether they should reduce the number of machines being manufactured. On 7 September Wenger sent the following message to Travis:

> Present production plans for bombes call for eventual total of 100 at current rate of 6 per week. 12 now assembled of which 6 are in actual operation. In light of known and contemplated developments would appreciate your views as to desirability of any downward revision of figures considering possible need for non Shark jobs such as Luftwaffe in which we shall be glad to assist.

Three days later the reply from Travis stated:

> In our view present favourable Shark position may not continue. Also your assistance in non Shark jobs may be very valuable. We should therefore be sorry if your production figure were reduced.

However the growing American involvement in the breaking of the Enigma code was not accomplished without frustration being experienced on both sides. When in December 1942 Alan Turing had been asked to advise the American engineers on the development of their bombe, he had laughed at their naive insistence that it was necessary to build one bombe for each of the 336 possible Naval Enigma wheel orders; Bletchley Park codebreakers knew that many of the wheel orders could be automatically ruled out day without having to check them out on the bombe. This was because of the predictable German habit of following strict rules when selecting the wheels to be placed in their cipher machines. So the American approach seemed unnecessarily extravagant. Only later did the Americans agree to scale down the number of bombes they intended to build. They eventually agreed that 96 would be a sufficient number.

It has to be said that what the British regarded as naivety was often the result of the British policy of revealing nothing concerning Enigma unless they were asked a specific question about a particular aspect of the cipher system. For example, in April and May 1942, at a time when the Americans were starting to investigate the feasibility of producing their own bombes, they were still asking the British fundamental questions such as did the Naval Enigma use the same wheels as the Army and Air Force Enigma.[15]

Later on, after the American bombes had begun to crack the U-boat ciphers, there was another gripe. Rather than immediately making their bombes available to deal with Army and Air Force Enigma ciphers, the Americans attempted to break U-boat keys using what Bletchley Park regarded as unsuitable cribs. If it had not been for the fact that the so-called 'reencodement' cribs from the Home Waters 'Dolphin' net, which have already been described, were bound to become available sooner rather than later, the American policy might have been perfectly rational. But reencodedments were being regularly produced. That explains why the writer of The History of Hut Eight described what the Americans were doing as the 'pure product of inexperienced enthusiasm', and went on to write the following devastating criticism:

right cribs were occasionally produced but, . . . the skill in cribbing is not so much finding a right crib as ignoring a wrong one and this Op-20-G signally failed to do; their weakness was not lack of ideas but a complete lack of judgement and sense of proportion and they were content to pour bombe time down the drain in the totally illusory hope that they had discovered a feasible method of breaking keys.[16]

The same writer continued:

The position was rather an embarrassing one. Milner Barry's [one of the senior cryptographers in Hut 6, the Army and Air Force Hut] axiom that 'Policy directing the use of the bombes is decided here [at Bletchley Park] on an inter-service level, and the bombes are in practice regarded as common property for the general war effort. Other considerations such as what service actually built the bombes and for what original purposes, are irrelevant' was clearly not being adhered to.

The transatlantic conflict between the two codebreaking units was only resolved towards the end of 1943 after a reliable crib based on a weather report was discovered. As the writer of the History of Hut Eight wrote: 'The effect of this crib was normally to break Shark currently and so in most cases to remove the problem of Op-20-G running bad cribs because there was nothing else to run.'

A month after the crib was identified, Howard Engstrom visited Bletchley Park, and sent back instructions that the Americans should henceforth send to Bletchley Park any crib which they wanted to run on their bombes; the Americans were then to comply with Bletchley Park's decision about which cribs should be tested.

Reining in the Americans while they picked up tips from Bletchley Park was evidently the answer to the problem. The writer of The History of Hut Eight who had criticised the Americans so harshly for the way they had behaved during the second half of 1943 was full of praise for their work in 1944, writing: 'by half way through 1944 they [Op-20-G] had taken over complete control of Shark and undoubtedly knew far more abcout the key than we did.' The fact that Op-20-G managed to break Shark in the 'cribless' days following the death of the weather report crib 'represent[ed] an extremely fine cribbing achievement' according to The History of Hut Eight.

So the British veterans ended up admiring the American cryptographers. The Americans in Op-20-G on the other hand were not quite so happy with the way the British carried on. Although they were keen to give credit to the British for what they had achieved, the Op-20-G bombe project managers were irritated by the British failure to keep to their commitment to build their share of the new fast bombes; they described the British production of four-wheel bombes as 'extremely unsatisfactory'. The following resentful comment was written in 1944 by Commanders Wenger, Engstrom and Meader: 'In the original discussions of the project with the British the US Navy was to assist GC&CS in thc Gcrman Naval problem. At present practically the entire burden of the naval problem is carried by the US Navy Bombes . . . From a position of domination the British have by their failures fallen behind in the submarine problem.' Their comments were backed up with facts: At the date of writing the British had only produced eighteen four wheel bombes, and these machines were so unreliable that an average of just three bombes were up and running at any given time. Worse still, there was little prospect of the British catching up with the Americans. A British note dispatched on 24 March 1944 frankly admitted:– 'Performance of our machine is still poor and likely to remain so. In view of your 4-wheel capacity being more than adequate, priority is being given here to the production of new 3-wheel machines.'

The Americans were given further grounds for dissatisfaction after Bletchley Park's Hugh Alexander visited Op-20-G in February 1944, and asked whether the Americans would be prepared to manufacture an additional fifty four wheel bombes! The new bombes were to make sure that a 'pessimistic outlook' on the Atlantic U-boat situation was catered for. However the Americans suspected that the main reason for the increased bombe request was the need for four wheel bombes to deal with Army and Air Force Enigma nets. This resulted 'from [the] British failure to carry through their obligation in building 4-wheel bombes', remarked Wenger, Engstrom and Meader acidly.[17]

The tension experienced within the Anglo-American relationship should not however be allowed to overshadow the progress they made together on the cryptographic front. The complete turnaround in the cryptographers' fortunes during the summer of 1943 was highlighted by the naval codebreaking units' ability to pass bombe time to Bletchley Park's Hut 6. The resulting increase in the bombe time allocated to Hut 6 was extremely helpful.

Although Hut 6's ability to read the Army Enigma was not as complete prior to the July 1943 invasion of Sicily as it had been during some phases of the North African battles, it provided valuable indications about the strength of the forces which the Allies had to overcome.[18] Air Force Enigma keys were also being read currently prior to the invasion. The intelligence gleaned from the combination of the two augured well for the coming invasions of the Italian mainland and, even more importantly, for the invasion of France.

By the time the Allied cryptographic units had sorted out their problems the crisis in the Atlantic had passed. That did not mean Naval Enigma could be neglected. The need for Naval Enigma intelligence was less acute after the end of May 1943, but it still had a vital role to play. Even though much of the offensive campaign against the U-boat tankers, conducted in July–August 1943, was carried out without the direct participation of Enigma decrypts, they nevertheless helped to identify the areas where the German supply boats were likely to be spotted. The Allies' long term victory over the Atlantic U-boats was to be further assisted by the fact that, after receiving several indications that the German Navy's intelligence arm was reading the Anglo-American Naval Cipher No. 3, the code used by the Allies for communications relating to transatlantic convoys, a new cipher was adopted by the Allies on 10 June 1943, a change which put an end to the damaging intelligence being used by the Germans to find Allied convoys.

At the beginning of 1944 a more direct role was played by Naval Enigma in ridding the Indian Ocean of the U-boat threat. The U-boats had begun to operate with some success there after another campaign in the North Atlantic had ended in failure. They were being supported by a surface fuel tanker, *Charlotte Schliemann*, which was sunk, thanks to Enigma information, on 12 February

1944. But it was the British willingness to stage a second ambush on *Brake, Charlotte Schliemann*'s replacement, a month later which was to alert the Germans that something strange was going on.

The men at the Admiralty were nervous from the start about the consequences of repeating the *Charlotte Schliemann* operation. The signals they sent to Admiral Sir James Somerville, the Commander-in-Chief of the Eastern Fleet, and the signals back to them give a fascinating insight into how operations were planned so as to minimise the risk of compromising the Allies' Enigma secret. 'The enemy is unaware that surface ships were used against *Charlotte Schliemann*,' the Admiralty cabled to Somerville on 21 February 1944, 'though he may presume Catalina patrolled in area. If surface ships are used again and should this time be reported near next fuel rendezvous enemy may infer their previous use and grave compromise is possible.'[19]

The Admiralty only relaxed the restraints they imposed on Somerville when U-boats made signals in the area where the tanker was operating, thereby providing the excuse for an anti-submarine sweep to be made. 'German U-boat signal interception particularly those at 2030 21st and 1730 22nd afford cover for Force which would be used for our anti-U-boat operation,' they told Somerville. '*Battler* [a jeep aircraft carrier] and *Quadrant* [a destroyer] can therefore be used in area mentioned provided that if actual rendezvous becomes known ship should not approach until enemy has been sighted by aircraft ... Cruiser should be kept in the background and not employed in the area until *Brake* has been sighted or broken W/T silence. Only after a suitable time interval could they then be used with security to our sources of information.'[20]

The Admiral in charge of the task force which was ordered to carry out 'Operation Covered', presumably so called because there had to be a good cover story for it, informed Somerville on 2 March 1944 what precautions he intended to take: 'No restriction on destroyers attacking tanker at any time nor on cruisers attacking outside supply area. If sighted inside supply area cruisers to avoid being seen by tanker until 4 hours after first sighting report.'[21] Somerville replied to the Admiral of the task force: 'If interval between aircraft sighting and appearance of cruiser repetition cruiser can be extended beyond 4 hours without risk of losing quarry this should be done.'[22]

On 4 March Somerville sent the following message to the Admiralty about the plan to sink the U-boats as well as the tanker: 'If tanker is sunk it is considered that the importance of denying to the enemy knowledge of the fact and how it was achieved outweigh the possible chances of success of Operation Stingaree against the U-boats. It is therefore only intended to carry out this operation if I am satisfied that tanker has reported her interception.'[23]

The written orders for Operation Covered included other precautions to prevent what was being planned ever becoming known to the Germans. At the top of the order under the words 'Most Secret' was the instruction: 'These orders are to be burnt on completion of the Operation', and there was also an instruction saying: 'Neither the sinking of the *Charlotte Schliemann* nor the name of the possible supply ship are to be mentioned to ships' companies.'[24]

As it turned out, a solitary destroyer, HMS *Roebuck*, was sent in to sink *Brake* after she was sighted by the escorting aircraft carrier's aircraft on 12 March 1944. *Brake* was eighteen miles away from *Roebuck* when the first report from the aircraft reached the destroyer's commander, John Lean, at about 3 p.m.[25] Two submarines were seen within half a mile of the tanker, as if they were waiting to receive supplies. *Roebuck*'s lookouts then sighted *Brake* for themselves a quarter of an hour later and began firing when there was about nine miles between the two ships. An hour later *Brake* sank, having been scuttled as most of its crew managed to escape in lifeboats. Lean had been forbidden to signal that he had sunk *Brake* until he was 100 miles clear of the rendezvous point. As soon as he had travelled the required distance, he sent the agreed coded signal: 'Covered Successful.' A signal came back from Somerville: 'Well done repetition well done.'

However it was not well done as far as the security of the Allies' Enigma secret was concerned. Some officers on the task force ships may have believed that a spy in Malaysia had provided the intelligence leading to the sighting of *Brake*; others put it down to a meteorological expert who was said to have identified the area where the rendezvous was situated because of its unusually temperate microclimate. But the Germans were not so easily convinced.[26] The commander of one of the U-boats at the rendezvous had sent a message – which had been read at Bletchley Park – stating that it presumed the refuelling had been 'basically compromised'. The U-boat commander had seen aircraft on the afternoon of 12 March which were thought to come from an aircraft carrier, as well as smoke to the south, which might have suggested to him that a task force was waiting there.[27]

It was partly because of this report that the Admiral from the task force wrote to Somerville stating that the 'cover intended for this operation is now inadequate. Even if suspicion has not been aroused I consider cover was weak, owing to very small chances success such an operation would have based only on D/F some 4 days old. I suggest it would now be most convincing if truth were told to effect that considerable force of surface ships with assistance of carrier borne A/C and A/C based on Indian Ocean Island . . . carried out continuous sweep for supply ships in likely fuelling areas during last three months.'[28] This conclusion was, he said, supported by the fact that the cruisers and carrier in the task force were 'most unlikely' to have been sighted by the U-boats, which had never been less than fourteen miles away from any Allied warships other than *Roebuck*.

This admission that the sinking was misconceived in the first place was borne out by the conclusions about it which had been reached inside Germany. 'It can be assumed that the enemy knew about the meeting point either by reading our messages or thanks to information provided by a traitor,' concluded the report on the affair. 'In the past repeated checks on our cipher system have confirmed that reading our messages is only possible after getting hold of all the codebooks including the Stichwort orders. The possibility that this has occurred cannot be excluded.'[29] As a safeguard, Dönitz sent out an emergency instruction to U-boat commanders instructing them to use settings which made use of the first letters of the names of their radio-electrician and third watch officer until new lists of settings could be handed out.[30]

Given that Bletchley Park was not relying on captured documents any more, this did not delay the codebreakers for very long. By 16 March 1944, they were already reading a message which gave details of two rendezvous to be attended by the last remaining supply U-boat in the area west of the Cape Verde Islands off West Africa. But this time the Admiralty, having realised that it had made a serious mistake, ordered all thirty-one commanders who were entitled to information based on Enigma decrypts to keep their forces clear of the area. Unfortunately, the Americans failed to comply, and a second U-boat was sunk there on 19 March, a first having already been sunk before the Admiralty's order was issued.

This led to a heated exchange of messages between Admiral King and Sir Andrew Cunningham, who had taken over as the First Sea Lord in September 1943, following Sir Dudley Pound's resignation. Cunningham stated that operating near a rendezvous mentioned in Enigma messages, even after the Germans had made modifications to the cipher, was liable to cause 'major changes' to be made to the Enigma procedure. King retorted that the rendezvous area had already been identified from Enigma decrypts before the change and he felt that, given that the jeep carrier groups had already been operating in the area for some time, their absence might raise more suspicions than their presence. He then stated that the British sinking of *Charlotte Schliemann* and *Brake* and the routing of convoys to evade the U-boats was the reason why the Germans were becoming suspicious.[31]

A report two months later by Kenneth Knowles, Rodger Winn's opposite number in the submarine tracking room in Washington, confirmed that King's bullish approach had turned out to be correct: 'Following the *Brake* sinking on 12 March 1944 in the Indian Ocean, the First Sea Lord requested that our contemplated A/S operations west of Cape Verde Islands be terminated,' he wrote, 'due to the danger of further arousing German suspicions as to cipher compromise. The position taken by Commander Tenth Fleet in continuing these attacks has been fully justified by subsequent operations, which resulted in the loss of six U/boats . . . Instead of arousing the suspicions of the enemy as to cipher compromise, they have merely confirmed his early fears that aircraft may be expected anywhere in the Atlantic North of 20° South.'[32]

The Germans' failure to realise that their cipher was compromised continued, in spite of another abortive attempt to seize Enigma documents from a U-boat. The opportunity arose at the beginning of March 1944, after a free ranging support group of warships which was escorting one of the transatlantic convoys to Britain made contact with the *U-744* about 200 miles south of Ireland. The idea behind having a support group of warships, in addition to the normal close escort, was that the support group was free to peel off after a U-boat was contacted in order to conduct a prolonged hunt; it did not have to abandon the search before it had been brought to a satisfactory conclusion, in order to return to the convoy, thereby allowing the U-boat to escape.

It was the *U-744*'s misfortune that it picked on one of these uncommitted groups of warships when it moved in for the kill on the morning of 5 March 1944.[33] Heinz Blischke, the twenty-three-year-old commander of *U-744*, had shot a torpedo at what looked like a solitary destroyer before submerging again. On the way down he and his crew heard an explosion, which led them to believe that the warship had been sunk. They then waited for the coast to clear. But shortly afterwards they heard the sound of ships passing above them. Then there was an eerie silence which was interrupted by the sudden crash of depth charges exploding. The lights in the U-boat were temporarily extinguished but, apart from that, no visible harm was done. The men would have been more concerned than they were at first if they had seen the number of ships which was being marshalled on the surface to pursue the attack against them. No less than six ships dropped depth charges during the next twelve hours.

The hunt went on all night; although the depth charges dropped did not damage the U-boat's hull, they did succeed in fouling her air circulation mechanism. By the morning of 6 March, half the crew were lying prostrate, either because they were attempting to conserve oxygen, which was achieved most successfully by resting and sleeping, or because they were unconscious after their air supply was contaminated by the growing amount of carbon monoxide. Blischke's room for manoeuvre was drastically curtailed during the early afternoon of 6 March when the U-boat's batteries began to run down. As the lights dimmed, he gradually became resigned to the fact that neither he, nor any of his men, would ever see daylight again. Perhaps influenced by the realisation that he was being pursued by so many warships, he let it be known to his officers that he was minded to remain under the water until he could no longer control the boat and until nature took its course.

A passionate debate ensued. The other officers ganged up on Blischke, telling him that there were a lot of young men in the crew who were entitled to be given the chance to survive. Their arguments softened Blischke's hardline approach, which was already being assailed by the thought that his young wife had just given birth to a baby, the subject matter of one of the last radio messages before the attack. Eventually Blischke was persuaded and orders were given to fix explosives fore and aft and inside the toilets. Once that was done, an attempt was made to rise to the surface. It was easier said than done. At the first attempt the U-boat plunged downwards bow first, before the blowing of tanks, and a judicious use of the last remaining reserves of battery power, restored *U-744*'s balance again. The second attempt to surface was more successful. The tanks were blown, and after a slow initial climb, the U-boat's bow shot up above the waves, before falling back into the water again. It was about 3.30 p.m. on 6 March, more than twenty-nine hours after the one-sided battle had begun.

As Blischke flung open the hatch and shouted to his men to abandon ship, he climbed up the conning tower and looked out. Before he could give any further orders, the gunners on the warships around the U-boat opened fire with every gun they could bring to bear. Blischke was hit by one of the first salvos, which clinically severed both his legs; after that he lay mercifully insensible to everything that followed on the U-boat deck, a horrific reminder to his comrades, who had to step over him, that bravery does not always win its just deserts. As the other men attempted to make it into the sea, emergency action was taken inside the U-boat. Two men attempted to light the fuses for the explosives; then, panicstricken, they too ran for their lives. They knew they had just under ten minutes to get off the boat. At the same time the head of the radio team lifted a plank on the inner deck and threw the moveable parts of the Enigma machine into the U-boat's bilge.[34]

Meanwhile a Canadian boarding party from the corvette HMCS *Chilliwack* arrived alongside the U-boat. Some of the Germans waiting on the outer deck thought that the small boat being rowed over was coming to rescue them. So they prepared to jump into it. This alarmed one of the Canadians so much that he pointed his revolver at a member of the U-boat's crew and pulled the trigger. The man crumpled into a heap as the shot rang out and the rest of the Germans, fearing they might also be shot, quickly made way so that the Canadians could board the U-boat without further obstruction. Whether the shooting represented a necessary act or a war crime, it certainly enabled the boarding party to climb onto the U-boat without any unnecessary delay. Three Canadians had already clambered down the conning tower before the last German emerged.[35] A fourth man, Wilfred Jenkins, was about to descend, when he was knocked over by a desperate German climbing out. As Jenkins prepared to enter the conning tower again, he pushed aside the white ensign flag which had been tied at the top, only to be frightened out of his wits by the sight of a German sitting with the conning tower hatch between his legs. His eyes were open and he appeared to be looking directly at Jenkins. It was some moments before Jenkins realised that the man must be dead.

Inside the U-boat the light was so dim, it was hard to see if there were any codebooks left. The three boarders had to rely on the light from their torches to see anything at all. In the radio room 'a machine similar to a typewriter probably a coding machine' was spotted. But the searching Canadians concentrated first on a couple of red codebooks, one of which had a yellow diagonal stripe on its cover, and some sheets of celluloid-like material about 8 inches by 10 inches, divided into lettered squares. 'These were thought to be part of the coding machine,' wrote Lieutenant Dunn, the officer in charge of the boarding party.

The codebooks and the sheets were passed to Bert Martin, the last man to board the U-boat. He had been told to jump back into the whaler, and that was where he was standing when he was handed *U-744*'s confidential books. 'Having no other place to put them,' he wrote later, 'I stuffed them under my life jacket.' But before he could row them over to *Chilliwack*, the whaler was capsized by a large wave, and Bert Martin, and the codebooks, fell into the water.

While this was going on, Jenkins' climb down into the conning tower was arrested by a shout from down below. 'We have to get off. She's taking on water. It's going to sink.' On hearing this, Jenkins and the three men down below, raced for the outer deck and jumped into the water. All members of the boarding party were subsequently rescued, but neither Martin, nor any of the other men ever saw the codebooks, or any of the other gear they had collected, again.

Although the commander of *Chaudière*, one of the other warships involved in the hunt, offered to send over another boarding party on a raft – three whalers had already capsized – the offer was declined by the commanding officer of the support group, and the *U-744* was sunk with a torpedo at 6.05 p.m.; the Germans' own scuttling charges had failed to explode.[36]

Fortunately for the Allies, no other German U-boats were in the vicinity to observe the Canadians going inside *U-744*. The Germans also failed to see through a misleading newspaper report which was published about the incident on 1 June 1944. In an article headed 'U-Boat Sunk by Canadian Warships', Lieutenant-Commander Coughlin, who was in command of *Chilliwack*, stated: 'our bow almost touched the U-boat's side at one time. You could see the terrified look on the Nazis' faces.'[37] But the report made it clear that the U-boat sank before the Canadians could board. Once again, Allied seamen had retrieved Enigma codebooks from a sinking U-boat without being caught in the act by the Germans; although they had failed to land the books they had brought out, the Allies' Enigma secret, at least, remained secure.

The Last Hiccough

Germany, France and the South Atlantic

MARCH–JUNE 1944

After Sir Stewart Menzies, the head of the British Secret Intelligence Service, heard that some of the Polish codebreakers, cipher experts and engineers had been captured, he waited anxiously to see how the Germans would react; the Poles knew that Enigma had been broken. One word from them would have been enough to persuade the Germans that Enigma was compromised, as Menzies well knew.[1] He would have been even more worried if he had known how close the Germans came to discovering from the Poles everything about the Allies' Enigma secret.

Antoni Palluth was the man they appeared to want to interview most of all. They knew all about his AVA company and its links with Polish Intelligence, and repeated attempts were made to trace him in Warsaw.[2] Fortunately for the Allies, after he was captured and imprisoned in the Sachsenhausen-Oranienburg concentration camp near Berlin, the Germans never realised that prisoner Number 64661 was the same Antoni Palluth as the man being hunted in Poland.[3]

Jadwiga Palluth, his wife, was the bait they dangled before him. She could have been imprisoned, or even shot, after she was caught storing AVA's radio equipment; the Germans had ruled that all such equipment should be handed in. But for some reason they accepted her implausible excuse; she had claimed the equipment was too heavy for her to carry down to the police station, and that she was only holding on to it until the Germans came to collect it. However there was always a lurking suspicion that the Germans had an ulterior motive for being so lenient, and that subsequently she was being watched, just in case her husband, Antoni, tried to get in touch. She assumed that the German authorities in Warsaw were not above trying to trick her into revealing his whereabouts. A Mr Pilarski, a man employed by Polish Intelligence before the war, began to visit her after the occupation of Warsaw. He always came for the same reason; he wanted to speak to her husband. Jadwiga Palluth quickly jumped to the conclusion that there was something fishy about the way he kept referring to her husband as 'Antoni'; Palluth had always insisted that everyone at work should refer to him as 'Mr Palluth'. So she told him nothing, and tipped off the Polish underground that Pilarski should be watched carefully.

It is unclear why after his arrest Palluth came to abandon his codename, 'Jean Lenoir', and began to use his real name again, but it very nearly helped the Germans who were looking for him to find out where he was. On one of the occasions when the German police visited Jadwiga Palluth in her flat, they asked her to empty out her bag. Inside were letters from her husband with the words 'Palluth Antoni' clearly written on the back. However, perhaps because her interrogators were put off the scent by the fact that the letters had been marked with the Oranienburg stamp, and by their conviction that Palluth was still at liberty, they failed to inspect the correspondence carefully after she told them that the letters were from a friend in the concentration camp. So they never saw the clue which would have told them where Palluth's 'hiding place' really was.

Jadwiga Palluth was able to send messages to her husband in the camp via another friend. One of the first messages she sent advised him, in a roundabout way, not to write letters to her at their flat. The message stated: 'Don't write to Mum because she is going blind.' Palluth did not at first fully understand the message and thought that his wife really was having problems with her eyes. Only later did he reveal that he had eventually understood what was meant; he then sent his letters via a friend living nearby in Warsaw.

Two of the guarded, but strangely moving, letters he sent are quoted below:

17/8/1943
Dear Friend,
I've already written more than once. I hope you received the letter. I am impatiently waiting for a message from you because I'm anxious to know if you, Junior and the children are all alive and well. Write to me about them because you'll understand how much I miss them. I'm always with them in my thoughts and in my heart. I'm allowed to receive food parcels with anything inside and without limitation as to their weight, but do not worry too much about me as I am well and because you and Junior are not

so well and don't have much to live on. I'm waiting for a long letter from you in German. Say hello and send my kisses to everyone. God bless you.
Your Antoni.

The second letter was dated 24 October 1943.

Dear Friend,
I hope Irene has received my letter and that it arrived in time for Junior's birthday. In the meantime I've received four more small parcels from Krysia . . . but please don't put tomatoes in with other products . . . I'm sorry you worry so much about me but if God permits I'll be OK.

I'm patiently waiting for your letter as I long for news about how you, Junior, the kids and everyone else are getting on, and how you are managing. Have the kids grown and do they study hard? It's not possible for me to put into words how much I miss you. I pray to God that he keeps an eye on you. Don't worry too much about me as I am in good health and I never lose hope. Write a lot. Greetings and kisses to Junior, the kids and everyone.
Antoni.

In this way Jadwiga and Antoni Palluth somehow managed to conceal where he was, until a terrible tragedy occurred on 18 April 1944. After the valiant struggle to stay out of German hands, and later to avoid being identified by them, Palluth eventually met his maker, not through any act done by the enemy, but thanks to a bombing raid carried out by his own side. The Heinkel factory where Palluth had been sent to work was bombed by the Allies and Antoni Palluth was one of the casualties.

Palluth's death was followed shortly afterwards by the death of his AVA partner, Edward Fokczyński, at the same camp. Fokczyński died of exhaustion. Their deaths meant that the Germans had two less potential informants who could tell them about the Allies' Enigma secret. But, as it turned out, it did not deny the Germans the opportunity to find out exactly what had been going on at Bletchley Park, and in France, after war broke out. For the Gestapo and the German Army signal experts, who were checking up on the security of Enigma, did eventually find Gwido Langer. He was a prisoner at Schloss Eisenberg, an internment camp near Brüx (now known as Most) in Sudetenland. No one has ever established how they found him there. Possibly his name had been identified in Warsaw, and then simply matched up with the records. Or perhaps Bertrand mentioned Langer's name after his arrest in January 1944. Whatever the reason, on 7 March 1944, Langer suddenly found that his case had been reopened and he was summoned to the camp kommandant's private quarters for an interrogation.

After the war Langer wrote up what happened next.

I was expecting the worst, for . . . all the prisoners' files had been closed when we were sent to this camp. Any renewed interrogation meant that some problem had been identified since then. I was sat down in front of a panel which included two army officers (a captain and a lieutenant as I was informed afterwards), and a Gestapo officer. They were all wearing plain clothes. The Gestapo officer spoke first: 'You were in the intelligence service,' he said. I was then made aware the panel wanted the answers to two questions. Firstly, would I work for the Germans in Poland? This was not asked directly, but when the army captain was talking, he happened to mention that they had already found other men to help them. At that point I interrupted, and said that you can only die once, and that I would never become another Redl [the Austrian Colonel Redl who agreed to spy for the Russians before the First World War]. After that, he did not persist. 'Oh I see,' he said.

The second question was about our work before 1940. When answering this, I made sure that I did not harm anyone, nor did my answer do any damage to our cause. When he asked me, without looking me in the eye, if we had read any machine ciphers during the war, I realized he must know something about what had happened. I told him that before the war, we conducted tests, and sometimes we did find a solution, but during the war, we didn't manage to decode anything, since the Germans had made changes, which they knew about, just before the war started.

I decided that I had to use the following strategy, given that I was dealing with experts, who knew who I was. I mixed truth with lies, and tried to present my lies in such a way that they had the veneer of truth. I then said that since I was dealing with experts, and since Major Ciężki knew more about the subject than I did, it was better that I did not try to go into details in case there was a conflict. That is why I asked the panel to summon Ciężki. They agreed, and Ciężki managed to convince them that the changes made before the war made decryption during the war impossible. I think they believed us, because although they were supposed to see us again, they never came.[4]

So it was that at a critical time in the Enigma story, Langer and Ciężki somehow managed to pull the wool over the Germans' eyes.

Even as they were being interrogated in Germany, a crucial plan, which was to play a decisive role in bringing the war to a successful conclusion for the Allies, was being acted upon in London. The plan – codenamed 'Fortitude' – represented an attempt to deceive the German Army over where the invasion of Europe by the Allies was to take place. One part of the plan was to persuade the Germans that the invasion would be concentrated in the Pas de Calais rather than in Normandy, the real target.[5] The Allies' ability to read Enigma messages and 'Fish', another code used by senior Nazi officials, which was also broken at Bletchley Park, was to play an important role; the decrypts enabled the Allies to check whether the Germans had been taken in by their deception.[6]

However Fortitude was called into question by the news that Bertrand had been captured by the Germans and then released in suspicious circumstances. Menzies realised that if Bertrand had told the Germans that the British had broken their Enigma cipher, Operation Fortitude might be turned on its head; the Germans might well be using it to deceive the Allies. The British Secret Intelligence Service (SIS) first heard about what had happened to Bertrand in the middle of January 1944, after his escape. However it was impossible to assess whether Bertrand had compromised the Allies' Enigma secret without interrogating him.

Unfortunately questioning Bertrand was not possible in the short term. Three months after his escape from the Germans, he was still in France. Only then did the SIS in London finally manage to inform him how to make contact with their evacuation agent.[7] The arrangement echoed what had happened when he had been arrested. He and Mary, his wife, were to stand outside the cathedral in Orléans, at midday on one of four consecutive days, starting on 8 May 1944. They were to wait for someone who was referred to as 'Fafa' in the signal sent from London. Like the last time when the SIS had arranged a rendezvous with Bertrand, London's agent was to carry a newspaper. The password this time was to be 'The train from Nîmes has arrived.'

As Bertrand and his wife hung around on the street by the cathedral on 8 May, waiting for a man whom neither of them had ever met before, they feared that the meeting had been compromised. Mary Bertrand overheard a blonde woman next to her speaking loudly to a friend about 'the train from Nîmes which must have arrived'. A man then walked up to Bertrand and asked him if he had come from Nîmes. Bertrand said that he had not and quickly walked away with his wife.

The next morning Bertrand went back to the same spot. When one of the men who had been there the day before drew up on a motorbike,

Bertrand went up to him and uttered the password. This time it had the desired effect. The all-important contact had been made. But before he could be evacuated, Bertrand was to have another very lucky escape. He was just returning to his hotel in Orléans, when a car passed slowly by. Inside was Monsieur Masuy, the Abwehr interrogator, who, according to Bertrand's subsequent account in his book *Enigma, ou la plus grande énigme de la guerre*, had allowed him his liberty if he collaborated with the Germans. Bertrand was fortunate that Masuy was looking away as the car went past.

It was 31 May 1944 before a coded message relating to Bertrand was sent out on the BBC from London. The message was: 'The white lilacs have flowered.' It told Fafa and his organisation that it was time to go to a field in the country near Lilas (French for lilacs), a rural area near Pithiviers, to wait for the aeroplane which was supposed to pick up Bertrand and his wife. The first time the Bertrands were taken to the field, no plane appeared, apart from a Messerschmidt, which, luckily, failed to react when they flashed their torches at it. It was 2 June, just days before the Allied landings in Normandy were due to begin, when the coded message about the lilacs was played over the radio again, and the expedition into the countryside was made once more, this time with better results. The plane arrived, and Gustave and Mary Bertrand were flown out of danger to England. That night another curious message went out on the BBC: 'Michel has shaved off his moustache', which was the signal to SIS and Resistance agents in France that Bertrand had arrived safely in England, and had shaved off the moustache which he had grown to disguise himself while he was on the run.

It was only then that Menzies, the head of the SIS, was able to look into whether Bertrand had compromised the Enigma secret, and whether the Fortitude deception plan, underpinning the whole strategy for the Allied invasion, was, in fact, fatally flawed. Menzies only had two clear days in which to check Bertrand's story; by the time Bertrand had had a good night's sleep and was available for his interrogation in London on 3 June, the first date pencilled in for the invasion was only two days away.[8]

The day before Bertrand was picked up by the plane in France, Menzies had asked Paul Paillole, the head of France's Counter-Intelligence division, whether he would conduct the interrogation. At the time Paillole was the only Frenchman who knew both the date when the invasion was due to start and its location. He was also privy to the Allies' Enigma secret, and Menzies' fear that Bertrand could have betrayed it to the Germans.

Bertrand was asked to write a report setting out what had happened to him since his arrest. The report was given to Paillole, who sat down to read it at 5.30 p.m. on 3 June 1944. In the report Bertrand described how following his arrest on 5 January, he had been interrogated by Monsieur Masuy, a saturnine character who wore a scarlet shirt and a black tie which he matched up with beige trousers.[9] He told Bertrand about the bath torture, and about the effects of giving prisoners anaesthetics until they were forced to tell everything they knew. Such talk terrified Bertrand; he knew he would not be able to remain silent if he were to be treated in this way.

The only way out was to pretend to collaborate, and in the process try to mislead Masuy, and even escape. It was then that Bertrand, and probably the Allies' Enigma secret, was saved thanks to an almost incredible coincidence. While waiting for his fate to be decided in a luxurious villa on the outskirts of Paris, Bertrand happened to see a face he recognised from the past. The face belonged to the all-powerful Otto Brandl, who was in charge of the German Purchasing Department in France. When Bertrand had met Brandl on a previous occasion, their roles had been reversed. Shortly before the invasion of France in May 1940, Otto Brandl had been arrested by the French police while attempting to travel across France to Germany. He claimed he was on the diplomatic staff in Belgium. However the police and counter-intelligence agents who interviewed him had quickly realised that he was not a real diplomat, something which was confirmed when he betrayed one of the secret agents he was running in an attempt to buy his freedom.

Although it is not clear whether Bertrand played any part in allowing him to be set free, Brandl, according to Bertrand, certainly believed that was the case. So when Bertrand reminded Brandl of their past meeting, Brandl was keen to help Bertrand in his turn. There was another fortunate coincidence in Bertrand's story: the fact that Brandl had been freed had enabled him in his turn to save Masuy's life. Both men recommended to their bosses that Bertrand should be used as a double agent. Under the deal which was eventually struck, Bertrand agreed to get in touch with his contacts in France before anyone realised that he had been arrested. Bertrand also agreed to arrange a meeting with another of London's agents so that Masuy's men could stage an ambush.

It was Bertrand's compliance with this arrangement which was to

put him very near the thin dividing line separating permissible trick-
ery in order to escape from impermissible collaboration. On 7 January 1944 he sent a telegram to London requesting a meeting with a
British agent for 15 January. He later claimed that he always planned
to cancel this meeting once Masuy allowed him to circulate freely;
he also intended to escape at the same time. Bertrand's ploy worked.
On 11 January he and his wife were permitted to be free for at least
forty-eight hours on condition that they reported back for duty on 13
January or, at the latest, the following day. By then Bertrand and his
wife were on the run. As well as securing his own liberty Bertrand
saved the British agent's life by cancelling the meeting he had
arranged. He also gave his contacts in France all the information he
had gleaned from his discussions with Masuy. On 27 and 28 January,
a message about the Bertrands, intended to confuse Masuy, was sent
out on the BBC. It stated: 'The Bertrands have arrived safely in London.'

On 3 June 1944 while Paul Paillole was considering whether this
story stacked up, he had to face up to a very difficult conflict of interest. On the one hand, he did not want to betray Bertrand, his former
colleague inside the Deuxième Bureau. On the other hand, he did not
want to have the deaths of hundreds of thousands of Allied soldiers
on his conscience just because he was being gullible, or too charita-
ble to Bertrand. There were parts of Bertrand's story which did not
seem very likely. For example, could Masuy really have been so foolish as to believe that once Bertrand was at liberty with his wife he
would ever voluntarily return to play the role of the double agent?
After Bertrand told Masuy what his real name was, and after Masuy
mentioned that he knew that Bertrand was involved with Hans Thilo
Schmidt, how was it that no questions were put to Bertrand about
what Schmidt had handed over to him, and in particular about
Enigma? Was it really true that Otto Brandl had been led to believe
that Bertrand had been responsible for his release in 1940? By
Bertrand's own account, Brandl was already involved in the process of
buying his freedom from the French counter-intelligence officers and
police by giving them information about his agents before Bertrand
arrived on the scene.

But Paillole was a man who believed in trusting his intuition.
Bertrand did not look like a man who was acting as a traitor. He
looked Paillole in the eye when telling him what happened, and was
so frank and so keen to tell him absolutely everything that Paillole
just could not believe that he had been turned. Bertrand's willingness

to include compromising and unlikely details in his account, when it might have been better for him to have excluded them, only served to reinforce Paillole's conviction that his former colleague had acted honourably.

In Paul Paillole's book *Notre Espion Chez Hitler*, Paillole did not mention that he had any doubts about what Bertrand had told the Germans. However by 1998, when I interviewed him, Bertrand and his wife had died. There no longer any need to cover anything up. The reality was that, in addition to some of the questionable features in Bertrand's account, there was something about what Bertrand said which Paillole found very disturbing. Time and again during Bertrand's discussions with Paillole, Bertrand tried to find out the date of the planned Allied landings in France. He wanted to know when and where, and then he wanted the information to be sent to his contacts in France over the radio. He asked for this to be done, even though he knew that the radio in question could, for all he knew, already be in German hands. It was this demand from Bertrand which persuaded Paillole that it would be wrong to give Menzies a totally positive verdict following the interview. Paillole did not believe that Bertrand had done anything discreditable such as betraying the Allies' Enigma secret. But he was not so sure of his judgement that he deemed it safe for Bertrand to be allowed to remain at liberty. So when he reported back to Menzies, he recommended a halfway house solution. Although Enigma was safe, as far as he could tell, Bertrand was to be placed under a form of house arrest until after the Normandy landings. At least that would ensure no further damage could be done by him.

There was, however, to be another twist to the story. In his attempt to be fair to both sides, Paillole felt that Bertrand needed to be protected from himself when dealing with Menzies and the SIS. When reading Bertrand's first account of what he had done for the Germans, Paillole came to the conclusion that his former colleague was being naô‹ve. Bertrand had admitted giving names of agents to the Germans, even though the names were of people who were in hiding or who had left the country. He had also admitted that he had set up a meeting with a British agent on 7 January 1944 and that he had passed details of the rendezvous to Masuy. This could have led to that agent being captured and shot if Bertrand had not managed to get away from Masuy in time. In other words Bertrand had admitted he had collaborated with the Germans in order to secure his own release. Given that Bertrand was trying to conceal the sensitive

Enigma secret, his strategy, if his story was true, was probably the right one. But, as Paillole pointed out, the British might not see it like that; if they were told that Bertrand had put the life of one of their agents at risk in order to save his own skin, they might want to lock him up immediately. It was to avoid this indignity, that Paillole advised Bertrand to tear up his original report. Instead Bertrand was instructed to write a more guarded account, with the bits mentioning collaboration taken out. This could then be passed on to Menzies without any fear that events would spin out of Paillole's control. In other words Paillole was prepared to tell Menzies and the SIS a white lie in order to help his former colleague. Paillole realised however that he would also be in serious trouble if Bertrand was not being straight with him after all. Only time would tell whether Paillole had read the situation correctly.

*

As the count down leading up to the Normandy landings was started, another drama relating to Enigma took place at sea. At 11.15 a.m. on 4 June 1944, the Asdic operator on USS *Chatelain*, a destroyer in an American hunter-killer task force operating off the coast of West Africa, picked up a U-boat on his set. His commander, Dudley Knox, who referred to his ship by its codename, 'Frenchy', sent the following message to the aircraft carrier, USS *Guadalcanal*, codenamed 'Blue Jay', where the task force's commander, Daniel Gallery, flew his flag: 'Bluejay from Frenchy we are investigating possible sound contact . . . We are attacking contact.'[10]

Chatelain fired her first hedgehogs and was just turning to make her next attack when her telegraphists received a message from one of *Guadalcanal*'s aircraft which was circling overhead: 'Ship that just fired hedghogs [depth charges] reverse course. I am firing at spot where sub is.' Helped by the advice from the air, *Chatelain* dropped a pattern of depth charges above the spot where the U-boat was thought to be lurking.

The second attack caused confusion, and in the case of some crewmembers even terror, inside the submerged *U-505*. All the lights were smashed. Even the emergency lights would not work. They were in the dark, apart from the beams given off by the officers' torches. That was enough to tell Harald Lange, the forty-year-old commander, that they were in real trouble. It was not just the light situation, or the fact that water was coming in at the stern. What bothered Lange most was that he might not be able to blow the water out of the tanks in order to take the U-boat to the surface. It would only take one more well aimed pattern of depth charges and they would be marooned hundreds of metres under the sea. The depth charges were still exploding around the U-boat when Lange saw his leading engineer looking at him enquiringly. Lange immediately understood what he was thinking, and decided there and then that they would have to go up quickly if they were to survive. It was too noisy to shout out the order, so he settled for giving an urgent thumbs up sign which said everything. Seconds later the U-boat's tanks were blown and *U-505* began her slow ascent to the surface.

As Lange made his decision, excited signals were flying through the ether above the still submerged U-boat. When *U-505* emerged, another message reached Frenchy (*Chatelain*) from the circling aircraft: 'You struck oil. Sub is surfacing . . . come in and have fun. It's a hell of a lot of fun. Let's get the bastard. I wish I had 10,000 rounds.' While the depth charges were being dropped, the aircraft carrier *Guadalcanal* had steamed away from the action, so as to be well clear of any trouble that might develop. However Captain Daniel Gallery still retained control over the five destroyers in his task force, which were collectively known as 'Blondie'. He proceeded to exercise that control by sending out the following order over the inter-ship radio: 'Bluejay to Blondie, I would like to capture that bastard if possible.'

But even as he spoke, his attempt to have the U-boat captured began to go seriously wrong. Dudley Knox, the commander of *Chatelain*, whose depth charges had brought the U-boat to the surface in the first place, suddenly found himself confronted with something of a crisis. He could see the U-boat was darting quickly towards him through the water. He also heard a lookout shouting that a torpedo had been fired at his ship. The action he took infuriated Gallery. Rather than contenting himself with taking emergency evasive action, he instead went onto the offensive himself and ordered his crew to fire a torpedo at the U-boat.

Fortunately for Gallery's plan, *Chatelain's* torpedo missed its target. But that was little consolation to the U-boat crew, who found themselves being subjected to bursts of murderous gunfire as they scrambled out of the conning tower. One of the shots hit Lange, the U-boat commander, in his legs. He fell unconscious onto the deck. By the time he came to, he was lying at the bottom of one of the U-boat's rubber boats, where he had been dragged by some of his men.

His first act was to call on his crew, most of whom were floating in the sea around him, to give three cheers for the *U-505*, which was expected to sink quickly. No one was more certain that this would occur than Hans Göbeler, the head machine operator in the U-boat's control room. Before leaving *U-505*, he had taken the cover off an 8-inch wide valve on the inner deck, thereby allowing seawater to come flooding into the boat. However Göbeler had made a mistake. Instead of taking the cover out of the conning tower with him, and throwing it into the sea, he merely tossed it down beside the valve, thereby giving an opportunity to anyone boarding the U-boat to shut off the incoming stream of water.

A boarding party had set off from USS *Pillsbury* within minutes of the U-boat coming to the surface. But the boarding also failed to go according to plan. One of the boarders, *Pillsbury*'s gunner's mate, fell between the motor whaleboat and the U-boat, hurting his legs in the process. As the other men pulled him back onto the U-boat, the tool box, which had been brought along to dismantle any apparatus discovered on *U-505*, also fell into the sea. Undaunted, the Americans jumped aboard and, disregarding the danger posed by booby traps, scuttling explosives and Germans left behind by their comrades, climbed down inside the U-boat's conning tower. There was just one dead German inside the conning tower. The U-boat's crew had evidently been surprised by *Chatelain*'s attack; their lunch, consisting of sausage and sandwiches was still on the table. Stanley Wdoniak, the radio man, and Wayne Pickels, *Pillsbury*'s twenty-one-year-old bosun's mate, rushed into the radio room, and immediately began collecting the codebooks. While they were working, they were told that water was flooding into the U-boat through a valve on the U-boat's inner deck, reminding them that the U-boat could sink at any minute. The codebooks were quickly passed up the conning tower to men waiting at the top and were carried along the outer deck to the whaler.

As the documents were being passed up, Zenon Lukosius, the engineer in the boarding party, spotted the cover for the valve which Hans Göbeler had left lying on the U-boat's inner deck. He moved to pick it up, but as he did so, he froze momentarily, after suddenly remembering that he had been told to watch out for booby traps. While he was thinking about what to do, he found himself looking into the anxious eyes of Wayne Pickels, who had temporarily abandoned the search for codebooks so that he could check out the leak. As Lukosius dithered, water continued to gush in through the valve.

Lukosius sweated as he decided to pick up the cover after all. 'Here goes nothing,' he said to himself, as he picked up the cover and placed it on top of the valve. There was no explosion, and the stream of incoming water was immediately cut off. Lukosius and Pickels sighed with relief.

After watching the last of the codebooks being passed up the conning tower ladder, Lukosius felt the U-boat shudder; the stern had settled lower in the water. From the top of the conning tower, Lukosius heard a shout. It was Lieutenant Albert David, the officer in charge of the boarding party, ordering his men, 'Come up, it's sinking.' Lukosius did not need to be told twice and raced up the conning tower ladder.

It was then that Gallery made what could have been a very expensive error of judgement. Given that the codebooks were already safely off *U-505*, he should have sunk the U-boat immediately. Instead he decided he would try to salvage her. In an attempt to satisfy himself that no explosives had been set on the U-boat, Gallery went down to *Guadalcanal*'s sickbay, where the wounded Harald Lange, *U-505*'s commander, was lying in bed.

'I'm sure you've heard about me,' Gallery began. 'I'm the man who captured Henke.' Gallery was referring to an incident two months earlier when he had captured the commander and crew of another U-boat sunk by his hunter-killer group. Lange who was too weak to respond just nodded.

Gallery commiserated with Lange about Lange's terrible wounds in his legs, and then continued, 'I could have you safely in a good hospital within twenty hours. But if that is to happen, you've got to help me. Is the U-boat safe? Or did you set explosives?'

At this Lange indignantly replied, 'Just imagine if you were the one lying in this bed and if you were asked such a question.'

Not to be so easily deterred, Gallery persisted. 'I can take you to Casablanca. Everyone tells me the French people there are on the side of the U-boat commanders.'

But this time Lange remained silent, and Gallery realised that nothing would be gained by carrying on with the interrogation. However, Lange's silence lest Gallery in a quandary; he needed to straighten *U-505*'s rudder, which was set at an angle, before attempting to tow the U-boat. Unfortunately, the rudder could only be operated from the compartment at the stern. The stern compartment hatch was shut and could only be opened if the door of a fuse box, on the wall outside, was closed. No one wanted to close the fuse box door in case it set off explosives.

On 5 June Gallery climbed onto *U-505* to see what had to be done. After inspecting the fuse box and its door, he was almost sure that no explosives were linked up to it. So he gritted his teeth and closed the door. There was no explosion, and the men around him laughed nervously. After checking that the rear compartment was not in fact flooded, Gallery had the rudder straightened and the U-boat made ready to be towed.

Gallery's initial plan was to attempt to tow *U-505* back to Casablanca, Morocco. But when his engineers told him he did not have enough fuel, he made another reckless decision. He would tow it into Dakar, the nearest neutral West African port, notwithstanding the fact that the news of the capture might easily be leaked from there back to Germany. He only reluctantly agreed it should be dragged across the Atlantic to Bermuda after receiving a signal telling him that Dakar was too dangerous. The towing was carried out successfully with the help of a tug, and an oiler ship, sent out to refuel *Guadalcanal*.

The codebooks captured from *U-505* only made it back to Bletchley Park on 20 June 1944, too late to affect the Normandy landings. They included the Offizier and regular Enigma settings for June 1944, the current short weather codebook for U boats, as well as the new versions of the bigram tables and the short signal codebook which were to come into effect on 1 August and 15 July respectively.[11] The 'address book' containing the code used by the U-boats to convert references on the grid chart into names and addresses was also picked up. The capture of this document meant that for the first time since the positions on the German charts had been encoded, the staff working in the submarine tracking rooms in London and in Washington were able to understand immediately the references to locations mentioned in decrypted Enigma messages.

However, in Washington Admiral King was furious with Gallery for jeopardising the Enigma secret, and he talked to his staff about having him court-martialled.[12] In London Sir Andrew Cunningham, the First Sea Lord, was equally concerned about Gallery's heroic, though reckless exploit. On 4 June, he cabled King: 'In view of the importance at this time for preventing the Germans suspecting a compromise of their cyphers, I am sure you will agree that all concerned should be ordered to maintain complete secrecy regarding the capture of *U-505*.'

It was an important point; unlike many of the other captures when the prisoners had been hustled into British warships before they knew what was happening, the POWs from *U-505* all knew that their U-boat had been captured. After being shipped back to America, the German submariners were isolated from other prisoners. Even the Red Cross was denied access to them; when Red Cross personnel visited the camp where the *U-505* men were being held, the prisoners were moved out before they could be seen. Back in Germany their parents were told that they had all been killed. Their parents only found out they were still alive in 1947 after the survivors were finally allowed to return to Germany.

*

As the armada of Allied ships sailed across the sea towards the Normandy beaches during the night of 5–6 June 1944, Harry Hinsley waited tensely in his office in Bletchley Park with only a map of France to keep him company. Although he was still only twenty-five years old, Hinsley had moved on from being just another intelligence officer analysing Enigma decrypts. He was now the assistant to Edward Travis, the head of the whole of Bletchley Park. However Hinsley still had one more important operational role to fulfil. It was down to him to inform the Allied commanders at their headquarters at Bushy Park and St Paul's School in London as soon as the first Enigma message was transmitted mentioning that the Allied ships had been sighted at sea.[13]

On the night of the invasion, Bletchley Park's mastery of the most important Naval Enigma nets was almost complete. For months, British codebreakers had been exploiting a regular stream of messages sent out by a weather station in the Bay of Biscay area which invariably started with the words: 'Wetter Vorhersage Biskaya . . .' (Weather forecast for Biscay . . .). It was an ideal crib, which enabled the Shark net to be broken quickly day in, and day out.[14] Prior to the first regular use of this crib, in October 1943, Bletchley Park had been breaking the Dolphin net first, and then using decrypted Dolphin messages as cribs to break Shark; some messages transmitted on Dolphin were also being transmitted on Shark. This had meant that Shark messages were usually broken after a time lag of one or two days.

There had been an agonising moment in January 1944 after the following reprimand, sent by the German security services to the

Biscay weather station, was intercepted in Britain, and read in Hut 8: 'Biscay Weather appears daily at an almost identical time, much of the text is identical, and it is repeated on the 'Ireland' frequencies.' Fortunately for the Allies, this rebuke had no significant effect; the Biscay weather messages were still going out on the day when Operation Overlord was commenced.

Another factor which led to the unprecedented speed with which Shark and Dolphin were being broken was the reduction in the number of wheel orders which had to be tested each day on the bombes, as a result of new research carried out by American cryptographers in Washington.[15] For example, the Americans pinpointed the German practice of not using wheel orders more than once during each six month period; as a result of this observation, any wheel order that had been identified by the Allied codebreakers could usually be ruled out on subsequent days during the six month period in question, without being tested on the bombes. Also, if a wheel was used in a particular position inside the Enigma, say, wheel 2 on the left, the American analysis revealed that on the next day there was an 80 per cent chance that the wheel on the left would be 6, 7 or 8, i.e. one of the three wheels not distributed to Army or Air Force Enigma operators. Statistics such as this, so painstakingly complied, could, it was hoped, result in a substantial saving of lives if the German U-boats attempted to spoil the Allied invasion plans by mounting a concerted attack while troops were being transported to France.

Bletchley Park's and the Americans' ability to break Naval Enigma ciphers more quickly was also helped by the large number of bombes coming on line; by the beginning of 1944, there were more than 330 three- and four-wheel bombes in Britain and America, a complete turnaround from the position at the end of 1941, when codebreakers had been forced to make do with just twelve.[16] The insistence by Frank Birch, the head of GC&CS' Naval Section, that aerials should be installed at Bletchley Park during the invasion, so that the interception of Enigma signals could be carried out on site, also helped to cut down the time between the interception of signals and the breaking of the code.[17]

As the hours ticked by, Hinsley's opposite number at SHAEF (the Supreme Headquarters of the Allied Expeditionary Force) rang him up from time to time to ask him if he had heard anything. Again and again Hinsley had to tell him that nothing had come through yet. 'I'll let you know the moment there's a sign,' he promised. As he spoke, he remembered a similar period of tension two years earlier when Ned Denning, at the Admiralty's OIC, had kept ringing him up to find out about *Tirpitz* and convoy PQ17. This time it was even more important that nothing should go wrong.

The first German Naval Enigma signal was decrypted shortly before 3 a.m. on 6 June. It was immediately teleprinted to London. Shortly afterwards, one of the three telephones on Hinsley's desk rang again.

'Is that Mr Hinsley?' enquired a disembodied woman's voice.

'Yes.'

'The prime minister would like to talk to you,' the woman told him. As Hinsley waited to speak to Winston Churchill, he remembered the last time he had seen the prime minister in the flesh, during the dark days of 1941, when Churchill had convened an emergency Battle of the Atlantic committee meeting to see what could be done about dealing with the U-boat menace. Hinsley had been surprised at how pink Churchill appeared in the flesh; he had looked like a big pink baby. Hinsley's memories were interrupted now by the familiar voice, heard so often on the wireless.

'Has the enemy heard we are coming yet?' it asked him.

Hinsley replied that the first message had just come through, and that Churchill would be getting it very soon via the teleprinter at Broadway. Then, without a word of thanks, Churchill put down the phone, leaving Hinsley gasping, and wondering whether he had done something wrong.

An hour and a half later the phone rang again; it was the prime minister ringing for another update.

'How's it going? Is anything adverse happening yet?' Churchill asked.

This time Hinsley was able to pass on to Churchill Naval Enigma intelligence which had recently been sent to the Allied commanders, just thirty-two minutes after the German signal in question had been transmitted. The Admiralty's message stated: 'EMERGENCY. At 0348B/6th 5th Torpedo Boat Flotilla were ordered to attack landing boats off Port en Bessin and Grandchamp.'[18] As soon as Hinsley finished speaking, the telephone was slammed down on him again.

By lunch time on 6 June the first wave of British troops were dug in on the Normandy beaches. Only then did Hinsley allow himself the luxury of abandoning the desk where he had been sitting for more than twenty-four hours. He walked out of his hut, went through the black gates in front of the Bletchley Park house and, after an exhilarating ride in the car which had been laid on to ferry him to his cottage, he slumped down into bed. Hinsley's war against Nazi Germany – and the battle for the Naval Enigma code – had been won.

Epilogue
Where did they go?

Significant events in the lives of the principal characters after they were mentioned for the last time in this book. (The information was up to date when this book went to press.)

THE SCHMIDTS
Charlotte Schmidt, the wife of Hans Thilo Schmidt, went to live in Vienna after her husband's arrest and death. But her and her family's torment was still not over. After her hiding place was betrayed to the invading Russians by a Viennese informer in return for a box of cigarettes, she was taken out into the street and raped. Her will to live already eaten away after what had happened to Hans Thilo, she swallowed some poison and committed suicide, dying an agonising death in the same street where she had been raped.

    Rudolf Schmidt, Hans Thilo's brother, was relieved of his command in the German Army in April 1943, shortly after Hitler found out about Hans Thilo Schmidt's treason.[1] After Rudolf Schmidt's dismissal, Joseph Goebbels noted in his Diary: 'He [Hitler] is totally fed up with the generals . . . They are not loyal to him . . . For example at the home of Colonel General Schmidt's brother, who was arrested for treason, a number of letters from the Colonel General were found which spoke very disparagingly of the Führer. Now he is one of the generals who was held in particularly high esteem by the Führer.'[2]

    After the War, Rudolf Schmidt was accused of ordering the murder of Russian prisoners when the Germans failed to capture Moscow in 1941. He was handed over to Russia where he was imprisoned until his release in 1955. He died two years later.

THE POLES

Jerzy Różycki drowned when *Lamoricière*, the ship carrying him and some fellow codebreakers back to France from Algiers, sank on 9 January 1942.

Gwido Langer travelled to England after being liberated by the Allies. But rather than being decorated for masterminding the breaking of the Enigma cipher, and for not giving anything away during his imprisonment and interrogation, the Polish officers to whom he attempted to report would not even deign to meet him for months after he arrived in England. They blamed him for not acting decisively when Bertrand was attempting to help him and his fellow Poles to escape from France. He attempted to defend himself in his Memoirs which were completed in 1945-6, but in 1948 he died, a bitter and broken man, before Enigma could be written about in the public domain. So he never had the chance to call up evidence which might have enabled him to clear his name.

Maksymilian Ciężki, like Langer, was never given the praise to which he was entitled for masterminding the breaking of the Enigma cipher. He decided not to live in Poland after the war, preferring to remain in Britain. He died in 1951.

Henryk Zygalski worked with Rejewski on the code used by the SS after arriving in England in 1943. He remained in England after the war teaching in London. He died in 1978.

Marian Rejewski helped Zygalski break the code used by the SS, after they arrived in England in 1943, but they were never allowed to break Enigma messages again. After the war, Rejewski went back to Poland, arriving there in 1946, only to find that the local Communists in Bydgoszcz, where he went to live – who knew nothing of his codebreaking work – suspected him of being decadent because he had lived abroad. They asked him to take a middle-ranking management position in industry rather than allowing him the opportunity to take up the high-flying academic mathematical post which should have been his due. This treatment represented one of the great injustices of the Enigma story. He completed the first part of his Memoirs in 1967, but he was only decorated for his groundbreaking wartime work two years before his death, when in 1978 he was given the Polonia Restituta, the equivalent of the French Légion d'Honneur.

In 1983 Rejewski, Zygalski and Różycki's part in the breaking of the Enigma cipher was finally commemorated in Poland with the issue of a special stamp. But by then all three men had died.

THE FRENCH

Rodolphe Lemoine refused to act as a double agent against France.[3] His excuse was that the Germans had kept him out of circulation for too long following his arrest in 1943 for him to be able to deceive the French. As the Allies invaded France he was taken to Berlin, where he was captured and interrogated by the French. He died in October 1946.

Gustave Bertrand retired from the French Secret Service in 1950 and went on to become a local councillor at Théoule in the south of France, where he also served as the mayor. He kept the Enigma secret until 1973, when, in order to correct erroneous accounts about the Enigma story in two books published in France and in Germany, his book, *Enigma, ou la plus grande énigme de la guerre*, was published. The book, which went on sale the year before F. W. Winterbotham's *The Ultra Secret* revealed the Enigma secret in England, gave for the first time, a detailed account of the French Deuxième Bureau's contacts with Hans Thilo Schmidt and the French role in the breaking of the Enigma. Bertrand died three years later.

Paul Paillole retired as the head of Counter-Intelligence as soon as the war was over in order to pursue a new career in industry. The company he worked for helped to re-arm Germany after the war. In 1985 his second book, *Notre Espion Chez Hitler*, was published giving a much more coherent account of the Hans Thilo Schmidt affair than that included in Bertrand's book. At the date of going to press, he was living outside Paris, making him the last man from the French Secret Service to have seen Hans Thilo Schmidt and to have lived to tell the tale.

THE BRITISH

Dilly Knox[4] went into hospital during 1942 after he was found to be suffering from lymph cancer. This did not stop him getting out of bed to receive the CMG which was his reward for his codebreaking successes. Knox told his family that if only he could go to the West Indies he was sure that he would recover, and there was a rumour that Churchill had agreed to make a warship available so that he could be taken there to recuperate. Whether or not this was true, the plan was never put into operation, and Dilly Knox died on 27 February 1943.

Alan Turing stopped working on the Enigma problem by mid-1943. He left Bletchley Park's Hut 8 in November 1942, when he travelled to the United States to advise the Americans on the development of their bombe machine, and he also worked on a machine designed to encipher speech.[5] After the war one of the official histories of Hut 8, written by Hugh Alexander, Turing's successor as the head of the Naval codebreakers' section, paid Turing the following tribute: 'It is always difficult to say that anyone is indispensable, but if anyone was indispensable to Hut 8, it was Turing. The pioneer work always tends to be forgotten when experience and routine later make everything seem easy, and many of us in Hut 8 felt that the magnitude of Turing's contribution was never fully realized by the outside world.'[6] After 1945 Turing played his part in the building of one of the world's first computers, thereby putting into practice the principles of the universal machine first outlined by him in an academic paper published during the 1930s. But ironically, the very innocence which had helped him to come up with his ideas in the first place – he worked some of them out without referring to other published material dealing with similar subject matter – led to an unfortunate incident in 1952. In the course of reporting a theft, he unwisely told the investigating detectives that he was having a homosexual relationship with the friend of the man who had done the thieving. Turing was prosecuted for indecent behaviour and, in spite of his OBE and a glowing character witness statement from Hugh Alexander, he only escaped going to prison by allowing himself to be injected with female hormones – so-called organotherapy – as a result of which he developed breasts, like a woman. Two years later he was found dead in his rooms, after he had poisoned himself with cyanide. No one was able to prove beyond a shadow of a doubt whether he had committed suicide – although this was the verdict of the coroner at the inquest – or whether he had inadvertently licked cyanide off an apple during an experiment; an apple coated with cyanide was found half eaten beside his corpse.

Turing's role in breaking Enigma was first revealed in 1982, when it was described in Gordon Welchman's *The Hut Six Story* (see under Welchman below), but it only became known to a wider audience after his life became the subject of Hugh Whitemore's play *Breaking The Code* which was first shown in London's West End in 1986.[7] The play was more recently shown on television; in the play and the TV adaptation, Turing was portrayed by the actor, Derek Jacobi.

Gordon Welchman emigrated to the United States after the war, where he ended up working for Mitre, a company used by the American defence ministry. He produced a new system which allowed groundstaff to keep in contact with their aircraft while they were airborne. But he very much wanted to demonstrate the lessons which he had learned as a result of working on Enigma at Bletchley Park. So in 1982 they were included in his controversial book, *The Hut Six Story*, which described how the Air Force Enigma was broken. Some of Welchman's former colleagues from Bletchley Park were appalled by what they saw as a blatant breach of the oath of secrecy which they had all taken when they had been hired by GC&CS. The American government obviously agreed, since Welchman lost his security licence. On 8 July 1985 the D Notice Committee, which advises the media on material with a possible bearing on national security, cleared a subsequent long article written by Welchman which further described the techniques used to break Enigma. The D Notice Committee appears to have suggested, however, that Welchman should submit his draft to his former department before publication. Four days later Sir Peter Marychurch, who was then Director of GCHQ, wrote accusing Welchman of causing 'direct damage to security' and of setting 'a disastrous example to others'. Nevertheless the article was published, and once more the Enigma secret was aired in public. Welchman, having told everything which he could remember, died of cancer later that same year.

Harry Hinsley was offered a special fellowship by St John's College, Cambridge during 1944, as it tried to find young men to fill the void left by the war years. One of his references was given by 'C', otherwise known as Sir Stewart Menzies, the head of the Secret Intelligence Service. Hinsley decided to accept St John's College's offer after the war, and went on to mastermind the writing of *British Intelligence in the Second World War*, the five-volume official history of the part played by intelligence, including information derived from Enigma decrypts, during the war. Subsequently, he became the Master of St John's College and Vice-Chancellor of Cambridge University, and he was knighted in 1985, after the Enigma story had become public. He died of lung cancer in 1998.

NAVAL ENIGMA

The Shark Enigma net was broken every day after 12 September 1943, as was the Home Waters (Dolphin) Enigma net.[8] Paradoxically, the breaking of these and other Naval Enigma nets was helped, rather than hindered, by the fact that the Germans began to use more and more different Enigma nets; the Allied cryptographers were assisted by the German decision to send out the same messages on more than one of the growing number of nets. Once one of the nets was broken, the messages decrypted acted as cribs for the other nets.

All the nets gradually stopped using three-wheel Enigma machines, and began to use four-wheel Enigmas, but the alteration which threatened to cause the codebreakers the biggest headache was made in May 1945, when new bigram tables were brought in at the same time as the Germans began to make use of more than one initial wheel setting (Grundstellung). As a result, bigram tables could not be reconstructed using the procedure specified in this book, which was only useable when one initial wheel setting was being used each day. A new system was devised to deal with the problem, but it would have taken at least two months for it to have become operational, by which time it was possible that the codebreakers would no longer have been able to identify the cribs necessary to work out the Enigma wheel orders and plug socket settings on the bombe machines. 'It is, I think, possible that we should not have survived this bigram table change,' wrote the author of 'The History of Hut Eight', one of the official histories about the breaking of the Naval Enigma. 'It would probably have been necessary to capture the bigram tables.'[9]

The fact that Germany surrendered and the war ended just as this problem came to light represented a final instance of the incredible luck which was experienced by the Enigma codebreakers in the course of the four-year period when one or more Naval Enigma nets were being broken.

Chronology

1931

8 November Hans Thilo Schmidt permits Rodolphe Lemoine and Gustave Bertrand, his French spymasters, to photograph the Enigma operating manuals which he has 'borrowed' from a safe in the German Defence Ministry Cipher Office.

8–10 December Bertrand delivers the photographs of the Enigma manuals to the Polish General Staff's Cipher Bureau in Warsaw, after the French and British experts have indicated that they cannot use them to break the Enigma cipher.

19 December Schmidt hands over an Enigma settings list to the French for the first time. Within days the list is sent to the Polish Cipher Bureau in Warsaw. But even with these documents, the Polish cryptographers cannot read the Enigma messages transmitted by the German armed forces; if they are to break to code, they will have to reconstruct the Enigma cipher machine itself.

1932

2–16 August Schmidt hands over two Enigma settings lists to the French, for September and October 1932. Once again, they are passed on to the Poles in Warsaw. These settings will, eventually, help the Poles to break the code for the first time.

December Marian Rejewski, the Polish cryptographer, works out the wiring inside the Enigma cipher machine, using the documents supplied by Hans Thilo Schmidt in November 1931 and August 1932. This is the crucial breakthrough which enables the Poles to break the code, and to read Enigma messages transmitted by the German armed forces. However, the French are to be kept in the dark for the next six and a half years.

1937

1 May The Enigma indicating system used by the German Navy is altered. As a result, the Polish cryptographers can no longer read Naval Enigma messages. The Naval Enigma will not be broken again regularly and currently for more than four years.

6 November A message from the French Ambassador in Berlin to the French Minister of Foreign Affairs in Paris, based on intelligence supplied by Hans Thilo Schmidt, is intercepted by the Germans. The Abwehr is told to track down the traitor who has leaked the information to the French. From that moment Schmidt's life and the security of the Polish Enigma secret is in peril.

1938

15 September The Enigma indicating system used by the German Army is altered, so that instead of all operators using a common initial wheel position (Grundstellung), each operator has to choose a different initial position for each message. This means the Polish codebreakers cannot carry on using the 'characteristic' method to break the code. However, within weeks, they have invented two new codebreaking tools, one of which, the bomby, can be used almost immediately, and the second, the perforated sheets, will, it is hoped, be 'manufactured' over the next few months.

15 December Two extra wheels for the German Army Enigma are issued, which means that Enigma operators each day use three wheels out of a total of five in circulation. As a result the Polish cryptographers cannot complete the task of producing the necessary number of perforated sheets with their existing resources; because of the two extra wheels, ten times as many perforated sheets would have to be produced.

1939

1 January The number of Enigma plugboard sockets connected to other sockets increases from between ten to sixteen to between fourteen and twenty. This change means that the bomby can no longer be relied on as the main tool to break the code.

24–25 July The Poles finally tell the French and British cryptographers that they have reconstructed the Enigma machine and have been reading the German armed forces' Enigma messages from 1933 to 1938. Although the Poles admit they are no longer reading the armed forces' messages, they reveal that the messages can be broken again if the perforated sheets are produced.

6 *September* The Polish cryptographers flee from Warsaw as Nazi Germany invades Poland. By October 1939 the Poles are installed at Château de Vignolles near Gretz-Armainvillers, north-east of Paris, where they wait for the perforated sheets which are being manufactured in Britain.

1940

17 *January* The first wartime Enigma messages are decrypted, after the perforated sheets are completed; the messages read are more than two months old. Enigma messages are not read within twenty-four hours of being transmitted until April 1940. The messages read have been transmitted after using the flawed indicating system used by the Army and Air Force; the Naval Enigma still cannot be broken.

12 *February* Two of the extra wheels supplied to German Naval Enigma operators, in addition to the five wheels used by all telegraphists in the German armed forces, are captured from the *U-33*, which is sunk off the west coast of Scotland. Although the wheels will one day help Bletchley Park, they do not immediately enable the British cryptographers to master the Naval Enigma; the indicating system is still baffling them.

18 *March* The first bombe machine, designed by Alan Turing, is installed at Bletchley Park. However, it does not incorporate the improvements subsequently suggested by Gordon Welchman, and by Turing himself, so it can only work out Enigma settings on the day in question, if the 'menu' produced for the bombe includes a 'closure' (see Appendix 2).

4 April Bletchley Park for the first time reads Enigma messages within twenty-four hours of their being transmitted by the Germans.

26 *April Polares*, a German trawler, is captured off the coast of Norway along with the Enigma operators' logs, some Enigma settings and the all-important explanation specifying how the Naval Enigma indicating system works. It is hoped that these documents will enable Bletchley Park to break the Naval Enigma cipher at last, using Alan Turing's Banburismus procedure. However Banburismus does not work at first; after some April 1940 messages are read – they are the first Naval Enigma messages to be read by British cryptographers during the war – no further Naval Enigma messages are broken, using Banburismus or any other procedure, until November 1940.

1 *May* The indicating system used by the German Army and Air Force

is altered so that, except in the Norwegian theatre, no operators encipher their message settings twice. This means that the perforated sheets can no longer be used to break the code, and Bletchley Park, and the Poles working on Enigma in France, are temporarily 'blinded'.

3–21 May Post-mortems carried out by the Germans on the disappearance of *Polares* conclude that the Naval Enigma cipher is unlikely to have been compromised; the German experts state that even if Enigma settings were captured, no settings were on board *Polares* for the period after 1 June 1940, so that whatever happened to *Polares*, cipher security will be re-established then.

16 May Preparations are made to evacuate the Polish codebreakers from the Franco-Polish codebreaking centre near Gretz-Armainvilliers in France, as the Germans invade France.

22 May Using cillis, and the Herivel Tip the cryptographers at Bletchley Park break their first Enigma messages outside the Norwegian theatre since the 1 May 1940 black out.

8 June Karl Dönitz questions whether the Naval Enigma cipher has been compromised by the sinking of *U-13* on 31 May 1940; he is told that the Enigma is unlikely to have been compromised.

20 June Rodolphe Lemoine, the French spymaster who had extracted the Enigma manuals and settings from Hans Thilo Schmidt, fails to leave France after being insulted by the commander of a British minesweeper; his refusal to flee to England could jeopardise the British and Franco-Polish Enigma secret; if he ever falls into the hands of the Germans, he might be forced or tempted to tell them everything he knows about the Enigma documents supplied by Schmidt.

24 June The Polish cryptographers, after being evacuated from Paris, are flown to Oran in Algeria. But in three months they will return to France, in spite of the risks.

1 July New Naval Enigma bigram tables come into effect. This means that no new messages can be broken using Banburismus until the new bigram tables are either captured or reconstructed. However, the reconstruction of the bigram tables is only possible if Naval Enigma settings are worked out using a crib and the bombe (which is unlikely to happen, given that no cribs have yet been discovered), or if the settings are captured.

8 August The first spider bombe, incorporating Gordon Welchman and Turing's improvements, is installed at Bletchley Park.

12 September Ian Fleming proposes plan to capture the Naval Enigma codebooks by crash landing a captured German aircraft in the English Channel, and then ambushing the German rescue boat; the plan, codenamed 'Operation Ruthless', is abandoned in October 1940 after it turns out to be impractical.

1 October The Polish codebreakers, having been shipped back to the unoccupied south of France from Algeria, are ready to start work at the new codebreaking centre at Château des Fouzes near Uzès. From the point of view of the Allies' Enigma secret, their presence in France is an accident waiting to happen.

1941

4 March Krebs, a German trawler, is captured off the Lofoten Islands in Norway, with the February 1941 Naval Enigma settings list. Using these settings, Bletchley Park is able to reconstruct the Naval Enigma bigram tables by the end of March thereby opening the way for the Banburismus procedure to be used to break Naval Enigma at the beginning of April 1941.

25–26 March Bletchley Park's cryptographers read the Italian Naval Enigma messages which help Admiral Cunningham, the Commander-in-Chief of the Mediterranean Fleet, defeat the Italian Navy in the Battle of Matapan on 28–29 March 1941. This is the first victory achieved thanks to Enigma intelligence.

7 May München, the German weather ship, is captured along with the June 1941 Naval Enigma settings; as a result, in June 1941, the Bletchley Park cryptographers will be able to read German Naval Enigma messages currently for the first time.

9 May U-110 is captured, along with the Offizier Enigma settings for June 1941. These settings enable the Bletchley Park codebreakers to work out how to break future Offizier messages, an important step, given that the Germans often use the Offizier procedure to announce changes to the general Enigma procedure.

4 June Gedania, a German supply ship, is captured by the British, along with some Enigma documents; the capture will lead the Germans to question whether Naval Enigma has been compromised.

15 June New Naval Enigma bigram tables are introduced; this threatens to delay the mastering of the Naval Enigma by another couple of months, while the new bigram tables are reconstructed at Bletchley Park. The only way to avoid such a delay is to capture the new tables at sea.

28 June Lauenburg, the German weather ship, is captured along with the July 1941 Naval Enigma settings; these settings enable Bletchley Park to read Naval Enigma messages currently during July 1941, and they also mean that the British cryptographers can reconstruct the new bigram tables without having to monopolise the bombes, which are badly needed by Hut 6, the Bletchley Park section dealing with the Air Force Enigma.

27 August U-570 is captured by the Allies along with some Enigma documents; the Germans question whether Naval Enigma has been compromised.

6 September Churchill's morale-boosting visit to Bletchley Park.

28 September The British submarine *Clyde* attempts to ambush three German U-boats in the Cape Verde Islands; when all three U-boats escape, Dönitz notes in his War Diary: 'The most likely explanation is that our cipher has been compromised.'

18–24 October The German Navy's Communications Service states that the capture of *U-570* on 27 August, and *Gedania* on 4 June 1941 could have led to the compromise of the Naval Enigma cipher, though they think that such a compromise is unlikely. The final conclusion reached by Erhard Maertens, the head of the German Navy's Communications Service, after also taking into account what happened in the Cape Verde Islands on 28 September 1941, is: 'The acute disquiet about the compromise of our Secret Operation cannot be justified. Our cipher does not appear to have been broken.'

21 October Bletchley Park's senior cryptographers write to Churchill complaining that they are not being given enough resources to do their codebreaking efficiently. Churchill immediately orders that their demands should be met.

31 October The Abwehr questions whether the 4 June 1941 capture of *Gedania* means that Naval Enigma is compromised. British witnesses subsequently captured by the Germans had stated that unspecified documents were taken from the German supply ship. The Abwehr concluded that it was 'worrying that codes . . . and sea maps with secret messages have been seen by the enemy'.

22 November After being tipped off by Enigma intelligence, the Royal Navy sinks the German supply ship *Atlantis* as it meets up with some U-boats. The subsequent British ambush of another supply ship nine days later will cause the Germans to question, yet again, whether Naval Enigma has been compromised.

29 November The Germans replace the bigram tables with a new set; until the new set is reconstructed or captured, Bletchley Park can only break the code by using cribs and bombes. As a result all possible wheel orders have to be tested on the bombe, a lengthy process. This is a major problem for the Bletchley Park cryptographers, given that bombes are in short supply.

31 November The Royal Navy's attack on the German supply ship *Python* leads the crew to scuttle the vessel and to report that the German Naval Enigma cipher might be compromised.

26–7 December In the course of the so-called Vågso raid, codenamed 'Operation Archery', carried out on the coast of south-west Norway, and in the course of another raid, codenamed 'Operation Anklet', in the Lofoten Islands, three German trawlers are captured with the new bigram tables on board. As a result, Banburismus can be used once again to break the code.

1942

20 January The Germans replace the short weather report codebook used by the U-boats with a new version; this act will mean that the Bletchley Park cryptographers cannot not use the old version, captured from *München* and *U-110* in May 1941, to help them break back into 'Shark', the Naval Enigma net used by the U-boats in the Atlantic and Mediterranean, following the black out on 1 February 1942.

1 February Bletchley Park can no longer break Shark after a new fourth wheel and a new reflector are used inside the Naval Enigma cipher machines distributed to U-boats in the Atlantic and Mediterranean. The black out will last for more than ten months.

18 March A German post-mortem on how *Atlantis* and *Python* came to be sunk in November 1941 states that Naval Enigma is probably not compromised; the investigators believe that the Royal Navy would have caught up with *Tirpitz* in January 1942 as she moved from Germany to Norway, and with *Scharnhorst* and *Gneisenau* as they moved from France to Germany in February 1942, if British cryptographers had been reading German Enigma messages.

4 July After a Naval Enigma black out, the Admiralty's OIC cannot assure Sir Dudley Pound, the First Sea Lord, that the German battleship *Tirpitz* has not set out from Norway to attack convoy PQ17. Pound orders the convoy to scatter; afterwards twenty-three of the thirty-five merchant ships in the convoy are sunk. It is one of the biggest convoy disasters of the war.

30 October Two heroic British seamen drown after *U-559* is boarded and some of her codebooks are seized. The documents captured include the short weather report codebook. It gives Bletchley Park's codebreakers the opportunity to break Shark once more; cribs can be worked out from the German weather reports now that the codebook is in British hands, and the cribs can be used to create menus for the bombes. However, no Shark messages are read until 13 December 1942.

8–9 November The Polish cryptographers, who know about the Allies' Enigma secret, are evacuated from Château des Fouzes, the codebreaking centre in France, after the Allied invasion of North Africa makes it certain that the Germans will move into the south of France. However while the Poles remain in hiding in France, there is a danger that they might be captured, and the Allies' Enigma secret compromised.

15 November The Abwehr decide to tail Rodolphe Lemoine, who has failed to leave the south of France after the Germans moved in.

13 December Shark is finally broken after Bletchley Park's cryptographers discover that the four-wheel Naval Enigma cipher machine being used by the U-boats in the Atlantic and Mediterranean is set up so that it is equivalent to a three-wheel Enigma; this means that cribs identified following the capture of the short weather report codebook can be used in conjunction with the existing three-wheel bombes to break the code.

1943

29 January Marian Rejewski and Henryk Zygalski, the Polish cryptographers, escape from France to Spain; they finally make it to England in July 1943. However there are still other Polish cryptographers and engineers stranded in France who know about the Allies' Enigma secret.

12 February Gustave Bertrand receives a message from Antoni Palluth, one of the Polish engineers who manufactured the replica Enigma cipher machines before and during the war, stating that he has been arrested by the Germans.

17 February U-205 is captured with some of her Enigma codebooks; these codebooks had already been captured. The decision to carry on capturing codebooks at a time when Naval Enigma was being read represented an unnecessary risk; if submariners in another U-boat had observed what was happening, the Allies' Enigma secret might have been compromised.

27 February Rodolphe Lemoine, the French spymaster who knows about Hans Thilo Schmidt and the Enigma manuals, is arrested by Germans in the south of France.

8 March Enigma intelligence warns Bletchley Park that the current version of the short weather report codebook, captured from *U-559*, is being replaced. The First Sea Lord, Sir Dudley Pound, is informed that as a result: 'The Tracking Room will be "blinded" in regard to U-boat movements for some considerable period.'

10 March The new short weather report codebooks comes into effect. This deprives the British codebreakers of the cribs which had been helping them to break Shark since 13 December 1942. During the codebreaking black out, there is another disaster at sea; twenty-two ships from convoys SC122 and HX229 are sunk. An Admiralty report, written at the end of the year, stated: 'Up to 20th March 1943, there seemed real danger that the enemy would achieve his aim of severing the routes which united Great Britain with the North American continent.'

13 March Polish Cipher Bureau bosses Gwido Langer and Maksymilian Ciężki are arrested by the Germans as they attempt to cross the border between France and Spain; like Palluth, they know all about the Allies' Enigma secret.

17 March Rodolphe Lemoine tells the Germans about Hans Thilo Schmidt and the Enigma manuals.

19 March Bletchley Park's codebreakers break into Shark again using the short signal codebook, which had also been captured from *U-559* on 30 October 1942, to help them identify cribs.

1 July A new fourth wheel and a new reflector are introduced for the Naval Enigma cipher machines being used by the Atlantic U-boats; British and American cryptographers work out their internal wiring by mid-July 1943.

10 August German intelligence in Switzerland warns that the Americans are reading Naval Enigma; although Dönitz admits that Naval Enigma messages might have been read at the end of July 1943 and the beginning of August 1943, he is sure that they have not been read thereafter because of a new security measure introduced.

20 August A Bletchley Park report states: 'We have had a record week on Shark, the whole month clearing up.' An official history of Hut 8, the Naval Enigma codebreaking section at Bletchley Park, stated: 'It indicated the end of the great Shark battle. From now onwards, there were always enough cribs and enough bombes to keep the situation under control.'

19 September Hans Thilo Schmidt commits suicide. The Germans never realised that the Enigma documents he had shown to the French were sufficient to compromise their Enigma ciphers during, as well as before, the war.

26 December The sinking of the *Scharnhorst*, thanks to Naval Enigma intelligence.

1944

5 January Gustave Bertrand is arrested by the Germans while working under cover for the Resistance in France. He admits to himself that he will not be able to remain silent if he is tortured, so, in order to obtain the chance to escape, he agrees to collaborate with the Nazis.

11 January Bertrand escapes from the Germans after they allow him his liberty so that his associates will not suspect that he is collaborating. When the British hear how he has hoodwinked the Nazis, they wonder if he has been turned.

6 March The Canadians seize Enigma documents from *U-744*, but the documents are lost after the boarding party's boat is sunk in the rough sea.

7 March Gwido Langer and Maksymilian Ciężki confess to the Germans that the Enigma cipher was broken before the war, but they convince their interrogators that the Polish cryptographers could not read any messages during the war.

12 March Brake, a German supply vessel, is sunk in the course of 'Operation Covered'. The sinking leads the Germans to conclude that their Naval Enigma cipher might have been compromised. 'The possibility that this has occurred cannot be excluded,' the German investigators stated.

18 April Antoni Palluth, one of the Polish engineers who manufactured the replica Enigmas before and during the war, is killed when a bomb dropped by Allied aircraft hits the Heinkel factory in Germany where he is working as a prisoner of war.

2 June Gustave Bertrand is, at last, picked up in France by a British aircraft and taken back to England.

3 June Bertrand's report on how he managed to escape from the Germans is seen by Paul Paillole, the French Counter-Intelligence chief; Paillole had been asked by Sir Stewart Menzies, the head of the British Secret Intelligence Service, to interrogate Bertrand to determine whether he has told the Germans about the Allies' Enigma secret. Paillole realizes that if Bertrand has tipped off the Germans, 'Fortitude', the British deception plan concerning the location of the Allied invasion of Europe, may have been compromised; the Germans could be using Enigma messages to convince the Allies that they have been taken in by Fortitude. Paillole concludes that Bertrand has not told the Germans any secrets about Enigma, but he asks Menzies to detain Bertrand for a few days until after the Allied invasion, just in case.

4 June U-*505* is captured by an American hunter-killer task force off the West African coast along with its Enigma codebooks. When the American Admiral King hears what has happened, he threatens to court-martial Captain Gallery, the leader of the task force, for endangering the security of the Allies' Enigma secret shortly before 'Operation Overlord', the invasion of France.

5–6 June As the Allied ships carry the troops over to France at the beginning of Operation Overlord, Naval Enigma is being read almost currently. This enables Bletchley Park to make sure no wolf pack attacks are being planned by U-boats, and it also means that Churchill and the Allied commanders can be warned as soon as the invading forces are spotted by the Germans.

Glossary

In this book the following meanings are ascribed to the following terms:

Banburismus – The procedure invented by Alan Turing which enabled codebreakers to narrow down the number of wheel orders which could have been in place when a series of messages was sent. The wheel orders not ruled out by Banburismus were tested on a 'bombe' machine, (defined below).

Bigram tables – A 'bigram' is a group of letters consisting of two letters of the alphabet such as, say 'AC'. In a 'bigram table' there are equivalent bigrams listed for each of the bigrams that could be formulated using all the letters in the alphabet. The Germans used a set of nine bigram tables; each table was different. The bigram tables were used by the German naval telegraphists to alter letters selected from a book when going through the Naval Enigma procedure necessary to create an indicator. (The word 'indicator' is defined below). The Bletchley Park codebreakers used the German bigram tables, which they captured or reconstructed, when following the Banburismus procedure. ('Banburismus' is defined above).

Bomba – the electro-mechanical device thought up by Polish cryptographers and engineers before the war. It consisted of six Enigmas wired together, and could only be used to break Enigma settings if the Germans were enciphering their message settings twice to produce indicators. ('Message settings' and 'indicators' are defined below).

Bombe – the electro-mechanical machine thought up by Bletchley Park codebreakers Alan Turing and Gordon Welchman to work out the daily Enigma settings. The first bombes consisted of a series of three-wheel Enigma replicas wired together; the Americans subsequently designed a bombe consisting of four-wheel Enigmas wired together. A bombe could only work out Enigma settings if it was programmed with information taken from a crib. (The word 'crib' is defined below).

Crib – Bletchley Park's cryptographers referred to the guessed plain-language German text of a message which matched up with a stretch of cipher text as a 'crib'. Without a crib the bombe machines mentioned above could not work out Enigma settings.

Grundstellung – German for 'initial position' which is defined below.

Indicator – The letters included in a coded message which 'indicate' to the recipient the message's 'message setting'. ('Message setting' is defined below).

In the case of Army and Air Force Enigma prior to 1 May 1940, the indicator was the result of tapping out the three letter 'message setting' used for the message twice with the Enigma wheels set initially to the Grundstellung. ('Grundstellung' is defined above). If the recipient then tapped out the indicator with his Enigma set up as specified in the settings list, the message setting would be lit up.

In the case of the Naval Enigma after 1937, the indicator was the result of looking up eight letters selected from a book in 'bigram tables', and then manipulating the resulting eight letters. If the recipient took the indicator, and carried out these steps in reverse order he would discover the eight letters chosen from the book; he then had to tap out three of these letters with the Enigma set to the Grundstellung to produce the message setting.

Indicating system – the procedure used by the German sender of a message when working out the relevant indicator. ('Indicator' is defined above).

Initial position – the English for the 'Grundstellung' defined above.

In the case of the Army and Air Force Enigma, it was the position at which the Enigma wheels were set by German telegraphists when the 'message setting' (as defined below) was tapped out on the keyboard to produce the 'indicator' (defined above).

In the case of the Naval Enigma, it was the position of the Enigma wheels when three of the letters chosen out of a book in the course of following the 'indicating system' (defined above) were tapped out on the keyboard to produce the 'message setting' (as defined below).

Menu – the chain of letters extracted from a 'crib', (defined above), which was used to programme a 'bombe' machine, (defined above).

Message setting – The setting of the Enigma wheels when the first letter in a plain-language, i.e. German, message was enciphered on an Enigma.

322

Net – A group of Enigma operators who used the same Enigma settings on a particular day were within a particular Enigma net or network. For example, after 1 February 1942 all the U-boat operators operating in the Atlantic were part of what I have referred to as the 'Shark' net or network.

Settings – the positions at which the variable elements in an Enigma machine were set. The variable elements included the wheels, the rings around the wheels, and the plugboard plugs.

Wheel order – When talking about a three-wheel machine this describes which wheel is on the left, which wheel is in the middle and which wheel is on the right.

Wheel setting – This describes the position of the wheels when a particular event happens. For example the 'wheel setting' ABC would mean that the left wheel had the letter 'A' showing through the window above the wheel, the middle wheel had 'B' showing through the window above the wheel, and the right wheel had 'C' showing through the window above the wheel.

Appendix 1

Polish Codebreaking Techniques

Part 1 – The 'Characteristic' Method of Reading Enigma Messages[1]

The 'characteristic' method of breaking the code, mentioned in chapter 4, was invented in 1936. Although it took over a year to put into practice, it was for a time one of the principal methods used to break the Enigma settings for the armed forces. It was made redundant, following a change in the Enigma indicator procedure on 15 September 1938.

The characteristic method exploited the fact that chains of letters of different length, made up as demonstrated below, could be produced from the first and fourth, second and fifth and third and sixth letters of the intercepted 'indicators' – the six letters lit up when the sender tapped the keys representing his 'message setting' twice on the Enigma keyboard; the 'message setting' comprised the letters showing through the windows above the wheels when the first letter in the German message was enciphered. The length of these chains varied depending on 'the wheel order' inside the Enigma (i.e. which wheel was on the right, which wheel was in the middle and which was on the left), and what was the 'initial position' (the Grundstellung) of these wheels on the day in question (the 'initial position' being, for Army and Air Force Enigma operators, the position of the wheels when the sender tapped the Enigma keyboard key representing the first letter of his message setting in order to light up the letters in the indicator).

Before any attempt was made to read Enigma messages using this method, a catalogue was prepared by the Polish cryptographers showing the length of the chains produced for each possible position of the Enigma wheels. Once the catalogue was complete, the cryptographers were able to use it to help them to break the code; this was often accomplished in less than twenty minutes. Each day the cryptographers had to work out the length of the chains which could be made up from the indicators intercepted on that day, and then they had to look up in the catalogue the chain lengths which they had spotted. The catalogue told them which Enigma wheel order and which initial position could produce the lengths of chains which they had found on the day in question. Once they had discovered these settings, the other settings, such as the connections between the plugboard sockets, could be worked out using other methods.

The chains, or cycles, of letters referred to above were made up as follows: Suppose that there were only two indicators intercepted on a particular day which were:

Indicator number 1 – dmq vbn
Indicator number 2 – von puy

The chain of letters which could be made from these two indicators would be made up with the following letters:

d – the first letter of the first indicator, which the cryptographers would know was produced by the sender tapping the Enigma keyboard key representing the first letter of his message setting. The cryptographers would not know what the first letter of the message setting was at this point.

v – the fourth letter of the first indicator, which the cryptographers would know was produced by the sender tapping the Enigma keyboard key representing the first letter of his message setting for a second time (i.e. the same letter as was tapped by the sender to produce d above).

v – the first letter of the second indicator, which the cryptographers would know was produced by the sender of the second indicator tapping the Enigma keyboard key representing the first letter of his message setting. This message setting would not be the same as the message setting used to create the first indicator.

p – the fourth letter of the second indicator, which the cryptographers would know was produced by the sender of the second indicator tapping the Enigma keyboard key representing the first letter of his message setting for a second time (i.e. the same letter which was tapped by the sender of the second indicator to produce v in the previous paragraph).

The resulting chain which could be produced from these letters is dvp. This chain would be extended if more indicators were intercepted on the day in question, until there were no more equivalent links.

The cryptographers could always make up more than one chain from the first and fourth letters of the indicators intercepted on a particular day. Similar chains would be made up for the day in question using the second and fifth, and the third and sixth letters in the indicators. Around sixty indicators were necessary to make up the series of chains, which were known as the characteristic cycles, for each particular wheel setting.

Part 2 – The Bomby[2]

The Polish cryptographers had noticed that a series of 'indicators' (defined in Part 1 of this Appendix), was being produced each day similar to the trio in Table 1 below. As can be seen, the first and fourth letters in the first indicator in Table 1 are identical, as are the second and fifth letters in the second indicator, and the third and sixth letters in the third indicator. In addition to the indicator for each message, the cryptographers also saw that an 'initial position' (defined in Part 1 above) was written, unenciphered, at the beginning of each message; let us say that the initial positions for the three messages referred to in Table 1 were as specified beside each of the three messages' indicators.

Table 1 – Example showing a series of the kind of indicators which were spotted by the cryptographers

	Indicator	Initial Position
Message no. 1	WAH WIK	AAA
Message no. 2	DWR MWR	AAG
Message no. 3	RAW KTW	AAL

The bomby, mentioned in chapter 4 ('bomby' is the plural version of 'bomba'), were machines which were designed to identify the wheel order and the initial wheel positions at which the series of indicators could have been produced; the initial positions specified in Table 1 did not give away the initial positions of the wheel 'cores', but only specified what letters on the rings around the wheels were showing through the windows above the wheels when the message settings were tapped on the Enigma keyboards to produce the indicators. The bomby could find the above mentioned positions of the wheel cores, which had to be identified if the code was to be broken for the day in question.

A bomba incorporated a series of six replica Enigmas wired together, without any rings around the wheels, and without any plugboard. It could test one wheel order at a time. If, say, the cryptographers decided to test the following wheel order first: 1 on the right, 3 in the middle, and 2 on the left, these wheels were placed in this order inside the bomba's six Enigmas. The wheels in the six Enigmas were then set to particular positions so that the 'distance' (as explained below) between the positions of the set of wheels in each Enigma reflected the distance between the wheel positions at which the six Ws in the above indicators were produced; this latter distance would have been betrayed by the series of initial positions in Table 1.

The following example explains what is meant by the 'distance': the initial position AAG is at a distance of six places from the initial position AAA; the six places represent the number of times the right-hand wheel has to turn one twenty-sixth of a revolution to go from the position where AAA is showing through the windows above the wheels to the position where AAG is showing through these windows.

Once the wheels were set as mentioned above, the bomba could be switched on, and, given the information in Table 1 for example, it would attempt to discover whether, starting at the positions set, the series of indicators in Table 1 could have been produced. If so, the bomba might have found the correct wheel order for the day in question, and the wheel positions at which the senders of the messages enciphered their message settings to produce their indicators. If not, then the right wheel in each of the Enigmas making up the bomba had to be moved on one place, so as to preserve the correct distance between the sets of wheels inside the bomba, and the same test was then applied again. This process was carried on until all possible wheel positions were tried out, or until the correct position was identified.

In 1938 when the bomba was introduced, there were six possible wheel orders. A bomba was set up for each of the six wheel orders, so that all six could be tested simultaneously.

To appreciate the fact that the cryptographers did not know the position of the cores of the wheels just because they knew the initial position, one only has to imagine the situation if the rings on the wheels were to be held still, so that AAA was always showing through the windows above the wheels, while the inner core of each wheel was turned manually to each of its twenty-six possible positions. At each position of the inner core of the wheel, the letters showing through the windows over the wheels would be the same AAA. In other words, the letters showing through the windows above the wheels give no evidence about the position of the core, unless the wheel ring settings are also known. The initial positions specified by the Germans merely betrayed the relative positions of the wheels, and it was these relative positions which were exploited by the bomby.

Appendix 2
The Bombe[1]

What was the bombe supposed to do?

As mentioned in chapter 5, the bombe was an electro-mechanical machine, designed to work out what sockets on the Enigma plugboard were connected to what other sockets on the day in question, and what was the wheel order inside the Enigma (i.e. which wheel was on the right, which wheel was in the middle and which wheel was on the left). Once this was deduced, the cryptographers at Bletchley Park were able to work out the other elements within the daily key for themselves – such as the settings for the rings around the wheels (the Ringstellung), and the initial position (the Grundstellung), as defined in Appendix 1.

How the first bombe invented by Alan Turing worked

Even Alan Turing could not design a machine which directly worked out the Enigma socket connections and wheel order. The bombe was next best thing. It was designed to rule out many of the plugboard socket connections and wheel orders so that only a few were left to try out manually. It did this by making logical deductions, as demonstrated in the following example, which necessarily followed on from certain assumptions made by the cryptographers. If one of these deductions was physically impossible, then it would be clear that one of the assumptions was incorrect, and the bombe would go on to test another set of assumptions, and then another, and so on, until it found a set of assumptions which did not produce impossible deductions; this would be one of the relatively few sets of assumptions which the cryptographers would try out manually on a replica Enigma to ascertain if one of them was correct.

Example illustrating how logical deductions were made from a set of assumptions and how the set of assumptions could be ruled out if some deductions were physically impossible

One set of assumptions made by the cryptographers
1   The wheel order is: wheel 1 on the left, wheel 5 in the middle and wheel 7 on the right.
2   The plugboard socket G is connected to plugboard socket A.
3   The cipher text and the matching crib are specified in Table 1 below. If the bombe were to start off by testing the message setting AAA (the message setting comprises the letters showing through the windows above the wheels when the sender tapped the first letter in the crib on the Enigma keyboard to light up the first letter of the cipher text), the wheel setting would be AAB when the second crib letter was tapped to produce the second cipher text letter, AAC when the third crib letter was tapped to produce the third cipher text letter, and so on.

Table 1

Relative Wheel Position	1	2	3	4	5	6	7
Cipher text	J	T	G	E	F	P	G
Crib	R	O	M	M	E	L	F

The chain of logical deductions which, without using a bombe, could be shown to follow on from the above set of assumptions, and how the deductions could be used to rule out the set of assumptions

In order to demonstrate how the bombe ruled out assumptions, I have specified below how the following deductions could have been made manually – albeit relatively slowly – by the cryptographers without a bombe. The bombe, which is described underneath, merely quickened the process.

Deduction 1
In Figure 1 I have illustrated the path which would be followed by the current inside a simplified picture of an Enigma if the settings in the assumptions were used, and if G, the third letter in the cipher

text, was tapped on the Enigma keyboard, so that M, the third letter in the crib was lit up on the Enigma lightboard. In line with assumption 3, the Enigma wheels would be set to 'relative position 3,' i.e. wheel position AAC if the bombe started off by testing the message setting AAA; I am calling the message setting AAA 'relative position 1'. In Figure 1 plugboard socket G is shown connected to plugboard socket A, which is assumption 2.

As is obvious from Figure 1, the only unknown, marked by a '?' in Figure 1, is the plugboard socket to which the M plugboard socket is connected. The cryptographers could easily work out what the '?' was. All they had to do was to set up a replica Enigma machine with no plugboard, so that its wheels were in the same position as those mentioned in the previous paragraph. They then had to tap the A keyboard key, the letter corresponding to the plugboard socket connected to G, the third cipher text letter, and watch which light lit up. Let us say that the P light lit up. That would be the first of the deductions which could be made from the above assumptions. It is illustrated in Figure 2.

Deduction 2

Deduction 1 above opens the way for a second deduction to be made; because of Deduction 1 above, it is known that when the keyboard key representing M, the fourth letter in the crib, is tapped, the current flows through the plugboard from M to P. Armed with this information, a similar illustration to Figure 1 can be drawn as Figure 3. It shows that when M, the fourth crib letter, is tapped to light up E, the fourth cipher text letter, with the wheels set to the 'fourth relative position', i.e. to AAD if the message setting being tested is AAA, the only unknown is the '?'. The '?' could be worked out by the cryptographers tapping P on the keyboard of the Enigma replica with no plugboard and observing which letter lit up. Let us say it is T; that would be the second deduction which is the logical result of the above assumptions. It is illustrated in Figure 4.

Deduction 3

Deduction 2 in its turn opens up the way for a third deduction to be made through using E and F, the fifth letters in the crib and cipher text; the third deduction is that the F plugboard socket is connected to the R socket, which is illustrated in Figures 5 and 6. It is this third deduction which opens the way for the cryptographers to see if an impossible fourth deduction is to be made.

Figure 1 – Concerning deduction 1

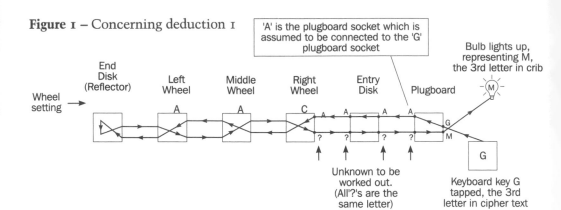

'A' is the plugboard socket which is assumed to be connected to the 'G' plugboard socket

Bulb lights up, representing M, the 3rd letter in crib

End Disk (Reflector) | Left Wheel | Middle Wheel | Right Wheel | Entry Disk | Plugboard

Wheel setting →

Unknown to be worked out. (All'?'s are the same letter)

Keyboard key G tapped, the 3rd letter in cipher text

Figure 2 – Concerning deduction 1

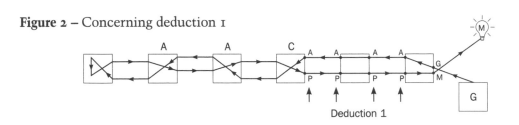

Deduction 1

Figure 3 – Concerning deduction 2

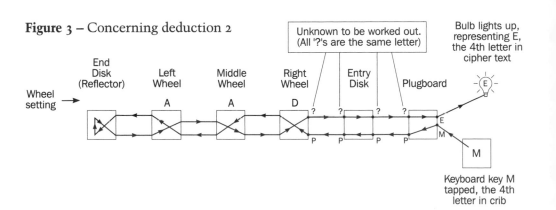

Unknown to be worked out. (All '?'s are the same letter)

Bulb lights up, representing E, the 4th letter in cipher text

End Disk (Reflector) | Left Wheel | Middle Wheel | Right Wheel | Entry Disk | Plugboard

Wheel setting →

Keyboard key M tapped, the 4th letter in crib

Figure 4 – Concerning deduction 2

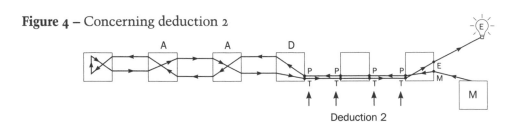

Deduction 2

332

Deduction 4

Because of Deduction 3, it is known that when the current flows into the plugboard at F, it comes out of the plugboard at R. Armed with this information, a similar illustration to Figure 6 can be drawn as Figure 7; it shows that when F, the seventh crib letter is tapped on the Enigma keyboard to light up G, the seventh cipher text letter, with the wheels set to 'relative position 7,' i.e. AAG if the message setting being tested is AAA, there is only one '?'.[2] It is at this point that the cryptographers would be able to see whether the above assumptions were incorrect. If when the cryptographers used the technique mentioned above to work out what was the '?', they discovered that it was an A, then nothing would have occurred which was inconsistent with assumption 2 above.[3] This is the position depicted in Figure 8. If, on the other hand, the cryptographers worked out that the '?' was, say, C, then they would have shown that at least one of the above assumptions must be incorrect, since the deduction that the '?' was C would be inconsistent with assumption 2 above, which states that it is A. In such circumstances, the set of assumptions being tested could be ruled out.

Ruling out the assumptions using a bombe

In the above example, I demonstrated how the cryptographers could manually work out whether a set of assumptions could be ruled out without using a bombe. The bombe merely performed the same task more quickly. This is how the bombe did it.

The bombe consisted of a series of Enigma replicas without plugboards; they were wired together so that the current coming out of one Enigma at a particular letter went into the next Enigma at the same letter. The wheels inside the series of Enigmas had to be set to starting positions consistent with those letters from the assumed crib and matching cipher text which were included in the chain of letters specified in the next paragraph. The assumptions specified above were then tested with the wheels in these starting positions. All the wheels were subsequently turned on one position, so that the distance between them was maintained, and the assumptions were then tested again. The testing was carried out at all 17,576 possible wheel settings, until the codebreakers were left with a limited number of settings which were not ruled out. These had to be tested manually by the cryptographers.

Figure 5 – Concerning deduction 3

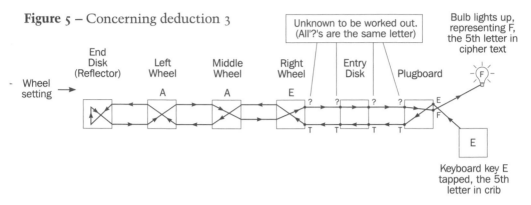

Figure 6 – Concerning deduction 3

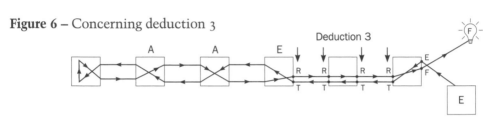

Figure 7 – Concerning deduction 4

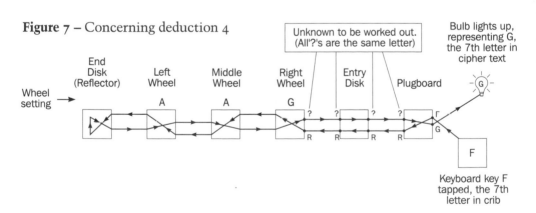

Figure 8 – Concerning deduction 4

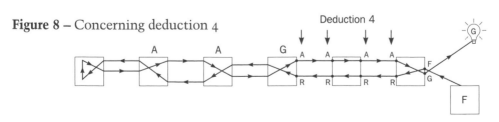

In the above example, the chain of letters from the crib and cipher text which would govern the starting position of the wheels inside the bombe, as mentioned in the previous paragraph, would be as specified in Figure 9; in practice, the cryptographers would not have drawn the chain around the cipher text and crib, but would have drawn it as shown in Figure 10. They referred to this kind of chain as 'a menu'; it regulated how the bombe wheels were set before the machine was switched on. The principle behind drawing the chain, or menu, was that after taking one vertical pair of letters from the cipher text and crib when written one above the other, the cryptographers would go on to find another pair of vertical letters from the cipher text and crib which had a letter in common with the previous vertical pair selected, and so on. The link in the chain shown in Figure 10 between the G and the M is the shorthand way of saying that the plug socket to which G, the third letter in the cipher text, is connected, will enable the bombe to make a deduction – which is the same as Deduction 1 above – about the socket to which the M, the third letter in the crib is connected, and so on. The number 3 written beside this link in the chain indicates that the deduction about the socket linked up to M is made with the Enigma wheels at 'relative position 3', i.e. if the bombe starts off by testing the message setting AAA, which for the purposes of the test is 'relative position 1', the wheels in the first Enigma in the bombe should be set to AAC, two places on from 'relative position 1', which makes it 'relative position 3'. The starting positions of the wheels inside the second, third and fourth Enigmas in the bombe, given the chain in Figure 10, could be determined in the same way. They are indicated in Figure 11, which illustrates how the current would flow through the wire circuit inside the bombe when making the Deductions 1–4 above.

How Gordon Welchman altered the bombe

The original bombe devised by Alan Turing used the procedure mentioned in the above example to rule out sets of assumptions. But it only worked in practice if the cryptographers identified cribs which led to menus with so-called 'closures', i.e. chains of letters which ended at the same letter at which the chains started. In practice, longer cribs were required than the one shown in Table 1. Sometimes, however, only short cribs could be identified, and these were not sufficient to enable the original bombe to break the code. Gordon Welchman worked out a way of adapting Turing's bombe so that more deductions could be made from a given cipher text and crib.

This meant that the bombe could be used on the shorter cribs. Welchman's adaptation is explained in the following extension of the above example.

Example showing how extra deductions could be made once Welchman's alteration was incorporated in the bombe

Welchman's alteration was prompted by the realisation that Turing's original bombe only made one deduction from a scenario such as that illustrated in Figure 3: Deduction 2, namely that if the E key was tapped on the Enigma keyboard, the current went from the E socket to the T socket.

Welchman said that the bombe could be adapted so that the extra scenario illustrated in Figure 12 could be taken into account by the bombe every time a scenario such as that represented in Figure 3 occurred. In other words if the T key was tapped, the current went from the T socket to the E socket or, as in Figure 12, when the current came out of the wheels at E, it was diverted to T as it went through the plugboard on the way to the lightboard. This extra scenario came about because of a feature in the plugboard which has not been mentioned before. If the E socket was plugged to the T socket, there was always a link between the two letters on the plugboard, whether it was the E key or the T key which was tapped on the keyboard.

The extra scenario depicted in Figure 12 opened the way for the cryptographers to use the second vertical pair of letters in the cipher text and crib in assumption 3 above, namely O in the crib and T in the cipher text to make Deduction 5, which is illustrated in Figure 13. Deduction 5 states that the O plugboard socket is connected to, say, the Y socket.

In Figure 14 I have illustrated more clearly the principle which is included in what Welchman was saying. Deduction 2 above, which was already taken into account by Turing's original bombe before Welchman's alteration, and which is represented in Figures 3 and 4, has been represented with an asterisk in Figure 14. The position of the asterisk in Figure 14 is found by identifying T (the point where the current comes out of the wheels when it is heading towards the

Figure 9

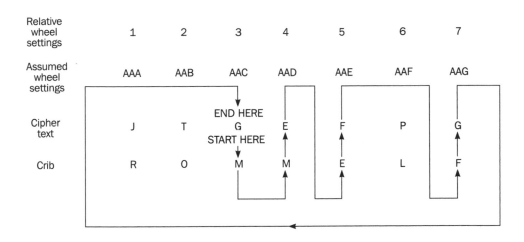

Relative wheel settings	1	2	3	4	5	6	7
Assumed wheel settings	AAA	AAB	AAC	AAD	AAE	AAF	AAG
Cipher text	J	T	G	E	F	P	G
Crib	R	O	M	M	E	L	F

Figure 10

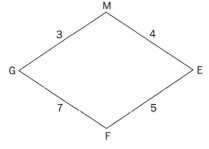

lightboard) on the horizontal axis, and the E point on the vertical axis, representing the cipher letter which is lit up.

The extra information, represented in Figure 12, which was derived from Deduction 2, but which was not taken into account by the bombe until Welchman made his alteration, is represented in Figure 14 with an asterisk in a circle. As can be seen, the information represented by the asterisk in a circle was the mirror image of that provided by the asterisk, with the diagonal line across Figure 14 acting as the mirror. The principle implied in Welchman's alteration meant that whenever a deduction made by the bombe led to an asterisk being entered on Figure 14, its mirror image was automatically filled in on the same figure. The diagram merely illustrates the principle behind the physical alteration which Welchman wanted to have made inside the bombe. The physical circuit board and wiring which ensured that the mirror image scenario referred to above was made was known as the 'diagonal board'.

Turing's altered bombe

The original bombe invented by Turing and altered by Welchman moved on to examine another set of assumptions when a deduction was made which was physically impossible on an Enigma. This situation could be illustrated in Figure 15 by two asterisks being put in the G row, i.e. in the A column and in the C column. As mentioned above under the heading Deduction 4, the G plugboard socket could not be connected to both the A and C sockets at the same time.

However Turing realised that the alteration to the bombe which Welchman was proposing opened the door to what Turing referred to as 'simultaneous scanning'. His original bombe design required the cryptographers to test one assumed plugboard socket at a time; if the cryptographers wanted to see if G was connected to either the A or B sockets, two separate runs on the bombe had to be made. Simultaneous scanning on the other hand permitted the cryptographers to conduct just one test to see if G was connected to any of the letters in the alphabet. Even if a set of assumptions was shown to be impossible, the bombe carried on running.

Sometimes if assumptions such as those mentioned in the above example were programmed into the bombe, the results were such that the whole of the G row in Figure 15 would be filled up with asterisks or asterisks in circles. This would suggest to the cryptographers that the wrong wheel order or wheel setting was being used; each finding that a particular socket was connected to the G socket was contradicted by another finding. That was an important result; millions of sets of assumptions were being ruled out simultaneously, i.e. all the possible plugboard socket combinations which could be linked with the use of the wheel order or setting which was being tested.

On other occasions only one point in the G row in Figure 15 would not have an asterisk or an asterisk in a circle on it. This would suggest to the cryptographers that the wheels were correctly positioned, but that the assumption about the plug socket connections was incorrect. It would also suggest that the one point on the G row with no asterisk in it represented the plugboard socket which had been connected with the G socket by the German Enigma operators on the day in question; it would never be one of the chain of deductions which contradicted each other.

On other occasions only one point in the G row in Figure 15 would have any asterisks in it. This would indicate to the cryptographers that the correct socket assumption, wheel order and wheel setting assumptions had been made.

Figure 11

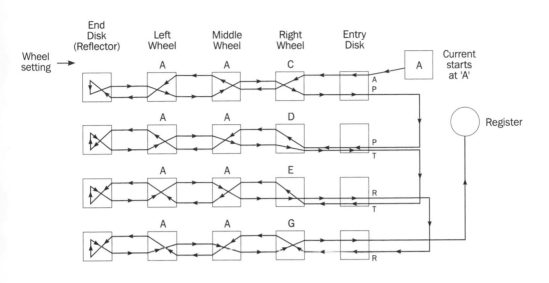

Figure 12

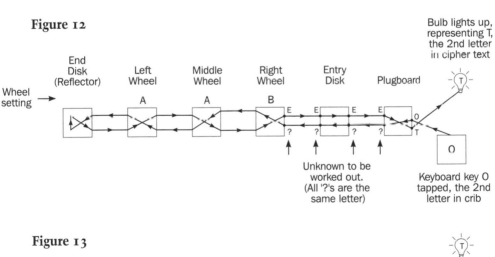

Figure 13

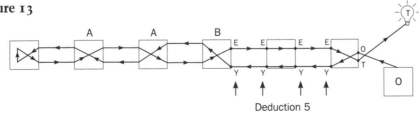

339

Figure 14

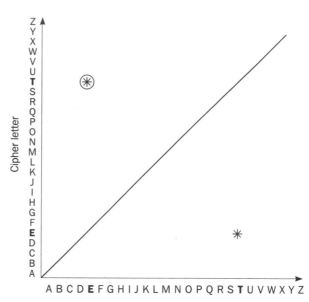

Letter at which current appears after going through
wheels, but before going through plugboard on way to lamp

Figure 15

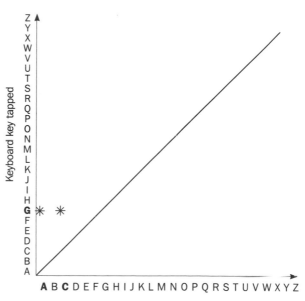

Letter at which current arrives after going through
the plugboard on the way to the wheels

Appendix 3
Naval Enigma

Laid out below is a description of the German Naval Enigma indicating system which baffled Alan Turing, and his colleagues at Bletchley Park, during the first twenty months of the War.[1] A document explaining the indicating system was captured in April 1940, as described in chapter 7, but the system was not mastered until the end of March 1941, when the elusive bigram tables were reconstructed in the manner described below.[2] Only then were the British cryptographers regularly able to use Alan Turing's Banburismus procedure, which is also explained below. Banburismus, used as it was in conjunction with Bletchley Park's bombes, was the main method used to break the Home Waters Enigma net until July 1943.[3]

Part 1 – The Naval Enigma indicating system

A. *Sending a message*

(1) The German sender chose two 'trigrams' (a trigram being a group of three letters from the alphabet) from a book (the Kenngruppen-buch). Let us say they were BFA and LXZ.

The sender added an extra letter (let us say C) to the beginning of the first trigram, and an extra letter (let us say B) to the end of the second. Then he wrote the two resulting groups of four letters one under the other as follows:

$$
\begin{array}{cccc}
\text{C} & \text{B} & \text{F} & \text{A} \\
\text{L} & \text{X} & \text{Z} & \text{B}
\end{array}
$$

The second group of four letters, which was to provide the most

assistance to the British cryptographers, was referred to as the Verfahrenkenngruppe (the procedure identification group of letters).

(2) The sender turned the wheels of his Enigma to the initial position
(the Grundstellung) – defined in Appendix 1 – given in his settings
list for the day, which might be, say, ABC, and tapped out on the
Enigma keyboard the first three letters of the second group of four
letters mentioned in 1 above, i.e. LXZ, so that three lights lit up. Let
us say they were RGL. This was the message setting, defined in
Appendix 1.

(3) The sender turned his keys to the message setting, and then enciphered his plain-language message by tapping out each letter of the
plain-language German message on the Enigma keyboard, noting
down the corresponding cipher letter.

(4) Before sending the enciphered letters in morse code to the recipient, the sender had to indicate to the recipient how to decipher it
without letting any eavesdroppers in on the secret. The sender
started off by transforming each of the four vertical bigrams specified
in 1 above, i.e.

$$\begin{array}{cccc} C & B & F & A \\ L & X & Z & B \end{array}$$

into the equivalent bigrams listed in the bigram tables.

Let us say the bigram equivalents are:

$$\begin{array}{cccc} R & V & M & K \\ E & Y & P & W \end{array}$$

In the excerpt from a bigram table shown in Table 1, it can be seen
that the bigram equivalent of CL is RE.

(5) These bigrams were then rearranged so they read as follows:

$$\begin{array}{cccc} R & E & V & Y \\ M & P & K & W \end{array}$$

This was the indicator which was sent in morse code by the sender
to the recipient, without being enciphered on the Enigma, immediately before the enciphered message referred to in 4 above.

Table 1 – Excerpt from a Bigram Table

AA=RN	BA=IK	CA=KJ	DA=PK	EA=TC
AB=KW	BB=RT	CB=PO	DB=EZ	EB=JX
AC=FM	BC=EY	CC=JV	DC=AW	EC=OM

AD=YE BD=AK CD=BM DD=JM ED=MJ
AE=NR BE=OW CE=MZ DE=WB EE=NY
AF=UC BF=WQ CF=EK DF=XY EF=AS
AG=KE BG=QA CC=KT DG=ZA EG=PU
AH=XU BH=ZZ CH=AZ DH=BS EH=WO
AI=PC BI=OG CI=ND DI=MT EI=KA
AJ=JP BJ=HQ CJ=TQ DJ=OE EJ=GZ
AK=BD BK=GC CK=GX DK=FP EK=CF
AL=QI BL=PR CL=RE DL=RI EL=FK
AM=HT BM=CD CM=WA DM=VV EM=LK

The entries in the bigram table are 'reversible' so that for example
if   AK=BD – see column 1, line 11
    BD=AK – see column 2, line 4.

B. How the Germans decoded Naval Enigma messages

(1) The recipient reversed the steps listed in 4 and 5 above as follows.
He firstly manipulated the letters in 5 above so that they were
arranged exactly as laid out in the last eight letters of 4 above, i.e.

R V M K
E Y P W

(2) The recipient looked up the bigram table equivalents of each of the
four vertical bigrams specified in 1 of this section (B), which were:

C B F A
L X Z B

(3) The recipient then did exactly what the sender did – as specified
in (2) of section A above – in order to discover the sender's message
setting. Once the recipient discovered that the message setting was
RGL, he turned his wheels to RGL, and tapped out the cipher text
on the Enigma keyboard, thereby lighting up on the lightboard the
plain-language German letters which had been sent to him in the
first place; the message was deciphered.

Part 2 – How the bigram tables were reconstructed

To reconstruct the bigram tables, the Enigma settings for the day in
question had to be known. The Enigma settings could either be

worked out with the aid of a crib and a bombe machine, or they could be captured. In the former case, the wheel order and the plugboard socket connections were worked out by the bombe (as described in Appendix 2), and the position of the rings around the wheels, the initial position for the day in question (Grundstellung), and the message setting for each message had to be worked out manually. The method used to work out the message settings is described in Part 3 of this Appendix.

The procedure used to reconstruct the bigram tables is specified below:[4]

(1) The wheels of a replica Enigma were set to the initial position (Grundstellung), for the day, which might be, say, ABC as specified in 2 of section A of Part 1 of this Appendix. The message setting for a message was then tapped out on the Enigma keyboard – let us say it was RGL, as specified in 2 of section A of Part 1 of this Appendix – and if the message described in Part 1 of this Appendix was being dealt with, the letters LXZ would be lit up, which were the first three letters of the Verfahrenkenngruppe, including the second trigram picked by the German sender out of the book as described in 1 of section A of Part 1 of this Appendix. At this stage, the following information about the two four-letter groups of letters specified in 1 of section A of Part 1 of this Appendix was known:

$$\overline{} \quad \overline{} \quad \overline{} \quad \overline{}$$
$$L \quad X \quad Z \quad -$$

(2) The cryptographers followed the same procedure with the indicator, which for the message being discussed was:

$$R \quad E \quad V \quad Y$$
$$M \quad P \quad K \quad W$$

as the German recipient followed with the same information, as specified in 1 of section B of Part 1 of this Appendix. This left the cryptographers with the two lines of letters:

$$R \quad V \quad M \quad K$$
$$E \quad Y \quad P \quad W$$

(3) The information in 1 and 2 of this Part, (2), of this Appendix was sufficient to enable the cryptographers to partially fill in three entries in the applicable bigram table: The first entry would be $\frac{\overline{}}{L}$ for $\frac{R}{E}$, the $\frac{\overline{}}{L}$ being all that was known of the first vertical pair of letters referred to in 1 of this Part 2, and the $\frac{R}{E}$ being the first vertical pair of letters

specified in the rearranged indicator referred to in (2) of this Part 2. The other entries which could be filled in in the bigram table would be:

$$\bar{X} \text{ for } \frac{V}{Y}, \text{ and } \bar{Z} \text{ for } \frac{M}{P}$$

Fortunately, partial bigram table entries such as this were all that the cryptographers needed to apply the Banburismus procedure, described below in Part 4 of this Appendix. The reversible characteristic of the bigram tables, i.e. if $\frac{C}{L} = \frac{R}{E}$, $\frac{R}{E} = \frac{C}{L}$, meant that once the cryptographers knew three of the four letters needed to make up an equation involving 2 vertical bigrams, i.e. $\frac{R}{E} = \frac{\bar{}}{L}$ the fourth letter could be deduced using what was gleaned from other bigrams, or partial bigrams, worked out.

Part 3 – The Eins Catalogue

Before a bigram table could be reconstructed, as described in Part 2 of this Appendix, the message settings for some messages had to be worked out. This was achieved through the use of the so-called 'Eins Catalogue'.

This catalogue consisted of the word 'eins', a common German word, enciphered at each position of the wheels, after the Enigma had been set up with the correct settings for the day. For example, with the wheels set to ABC, EINS tapped out on the Enigma might give the cipher text LBGT. This, and all the other 17,575 enciphered versions of EINS were then put in alphabetical order into the Eins Catalogue. LBGT would have the wheel setting ABC (or 123, ABC's equivalent in numbers) written beside it. This would indicate that if ever LBGT was discovered in the cipher text, it may well have been produced by the sender tapping out EINS with his wheels set to ABC.

The cryptographer then had to see whether each consecutive series of four letters in the cipher text appeared in the catalogue. To illustrate this, let us assume that the first letters in the message were VLBGTXSY. The cryptographers would first look in the catalogue for VLBG, the first series of four letters in the cipher text. Then, assuming that they could not find VLBG listed, they would look for LBGT, the second series of four letters in the cipher text. When they found LBGT in the catalogue with ABC written beside it, they would know that the sender might have tapped E in the word 'eins' on his keyboard to produce the L in LBGT when the wheels were set to

ABC. If the wheels were set to ABC when the second letter in the cipher text was produced, then the first letter in the cipher text, V, must have been produced with the wheels set to ABB, i.e. after turning the right wheel back one place. This could be the message setting.

The cryptographers still had to check whether this possible message setting was the correct one. To do this they could set their wheels to ABB, and tap the letters making up the enciphered message on their keyboard keys. If this produced plain-language German even after the appearance of 'eins', they would know they had discovered the correct message setting.

Part 4 – Banburismus

The reason for using Banburismus

The object of the Banburismus procedure was to rule out most of the 336 possible wheel orders which could be in place inside the Enigma on the day in question. (A typical wheel order would be wheel 6 on the left, wheel 5 in the middle and wheel 1 on the right.) If, as could happen, all but three wheel orders were ruled out by the Banburismus procedure, the amount of time which it took the bombe to break the Naval Enigma settings for the day in question could be kept to a minimum. This was very important until the summer of 1943, when, for the first time, there were enough bombes to break the Home Waters Naval Enigma by testing the menus derived from cribs against all possible wheel orders, without depriving the Army and Air Force cryptographers of bombe time.

How Banburismus worked[5]

Stage 1 – Working out the distance between the message settings
(1) The cryptographers picked out pairs of messages intercepted on the day in question, whose Verfahrenkenngruppe (as defined in 1 of section A of Part 1 of this Appendix) had the first two, or at least the first, letters in common, i.e. the Verfahrenkenngruppe for the two messages might start: BBC and BBE. The cryptographers did not, in the first place, know what the message settings for these messages were, but they did know that senders of messages which had Ver-

fahrenkenngruppe with the first two letters in common had used message settings which also had the first two letters in common.

This was obvious, if one took into account the Naval Enigma indicating procedure specified in 2 of section A of Part 1 of this Appendix: the cryptographers knew that the sender of the first of a pair of messages, with the first two letters of their Verfahrenkenngruppe in common, would have tapped out the first two letters of the Verfahrenkenngruppe, i.e. BB in the example given in the previous paragraph, in order to produce the first two letters of his message setting. At the time when the sender tapped the keyboard key marked with the first letter in the Verfahrenkenngruppe, his Enigma wheels would have been set to the initial position (Grundstellung) given in the settings list for the day in question. The right wheel would have turned on one place before the sender would have tapped the keyboard key marked with the second letter in the Verfahrenkenngruppe. The sender of the second message would have done exactly the same with the identical first two letters of his Verfahrenkenngruppe, i.e. BB in the example mentioned in the previous paragraph, with the wheels of his Enigma set to the identical positions. The result would have been that the first two letters of the message settings for both messages would have been the same.

The cryptographers also knew that the third letters of the message settings for the two messages referred to above were different; the third letter of the first message's message setting was arrived at by tapping the Enigma keyboard key C, from the Verfahrenkenngruppe letters BBC, with the right wheel turned two places on from the initial position, and the third letter of the second message's message setting was arrived at by tapping a different letter, E, from the Verfahrenkenngruppe letters BBE, with the right wheel also turned two places on from the initial position. However the cryptographers knew that these third letters of the two message settings could not be more than twenty-five letters apart; the 'distance' between them would be exactly twenty-five letters, if, for example, the first message's message setting's third letter was A and the second message's message setting's third letter was Z.

The cryptographers made use of the following procedure to work out the distance between the unknown third letters of the message settings. The letters in the first enciphered message were punched onto a so-called 'Banbury Sheet', a sheet made in Banbury with a series of vertical columns of letters of the alphabet printed on it, so that if, for example, the first letter of the cipher text was, say, C, then a hole was punched in the first column of the Banbury sheet in row C, and if the second letter was, say, G, then a hole was punched in the second column in row G, and so on. Then the letters in the cipher text in the second enciphered message were punched onto another Banbury sheet. The two Banbury sheets were placed one on top of the other, so that their starting positions were on top of each other. Then the Banbury sheet for the first message on the bottom was held still, while the second message's Banbury sheet on top was slid one place to the right, so that a test could be carried out as mentioned below, then two places to the right so that the same test could be carried out, and then three places to the right, and so on, until the test could be carried out at each position arrived at as the top sheet was slid twenty-five places to the right and left.

At each position the cryptographers wrote down how many lined up pairs of letters there were, where the letter on top was the same as the one underneath. This could be spotted at a glance, because there would be a hole going through both sheets wherever the cipher text letter on the top sheet was the same as the letter on the bottom sheet. If there were lots of pairs of such letters after the second message's Banbury sheet had been slid to a particular position, the cryptographers might conclude that identical cipher text letters had been produced by the two Enigma message senders tapping identical keys on their keyboards with their Enigma wheels set to identical positions. This conclusion sprang from the known fact that two lines of cipher text produced by tapping out plain-language German on Enigmas whose wheels were set to the same position tended to have more letters in common than if the cipher text was produced on Enigmas with their wheels in different positions. In the former circumstances, the two messages were said to be positioned 'in depth'.

(2) It should be pointed out that the finding of several holes lined up after sliding the Banbury sheets against each other was not enough to prove that the two messages were in depth. The cryptographers were only convinced if the lined up holes resulting from sliding the two messages against each other achieved a high score according to a system devised by Alan Turing. According to this system, for example, five consecutive lined up holes produced by sliding the Banbury sheets a particular number of places against each other, would result in a higher score than if only four or three consecutive lined up holes were discovered. And if the sheets had lined up holes in 20 per cent of the columns, that would result in a higher score

than if lined up holes were only to be found in 10 per cent of the columns.

(3) After working out the distance between the message settings for the pairs of messages mentioned in (1) of this Stage 1, using the procedure in (2) of this Stage 1, a chain could be drawn showing the distance between a series of these message settings. So, for example, if it was discovered that the distance between the message setting for the message whose Verfahrenkenngruppe was BBC, and the message setting for the message whose Verfahrenkenngruppe was BBE, was two places, that would be written as C.E. The chain, as written, was shorthand for saying what was written in the previous sentence; the dot in between the C and the E represented the distance between the two message settings. If, on the same day, it was discovered that the message setting for another message, whose Verfahrenkenngruppe was RWE, was eleven places in front of a message whose Verfahrenkenngruppe was RW'L', then the chain C.E could be extended, so that it became 'C.E. . . . . .L'.

Using the same shorthand, the conclusions about the distances apart of the message settings of other pairs of messages on the same day might lead to the chain being extended, so that it read as follows:
R. . . .X. . . .C.E. . . . . .L. .R

Stage 2 – Working out the message settings using the distances between the messages' message settings and assumptions about one such message setting
(1) The message settings themselves were worked out in the following way. An assumption was made that, say, A was the third letter of a message setting for a message whose Verfahrenkenngruppe's third letter was R, R being the first letter in the chain mentioned at the end of (3) of Stage 1 above. Then, using the information mentioned in the chain, the logical consequences flowing from that assumption were filled in. These consequences are listed in Table 2 below:

Table 2

Third letter of Verfahrenkenngruppe	R*	X	C E	L
Third letter of message setting	A*BCDEFGHIJKLMNOPQRSTUVWXYZ			

What is being assumed is that if the sender of a message, whose Verfahrenkenngruppe was, say, ZD'R', tapped the keyboard key R, the third letter of the Verfahrenkenngruppe, with his Enigma's right wheel turned on two places from the initial position (which I will refer to as the 'initial position +2'), the A light, representing the third letter of the message setting, would light up on the Enigma light-board.

Because the information summarised in the chain laid out at the end of (3) in Stage 1 above stated that the distance between the third letter of the message setting for the message which had R as the third letter of its Verfahrenkenngruppe, and the third letter of the message setting for the message which had X as the third letter of its Verfahrenkenngruppe, was five places, it followed that if A was assumed to be the third letter of the former message's message setting, then F (which was five places on from A) was the third letter of the latter message's message setting. This deduction is depicted in Table 2. The position of the other letters in the top line of Table 2 were worked out in the same way.

(2) The information in Table 2 could be built up using the known Enigma rules. So, for example, because of the reversible character of the Enigma machine, if R in line 1 of Table 2 = A in line 2, then R in line 2 of Table 2 = A in line 1. Using this principle of reversibility, the underlined letters in line 1 of Table 3 below could be written in.

Table 3

Third letter of Verfahrenkenngruppe	R K̲ M̲X		CX̲E	A̲	$\frac{F}{L}$
Third letter of message setting	ABCDEFGHIJKLMNOPQRSTUVWXYZ				

One item in the underlined data specified in Table 3 shows that the initial assumption marked with an '*' in Table 2 cannot be correct; that assumption leads to the deduction that if the X keyboard key is tapped at the initial position +2, either F or L is lit up. That is impossible on a Enigma machine; only one letter can be lit up if a particular keyboard key is tapped with the wheels set to a particular position.

(3) Once one assumption was found to be incorrect, other assumptions would be tested in the same way to see if they were correct, i.e. when 'R', the third letter of the Verfahrenkenngruppe, was tapped at the initial position +2, 'B', the next letter in the alphabet, would be lit up. If that was also shown to be incorrect, the assumptions that

tapping 'R' would cause 'C', 'D', or 'E' to light up would be tested, and so on, until each letter of the alphabet had been tried out.

I am going to assume that each assumption mentioned in the last paragraph gave a result which infringed the Enigma rules, except for one, which is that when R, the third letter of the Verfahrenkenngruppe, was tapped on the keyboard, at the initial position +2, the T light lit up. If this assumption is made, the letters which could be filled out, given the information in the chain in (3) of Stage 1, and taking into account the reversible character of the Enigma, are specified in Table 4 below; once again the figures arrived at using the reversible character of the Enigma are underlined.

Table 4

Third letter of Verfahrenkenngruppe	DCFE	Q	LT R	YX
Third letter of message setting	ABCDEFGHIJKLMNOPQRSTUVWXYZ			

I am also going to assume that the distance information taken from other pairs of messages enabled the cryptographers to fill in other letters in Table 4. These extra letters are filled in on Table 5 below.

Table 5

Third letter of Verfahrenkenngruppe	DCFE	Q	LTURS	YX
Third letter of message setting	ABCDEFGHIJKLMNOPQRSTUVWXYZ			

Stage 3 – How wheels could be ruled out by taking into account the known turnover positions for each of the Enigma wheels, and the third letters of the message settings which had been worked out during Stage 2 above.

(1) The information in Table 5 was used to work out which of the eight Naval Enigma wheels was being used on the day in question on the right hand side of the Enigma machine. To do this, the 'turnover position' of each of the eight wheels had to be taken into account. By the turnover position of a wheel, I mean the letter of the alphabet on the ring around the wheel which had to be showing through the window above the wheel for the wheel's turnover action

to be activated when the next keyboard key was tapped; when the turnover action of a wheel was activated, the wheel on its left was turned over one place. These turnover positions are specified in Table 6 underneath the information gleaned from Table 5.

Table 6

Third letter of Verfahrenkenngruppe	D̲CF̲E	Q̲	LT̲U̲RS	Y̲X
Third letter of message setting	ABCDEFGHIJKLMNOPQRSTUVWXYZ			

Wheels	2*	4	6	1	3	5
			7			6
			8			7
						8

* The 2 under the E indicates that the notch on the ring of the wheel labelled number 2, when wheel 2 was placed inside the Enigma on the right-hand side, ensured that the middle wheel was turned over one place when the letter showing through the window above the right-hand wheel changed from E to F. The same principle applies to the other wheel numbers which are under other letters of the alphabet in Table 6.

(2) The cryptographers also made use of the following conclusion, mentioned in (3) of Stage 1 above, when the chain was being constructed: the chain took into account the fact that the third letter of the message setting for the message whose Verfahrenkenngruppe was RWE was eleven places in front of the third letter of the message setting for the message whose Verfahrenkenngruppe was RWL. This conclusion in its turn implied that the right wheel did not reach its turnover position as it turned between F, the third letter of the message setting, which, as can be seen from Table 6, was arrived at when the sender hit the E of RWE at the initial position +2, and Q, which, as can be seen from Table 6, was arrived at when the sender hit the L of Verfahrenkenngruppe RWL at the initial position +2.

The latter conclusion could be reached because, if the right wheel had reached its turnover position as it turned between F and Q, the middle letter of the message setting for the message with RWL as its Verfahrenkenngruppe would have been one place on from the position of the middle letter of the message setting for the message with RWE as its Verfahrenkenngruppe. And that could not have happened, because, as has been pointed out in (1) of Stage 1 above, the middle letters of the message settings with Verfahrenkenngruppe RWE and RWL were identical. If the right wheel's turnover position was not reached as the wheel turned between F and Q, the right wheel could not have been wheels 4, 6, 7, or 8, since, as specified in Table 6, wheels 4, 6, 7 or 8 would have reached their turnover points as they turned between F and Q. As a result of this logic, four of the wheels could be ruled out as the right wheel for the day in question. Using similar principles, some of the other wheels might be ruled out. A similar process could be applied to rule out wheels placed inside the Enigma in the middle. At the end of the Banburismus procedure, so many wheels might be ruled out, that there could be as few as three wheel orders to try out on the bombe, i.e. if the right wheel was, say, 1, and the middle wheel was, say, 5, the left wheel was likely to be 6, 7 or 8; Bletchley Park's cryptographers had observed that one of the wheels was usually 6, 7 or 8. If none of these three wheels was on the right, or in the middle, then one of the three had to be on the left. (3) The information in Table 6 would have enabled the bombe to work out which of the remaining wheel orders, that had not been ruled out, was the correct one. The same information could also be used to create a menu for the bombe; the information was as useful as if a normal crib had been worked out. The only difference was that neither the letters in line 1 or line 2 of Table 6 represented the letters in a plain-language German message. That was irrelevant as far as the bombe was concerned; it worked as long as the cryptographers made up the bombe menu using information about which keyboard keys lit up specific lights on the Enigma lightboard when the keys on the Enigma keyboard were tapped.

Appendix 4
Cillis[1]

The German mistakes known as cillis, mentioned in chapter 8, helped the Bletchley Park cryptographers to break Air Force Enigma messages on and after 22 May 1940. They are said to have been spotted by Dilly Knox in January 1940 at a time when Enigma messages were already being broken, and they were already being used prior to the 1 May 1940 codebreaking black out in order to speed up the breaking of the code with the perforated sheets.[2]

The cillis are best explained with reference to long German messages which were split into several parts. The German manuals did not permit messages to be longer than 250 letters. Knox noticed that if the wheels were set to, say, ABC when an operator finished enciphering the first part of his message, that same setting was being used as the initial position (defined in Appendix 1) for the next part of the message. When this occurred, cryptographers merely had to look at the unenciphered initial position used for the second part of the message in order to know what were the letters showing through the windows above the wheels when the last letter in the first part of the message was enciphered. This, subject to what is said in the next paragraph, enabled the cryptographers to work out what letters were showing through the windows above the wheels when the first letter in the first part of the message was enciphered; for ease of reference, I will refer to these letters as the message setting although, as has been noted in Appendix 1 Part 2, the cryptographers would not know the position of the wheel cores until the ring settings were also worked out by, for example, using the Herivel Tip, as described in chapter 8.

The cryptographers used the following reasoning to work out the message setting of the first part of the message: the cryptographers knew what letters were showing through the windows above the wheels when the last letter in the first part of the message was enciphered; let us say they were ABC. The cryptographers also knew the number of letters in the first part of the message, since the Germans specified this information at the beginning of the message; let us say it consisted of 240 letters. Given what the cryptographers knew, all they had to do was to turn the wheels back 240 places from ABC to arrive at the message setting for the first part of the message.

There was a complication, although, ironically, this complication, which was presumably intended to make the cipher harder to break, was the factor which helped the cryptographers to exploit the cillis and to work out the wheel order for the day in question. The position to which the Enigma wheels would be turned when they were rotated back 240 places depended on which wheels were in the Enigma machine. Each of the five wheels given to Army and Air Force operators had a different 'turnover position'. A turnover position refers to the letter of the alphabet on the ring around the wheel which had to be showing through the window above the wheel for the wheel's turnover action to be activated when the next keyboard key was tapped; once the turnover position of a particular wheel was reached a notch on the ring around the wheel ensured that the wheel on its left was rotated 1/26th of a revolution when the next keyboard key was tapped. For example, wheel 1's turnover position was Q, and wheel 2's was E. So when using the procedure mentioned in the previous paragraph, the cryptographers, who did not in the first place know which wheels were inside the Enigma, could not immediately work out the exact message setting for the first part of the message; they could only deduce that the message setting must be one of a selection, albeit a small selection, of message settings.

The following procedure enabled the cryptographers to guess which of the small selection of message settings identified was the correct one. Knox had noticed that the German operators were not only making the mistake specified above, but they were also committing a second error. They were using one of a series of obvious message settings for each part of their multi-part messages. For example some operators used parts of German sayings, such as MAR IAI STM EIN LIE from 'Maria ist mein liebling' (Mary is my darling), and other operators used the letters making up the diagonals on the Enigma keyboard, such as QAY and WSX.[3] The letters appearing on the Enigma keyboard are laid out in Table 1 on the next page.

Table 1

The Enigma keyboard was arranged as follows

Q W E R T Z U I O

A S D F G H J K

P Y X C V B N M L

This habit was exploited by the cryptographers as follows. They might have worked out that one of the possible message settings for the first part of a message was QAY, which could only have been arrived at, when rotating back the wheels 240 places, if, say, wheels 1 and 3 were inside the Enigma in the middle and on the right. The cryptographers might also have found that one of the possible message settings for the second part of the message was WSX, which could only have been arrived at with, say, the same wheels, 1 and 3, in the same place inside the Enigma. This would have enabled the cryptographers to guess that a German operator had picked letters making up the diagonals on the Enigma keyboard as the message settings for part one and part two of his message; he could then rule out the other possible message settings.

Once the middle and right wheels were identified as 1 and 3, the wheel on the left could only be 2, 4, or 5. The correct one could be quickly identified by trial and error. Thus the cillis enabled the cryptographers to work out the wheel order for the day, as well as the message settings for particular messages.

These German mistakes came to be known as cillis, because one of the first message settings worked out in this way was CIL. The word cilli was a cross between CIL, and 'Silly', which describes what the Bletchley Park cryptographers thought of the Enigma operators making the mistakes. The mistakes were made notwithstanding the fact that both practices mentioned in this Appendix were expressly forbidden in the German Enigma manuals.

Appendix 5
Rodding[1]

Part 1 – The rodding procedure and the Battle of Matapan

Rodding was the manual procedure used by Bletchley Park's cryptographers to break the Italian Navy's Enigma cipher, as mentioned in chapter 10. The procedure enabled the British to read two crucial Italian messages on 25–26 March 1941; the intelligence in the decrypts helped Admiral Cunningham, Commander-in-Chief of the Mediterranean Fleet, to ambush the Italian Fleet and to win the historic Battle of Matapan on 28–29 March 1941.

Rodding enabled Bletchley Park to work out the wheel order inside the Enigma on a particular day, as well as the position of the Enigma wheels when the first letter in a particular message was enciphered. The way this was done is illustrated by the example below. To follow what is said in the example, the reader needs to take on board the following elements of a simplified Italian Naval Enigma; the reader is advised to draw three of these elements on three pieces of paper, and then to manoeuvre the drawings, as directed below.

The simplified Italian Enigma, shown in Figure 16, includes a keyboard, an entry disk, three wheels and a reflector end disk. Also included in Figure 16, on the left of the right wheel, is an imagined unmovable disk, hereafter referred to as the 'imaginary disk', which does not divert the current when the current passes through it{iu1,1}. Unlike the German armed forces Enigma, the Italian cipher machine did not incorporate a plugboard; that was the reason why it could be broken by a manual procedure such as rodding. The letters QWERTZU . . . L (i.e. the letters of the alphabet in the order they appeared on the Enigma keyboard) are arranged clockwise around the right-hand faces of the disks and wheels mentioned above, when, as

Figure 16

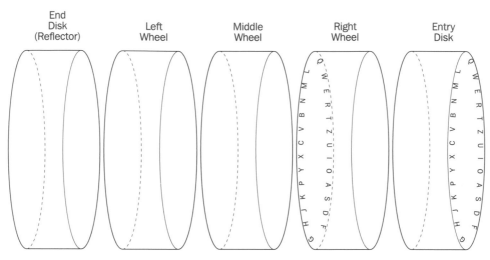

| End Disk (Reflector) | Left Wheel | Middle Wheel | Right Wheel | Entry Disk |

All the wheels and disks have the same lettering

Lightboard

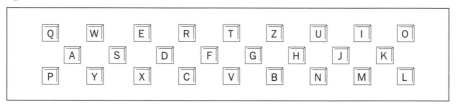

Keyboard

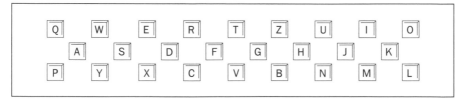

Note. Wheels in this simplified drawing of an Italian Enigma are observed from the front/right.

shown in Figure 16, they are looked at from the right; the same letters are arranged anti-clockwise around the left-hand faces of these disks and wheels, when they are viewed from the left, so that the Qs on the left faces are behind the Qs on the right faces, and the Ws on the left faces are behind the Ws on the right faces, and so on. The right-and left-hand faces of the entry disk should be drawn by the reader on one piece of paper, with the letters marked on the two faces as mentioned above; the letters on the right face should be represented on one side of the piece of paper, and the letters on the left face, on the other side. The letters on the two faces of the right wheel should be drawn onto a second piece of paper, and the letters on the two faces of the imaginary wheel should be drawn onto a third piece of paper, in the same way.

Example illustrating how rodding was done

Rodding could only be brought to a successful conclusion if a crib was identified (i.e. if the cryptographers knew the Italian plain-language meaning of an enciphered message which had been intercepted), or if the meaning of the intercepted message was guessed or worked out. In this example, I have assumed that the crib and matching cipher text were as specified in Table 1 below.

Table 1 – Matching crib and cipher text

Cipher text	D	A	C
Crib		P	E	R

The cryptographers started off the rodding procedure by attempting to establish which of the three wheels being used by the Italian Naval Enigma operators was placed inside the cipher machine on the right on the day in question, and what was the message setting (defined in Appendix 1) of the message being rodded. To do this, the path followed by the current had to be analysed as it passed through one of the wheels, which was assumed, for the purposes of the analysis, to be on the right, while the crib, or guessed meaning, was tapped out on the Enigma keyboard to produce the cipher text; the same analysis was carried out in relation to each of the three wheels in turn, and with each of the three wheels starting at each possible position. In this example, I have assumed the internal wiring for the wheel being analysed first was as specified in Table 2 below; this shows which current entry/exit points on the right face of the wheel are connected to which points on the left face.

Table 2 – Which points on right face of wheel are connected to which points on left face

| Right face | QWE R T Z U I OA S D F GH J K P Y X C V B NML |
| Left face | A H I U E W S L QG P K V X NMOZ F C B T Y RD J |

The cryptographers began by looking at the first vertical pair of letters produced by writing the crib under the cipher text, i.e. as shown in Table 1:

| Cipher text | D |
| Crib | P |

The cryptographers worked out which current entry/exit point on the imaginary disk would be entered by the current if firstly P, the first letter in the crib, and secondly D, the first letter in the cipher text, were tapped on the Enigma keyboard with the right wheel set so that the Q on its right and left faces was lined up with the Qs on the entry disk and on the imaginary disk. This will be hereafter referred to as 'Position 1' of the right wheel. The reader will see, if he holds up the three pieces of paper described above in the wheel/disk order specified in Figure 16, and in the positions described above, and if he takes into account the wiring connections specified in Table 2 above, that the current's path, as it goes from the keyboard to the imaginary disk, would be as specified in Table 3 if P or D were tapped. (When following the current's path, the reader should look at the right-hand column in Table 3 first.) So, for example, when the P keyboard key is tapped, the current passes through the entry disk at point P, through the right wheel's right face at point P, through the right wheel's left face at point Z, before arriving at the right face of the imaginary disk at point Z.

Table 3 – Current's paths when keyboard keys specified in this table are tapped with the right wheel in Position 1

Imaginary disk Right face	Right wheel Left face	Right wheel Right face	Entry disk Right and Left faces	Letter on keyboard Tapped
Z	Z	P	P	P
K	K	D	D	D

The letters in the left column in Table 3 are the two points on the imaginary disk which the current passes through when P is tapped to produce the cipher text letter D; the current goes through point Z when going from right to left on the way to the reflector disk, and through K when going from left to right after being reflected back by the reflector disk towards the D lamp. These two points on the imaginary disk can be said to be paired together; if the wheels and disk on the left of the imaginary wheel are assumed to remain in the same position, then whenever the current, going through the Enigma from right to left, reaches point Z on the imaginary disk, it will always run on to the reflector end disk, and then bounce back to K on the imaginary disk. This kind of pairing is at the heart of the rodding procedure, as will be demonstrated below.

The cryptographers would then work out what points on the imaginary disk are similarly paired together when A and E, the next vertical pair of letters produced when the cipher text in Table 1 is written on top of the crib, are tapped out one by one on the Enigma keyboard, assuming that no wheel or disk moved when P was tapped to give D, other than the right wheel, which moved one place anticlockwise to what is hereafter referred to as 'Position 2'. To work out the current's paths when keyboards keys A and E are tapped as mentioned above, with the right wheel in Position 2 in each case, the reader should hold up his three pieces of paper in the position they were in when working out the path followed by the current when P was tapped to light up D, and he should then move the drawing on the paper representing the right wheel one place anti-clockwise, viewed from the right. The current's resulting paths are laid out in Table 4 below. Once again points Z and K on the imaginary disk are paired together.

Table 4 – Current's paths when keyboard keys specified in this table are tapped with right wheel in Position 2

Imaginary disk	Right wheel Left face	Right wheel Right face	Entry disk Right and Left faces	Letter on keyboard Tapped
Z	U	R	E	E
K	P	S	A	A

If that was the pairing discovered, there would be no problem; the path of the current, as it goes from right to left from point Z on the imaginary wheel through the middle and left wheels to the end disk, and then, after it is reflected by the end disk, as it goes back from left to right to point K on the imaginary wheel, is consistent with the pairing discovered when P was tapped on the keyboard to light up D (see Table 3 above). If a consistent pairing like this was discovered, the cryptographers would carry on by working out the equivalent pairings for the other pairs of letters in the crib and cipher text.

However, if instead of K, the current passed through, say, M on the imaginary disk when A was tapped, while the current still passed through Z on the imaginary disk when E was tapped, (which are the paths laid out in Table 5 below), the cryptographers would have highlighted an inconsistency, enabling them to rule out the starting position of the right wheel they were testing, i.e. Position 1. The inconsistency can be explained as follows: if the wheels to the left of the imaginary disk had not moved, which was what the cryptographers were assuming, the path of the current, as it went from right to left from the imaginary disk through the middle and left wheels to the end disk, and as it went back to the imaginary disk after being reflected by the end disk, could not change. So it was impossible, given the cryptographers' assumption that no wheels to the left of the imaginary disk had moved, that the current, going from right to left, should go from Z on the imaginary disk through the middle and left wheels to the end disk, and then back to point K on the imaginary disk, as specified in Table 3, and also that the current, going from right to left, should go from Z on the imaginary disk through the middle and left wheels before being reflected by the end disk back to M on the imaginary disk, as specified in Table 5.

Table 5 – Current paths when the keyboard keys specified in this table are tapped with right wheel in Position 2

Imaginary disk Right face	Right wheel Left face	Right wheel Right face	Entry disk Right and Left faces	Letter on keyboard Tapped
Z	U	R	E	E
M	P	S	A	A

After the cryptographers, adopting the procedure specified above, had ruled out a particular right wheel position as being the correct wheel starting position for the message, they would move on to test what would happen if they assumed that the starting position of the right wheel was Position 2, i.e. where W on the right wheel was opposite Q on the entry and imaginary disks. If there was a similar inconsistency in the equivalent pairings discovered with the right wheel in Position 2, then the cryptographers would go on to test the next starting position, 'Position 3', where E on the right wheel was opposite Q on the entry and imaginary disks, and so on, until a position was tested which showed no inconsistencies; that might be the correct position of the correct right wheel.

It should be noted that for two of the three Italian Naval Enigma wheels which had to be tested for a particular day, the cryptographers might not be able to find any positions without similar inconsistencies to those described above. In such circumstances, the two wheels being tested would be ruled out, and then the third wheel would be tested until the correct starting position was identified. A similar, but not identical, consistency test was applied to identify the middle wheel being used on the day in question, and its starting position for the message being rodded. Once that was identified, the cryptographers had successfully worked out the wheel order; the remaining wheel had to be the left wheel. With this information, the cryptographers would go on to work out the meaning of the messages transmitted on the day in question.

Rodding in practice

The above example explains the rodding principle. In practice, the cryptographers at Bletchley Park used a shortcut. They did not have to work out the points reached by the current on the imaginary disk every time they discovered a crib and matching cipher text. Instead they prepared a table for each of the three wheels (i.e. there were three tables) which set out these points. The cryptographers could then quickly check whether the kind of pairings referred to in the previous paragraphs showed any inconsistencies. It was the rows in these tables which were referred to as 'the rods'; the letters in a particular row were originally written on long cardboard sticks, or rods. The letters on the imaginary disk which were paired together, as indicated above, were sometimes referred to as 'the rod couplings'.

A portion of one of the tables, which would have been produced for a wheel with the internal connections mentioned in Table 2 above, is specified in Table 6.

Table 6 – Table used for Rodding

Right wheel positions

		1	2	3	4	5	6	7	8	9	10	11
	Q	O	T	E	C	P	F	N	V	O	P	B
	W	Z	R	V	Y	G	M	B	A	Y	N	H
	E	T	B	X	H	L	N	S	X	M	J	C
	R	N	C	J	Q	M	D	C	L	K	V	L
	T	V	K	W	L	F	V	Q	P	B	Q	P
	Z	P	E	Q	G	B	W	Y	N	W	Y	J
	U	R	W	H	N	E	X	M	E	X	K	W
Points on	I	E	J	M	R	C	L	R	C	P	E	Q
Imaginary	O	K	L	T	V	Q	T	V	Y	R	W	F
wheel	A	Q	Z	B	W	Z	B	X	T	E	G	R
	S	U	N	E	U	N	C	Z	R	H	T	A
	D	M	R	I	M	V	U	T	J	Z	S	E
	F	Y	O	L	B	I	Z	K	U	D	R	S
	G	A	Q	N	O	U	P	I	F	R	D	T
	H	W	M	A	I	Y	O	G	Z	F	Z	Z
	J	L	S	O	X	A	H	U	G	U	U	N
	K	D	A	C	S	J	I	H	I	I	M	M

The intersection of row Q and column 1 shows that electric current goes from Q on Imaginary Disk to O on entry disk, and vice versa, when right wheel is at position 1.

The intersection of row Q and column 2 shows that current goes from Q on Imaginary Disk to T on entry disk, and vice versa, when right wheel is at position 2.

If the cryptographers wanted to use this Table, to find the point on the imaginary disk which the current, going from right to left, would pass through when P, the first letter in the crib, was tapped, assuming that the right wheel was set to Position 1, as specified above, they would look down column 1 in the Table, until they found P, and they would find it was in the Z row. This indicated that when P was tapped on the keyboard, the current went to Z on the imaginary disk – which is the same answer as is specified in Table 3 above.

When using the Table to find the point on the imaginary disk which the current, going from right to left, would pass through when D, the first letter of the cipher text, was tapped with the right wheel set to Position 1, the cryptographers would look for D in column 1, and they would find that it was in the K row, which is also the same answer as specified in Table 3.

Part 2 – How the Italian Naval Enigma was broken for the first time

The intercepted cipher text rodded by Mavis Lever, the Bletchley Park cryptographer who broke the code for the first time in 1940, has yet to be declassified; so the precise steps she followed to work out the first words of the message, as mentioned in chapter 10, cannot be described. However, by interviewing cryptographers who helped to break the Italian Naval Enigma cipher, I have pieced together the technique she used; it is illustrated by the following example.

I have assumed that the Bletchley Park cryptographers were attempting to use rodding to read the cipher text mentioned in Table 7 below. P-E-R-X, the guessed meaning of the first four letters of the cipher text, were the letters actually used by Mavis Lever in 1940 when she was breaking her first message.

Table 7 – Cipher text and guessed meaning

```
H Z L A B Y E F S E K I S T V X B G L S E  - Cipher text
P E R X                                    - Guessed meaning
```

I have also assumed that the cryptographers, when testing a particular Enigma wheel and a particular starting position of that wheel, discovered that the rod couplings (defined in the first part of this Appendix), for the first three vertical pairs of letters formed by writing the guessed meaning under the cipher text, were as specified in Table 8 below. Beside the rod couplings in Table 8, I have listed the letters I have assumed were in the relevant row of the rod table, i.e. the row used to identify the above-mentioned rod couplings; the rod table is equivalent to the table laid out in Table 6, which is explained within the first part of this Appendix. To work out the rod coupling for the first vertical pair of letters made up by writing the guessed meaning under the cipher text, i.e. for:

H

P

the letters H and P would have been looked up in the appropriate column of the rod table; I have assumed they would have been found in the Z and U rows of the rod table, which is why Z and U are shown as the rod coupling in Table 8. This follows the procedure explained in Part 1 of this Appendix for using the rod table shown in the afore-mentioned Table 6. However it was the other letters in the rods coupled together which helped Mavis Lever to break the code; the way this happened is illustrated below.

Table 8 – Rod couplings for the first three vertical pairs of letters produced by writing guessed meanings under cipher text

Rod
Coupling

Z	H̲	L	G	S	J	N	B	G	V	T	E	S	G	N	V
U	P̲	T	F	U	L	K	L	T	B	A	B	R	F	M	S
D	L	Z̲	K	G	D	T	Y	E	X	G	S	P	S	
M	K	E̲	T	Y	F	B	C	K	T	A	Y	E	R	
F	S	U	L̲	S	G	P	Q	D	F	X	Z	U	P	K
G	T	V	R̲	A	L	C	D	X	M	E	T	M	N	O

After working out the first three rod couplings, the cryptographers would see that the fourth letter of the cipher text, i.e. A in Table 7 above, appeared in one of the coupled rows in the rod table. The A is in the fourth column of the G row, which has been shown in Table 8 to be coupled to the F row. This is significant. There was a rule of thumb – which was merely a particular application of the rodding principles outlined in the first part of this Appendix – which stated that if a cipher text letter appeared in a particular column on one of a pair of coupled rods in the rod table, then the matching plain-language letter must be the letter in the same column on the other rod in the pair. If this were not to be the case, an inconsistency of the kind demonstrated in the first part of this Appendix would have been highlighted. Applying this rule to the example being looked at, the discovery of A, the fourth letter of the cipher text on the G rod meant that the fourth plain-language letter must be the letter in the fourth column of the coupled F rod, which was an S, and not an X as guessed.

That might lead the cryptographers to start looking at PERS rather than PERX, as the possible guessed meaning of the first four letters of the cipher text. It would be a short step from that to guess that the message might begin with the word 'Personale', followed by X; the X would represent the gap between 'Personale' and the next word. Once these extra letters were guessed, the cryptographers would be able to look up the rod couplings for the vertical pairs of letters produced by writing PERSONALEX under the cipher text in Table

7. This would in its turn open the way for them to use the same rule of thumb mentioned above to 'suggest' extra letters, which in their turn might enable the cryptographers to guess a few more letters. Using this approach, the cryptographers might be able to guess and work out several words at the beginning of the message at the same time as breaking the code.

Appendix 6

Naval Enigma Offizier – How It Was Broken[1]

As mentioned in chapter 24, the Bletchley Park cryptographers' failure to quickly break Offizier, as well as the general Naval Enigma settings, could have had disastrous consequences immediately prior to the sinking of the *Scharnhorst* in December 1943. If Offizier messages had been read currently, Admiral Bruce Fraser, the Commander-in-Chief of the Home Fleet, would have discovered that *Scharnhorst* was about to make a sortie approximately twelve hours before the Admiralty sent out its signal at 3.39 a.m. on 26 December 1943 confirming that she was at sea. On the other hand, the breaking of the Offizier Naval Enigma settings – referred to by the British as 'Oyster' and 'Limpet' in respect of signals sent on the Home Waters (Dolphin), and the Atlantic U-boat (Shark) nets – helped British cryptographers keep up with changes in the procedure being used on these nets.

Laid out below is how signals were sent by the Germans on the Oyster and Limpet Offizier nets, and how these signals were broken.

Part 1 – How Offizier was used by the Germans

(1) The Offizier settings, in areas where Dolphin and Shark were used, were the same as the general settings, apart from the plugboard socket connections. However, rather than the sender using the Naval Enigma sending procedure, mentioned in Appendix 3, to work out his message setting, the Offizier message settings were chosen for each message from a list of twenty-six, which was changed each month. Each message setting in the list was designated by a letter of the alphabet. The message sender indicated which setting he had chosen by placing a code word at the beginning of his message whose first letter was the letter of alphabet beside the setting chosen from

the list, i.e. if the sender chose the message setting ABC which was beside the letter P in the settings list, he might start his message: Offizier Paula. (The P in Paula would not have been underlined in the message.)

(2) After setting the Enigma to the correct settings, the Offizier message was enciphered.

(3) The cipher text mentioned in 2 above, was then enciphered again using the general Enigma settings and procedure, and transmitted in morse code.

Part 2 – How Offizier settings were broken

(1) The first break into the Offizier each month had to be made using a crib and bombe. Once the wheel, ring and plugboard socket settings were discovered, some of the message settings in the list of twenty-six mentioned in Part 1 above could be worked out.

(2) After the first break had been made during a particular month, Offizier settings for the rest of the month could be worked out without a crib. Firstly, the general settings for the day in question were worked out using a crib and bombe, or Banburismus and a bombe.

(3) A message was identified whose message setting had been worked out as mentioned in 1 above. After this was done, the cryptographers only had to work out the Offizier plugboard settings for the day in question.

(4) A so-called 'dottery' was filled in to work out some of the Offizier plugboard socket settings used when the Germans enciphered the message mentioned in (3) above. The cryptographers filling in a dottery tapped out the cipher text letters making up the message on a replica Enigma with no plugboard sockets connected to other sockets, and with its wheels set initially to the message setting mentioned in (3) above, and recorded the Enigma lamps which lit up on a graph similar to the graph in Figure 17; the right wheel turned around one place each time a keyboard key was tapped. If, say, the keyboard key representing the cipher text letter D was tapped, and the J lamp lit up, a dot was placed in the intersection of the D row and the J column. After the results were recorded in the Figure 17 graph, the cryptographers would expect to find the following results.

In one column, say, the J column, as specified in Figure 17, there would be more dots than in all the other columns. Most of these dots would be in a limited number of rows, such as rows D, F, L, M, R and Z, as specified in Figure 17. These two observations would tell the

Figure 17

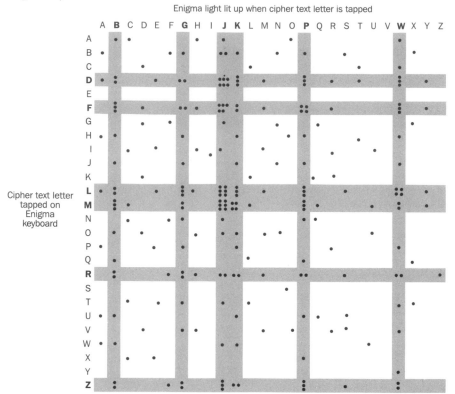

cryptographers that J was, probably, the plugboard socket connected to the E socket; E was the most common letter in German plain-language texts. The cryptographers would also deduce that the six rows, where most of the dots in the J column were situated, represented plugboard sockets which were not connected to other sockets; the cryptographers would say that these sockets were 'self-steckered'.

The cryptographers' deductions mentioned in the previous paragraph assumed that the following had taken place:

(a) The E keyboard key had been tapped several times by the message sender on the Enigma with a plugboard in the course of sending his message. On many of these occasions, this had led to the current lighting up some, or all, of the limited number of letters, such as D in Figure 17, whose plugboard sockets were self-steckered. Usually there were six such sockets. In such cases, the current would have flowed from E on the keyboard to the plugboard, at which point, the current would have been diverted to the plugboard socket to which E was connected, i.e. J in Figure 17, which the cryptographers referred to as 'the stecker of E', before entering, and being diverted as it passed through, the wheels. These wheels would have rotated one place further away from the message setting, specified in code by the message sender at the beginning of the message, each time a keyboard key was tapped.

(b) Because of the reversible properties of the Enigma, a consequence of (a) above was that when, in the course of doing the dottery illustrated in Figure 17, the plugboardless Enigma wheels were placed in the positions mentioned in (a), and when a keyboard key representing a self-steckered letter in the cipher text, such as D, was tapped, the current would, on many occasions, have flowed back through the wheels to light up the letter representing the stecker of E: J. This means that the current would have followed the identical path when flowing through the wheels – set to a particular position – on the plugboardless Enigma, when D was tapped, to that followed when E was tapped on the Enigma with a plugboard, and with the wheels set to the same position, except that the current would have flowed in the opposite direction.

Using the reasoning in (a) and (b) above the cryptographers were able to deduce that the six rows in Figure 17 with lots of dots in them in the J column were self-steckered, since the phenomenon observed, i.e. lots of dots in the J column with most of the dots in up to six rows, would not have taken place if the plugboard sockets corresponding to the letters beside these rows had been connected to other plugboard sockets.

For example, if plugboard socket D had been connected to, say, plugboard socket C, then, when the keyboard key representing cipher text letter D was tapped on the plugboardless Enigma with its wheels at a particular position in the course of doing the dottery, the current would not have flowed along the same path – albeit in reverse – through the wheels to that followed when E was tapped on the Enigma with a plugboard with its wheels at the same position. In the latter case, the current would have gone from E to E's stecker, i.e. J in Figure 17, before going into the wheels at J and coming out of them at C, before being diverted by the plugboard once more on its way to D. When the D keyboard key was tapped, the current would have gone into the wheels at D, instead of C, and would have ended up coming out of the wheels, not at J, E's stecker, but at another letter, say, T. In these circumstances, the dot in the Figure 17 graph would not have been in the J column, but in the T column. The same would have happened in relation to the other letters: F, L, M, R and Z mentioned above, if they had also been connected to other sockets, so there would not have been a large group of dots in the intersection of the rows representing these letters, and E's stecker, J.

After completing and analysing the dottery, the cryptographers would have known some or all of the sockets which were self-steckered, and which socket was connected to the E socket. They might also have had some idea about which other sockets were connected to the: T, O, N, I and A sockets; like E, these letters appeared frequently in German, and using letter frequency statistics, the cryptographers could observe which columns in the dottery had the number of dots in them which complied with these statistics.

(5) Extra plug socket connections used when the German sender sent the message mentioned in (3) above, could be gleaned by using the following procedure, which came to be known as 'Yoxallismus' after Leslie Yoxall, the Bletchley Park cryptographer who first applied it to the Offizier settings problem. The keyboard key representing the stecker of E, i.e. J, as discovered through doing the dottery in (4) above, was tapped on the plugboardless Enigma at each position of the wheels at, and after, the message setting for the message in question, and the enciphered version of J could be written in a line above the line representing the cipher text intercepted, or the information could be represented on a graph; let us say the two lines were as specified in Table 1 below:

Table 1

Wheel Positions	1	2	3	4
Enciphered Version of J	D	G	K	G
Cipher Text Intercepted	D	K	G	K

The information under Wheel Position 1 in Table 1 merely confirms what could already be gleaned from the dottery in Figure 17, that D is self steckered: the D in the Enciphered Version of J row would have told the cryptographers that when J was tapped, the current flowed through the wheels on the plugboardless Enigma, and came out of the wheels at D. The D in the Cipher Text Intercepted row would have told the cryptographers that when a keyboard key, which might well have been E, was tapped on the Enigma with a plugboard, the D light lit up. The combined information in the two rows would have suggested, but would not have proved, that D might be self steckered.

The information in the Enciphered Version of J row under Wheel Position 2 would have told the cryptographers that the current flowed out of the wheels on the plugboardless Enigma at G when J was tapped. The information in the Cipher Text Intercepted row would have told the cryptographers that when a keyboard key, which might well have been E, was tapped on the Enigma with a plugboard, the K light lit up. The combined information in the two rows would have suggested, but would not have proved, that G was the stecker of K.

The evidence that the G and K sockets were connected would have been strengthened by what is under Wheel Position 3 in Table 1: on this occasion, the information in the Enciphered Version of J row would have told the cryptographers that the current had flowed out of the plugboardless Enigma wheels at K when J was tapped. The information in the Cipher Text Intercepted row would have told the cryptographers that when a keyboard key, which might well have been E, had been tapped on the Enigma with a plugboard, the G light lit up. The combined information in the two rows would have suggested, but would not have proved, that K was the stecker of G. This is consistent with the information in the previous paragraph, given the reversible character of the Enigma plugboard; and it would have lent more weight to the growing evidence that the G and K plugboard sockets were connected when the message under consideration was enciphered.

The information under Wheel Position 4 in Table 1, which repeats the information specified under Wheel Position 2, would also have supported the deduction referred to in the last sentence of the previous paragraph.

In the case of a longer stretch of cipher text than that specified in Table 1, more evidence, such as that in Table 1, might have indicated that the G and K sockets were connected, and similar deductions about some of the other plugboard socket connections might have been made. Then, the cryptographers would have been able to tap out the letters in the cipher text with the worked out socket connections in place inside the replica Enigma, in order to light up some of the letters in the plain language message sent. Using this information, the cryptographers might have been able to guess the missing letters in the plain-language German message, and in the process, to work out the remaining plugboard socket connections for the day in question.

Notes

Introduction (pp. 1–7)

1 Cryptographers usually refer to the letters of the alphabet produced by scrambling a plain-language message on an Enigma machine as 'cipher text', rather than as 'code'. When they talk about code, they are generally referring to what is produced when a plain-language word is replaced by another word or symbol, whereas the Enigma scrambles the letters in each word one by one. However, because we have become accustomed to talking about breaking 'the code', when talking about reading Enigma messages, I have sometimes written code rather than cipher text where I felt this was appropriate.
2 The Enigma cipher was broken for the first time by the Polish Cipher Bureau at the end of 1932, or at the beginning of 1933. Many messages were broken between 1933–8, but changes made to the Enigma machine in 1938 made it difficult for the Polish codebreakers to carry on reading the messages. Marian Rejewski, the Polish codebreaker who reconstructed the Enigma machine (the vital breakthrough enabling him to read Enigma messages), stated that he would not have broken Enigma when he did without the documents provided by Hans Thilo Schmidt. Schmidt passed his documents to the French Secret Service, which passed them on to the Poles. Rejewski's admission was made in a 24 July 1978 interview by Richard A. Woytak. An edited version of Woytak's interview appear in Władysław Kozaczuk's *Enigma: How the German Cipher Machine Was Broken, and How It Was Read by the Allies in World War Two* (London, 1984), referred to hereafter as 'Kozaczuk, *Enigma*'. The relevant passage is on p. 233. Kozaczuk gave the author a copy of the transcript of the original Woytak interview.
3 If it had not been for Schmidt's and the Poles' contributions, it is likely that no Army and Air Force Enigma messages would have been read by British codebreakers prior to the fall of France in June 1940. This is the conclusion reached on p. 956 of vol. 3(2) of the official history, *British Intelligence in the Second World War* by F. H. Hinsley, E. E. Thomas, C. A. G. Simkins, R. C. Knight and C. F. G. Ransom (London, 1979–88), hereafter referred to as 'Hinsley' with the relevant volume number added. Thanks to Schmidt and the Poles, some Army and Air Force Enigma messages were read by the British and Poles between January 1940–1 May 1940. A change in the Enigma procedure then led to a

codebreaking black out on some Enigma networks until 22 May 1940, when the British managed to break the code used on these networks again.

Even after June 1940 it is by no means certain when the Air Force and Army Enigma codes would have been broken without Schmidt and the Poles' involvement. Hinsley vol. 3(2) p. 956 states that there was 'enough external evidence' to have enabled the break into Air Force Enigma to have been achieved, even without the Poles' involvement, shortly after the fall of France, through using a particular type of cilli (a German encrypting mistake explained in chapter 8). Hinsley however admits that the British codebreakers only managed to identify these cillis in January 1940 because Bletchley Park's codebreakers were reading the German messages at the time. This was thanks to information provided by Schmidt and the Poles. So Hinsley's assertion should be treated with some caution.

The way in which a similar German enciphering mistake led to the creation of the so-called Herivel Tip procedure (also described in chapter 8), used by the British codebreakers in conjunction with the cillis, gives a clue as to what knowledge was needed for such mistakes to be identified. John Herivel, inventor of the Herivel Tip procedure, has stated that he thought it up after he knew about the Enigma's indicating procedure (the procedure adopted by a German message sender when informing the message receiver how both of them should set up their Enigma machines). In a 1999 letter to the author he confirmed that he would never have thought up the Herivel Tip if he had had no idea what the indicating procedure was. He would not have known what it was without Schmidt's and the Poles' assistance. The same is true of the cillis.

If the Air Force Enigma had not been broken by the Poles before the war, or through the use of the Herivel Tip and the cillis during May 1940, then it is possible that the Enigma code in question would not have been broken regularly until both an Enigma machine and a document giving a month of Enigma settings had been captured. Enigma machines were captured in Norway and were in Bletchley Park by 17 May 1940 (Hinsley vol. 3(2) p. 955), and some Army Enigma settings for November 1941 were captured on 28 November 1941 (Hinsley vol. 2 p. 295). This would have enabled the British codebreakers to read the Army Enigma November 1941 messages during December 1941, even without Schmidt and the Poles' involvement, and would have given the codebreakers a perfect opportunity to spot both the cillis and the mistake that led to the invention of the Herivel Tip. So it is quite possible that the first substantial breaks into the Army and Air Force Enigmas might only have taken place after November 1941 had it not been for Schmidt's contribution.

4 According to Hinsley vol. 3(2) p. 958, it was unlikely that the Polish contribution affected the date when the Naval Enigma was first mastered by the British codebreakers, between August–October 1941. But once again Hinsley's statement, which he admits is just his subjective opinion, should be treated with some caution. As stated in note 3 above, without Schmidt and the Poles, there might not have been any breaks into Army or Air Force Enigma until the end of 1941. In those circumstances it is quite feasible that Alan Turing's bombe machine, which helped to break the code during the war, would not have been thought of and manufactured until Bletchley Park discovered the wiring inside the Enigma from a captured machine and demonstrated that there would be a

regular supply of 'cribs' (guessed meanings of Enigma messages), necessary for a machine such as the bombe to break the Naval Enigma. That combination could not have been demonstrated until, at the earliest, after the capture of the Enigma machines in Norway (note 3 above), and until the capture of Enigma documents from *Polares*, a German trawler, in April 1940 led to the reading of a limited number of German Naval Enigma messages. However evidence that cribs would become regularly available may not have been persuasive enough to satisfy the government that bombes should be manufactured until a larger number of messages were read following the capture of *Krebs*, another German trawler with its Enigma documents on board, in March 1941. In the former case, where the bombe invention and manufacture would have proceeded only following the capture of *Polares* and the Enigma machines in Norway, the mastering of Naval Enigma would probably not have been delayed for long. On the other hand in the latter case, Naval Enigma might well only have been mastered in line with the following schedule (assuming that the same amount of time was taken to carry out the stages as these steps actually took). Since the invention and building of the final version of the bombe took around one year (August 1939–August 1940), and since it seems that only the final version of the bombe could break Enigma settings regularly and quickly enough to be useful operationally, it is likely that no suitable bombe would have been available to help crack any of the Naval Enigma networks' messages until March 1942, one year after *Krebs'* capture. Because it took another five months after the *Krebs'* capture for the British codebreakers to learn how to use Alan Turing's Banburismus procedure, which reduced the number of bombe hours needed to break each day's Enigma settings, and it took them another two months to learn to read the messages quickly, it is not unreasonable to say that the mastering of a Naval Enigma network for the first time would not have taken place until seven months after the notional March 1942 delivery of a bombe, in October 1942, if Schmidt and the Poles had not been involved. By that time the German Atlantic U-boats might have been using an adapted Enigma machine with four wheels – as actually happened. This four-wheel Enigma was only broken into for the first time, following another capture, in December 1942. If it had not been for Schmidt and the Poles, the Naval Enigma used in the Atlantic might not have been read regularly and quickly until then.

5 This is a simplification of the real position. In fact, five wheels had different turnover positions, and the other three had the same turnover positions. However enough of the wheels were different to enable Turing to break the Naval Enigma because of the differences using his Banburismus technique. It is described in Appendix 3.

6 Alexander, *Naval Enigma History* p. 52.

7 Hinsley vol. 2 p. 174.

8 Sir Harry Hinsley, 'The Influence of Ultra in the Second World War', the annual lecture given to the Liddell Hart Centre for Military Archives, 18 February 1992, p. 7.

9 *ibid.* p. 13.

10 Of course the use of the atomic bomb might have ended the war before 1946, even if Operation Overlord had not taken place during 1944. But it is not certain that the Allies would have allowed its use in Germany because of the fall out repercussions.

Prologue (pp. 9–13)
1 The way in which the British captured the Enigma wheels is not entirely clear, as is mentioned in chapter 6.
2 Public Record Office (PRO) ADM1/14256.

Chapter 1 The Betrayal (pp. 15–20)
1 Details about Hans Thilo Schmidt in this chapter come from: the author's 1998 interview with Paul Paillole who rose to become head of French Counter-Intelligence during the Second World War; pp. 1–39 of Paillole's book *Notre Espion Chez Hitler* Paris, 1985 (hereafter referred to as 'Paillole'); and from the author's 1998 interview with Hans Thilo Schmidt's daughter, Gisela.
2 Before the war the French Army's 'Deuxième Bureau' was responsible for deciding what intelligence was needed, and for analysing and interpreting any intelligence passed to it. The French Army's autonomous Service de Renseignement – officially known as the 'Deuxième Bureau SR-SCR' – was responsible for gathering intelligence and carrying out counter-espionage; the Deuxième Bureau was in effect a client of the Service de Renseignement. Their chiefs reported to the same department in the Army. During the war the Service de Renseignement came to be known as the Cinquième Bureau. In this book I have adopted the simple solution of refer-ring to both the Deuxième Bureau and the Service de Renseignement as the 'Deuxième Bureau '.

Chapter 2 The Leak (pp. 21–30)
1 One source for this anecdote is a written account by Leonard Danilewicz, the brother of Ludomir, which was sent to Marian Rejewski on 28 February 1975. Leonard Danilewicz co-owned the AVA company with Ludomir, Antoni Palluth and a fourth partner, Edward Fokczyński. Another verbal account given to the author by Maria Danilewicz-Zieliński, Ludomir Danilewicz's widow, slightly contradicts the date for the incident given in Leonard Danilewicz's account. He thought it occurred in 1927 or 1928. She is sure that it occurred on the last Saturday in January 1929 which was while she was finishing off a thesis she was writing at Warsaw University. Although memories are not always accurate, I have preferred her account because it is linked to such a definite event in her life whose date can be ver-ified. A translation of the original account by Leonard Danilewicz was made available to the author by Maria Danilewicz-Zieliński and by Leonard Danilewicz's son, John.
2 *ibid.*
3 The date for the cryptology course and an account of how it was set up comes from Kozaczuk, *Enigma*, and from Marian Rejewski's 'Memoirs' (hereafter referred to as 'Rejewski, Memoirs'), the first part of which was completed in 1967.
4 The source is Marian Rejewski's 'Remarks on Appendix 1 to *British Intelligence in the Second World War*, vol. 1 by F. H. Hinsley', *Cryptologia*, January 1982 (hereafter referred to as 'Reyewski on Hinsley').
5 Kozaczuk, *Enigma* p. 6.

6 Paillole pp. 40–1.
7 Paillole p. 46.
8 Paillole pp. 47–8.
9 Paillole pp. 56–7.
10 Paillole pp. 58–9.
11 Paillole p. 55.
12 Paillole p. 88.
13 Paillole p. 106.
14 Paillole pp. 104–5.
15 Paillole pp. 107–12.
16 *Documents Diplomatiques Français 1932–1939, Deuxième Série 1936–39*, vol 7 pp. 343–4, Paris, 1972.
17 Paillole pp. 278–83.
18 Paillole p. 120.
19 Paillole p. 121.

Chapter 3 An Inspired Guess (pp. 31–38)

1 Paillole p. 163 and Bertrand, *Enigma, ou la plus grande énigme de la guerre* (hereafter referred to as 'Bertrand') p. 57.
2 There is a difference of opinion as to the date when this plan emerged and who was the author. Paillole suggests it was put to the Poles in August 1938, and that it was the Counter-Intelligence department of the Deuxième Bureau who thought it up. Bertrand says that he thought up the plan, and subsequently put it to the Poles in December 1938.
3 Interview with Rejewski given to Richard Woytak in July 1978. See Kozaczuk, *Enigma* pp. 229–36.
4 Rejewski's story about how he reconstructed the Enigma machine in 1932 suggests that he could not remember the precise dates when Ciężki gave him information on the cipher machine, or the exact order in which the information was given to him. The main source for my description of how Rejewski did it is to be found in Kozaczuk, *Enigma* pp. 254–9.
5 The manuals which Schmidt showed to the French Secret Service do not appear to be available for inspection in the German, British or American archives. Most historians refer to the earliest Army Enigma manuals which are available, which are those created in 1937 and 1940. See Paillole pp. 35–7.
6 Enigma operators working at the time when Schmidt was providing manuals and settings lists to the French Secret Service placed three wheels in their cipher machines. They only had three wheels to choose from. Subsequently operators were supplied with two extra wheels. Some Naval Enigma operators used four wheels after 1 February 1942. By then these Naval Enigma operators had eight wheels to choose from, in addition to the special fourth wheel.
7 The figure of around 17,000 is arrived at by working out the calculation 26 x 26 x 25 = 16,900. The calculation would have been 26 x 26 x 26 were it not for an extra complication which I have not mentioned in the main text in order to keep the explanation simple: at one point in its cycle the middle wheel turned over not only when the right wheel rotated through its turnover

position, but also when the very next keyboard key was tapped if, before the key was tapped, the middle wheel had reached its own turnover position. This latter situation would mean that all three wheels would turn one twenty-sixth of a revolution at the same time.

8 The formula adopted by Rejewski is laid out in full in Kozaczuk, *Enigma* pp. 254–5. It consisted of six equations, each of which represented the path of the electric current inside an Enigma when a keyboard key was pressed six times consecutively. Professor David Rees, who worked at Bletchley Park after graduating in mathematics from Cambridge University, told me in 1999 that the mathematics used by Rejewski to make up the formula could have been understood by any university mathematics undergraduate who had specialised in group theory. What was clever, according to Rees, was Rejewski's idea that the group theory in question could be applied to the problem of reconstructing an Enigma.

9 Paillole p. 53, and Kozaczuk, *Enigma* p. 233.

10 Rejewski account in Kozaczuk, *Enigma* p. 257.

11 *ibid.* p. 258. It has to be said that Rejewski's initial assumption that there was a diversion inside the entry disk is surprising. The illustration in the Enigma manual *Gebrauchsanleitung für die Chiffriermachine Enigma Vom 12.1.1937*, which is the earliest Enigma manual still available in the German archives, suggests that there was no diversion inside the entry disk. Perhaps this illustration was not in the version handed over by Hans Thilo Schmidt to the Poles, or perhaps Rejewski was not shown the illustration in question.

12 *ibid.* p. 258.

Chapter 4 A Terrible Mistake (pp. 39–45)

1 Leonard Danilewicz's account referred to in chapter 2 note 1 and the author's 1998 interview with Jerzy, son of Antoni Palluth.

2 Rejewski's account in Kozaczuk, *Enigma* p. 265.

3 According to Rejewski in Kozaczuk, *Enigma* p. 266, the two new tools for breaking Enigma were thought up within weeks of 15 September 1938.

4 The reference to the bomby being so named because a weight was dropped to show that the correct solution had been found is in a note dated 11 October 1943 in Record Group in Historic Cryptographic Collection (RG) 457 Box 705 in the National Archives and Records Administration (hereafter referred to as the 'National Archives') in Washington.

5 Kozaczuk, *Enigma* p. 267.

6 Rejewski on Hinsley p. 79 states that breaking the Enigma using the bomby took 110 minutes 'at most'; that was the time it took for the bomby to run through a complete cycle.

7 *ibid.* p. 78. Rejewski said that the wheel order was changed daily after 1936. After October 1941 the Air Force Enigma wheel order was changed three times during each twenty-four hour period. This is confirmed on page 37 of William F. Friedman's 'Report on E Operations of the GC and CS at Bletchley Park', filed in RG 457 at the National Archives in Washington. The Army Enigma wheel order was only changed once a day even after October 1941.

8 Rejewski in Kozaczuk, *Enigma* p. 266 mentioned that there were only five to eight plugboard socket connections in the autumn of 1938, i.e. a minimum of five sockets were connected to five other sockets.

9 Females was the name given to them by the British codebreakers. According to Dilly Knox, one of the senior British codebreakers, this was because the codebreakers identified them on the perforated sheets by finding places where there were holes: 'C'est comme les femmes. On cherche les trous,' he would say, speaking in French presumably because he felt it would be indelicate to make his mildly dirty joke in English.

10 The 40 per cent figure comes from the author's 1999 interview with Professor David Rees who worked at Bletchley Park during the war at a time when the perforated sheets were being used.

11 Rejewski's account in Kozaczuk, *Enigma* pp. 267–8 and pp. 59–71 of Gordon Welchman's *The Hut Six Story*, London, 1982, hereafter referred to as 'Welchman'.

12 If each socket on the plugboard was connected by a wire to one of the other twenty-five sockets, the number of different socket combinations which could be produced was almost 8,000,000,000,000 (8 trillion). In fact at various times there were different rules nominating the number of sockets which could be linked to other sockets. Prior to 1939 ten to sixteen sockets were linked to other sockets on the plugboard. After 1 January 1939 the number of sockets which could be linked to other sockets rose to between fourteen and twenty. However the number of socket combinations from which the German Cipher Office could select the Enigma's plugboard setting was always enormous.

13 Rejewski in Kozaczuk, *Enigma* p. 268.

14 *ibid.*

15 *ibid.*

16 Kozaczuk, *Enigma* p. 242 says that fourteen to twenty of the plugboard sockets had to be connected to other sockets after 1 January 1939. From 1 October 1936 the rule was that ten to sixteen plugboard sockets had to be connected.

17 Rejewski in Kozaczuk, *Enigma* pp. 268–9.

18 This is mentioned in Rejewski's article 'How the Polish Mathematicians Broke Enigma' which appears in Kozaczuk, *Enigma* p. 257.

19 Memorandum from Lt.-Col. Telford Taylor about the Early 'E' [Enigma] History, 22 January 1944, Box 1364 in RG 457 in the National Archives, Washington.

20 Paillole p. 166.

21 Paillole pp. 58–106.

22 Paillole pp. 128–32.

Chapter 5 Flight (pp. 46–58)

1 The details in this chapter about Hinsley's movements in 1939 have been taken from an interview he gave to Dr Jonathan Steinberg, a history fellow at Trinity Hall, Cambridge in January 1996, hereafter referred to as the 'Steinberg Hinsley interview'.

2 The sources for the Polish cryptographers' escape from Warsaw are: an unpublished post-war account by Kazimierz Gaca, one of the younger cryptographers who worked on Enigma at Pyry and then in France; a 20 October 1980 letter from Gaca to Professor Jean Stengers; the author's 1998 interviews with Wanda Grodecka (Jerzy Różycki's niece), with Jerzy Palluth (Antoni Palluth's son), and with Janina Rejewski (Marian Rejewski's daughter); Kozaczuk, *Enigma* pp. 69–80; Rejewski's unpublished 1967 Memoirs; Basia Różycki's unpublished post-war account; an unpublished post-war account by Tadeusz Suszczewski, who worked with the Polish cryptographers in Warsaw and in France; and Henryk Zygalski's Diary entries which are to be found in his and his wife's correspondence with Marian Rejewski during 1974 – given to the author by Rejewski's grandson Wojtek.

3 PRO HW14/1.

4 The information about the breaking of the first Enigma message by an Englishman comes from the author's 1998–9 interviews with Peter Twinn. Hinsley vol. 3(2) pp. 950–1 mentions that Bertrand handed over some intercepts and settings to the British codebreakers during 1938.

5 PRO HW14/3.

6 Hinsley vol. 3(2) p. 952.

7 Gwido Langer's unpublished Memoirs entitled 'Report on the work of Lieutenant-Colonel Langer's team during the French Campaign from 1 October 1939 to 24 June 1940', (hereafter referred to as '1 October 1939–24 June 1940 Langer Memoirs'), which are filed in the Polish Institute and Sikorski Museum in London, give the dates when the Allies broke the Enigma code during the period 17 January 1940 until 21 June 1940, but they do not reveal which days were broken in France and which in Britain, except for one break: on 17 January 1940, it was the Poles in France who broke the code for 28 October 1939.

8 Kozaczuk, *Enigma* p. 97 mentions the meeting with Turing, but does not give a precise date for it. Kozaczuk says that Rejewski told him about the meeting. It was obviously after the Poles received the first portion of their perforated sheets from the British, which Hinsley vol. 3(2) p. 952 says was sent with a covering note dated 28 December 1939, since in the course of the meeting, the sheets are referred to by Zygalski. But no more precise date can be gleaned from Kozaczuk's text. It is possible that the meeting took place around 17 January 1940. Langer in the '1 October 1939–24 June 1940 Langer Memoirs' states that an English codebreaker was staying with the Poles in France when the first wartime Enigma message was broken on 17 January 1940.

9 Hinsley vol. 3(2) p. 954.

10 Anecdote about Turing provided by Professor Jack Good during 1998 interview with the author. Good worked under Turing at Bletchley Park.

11 Hinsley vol. 3(2) p. 954.

12 Welchman p. 81.

13 Joan Clarke, who was to become Joan Murray, in her chapter 'Hut 8 and naval Enigma Part 1' in *Codebreakers*, edited by F. H. Hinsley and Alan Stripp, Oxford, 1993 hereafter referred to as 'Codebreakers'. See p. 115 of the paperback edition, Oxford, 1994.

14 Author's 1999 interview with Richard Pendered. The crib and matching cipher text used by Pendered when he tested the spider were taken from

the Blue Enigma network. Blue was the colour given by Bletchley Park's codebreakers to Enigma messages sent out by Germany's armed forces while they were being trained. The menu produced using this crib could not have been used to break the code on the original bombe devised by Turing. That bombe only worked if the menu comprised a so-called closure, which meant that the chain of letters making up the menu started with a particular letter and ended with the same letter (see Appendix 2). The menu made up from the crib used by Pendered did not include such a closure. So Pendered was applying a rigorous test when he used his crib on the spider.
15 Hinsley vol. 3(2) p. 955.

Chapter 6 The First Capture (pp. 59–68)
1 The most important sources for the story told in this chapter are: PRO ADM186/805, which includes an account of U-33's 'last Cruise'; an account of the U-33's last patrol by Friedrich Schilling which can be found in PG30030 at the Ministry of Defence in London; pp. 104–111 of the paperback version of David Kahn's *Seizing the Enigma*, London 1996 (hereafter referred to as 'David Kahn'); and the author's 1999 interview with Max Schiller, one of the crew on the U-33 on the day it was sunk.
2 U-boat measurements taken from p. 57 of Clay Blair's *Hitler's U Boat War: the Hunters 1939–1942*, London 1997 (hereafter referred to as 'Blair vol. 1').
3 Blair vol. 1 p. 84 and Dönitz's War Diary, 10 September 1939 and 22 October 1939.
4 Blair vol. 1 p. 54.
5 Shipping losses are from p. 615 of vol. 1 of the official naval history *The War At Sea, 1939–1945*, London 1954–61, by Stephen Roskill (hereafter referred to as 'Roskill'). It should be pointed out that Roskill's figures have been challenged as more information has become available since publication. For example Jürgen Rohwer in his *U-Boote, Eine Chronik in Bildern*, Germany, 1962 (hereafter referred to as 'Rohwer'), stated that around 563,000 tons of merchant shipping (170 ships) were sunk by U-boats during the first five months of the war, in addition to the 131,000 tons (35 ships) sunk by mines released from U-boats. Since these figures arc still being corrected as new research is carried out, the tonnage and numbers of ships which are said to be sunk in these sources should be treated as the best estimates possible at the date the books were written.
6 *Statistical Digest of the War* ed. by W. Keith Hancock, London, 1975 pp. 173–4 quoted in Blair vol. 1 p. 99.
7 The account of what was happening aboard *Gleaner* is to be found in a report dated 13 February 1940 written by Lieutenant-Commander Hugh Price, the commanding officer, PRO ADM199/123. A second unsigned report describing the incident is to be found in the Imperial War Museum.
8 David Kahn pp. 109–11.
9 The author's 1999 interview with Peter Turfrey, son of Les Turfrey, one of the crewmembers aboard *Gleaner* when the U-33 was sunk.

Chapter 7 Mission Impossible (pp. 69–78)

1 Hinsley vol. 3(2) p. 957 and vol. 1 p. 336 lists the wheels captured.

2 The Naval Enigma operators only used a fourth wheel in their cipher machines after January 1942. It is not clear when the three new wheels made available to Naval Enigma operators, in addition to the five already available, were handed out.

3 Hinsley vol. 3(2) p. 957.

4 The seven indicators and message settings are laid out on p. 136 of Turing's unpublished 'Treatise on the Enigma' (hereafter referred to as 'Turing's Treatise') which is said to have been written between 1939–42; the contents of the Treatise suggest it was written in 1940. A copy is filed in the National Archives in Washington, Box 201 of RG 457.

5 Turing's account of how he identified the new indicating system is on pp. 129–42 of Turing's Treatise.

6 PRO HW14/2.

7 PRO ADM199/124.

8 Churchill's opinion that troops should be evacuated from the south of Norway is recorded in Martin Gilbert's biography, *Winston S. Churchill*, vol. VI *Finest Hour*, p. 269 of the Minerva paperback edition, London, 1989 (hereafter referred to as 'Gilbert, *Finest Hour*').

9 This account of the capture of *Polares* is based on: PRO ADM186/805 Second and Last War Cruise (of *Schiff 26*); PRO ADM199/476 War History; an unpublished account by Alec Dennis which is filed in the Imperial War Museum; and the author's 1998 interview with Dennis.

10 PRO ADM199/476.

11 PRO ADM199/476 Report by Lieutenant Commander John Barber. A note by the late Jon Walley, *Griffin*'s doctor, stated that he and another man with the aid of a German dictionary looked at the documents recovered from the bag captured by Foord and came to the conclusion that he had rescued the current German codebooks. The Walley document was shown to me by his son, Jon Walley junior.

12 PRO ADM1/10603.

13 PRO ADM223/297.

14 The unpublished 'The History of Hut Eight, 1939 1945' by Patrick Mahon (hereafter referred to as 'History of Hut Eight'), p. 22, in Box 4685 RG 457 in the National Archives in Washington, and documents filed at the Naval Historical Branch, Ministry of Defence (hereafter referred to as NHB).

15 PRO ADM199/476.

16 The description of how the documents captured from *Polares* were exploited comes from Alexander, *Naval Enigma History* pp. 24–6 and 'History of Hut Eight', p. 22.

17 Ralph Erskine's 'First Naval Enigma Decrypts of World War 2' in *Cryptologia* January 1997 pp. 43 and 45.

18 History of Hut Eight p. 22 says that the first bombe arrived in April 1940. However Hinsley vol. 3(2) p. 954 states that the first bombe was installed on 18 March 1940.

19 Alexander, *Naval Enigma History*, p. 26, reveals that there were only four cryptographers, including Turing, working on Naval Enigma at this stage.

20 In Turing's Treatise p. 139, he says that he had correctly 'inferred' what the indicator system was, except that he had not known about the second trigram looked up by the sender which was known as the Schlüsselkenngruppe. See Appendix 3.

21 Alexander, *Naval Enigma History*, p. 14.

22 'History of Hut Eight' p. 22.

23 'History of Hut Eight' p. 26.

24 PRO HW14/8.

Chapter 8 Keeping the Enigma Secret (pp. 79–92)

1 Hinsley vol. 1 p. 143.

2 Details about Rees's and Herivel's work at the beginning of 1940 were provided by Professor David Rees himself in the course of his 1999 interview by the author.

3 The account of John Herivel's invention of the Herivel Tip is taken from his own account in *Station X* by Michael Smith pp. 42–3, London, 1998, and from Welchman pp. 98-9.

4 Hinsley vol. 1 p. 144.

5 Welchman pp. 52–4. Each network had its own settings. Sometimes historians and cryptographers refer to these networks as keys. I found this practice confusing given that there are keyboard keys, and also given that sometimes the settings themselves are referred to as keys.

6 Hinsley vol. 1 p. 109.

7 Hinsley vol. 1 pp. 137–140 and 143–5.

8 The account of what happened on *Seal* comes from *Will Not We Fear* by C. E. T. Warren and James Benson, London, 1961.

9 *ibid.* p. 162.

10 The reference to the chart being found is in Rainer Esterer's account of the capture of the crew from the *U-13*. Rainer Esterer was an officer on the *U-13* when it was captured. The undated account is filed at the U-boat Archiv in Cuxhaven-Altenbruch in Germany, hereafter referred to as the 'U-Boot Archiv'.

11 This account of the last cruise and sinking of *U-13* comes from the following sources: PRO ADM186/805 and ADM199/2057; the author's 1999 interviews with Max Schulte, commander of the *U-13*; Charles Emerson who at the time was a sub-lieutenant on *Weston*; and a series of reports and diaries collected together and filed at the U-Boot Archiv, including a report by Max Schulte, by Hans Grandjean the engineer, Rainer Esterer, an officer, and by Sub-Lieutenant Richard Richardson. I am indebted to Donald Tuke, son of Seymour Tuke, commander of the *Weston* at the time, who furnished me with an English translation of these German reports.

12 There is a divergence of opinions over where the U-boat was encountered. The official British reports of the sinking of the *U-13* say that it happened about fourteen miles south-east of Lowestoft, but there is some doubt about their accuracy. For example, they also say that *Weston* was ahead of a convoy, whereas Charles Emerson, who at the time was a sub-lieutenant on *Weston*, remembers that it was ten miles behind the convoy. A report also exists which says that the *U-13* surfaced for the last time near Orfordness. It refers

to a strong current which might have altered the position of the ships during the hunt for the U-boat.

13 Documents at the Naval Historical Branch at the Ministry of Defence in London hereafter referred to as 'NHB, MOD' support the conclusion that no useful Enigma material was recovered, but there is no positive statement in these documents that this was the case. For example, the author was unable to find a report stating what happened during the salvage operation. There is always the chance that one day a more specific document will turn up giving the precise findings of the team which carried out the salvage operation on *U-13*.

14 The investigation into whether Enigma was compromised by the sinking of the *U-13* was brought to my attention by Ralph Erskine, a historian who specialises in Naval Enigma. The investigation can be found in the entry for 11 June 1940 in 2 SKL KTB, which is the War Diary for the Seekriegsleitung (Naval War Staff). This is on Microfilm 319 at the Ministry of Defence hereafter referred to as the 'MOD'.

15 The investigation following the sinking of the *U-33* is in a report which appears to have been written between 15 March 1940 and 30 June 1940. It is to be found in 2 SKL/KTB, which is on Microfilm 319 at the MOD. This investigation was again brought to my attention by Ralph Erskine.

16 The 3 May and 8 May reports about the disappearance of the two trawlers off Norway are to be found in 2 SKL/KTB, which are on Microfilm 319 at the MOD. Ralph Erskine brought this investigation to my attention.

17 Report in 2 SKL KTB for 21 May 1940, which is on Microfilm 319 at the MOD. This report was brought to my attention by Ralph Erskine.

18 The date is taken from Zygalski's Diary which was transcribed in 1974 correspondence with Rejewski. The correspondence actually states there was a withdrawal 'from' Paris. It must have meant 'to' Paris.

19 Bertrand, pp. 88–9 states that Enigma was being read by 20 May 1940, which contradicts the date mentioned by Hinsley. (See note 4 above.) The 1 October 1939–24 June 1940 Langer Memoirs appear to suggest that the failure to read Enigma due to the change in the indicator procedure only applied to messages transmitted between 14 May and 20 May 1940. However Langer's note is ambiguous. Perhaps he meant to say that the Poles in France were only affected on the above mentioned dates. It is possible that before that date they were concentrating on messages relating to Norway where the Enigma procedure was not altered in May 1940.

20 Rejewski *Memoirs*.

21 Rejewski *Memoirs*.

22 Gilbert, *Finest Hour* pp. 456–8.

23 Kozaczuk, *Enigma* p. 109.

24 Paillole pp. 191–2.

25 PRO HW14/6.

26 *ibid.*

27 *ibid.*

Chapter 9 Deadlock (pp. 93–102)

1 Blair vol. 1 p. 144.
2 Figures taken from Roskill vol. 1 p. 616.
3 The fluctuating estimates of U-boat numbers comes from *Very Special Admiral: the Life of J. H. Godfrey* by Patrick Beesly, London, 1980.
4 The anecdotes and information about Alan Turing in this chapter come from the author's 1998 interviews with the following codebreakers who worked with him at Bletchley Park: Jack Good, Peter Hilton, Donald Michie, Peter Twinn and Shaun Wylie and from the author's 1999 interview with Gershon Ellenbogen, a contemporary of Turing's at Cambridge University. Some of the anecdotes are also referred to in Andrew Hodges' biography, *Alan Turing, the Enigma*, London, 1992 (first published, London, 1983). The 1992 paperback version is hereafter referred to as 'Hodges'.
5 PRO HW14/1.
6 Hodges p. 114.
7 History of Hut Eight p. 14.
8 *ibid.* p. 14.
9 *ibid.* p. 23.
10 *ibid.* p. 23.
11 *ibid.* p. 28.
12 *ibid.* p. 29.
13 *ibid.* p. 29.
14 *ibid.* p. 23.
15 PRO HW14/8.
16 History of Hut Eight p. 25.
17 CAFO 1544 – German Cyphering Machines, dated 29 August 1940.
18 PRO HW17/7 31 October 1940.
19 Memo quoted in a report by C. Morgan (hereafter referred to as 'Morgan') in PRO ADM223/463. It should be mentioned that the same memo is quoted in the History of Hut Eight p. 25. There it is said that Birch sent an identical letter to Godfrey. It is possible that both men sent in the same suggestion, perhaps after discussing it together. I am inclined to believe Morgan's account, which mentions that the memo was signed 'F 12/9/40'.
20 *ibid.*
21 History of Hut Eight p. 22 states that Turing wrongly thought that new bigram tables had been introduced on 1 June 1940; page 26 states that it was only in November 1940 that a message, sent by the Germans on 26 June 1940, was decrypted, revealing that new bigram tables were introduced on 1 July 1940.
22 Morgan, PRO ADM223/463.

Chapter 10 The Italian Affair (pp. 103–116)

1 Penelope Fitzgerald, *The Knox Brothers*, pp. 144–5, London, 1977.
2 The anecdotes about Dilly Knox come from the author's 1998–9 interviews with codebreaker Mavis Batey (née Lever); Josh Cooper's 'Reminiscences' in PRO HW3/83; his son Oliver Knox; and *The Knox Brothers*.
3 This story was told by Professor E. R. Vincent to Stephen Roskill and is recorded in Roskill's papers at Churchill College, Cambridge.

4 There is some dispute as to the exact date when the Italian Naval Enigma was first broken. Hinsley vol. 1 p. 210 says it was in September 1940 without citing any document in support of this date. Mavis Lever agrees that this date is probably accurate, and her husband Keith Batey told the author during the year 2000 that he worked for Dilly Knox for a week during August 1940, and it had not been broken by then. However in the PRO HW14/11, there is a wartime summary of what Italian codes were broken, which states that the Italian Naval Enigma was broken in July 1940.

5 Hinsley vol. 1 p. 210.

6 Alberto Santoni's *Il Vero Traditore* pp. 308–9, Milan, 1981, (hereafter referred to as 'Santoni').

7 Hinsley vol. 1 p. 404 lists these early signals suggesting that something was afoot.

8 PRO ADM223/76 X PO9755.

9 *ibid.*

10 Archivo Ufficio Storico Marina in Rome (hereafter referred to as 'AUSM'), file 28bis, message number 53148; also Santoni pp. 306–7.

11 AUSM file 27 message number 51106; also Santoni p. 74.

12 On p. 73 of the paperback version of Santoni, the most authoritative history of how Enigma and Ultra affected Italy, it is stated that all orders were sent to Iachino by radio. On the other hand on p. 18 of the transcript of the Supreme Court judgement in the Montgomery Hyde–Lais libel case referred to at the end of this chapter, reference is made to a previous enquiry which suggested that the British could not intercept the order because it was not sent by radio. Further research carried out by Alberto Santoni has subsequently revealed that his earlier account in *Il Vero Traditore* was incorrect. The 23 March message was sent by 'telcarmonica' (teleprinter), as Alberto Santoni confirmed in a letter to the author in 1999. On p. 218 of his book *Storia E Politica Navale Dell'eta Contemporanea* (Contemporary Naval History and Policy), Rome, 1993, he corrected his previous error. The existence of the 23 March 1941 signal and its amendments were first pointed out to me by Giulio DiVita, who was commissioned by Italy's Naval Historical Branch to investigate how Bletchley Park's deciphering of Italy's messages had contributed to the Italian defeat during the battle of Matapan.

13 PRO ADM223/88.

14 PRO ADM199/781.

15 PRO ADM223/88.

16 *ibid.*

17 The sources for what happened in Cunningham's presence from mid-morning on 27 March 1941 until the end of the Battle of Matapan are: PRO 199/781, Lieutenant Hugh Lee, as he then was, who was Cunningham's flag lieutenant on *Warspite* at the time, and John Winton's biography *Cunningham: the greatest admiral since Nelson*, London, 1998.

18 PRO ADM223/88.

19 According to PRO ADM233/88, the Italian Fleet was sighted at 12.20 on 27 March, and the message from Cunningham to Pridham-Wippell was sent at 12.19, one minute earlier.

20 This anecdote is in a letter which Edward Clarke, who later became His

Honour Judge Edward Clarke, wrote to Giulio DiVita, on 19 February 1980. The letter stated that victory was due to Dilly Knox and his 'guts'. He must have meant his 'girls'.

21 PRO HW14/7.

22 PRO HW14/22.

23 *ibid.*

24 PRO HW14/24. The surviving copy of the note does not reveal to whom it is addressed.

25 *The Quiet Canadian: the secret service story of Sir William Stephenson* by H. Montgomery Hyde, London, 1962.

26 I am indebted to Giulio DiVita who made the court judgements for the Montgomery Hyde-Lais libel case available to me.

Chapter 11 The End of the Beginning (pp. 117–122)

1 The account of what happened during Operation Claymore comes from Commander John Freeman who, when he was Sub-Lieutenant Freeman, took part in the Operation aboard *Somali*; the official report of the operation in PRO DEFE2/142; and David Kahn pp. 127–36.

2 Ralph Erskine's article 'Naval Enigma: A Missing Link' in the *International Journal of Intelligence and Counter Intelligence* 1989 vol. 3 No. 4 p. 498 (hereafter referred to as 'Ralph Erskine, Missing Link').

3 History of Hut Eight p. 26.

4 Ralph Erskine, Missing Link p. 498.

5 History of Hut Eight p. 26.

6 *ibid.*

7 Ralph Erskine, Missing Link p. 497, contradicting Hinsley's vol. 1 p. 337 which had said that all of the April 1941 Naval Enigma messages were read by 10 May 1941.

8 PRO DEFE2/142.

9 Kriegstagebuch des Befehlshabers der Unterseeboote (hereafter referred to as 'KTB/BDU') 21/1/1941.

10 KTB/BDU 18/4/1941 which is to be found in PG30287 at the MOD.

11 The account of the German realisation that there had been leaks from the Cipher Office and the Research Office, their search for Lemoine, and Paillole's decision to ask Lemoine to go underground, all come from Paillole pp. 204–16.

Chapter 12 Breakthrough (pp. 123–131)

1 The personal information on how Hinsley's fortunes changed, on his dealings with the OIC, including the warning he gave prior to the sinking of HMS *Glorious*, and on how he came to propose that the weathership *München* should be captured, came from the Steinberg Hinsley interview, and the author's interview with Harry Hinsley in 1997. Edward Thomas mentioned Hinsley's nickname on p. 43 of *Codebreakers*.

2 Hinsley vol. 1 p. 123.

3 Hinsley vol. 1 pp. 141–2 tells the story of how he tried to warn the OIC about the movement of German ships which culminated in the sinking of *Glorious*.

4 Hinsley vol. 1 p. 142.

5 A post-war report by R. T. Barrett for the Naval Intelligence Division stated that by the spring of 1940, the Germans could read between 30 and 50 per cent of Britain's traffic in the naval cypher, and had free run of everything of importance in connection with the Norway expedition. See PRO ADM223/297.

6 National Archives Record Group 457 Item no. 1862 Box no. 743 'The German Navy's Use of Special Intelligence', a post-war study of the use the German Navy made of the British messages which the Germans decoded and read. It is hereafter referred to as 'The German Navy's Use of Special Intelligence'.

7 It is not absolutely clear whether the German cruisers were attempting to attack the British aircraft carriers thanks to the intercepted British messages, or whether they came across the carriers in the course of trying to find and attack British convoys.

8 The German Navy's Use of Special Intelligence.

9 The German Navy's Use of Special Intelligence mentions the time of the broadcast, and Hinsley vol. 1 p. 143 mentions that the Home Fleet only found out about the sinking from a German broadcast.

10 PRO HW14/7. Letter dated 21 October 1940.

11 PRO HW14/7. Letter dated 23 October 1940.

12 Roskill vol. 1 p. 616.

13 Blair vol. 1 p. 245.

14 Blair vol. 1 p. 266.

15 The account of the capture of *München* is taken from Vice-Admiral Holland's report in PRO ADM199/447; interviews with John Freeman, Eric Tubman, Samuel Gregory, Jack Willis and Nick Carter who were all on *Somali* at the time of the capture; Colin Kitching who was a member of the HMS *Edinburgh* boarding party; and David Kahn pp. 153–60.

16 PRO ADM223/88.

17 According to the NHB, MOD the papers were handed in to Peter Twinn on 10 May 1941.

18 PRO ADM199/447.

Chapter 13 Operation Primrose (pp. 132–146)

1 The sources for the account of Operation Primrose come from the following: David Balme's 11 May 1941 report about boarding *U-110* PRO ADM237/33; Joe Baker-Cresswell's 13 May 1941 report of proceedings of the 3rd escort group with convoy O.B.318 and his 10 May 1941 report about the capture of *U-110* PRO ADM1/11133; report about *U-110* in PRO ADM199/2058 and PRO ADM186/806; author's 1998–9 interviews with the following men who were on *U-110* when it sank: Herbert Langsch, Helmut Ecke, Heinz Vocke, Heinz Brandl, Heinz Wilde, Georg Högel; author's 1998–9 interviews with David Balme who led *Bulldog*'s boarding party; reports by: Allon Bacon, given to the author by his family, by Joe Baker-Cresswell and G. E. Dodds, the engineer on *Bulldog*, which are to be found at Churchill College, Cambridge, and by V. Funge Smith, *Aubretia*'s commander, in the Imperial War Museum, along with signals sent to his ship; Stephen Roskill's *The Secret Capture*, London 1959, hereafter referred to as 'Roskill, *Secret Capture*'; David Kahn pp. 1–14 and 161–9; Blair vol. 1 pp. 278–85; a series of articles about the life of Joe Baker-Cresswell which was published in the *Northumbria Weekender*, supplied to the author by Margaret Aitken, wife of John Aitken, first lieutenant on *Bulldog* when the *U-110* was captured.

2 Blair vol. 1 p. 213.

3 No one has ever established for certain what happened to Lemp. There was speculation about whether he was shot by the boarding party to stop him revealing the Enigma secret. But these allegations were withdrawn after David Balme, who led the boarding party, said that he never saw Lemp, let alone shot him. So we can only speculate on what happened to him. Perhaps he was shot from one of the destroyers, or perhaps he committed suicide when he realised that the U-boat was not sinking. Perhaps he simply drowned.

4 Ralph Erskine's article 'The Breaking of Heimisch and Triton' in *Intelligence and National Security* 3(1) 1988 p. 165 specifies when Naval Enigma messages were sent to the Admiralty between 10–24 May 1941. His article 'Naval Enigma: A Missing Link' in *International Journal of Intelligence and Counter Intelligence* vol.3(4) 1989 p. 497 specifies the time when the first decrypt was sent to the Admiralty on 13 May 1941. As he says in that article, there is no evidence in the public domain which suggests that the bigram tables recovered from *U-110* helped the codebreakers to break the Enigma messages sent to the Admiralty on 13 and 14 May 1941. The fact that messages began to be decrypted just minutes after Bacon's arrival at Bletchley Park might suggest that the bigram tables which he brought with him did break the deadlock. However, it has to be said that according to the History of Hut Eight, the codebreakers had already reconstructed most of the bigram tables even before *U-110*'s capture. So it is possible that the timing of the decrypts being sent represented a coincidence.

5 G. E. Dodds, who reported what the King said when he wrote to Roskill on 19 April 1958, did not mention the exact words, which were quoted on p. 154 of Roskill, *Secret Capture*, and which have been copied from that book by other writers. According to Dodds: 'I was told by the late King George VI that the value of this operation to the country and naval services was the most important single event that had ever taken place and that its value to the war effort and country limitless.'

6 Balme could not have been awarded the Victoria Cross for going down the conning tower into *U-110*. This was not because he did not show the required amount of heroism, but because, unknown to him, as he began his descent into *U-110*, all the enemy had abandoned the U-boat. The Victoria Cross can only be given to people who are heroic in the face of the enemy.

7 David Kahn p. 169.

8 NHB MOD holds documents which specify what was captured from *U-110*.

9 History of Hut Eight p. 26 summarises the position regarding the bigram tables at the end of March 1941. P. 27 states that the new bigram tables, which came into operation on 15 June 1941, were reconstructed by the end of July 1941, i.e. it took about six weeks to reconstruct them at this stage in the war. The television documentary referred to was *Station X*, which was shown on Channel 4.

10 Also captured on *U-110* were: the document which explained how Enigma settings were adjusted, if it was thought the Enigma cipher had been compromised, by the transmission to the U-boat of a message containing a cue-word; the Kenngruppenbuch, from which the trigrams were chosen in order to create the indicator, and in order to work out the message setting for particular Naval Enigma messages (see chapter 7); and a chart which indicated the position of minefields along the coast of France.

11 The story about Loewe's reports back to Germany relating to the capture and sinking of *U-110* comes from his own account, filed in PG 30106. It is on microfilm reel number 1081 at the Ministry of Defence in London. The inference that British intelligence officers were masterminding his meetings with survivors from *U-110* is arrived at by applying common sense to what is stated in Loewe's account, and the knowledge that the POW code used by the Germans was broken by the British.

Chapter 14 The Knock-Out Blow (pp. 147–155)

1 The account of how Turing told Hinsley he needed another capture and the subsequent capture of *Lauenburg* is based on the author's 1997–2000 interviews with Hinsley, and with the following men who were on HMS *Tartar* when the *Lauenburg* was captured: Sir Ludovic Kennedy, Hugh Wilson and Tom Kelly; the author's 1998–9 interviews with Georg Klarman, one of the *Lauenburg* crew; the 1 July 1941 report about Operation EC by Admiral Burrough, a copy of which was given to the author by his daughter Pauline Lee; David Kahn pp. 170–182.

2 Hinsley vol. 2 p. 569.

3 The source for this is the author's 1997 interview with Hinsley.

4 Hinsley's *The Influence of Ultra In the Second World War*, a publication produced for the Liddell Hart Centre For Military Archives in 1992.

5 A copy of this document was given to me by Admiral Burrough's daughter, Pauline Lee.

6 *ibid.*

7 *ibid.*

8 *ibid.*

9 NHB, MOD.

10 Document provided by the family of the late Allon Bacon.

11 *ibid.*

12 *ibid.*

13 Alexander, *Naval Enigma History*, p. 31.

14 The time to break Enigma in August 1941 was around fifty hours according to Hinsley vol. 2 p. 173.

15 Alexander, *Naval Enigma History*, pp. 32 and 68.

16 *ibid.* p. 12. The label on the German Enigma wheels was usually inscribed in roman numerals. I have not used roman numerals however in my text since some readers find it hard to understand them.

17 This account describing how Noskwith discovered the crib which broke the Offizier system is based on the author's interview with Rolf Noskwith earlier this year, on Noskwith's account on p. 120 of *Codebreakers*, and on Alexander, *Naval Enigma History*, p. 34.

18 Alexander, *Naval Enigma History* p. 33.

Chapter 15 Suspicion (pp. 156–167)

1 Hinsley vol. 1 p. 344.

2 Hinsley vol. 2 p. 337.

3 Hinsley vol. 1 p. 341.

4 The source for this is Hinsley vol. 1 p. 345. A slightly different account is given in Beesly, *Very Special Intelligence*, London 1977, p. 84 where he refers to a high-ranking Air Force officer whose son was on *Bismarck*, and on p. 203 of Ronald Lewin's *Ultra Goes To War*, London 1978, there is only reference to a 'senior personality' whose nephew was on board.

5 This analysis is based on Hinsley vol. 1 pp. 344–5. The Batey story comes from the author's 1999–2000 interviews with Keith Batey. Keith Batey has pointed out to the author that even if Tovey had decided that *Bismark* was heading for France before Bletchley Park broke the Air Force Enigma message specifying the German battleship's destination the latter Enigma message must have been a comfort for Tovey and may have prevented him from changing his mind since it confirmed he had made the correct decision.

There is also some evidence to back up the fact that the Air Force Enigma message did play its part after all. According to Jean Howard, who worked at Bletchley Park, the First Sea Lord, Sir Dudley Pound, visited Hut 3 after the sinking of the *Bismarck* to congratulate the Enigma intelligence analysts. This suggests that either Tovey may have come to his decision after receiving the contents of the Air Force Enigma message, notwithstanding the evidence to the contrary, or that there may have been more information in the Air Force Enigma message decoded than in the message sent out to Tovey at 18.12 on 25 May; only the latter message – which merely stated that *Bismarck* was heading for the west coast of France – is to be found in the PRO, in file ADM 223/78. This point can only be cleared up if the decrypt of the Air Force Enigma message is declassified or discovered. Hunsley vol. 1 p. 345 states that the aircraft which found *Bismarck* on 26 May had been briefed in the light of the Air Force Enigma message; if the message had, for example, given *Bismark*'s position and if it had specified that the German battleship was heading for Brest, this would have narrowed down considerably the area where the aircraft had to look, and would have enabled the aircraft to find *Bismarck* more quickly than would otherwise have been the case.

6 Hinsley vol. 1 p. 344 mentions the identification of the change in *Bismarck*'s base, and more details are given in the Steinberg Hinsley interview. Unfortunately, no document has yet revealed the exact time when Hinsley rang up Denning to give him this information. The records also do not prove whether the information was decisive when it came to finding *Bismarck*. Pp. 80 and 84 of Beesly suggests that the direction-finding information was sufficient to enable the OIC to decide that *Bismarck* was going to Brest. On the other hand, Beesly suggests that the OIC relied on other information, including Hinsley's. The truth is likely to be that all the information available helped the OIC to reach its conclusion.

7 PRO ADM 223/88 and Hinsley vol. 1 p. 345.

8 The Abwehr investigation and its report dated 31 October 1941 were brought to my attention by Timothy Mulligan, a historian who works for the National Archives in Washington.

9 Martin Gilbert, *Finest Hour* p. 849 mentions how in October 1940 Churchill asked for the list of people who saw Enigma decrypts to be cut back.

10 This document, a copy of which is filed in the Imperial War Museum, is mentioned on p. 296 of *The Lost Battle: Crete 1941* by Callum MacDonald, London, 1995. It was given to me by the historian Ralph Bennett. It was brought to my attention by John Gallehawk, an archivist at the Bletchley Park Trust Museum. A copy of the original English telegram and its German translation were amongst a batch of German documents filed under the heading 'Kreta: Dokumente des Britischen Generalstabs' which were captured at the end of the war.

11 Churchill anecdote provided by Pauline Elliott, who worked in Hut 8, in the 1998–9 interviews she gave to the author.

12 The words were remembered by Baroness Jean Trumpington who as Jean Campbell Harris worked at Bletchley Park as a typist.

13 The writers of the letter included Gordon Welchman, and Stuart Milner-Barry, as well as Turing and Alexander. It is laid out in full in Hinsley vol. 2 pp. 655–7.

14 Martin Gilbert, *Finest Hour* p. 1186.

15 Hinsley vol. 2 p. 171 and 173.

16 There were eighty operational U-boats in October 1941, compared with forty nine at the beginning of the war, according to Roskill vol. 1 p. 614. There were also 118 U-boats training and in trials in October 1941 compared with just eight in September 1939. Shipping sunk figures are also from Roskill vol. 1 p. 616.

17 Hinsley vol. 2 p. 174 specifies the time to break Naval Enigma in October 1941. It took forty-eight hours during the first day in each pair of days, and just a few hours for messages intercepted during the second day in the pair. The reason was that during the second day, only the plugboard connection settings were changed, whereas during the first day, all the settings were changed.

18 The figures giving the percentage of North Atlantic convoys spotted and successfully attacked by wolf packs came from '"The Most Thankless Task" Revisited: Convoys, Escorts, and Radio Intelligence In the Western Atlantic, 1941–3' by W. A. B. Douglas and Jürgen Rohwer (hereafter referred to as 'Douglas and Rohwer "Thankless Task"') in *The Royal Canadian Navy In Retrospect 1910–68* edited by James Boutilier, Canada 1982.

19 Hinsley vol. 2 pp. 681–2.

20 Hinsley vol. 2 p. 174.

21 BDU KTB 27 August 1941.

22 This account of the capture of the *U-570* is taken from the following sources: PRO ADM186/806; PRO ADM199/2058; interview with Bill

Arnold, who was on *Burwell* at the time of the capture; Blair vol. 1 pp. 339–48.

23 Documents at the NHB, MOD suggest that matching plain-language German and cipher text was recovered from the *U-570* for 21, 26 and 27 August 1941. There is also a reference to 'settings' having been recovered. It is not clear what settings these were.

24 BDU KTB 11 November 1941.

25 Both the 18 and 20 October 1941 reports are on Microfilm Reel 40 at the MOD.

26 If under the Stichwort procedure 4 was to be added to 7, the German telegraphists did not simply add 4 to 7 which equals 11. Instead they jumped back to the number '1' when their addition led to a number greater than '8', (8 being the number of wheels distributed to Naval Enigma operators, and then the telegraphists carried on adding on to 1. Thus 4 added on to 7 equals 3.

27 Alexander, *Naval Enigma History*, p. 6.

28 NHB, MOD information states that the 'Teich' bigram tables were discovered by the British on *Gedania*.

Chapter 16 A Two-Edged Sword (pp. 168–177)

1 Information from Leading Wren Mary Carlisle who is quoted on p. 204 of *Convoy: the Battle for Convoys SC122 and HX229* by Martin Middlebrook, London, 1976 (hereafter referred to as 'Middlebrook').

2 Douglas and Rohwer "Thankless Task" is the basis for this description of what happened to SC42. All decrypts cited are from PRO DEFE 3/27. The official report describing what happened to the convoy is in PRO ADM199/1991.

3 Blair vol. 1 p. 364.

4 This account of what happened to convoy SC42, and the boarding and sinking of *U-501* is taken from the following sources: PRO ADM199/1129 Statement of Lieutenant Freddie Grubbe, the commander of the *Moose Jaw*, on 18 September 1941; PRO ADM199/1129 Statement of Commander Douglas Prentice on 14 September 1941 and statement of Lieutenant Ted Simmons about boarding the U-boat; PRO ADM199/2058 and ADM186/806 reports about the sinking of U-501; Blair vol. 1 pp. 362–3; Commander Tony German, *The Sea Is At Our Gates: the History of the Canadian Navy*, Toronto 1991 pp. 90 and 100–8; Douglas and Rohwer, "Thankless Task"; author's 1998 interviews with Fritz Weinrich and Adolf Natzheim who were on *U-501* when it was boarded and sunk, and interview with Eugene Tobin who was a member of the boarding party; a letter from Douglas Prentice, dated 15 January 1947, sent to the author by the Canadian Ministry of Defence Historical Department. The times mentioned are Greenwich Mean Time.

5 This account of the Tarrafal Bay encounter is taken from the following sources: PRO ADM186/806; *Clyde's* service history supplied by Margaret Bidmead, from the Royal Navy Submarine Museum at Gosport, Hampshire; author's 1998–9 interviews with George Gay, Hedley Kett and Ernie Turner who were all on *Clyde* during the encounter; Wilhelm Blott, Wilhelm

Feldges, Günter Wulff, and Kurt Schönthier who were on *U-111* during the encounter; Kurt Schönthier also allowed the author to see his account of *U-111's* last patrol which included an account of this incident; Gottlieb Baumann, Heinrich Lüdmann who were on *U-68* during the encounter; Karl-Heinz Wiebe, Hans Burck, Heinrich Hossmann, and Martin Beisheim who were on *U-67* during the encounter; Blair vol. 1 pp. 383–5.

6 Maertens' letter dated 24 October 1941, and his 20 October 1941 report, where he analysed the Tarrafal Bay incident, are to be found on Microfilm Reel 40 at the MOD. Ralph Erskine told the author where the documents are filed, and Timothy Mulligan, an employee of the National Archives in Washington, alerted him to the existence of the reports in his article 'The German Navy Evaluates Its Cryptographic Security, October 1941' which is to be found in *Military Affairs* 49, April 1985 pp. 75–9.

Chapter 17 Living Dangerously (pp. 178–187)

1 Hinsley vol. 2 p. 166 refers to a message from the Admiralty telling the Navy where *Atlantis* was supposed to meet up with the U-boat. This account of the sinking of *Atlantis* is based on the following sources: a report of the sinking in a supplement to the 9 July 1948 *London Gazette*; *War in the Southern Oceans 1939–1945* by L. C. F. Turner, H. R. Gordon, and J. E. Betzler, London, 1961. The latter two sources were made available to the author by Sheila, the widow of Michael Craig Waller who was the gunnery officer on HMS *Dorsetshire*.

2 This account of the rendezvous with *Python*, and the sinking of *Python* is based on the following sources: a supplement to the 9 July 1948 *London Gazette*; reports by Karl-Friedrich Merten, the commander of *U-68*, Hans Eckermann, the commander of *U-A*, G. Lüders, the commander of *Python*, and by J. G. Braync and L. R. R. Foster, who were both on *Dorsetshire* when *Python* was sunk; *War in the Southern Oceans 1939–1945*; *Atlantis – The Story of a German Surface Raider* by Ulrich Mohr, London, 1955; *Footprints in the Sea* by Captain Augustus Agar, London, 1961; Log of *U-A*. All of these sources were made available to the author by Sheila, the widow of Michael Craig Waller.

3 Details about what British messages could be read are from The German Navy's Use of Special Intelligence.

4 The Bonatz report is filed on Microfilm Reel 320 at the MOD.

5 The report by Fricke is to be found at the Bundesarchiv Militärarchiv in Freiburg under Ref no. RM 7/121.

6 Hinsley vol. 2 pp. 201–2.

7 Account of *Scharnhorst* and *Gneisenau* break out taken from Hinsley vol. 2 pp. 179–88; Correlli Barnett's *Engage the Enemy More Closely*, pp. 445–55 London, 1991; and Beesly pp. 117–23.

8 British Summer Time, one hour ahead of Greenwich Mean Time.

9 *The Times'* verdict on the German battle-cruisers' dash up the English Channel was quoted on p. 123 of Patrick Beesly's *Very Special Intelligence*, London, 1977, (hereafter referred to as 'Beesly'). As was the story about not revealing that the two battle-cruisers had been damaged by mines in order

not to reveal that Enigma messages had been read. This latter story was also mentioned in Hinsley vol. 2 p. 187.

10 PRO HW14/27 Letter to Travis is dated 26 January 1942.

11 PRO HW14/31 11 March 1942.

12 Hinsley vol. 2 p. 321.

13 Hinsley vol. 2 pp. 294–5 states that Army Enigma 'keys' used in north Africa were broken regularly for the first time from 17 September–19 October 1941, and then again from 2 November–6 December 1941. GC&CS referred to the three 'keys' in question as 'Chaffinch'. They were often broken a week or more after the messages in question were sent. The Army 'key' used on the Russian front had first been broken in June 1941. It was referred to as 'Vulture'.

14 PRO HW14/14.

15 PRO HW14/24.

Chapter 18 The Hunt for the Bigram Tables (pp. 188–201)

1 The June 1941 date is mentioned in Christopher Morris's chapter, 'Navy Ultra's Poor Relations' on p. 238 of *Codebreakers*. Documents at NHB, MOD confirm that RHV offizier documents were captured on *U-110*.

2 The date when Werftschlüssel was broken is mentioned in Christopher Morris's chapter, 'Navy Ultra's Poor Relations' on p. 233 of *Codebreakers*. The problems caused by the creation of a new net for the U-boats is referred to in History of Hut Eight p. 48.

3 PRO HW1/118 and 122.

4 History of Hut Eight, pp. 45–6.

5 The account of how the codebreakers identified which bigram table was being used is based on the author's 1998–9 interviews with Jack Good, and a letter to Good from Joan Clarke dated 26 September 1993.

6 History of Hut Eight p. 48.

7 Alexander, *Naval Enigma History*, p. 13.

8 The History of Hut Eight p. 20.

9 Alexander, *Naval Enigma History*, p. 35.

10 *ibid.*, p. 34 lists the number of cryptographers in Hut 8.

11 Document provided by the late Allon Bacon's family.

12 This account of what happened on *Onslow* during Operation Archery comes from the following sources: Rear-Admiral H. M. Burrough's report dated 2 January 1942, given to the author by his daughter, Pauline Lee; report by Captain Armstrong, given to the author by the family of Allon Bacon; as was Allon Bacon's own report stating what he recovered in the course of Operation Archery; G. G. Connell, *Arctic Destroyers: The 17th Flotilla*, London, 1982; Donald Grant, *A Working Holiday*, Gisborne, New Zealand, 1992; author's 1998–99 interviews with B. S. Pemberton, who was on *Onslow* during Operation Archery.

13 This anecdote has been improved in the telling since it was first mentioned to Rear-Admiral Burrough in a note from Brigadier Charles Haydon dated 6 January 1942. The note was given to me by Pauline Lee, Admiral Burrough's daughter. In the note Haydon said that the story came from the intelligence officer who landed on Måloy Island to interview prisoners during

Operation Archery. The original note did not include the extra twist which was subsequently added to the story. This filled in the reason why the batman did not disturb his master: he was said to have woken his master unnecessarily the previous morning and received such a telling off that he decided not to risk doing it again. While this may be true, I have not included it in the main narrative, since it is not backed up by the original note from Haydon.

14 G. G. Connell in *Arctic Destroyers* says that Bacon was on *Offa*. This is contradicted by Bacon's own report which quite clearly says that he was on *Onslow*, and that he recovered Enigma documents from *Föhn*.

15 Allon Bacon's report describing what he found on *Föhn* mentions an Enigma settings list as well as the bigram tables. NHB, MOD confirms that two sets of bigram tables were captured at the end of December 1941, and suggest one set, referred to as 'Strom', was from *Donner*. The NHB documents do not specify where the other set, referred to as 'Ufer', came from. The NHB documents also confirm that some Enigma settings were captured at the end of December 1941, without clearly identifying where they were captured.

16 The account of the capture of documents from *Donner* comes from the following sources: report by Admiral Sir William O'Brien; author's 1998–9 interviews with Admiral O'Brien, Danny Daniels, and Dr G. M. Forsyth who were on *Offa* during Operation Archery.

17 The source for this is NHB, MOD. The bigram tables captured from *Donner* were labelled 'Strom'.

18 The officer was William O'Brien and the sailmaker was Able Seaman Tucker.

19 This account of how *Ashanti* captured Enigma codebooks from *Geier* comes from the following sources: author's 1998–9 interviews with Reg Swann who was on *Ashanti* during Operation Anklet; report by E. A. S. Bailey who was a lieutenant on *Ashanti* during Operation Anklet, made available to the author by his son, Mark Bailey.

20 Documents in the NHB, MOD specify what documents were captured from *Geier*. The bigram tables captured from *Geier* were named 'Ufer' and 'Strom'.

Chapter 19 Black Out (pp. 202–218)

1 Hinsley vol. 2 pp. 663–4.
2 Ludovic Kennedy, *Menace: the Life and Death of the Tirpitz*, London, 1979 p. 40.
3 Hinsley vol. 2 p. 209.
4 Hinsley vol. 2 p. 201 says that the average delay was thirty-two hours by January 1942, although, as is demonstrated in this chapter, the settings might take up to fifty hours to break on the first day in each pair of days, and on the second day, a much shorter period might be taken.
5 History of Hut Eight p. 56.
6 *ibid.*
7 Richard Woodman, *Arctic Convoys*, London, 1994, (hereafter referred to as 'Arctic Convoys').

8 Hinsley vol. 2 p. 213.

9 *ibid.*

10 Ned Denning stated that the British did not know during the PQ17 affair that the Swedes were tapping German land lines to the Naval Commands in Norway. This statement appears in Denning's account of the PQ17 disaster in the National Maritime Museum under Reference MS/84/192 File 38, made available courtesy of the museum's trustees (hereafter referred to as 'Denning on PQ17').

11 Tovey's account is to be found in the Churchill Archives Centre, Churchill College, Cambridge.

12 The main sources used to describe what happened to convoy PQ17 are: Denning on PQ17; *Arctic Convoys* pp. 189–257; Hinsley vol. 2 pp. 214–23; Beesly pp. 128–41; and David Irving, *The Destruction of Convoy PQ17*, London, 1968 (hereafter referred to as Irving). All page references in Irving are to the 1980 edition.

13 The German aircraft's first sighting of PQ17 is mentioned in Hinsley Vol. 2 page 215.

14 Denning on PQ17.

15 A. Hutchinson remembered the term. His correspondence is in Churchill Archives Centre, Churchill College, Cambridge.

16 Beesly p. 135.

17 Denning on PQ17.

18 'History of Hut Eight' p. 56 says that this so-called 'flap' procedure was adopted during the *Tirpitz* flaps and the PQ convoy flaps.

19 Alexander, *Naval Enigma History*, p. 12.

20 The reference in this signal to Vågsfjord did not make sense. Denning thought that the sender had probably intended to refer to Langfjord which was another fjord branching westward nearer the mouth of Altenfjord. Where in this chapter it is stated that a message was 'originated', or sent to the Operational Intelligence Centre, or British Fleet at a particular time, the time specified is according to Double Summer Time (i.e. Greenwich Mean Time plus two hours).

21 PRO DEFE3/110 p. 896.

22 PRO DEFE3/110 p. 894.

23 Denning on PQ17.

24 Roskill vol. 2 p. 138.

25 PRO DEFE3/110 p. 919.

26 PRO DEFE3/110 p. 945.

27 Irving pp. 121–7. It is the same as Denning's account told in this chapter, except that some of the events are said to have happened at different times. Irving says that Dudley Pound's meeting with Denning, at which Denning said he could not be absolutely sure that *Tirpitz* was at Alta, took place at 8.30 p.m., whereas Denning says it was before 7.18 p.m., when a message was sent to Tovey and Hamilton stating that *Tirpitz* had arrived at Altenfjord at 9 a.m. Irving then implies that Pound's message telling Hamilton to withdraw westward, which was sent at 9.11 p.m., was sent before the all-important meeting at which Dudley Pound decided to disperse the convoy. According to Irving, after the 9.36 p.m. signal drafted by Admiral Moore telling the convoy to scatter, Denning received the decrypt of the signal which had been sent by the Admiral Commanding Arctic at 11.30 a.m. stating that there were no naval forces near the convoy. Denning on the other hand says he received this message, which in fact was originated by the 'Admiral Commanding Northern Waters', at about 8.30 p.m., which was approximately when it arrived at the OIC. Denning says he received it just in time to give a copy to Clayton before Clayton attended the meeting convened by Pound at which the decision to scatter the convoy was taken. Denning, says Irving, used this message to confirm his gut feeling that *Tirpitz* was not at sea, and when Clayton arrived back from the meeting at which it was decided the convoy should disperse, Denning suggested that he should go back to Pound again to try to change his mind.

Some of the times mentioned in Irving's account do not square with the times given in official documents now available in the PRO. Irving's assertion that Denning received the 11.30 a.m. signal stating that there were 'no own naval forces' in the area after the 9.36 p.m. 'convoy to scatter' signal appears to be inconsistent with the decrypt of the 11.30 a.m. signal in the PRO which states that it was sent to the Admiralty at 8.31 p.m. Although it is possible that it took over an hour for the signal to be handed to Denning after it had been received by the OIC, it is most unlikely, considering that Denning was anxiously waiting for decrypts to arrive from Bletchley Park, and was in frequent contact with Hinsley on the telephone so that he could be kept up to date with what was happening.

If Denning is correct when he says that he did not send out the message to the Home Fleet mentioning the 11.30 a.m. signal until after Clayton returned from the meeting at which it was decided the convoy should disperse, then Clayton must have returned from the latter meeting shortly before 9.10 p.m., which was the time when Denning's message was finally sent out to the Fleet. It would follow on from this that Irving cannot be right when he asserts that the signal telling Hamilton to leave the convoy and to go westward, which was sent at 9.11 p.m., was sent before the meeting at which Pound decided to order the convoy to disperse. If Denning's account is accurate, the signal to Hamilton must have been sent shortly after Pound had made the decision at the meeting convened by him to order the convoy to be dispersed.

These points of detail are not intended to call into question the substance of Irving's classic and dramatic account. They are only included to explain why I have preferred Denning's account to Irving's in certain respects.

28 PRO DEFE3/110 p. 937.
29 Author's 1997 interview with Hinsley.
30 Correspondence dated 26 April 1967 in Churchill Archives Centre, Churchill College, Cambridge.
31 Account based on Irving pp. 220–9.
32 The account of what happened to Jackie Broome after he was given the scatter signal comes from his book *Convoy Is To Scatter*, London, 1972.
33 Irving pp. 146–8. Decrypt is filed in PRO DEFE3/111.
34 *ibid.* pp. 220–9.
35 Message laid out in Hinsley vol. 2 p. 689.

36 Hinsley vol. 2 p. 221.
37 Irving p. 151.
38 Alexander, *Naval Enigma History*, p. 12.
39 *ibid.*, p. 36.
40 Hinsley vol. 2 p. 749.
41 Alexander, *Naval Enigma History*, p. 11.
42 PRO ADM 223/92.
43 Irving p. 283.
44 Roskill vol. 2 p. 485.
45 Hancock *Statistical Digest* p. 184, London, 1975.
46 Hinsley vol. 2 p. 636.

Chapter 20 Breaking the Deadlock (pp. 219–232)
1 PRO HW 14/8.
2 PRO HW 1/2.
3 PRO HW 14/45, and Robert L. Benson's *A History of U.S. Communications Intelligence during World War II: Policy and Administration*, Series IV, World War II, Vol. 8, Centre for Cryptological History, National Security Agency, 1997.
4 PRO HW 14/45.
5 PRO HW 1/6 24 June 1941 note from Menzies to Churchill.
6 Minutes of Conference, 16 August 1941 Historic Cryptographic Collection, Number 2738.
7 National Archives in Washington RG 457 Box Number 1414 'History of the Bombe Project' dated 30 May 1944 by Joseph Wenger, Howard Engstrom and Ralph Meader, (hereafter referred to as the 'Bombe History'), pp. 2–3.
8 *ibid.* p. 3.
9 *ibid.* p. 3.
10 14 September 1942 memorandum from William Friedman to Colonel Bullock through Colonel Minckler filed in National Archives RG 457 Box 1283.
11 Bombe History p. 4–5.
12 3 September 1942 Memorandum for Op-20 filed in National Archives RG457 Box 1283.
13 An agreement signed on behalf of Britain and the US in relation to Naval Enigma has yet to be declassified. However a letter including terms which were in the agreement are to be found in the 2 October 1942 letter from Captain C. F. Holden to Travis which is quoted in Ralph Erskine's article: *'The Holden Agreement on Naval Sigint: The First BRUSA?'* in Intelligence and National Security Vol. 14 No. 2 1999 p. 187–197. It is not clear whether this is the complete agreement. References in other documents filed in the National Archives suggest that this letter only includes part of the extended agreement entered into by Travis and Harry Hinsley. What is missing in the 2 October letter mentioned above is a statement confirming that Britain should have overall control in relation to the breaking of the Naval Enigma. In Bradley F. Smith's *The Ultra-Magic Deals and the Most Secret Special Relationship 1940–1946*, US and UK, 1993 p. 128 there is a reference to Hinsley's meeting with Wenger in Washington shortly after Travis' return

to the UK. Smith writes that it was agreed that both countries would have the unlimited fight to intercept Shark traffic while Bletchley Park would have overall control when it came to deciding which country was to deal with traffic intercepted. Smith also describes the difficulty in obtaining a similar agreement in relation to Army and Air Force Enigma. Some of the documents he refers to are in National Archives RG 457 Box 1283.

The Anglo-American agreement concerning the Air Force and Army Enigma, often referred to as the 'BRUSA' agreement ('BR' standing for British, and 'USA' for America) was reached on 17 May 1943 and a copy is filed in the Historic Cryptographic Collection NR 2751 at the National Archives. Telford Taylor's 5 April 1943 note is in the Historic Cryptographic Collection NR 4632.

14 Roskill vol. 2 p. 485.

15 Blair vol. 2 p. 23.

16 This description of Thornton comes from the following sources: G. G. Connell's *Fighting Destroyer HMS Petard*, London, 1976 (hereafter referred to as 'Connell, *Petard*'); interviews with the following crew members who served on *Petard* under Thornton: Reg Crang, Douglas Freer, Jeff Richards, Jack Hall, Eric Shove, Charlie Sewell, Ken Lacroix.

17 This account of the capture of *U-559* comes from the following sources: PRO ADM199/1259; Connell, *Petard*; an account by Connell written in 1973, before his book on *Petard* was commissioned. It was given to the author by Sheena d'Anyers Willis, Tony Fasson's sister; author's 1998–9 interviews with: Hermann Dethlefs who was on the *U-559* when it was captured and sunk; Donald Bush who was on HMS *Dulverton* during the capture; Stanley Reynolds and Ken Lacroix who were in *Petard*'s boarding party; Reg Crang, Anthony Creery-Hill, Douglas Freer, Jack Hall, John Macness, Robert de Pass, Geoffrey Richards, Mervyn Romeril, Charlie Sewell, Eric Shove, Trevor Tipping and Charles Underwood who were on *Petard* on the day of the capture; Patrick Murray, a friend of Tony Fasson; Joan and Mike Connell, Gordon Connell's widow and son, who helped the author to get in touch with some of *Petard*'s crew, and gave the author permission to refer to passages from Connell, *Petard*.

18 Cited in Blair vol. 2 p. 86.

19 Connell, *Petard*, p. 119.

20 Hinsley vol. 2 p. 750.

21 Alexander, *Naval Enigma History*, pp. 44–5.

22 Hinsley vol. 2 p. 233.

Chapter 21 The Turning Point (pp. 233–245)

1 Bertrand, pp. 136–41.

2 *ibid.* p. 138.

3 This account of the events leading up to Lemoine's arrest are based on Paillole pp. 221–9.

4 This account of the capture of *U-205* is based on the following: PRO: ADM199/432, ADM199/2060, ADM1/14342; author's 1998–9 interviews with Roger Morgan, William Murdoch, Nick Carter, Cyril Dawson and Ron Maflin, all of whom were serving on HMS *Paladin* at the time of the capture;

author's interviews with Friedrich Bürgel, the commander of *U-205* and Horst Georgy, the engineer on *U-205* at the time of the capture.

5 NHB, MOD.

6 These two quotes are laid out in Blair vol. 2 p. 241.

7 Middlebrook p. 250.

8 Second-Officer Clarke-Hunt, a survivor from *Canadian Star*, quoted on p. 250 of Middlebrook.

9 *ibid.* p. 250.

10 Able Seaman T. Napier, who was on the *James Oglethorpe* when it was sunk during the passage of HX229, quoted in Middlebrook p. 251.

11 Second-Officer G. D. Williams, who was aboard *Nariva* during the passage of HX229, quoted in Middlebrook p. 252.

12 Lieutenant D.C. Christopherson quoted in Middlebrook, p. 252.

13 Middlebrook pp. 252–3.

14 Middlebrook p. 303.

15 Roskill vol. 2 p. 485.

16 PRO ADM199/2060.

17 Hinsley vol. 2 pp. 562–3 specifies the date when the Shark settings were broken. The numbers in the Naval Enigma codebreaking section are specified in Alexander, *Naval Enigma History*, p. 52.

18 Quoted in History of Hut Eight pp. 68–9.

19 Hinsley vol. 2 p. 552. Two or more cribs were normally needed.

20 PRO HW1/1482. This is mentioned in Ralph Erskine's article 'Kriegsmarine Short Signal Systems – And How Bletchley Park Exploited Them' in *Cryptologia*, January 1999, vol. xxiii, no. 1, pp. 84–5.

21 Alexander, *Naval Enigma History*, p. 52 and History of Hut Eight, p.-93.

22 Quoted in Hinsley vol. 2 p. 549.

23 Quoted in Blair vol. 2 p. 310.

24 Hinsley vol. 2 p. 566.

25 Hinsley vol. 2 pp. 594–6 stated that the Enigma decrypts were of 'decisive importance' in the defeat of Rommel at Medinine.

26 Blair vol. 2 p. 339 states that the actual number of sunk U-boats or U-boats which had to abort before carrying out their mission prior to 23 May 1943 was thirty-three, not thirty one, as Dönitz had estimated.

27 Karl Doenitz, *Memoirs: Ten Years and Twenty Days*, p. 341, London, 1990. This book was first published in 1958 in Germany and in 1959 in England.

Chapter 22 Trapped (pp. 246–252)

1 Bertrand, p. 141.

2 Langer's 1946 'Memoirs' (hereafter referred to as 'Langer's 1946 Memoirs') a copy of which is filed in the Polish Institute and Sikorski Museum.

3 This account of the attempts to evacuate the Poles is based on Langer's Memoirs.

4 This account of how Rejewski and Zygalski escaped is to be found in Rejewski, Memoirs and in Kozaczuk, *Enigma* pp. 149–55.

5 Bertrand, p. 142.

6 Paillole p. 243.

Chapter 23 The Arrest (pp. 253–257)
1 Paillole pp. 234–7.
2 Paillole p. 285.
3 This account about what happened after Hans Thilo Schmidt's arrest is based on the author's 1998–9 interviews with his daughter, Gisela.

Chapter 24 Sinking the *Scharnhorst* (pp. 258–266)
1 Author's 1999 interview with Admiral Tom Homan who in December 1943 was a lieutenant on *Duke of York*.
2 Details of this and all other Enigma intelligence mentioned in this chapter which was passed to Fraser is to be found in PRO ADM 223/186.
3 Alexander, *Naval Enigma History*, p. 34.
4 *ibid.*, p. 33.
5 A copy of Fraser's report is filed at the National Maritime Museum in MS/83/158 File 18.
6 This, and all other Enigma messages quoted in this chapter, can be found in PRO ADM223/36. Where, in this chapter, it is stated that a message was 'originated', or sent to the Operational Intelligence Centre or British Fleet at a particular time, the time specified is according to British Summer Time (i.e. Greenwich Mean Time plus one hour).
7 Hinsley vol. 3(1) p. 266.
8 Beesly p. 215.
9 Author's 1999 interview with Richard Pendered.
10 Hinsley vol. 3(1) p. 267.
11 Letter from Captain A. G. F. Ditcham to John Winton, dated 10 November 1984, ROSK 5/77 amongst Roskill's papers in Churchill College, Cambridge. The quotation is also to be found Correlli Barnett's *Engage the Enemy More Closely*, London, 1991 on p. 743. This description of the engagements of the ships leading up to the sinking of *Scharnhorst* is partly based on Barnett's account.
12 Lieutenant B. B. Ramsden on HMS *Jamaica* in John Winton's *The War At Sea, 1939–45*, London, 1994. The book was first published in 1967.
13 *Arctic Convoys*, Richard Woodman, London, 1994, p. 373. This account of *Scharnhorst*'s last moments and the aftermath is based in part on Woodman's account. The anecdotes about Fraser, and about his minder were mentioned to the author by Admiral Homan.

Chapter 25 Operation Covered (pp. 267–285)
1 This account of Bertrand's arrest is taken from Bertrand pp. 149–59.
2 This report is included in the BDU War Diary for 13 August 1943 and a translation is to be found in the National Archives RG 457 item 908 Box number 192. It is also included in file OKM: Akte Geheimhaltung (OKM:4.Skl, Operative Geheimaltung 1941–4) at the Naval Historical Branch in the Ministry of Defence in London. It was made available to the author by Dr. Phil. Berthold J. Sander-Nagashima, Korvettenkapitän from Militärgeschichtliches Forschungsamt in Potsdam. The information about Karl Stein comes from answers he has given to the author in 2000, via his

son Ulrich, and from a document summarizing his conclusions about Enigma Security which was completed in 1944.

3 RG 38, Crane Naval Security Group ('CNSG') 5750/441, Crane Files, National Archives, brought to my attention by Stephen Budiansky in his book *Battle of Wits: The Complete Story of Codebreaking in World War II*, US and London, 2000.

4 Alexander, *Naval Enigma History*, p. 60.

5 History of Hut Eight p. 87.

6 Alexander, *Naval Enigma History*, p. 54 and *ibid.*, p. 95.

7 Roskill vol. 3(1) p. 388.

8 Alexander, *Naval Enigma History* p. 53 states that Pendered worked out one set of Shark settings on 27 May 1943 by using a 400-letter re-encodement (crib). Pendered himself, when interviewed by the author in 1998–9, stated his crib comprised around 280 letters.

9 Author's 1998–9 interviews with Richard Pendered, and History of Hut Eight p. 87.

10 Alexander, *Naval Enigma History*, p. 61.

11 The conference is referred to in a Memorandum dated 19 March 1943 from Leo Rosen in the Signal Corps to Colonel W. Preston Corderman which is filed in the National Archives in RG 457 Box 1283.

12 Professor Colin Burke wrote up his account of what he had seen about the engineering problems concerning the American bombes in his book *Information and Secrecy*, Metuchen, New Jersey, 1994 pp. 287–302. It should be pointed out that the Bombe History version of the events described does not always coincide with what is in Burke's book. The Bombe History states that the test models were immediately successful in May 1943, and says that production models were put into operation in early June 1943. This version is unlikely to be accurate given the specific memos about major engineering problems in May and June 1943 cited by Burke and shown by Burke to the author. Other evidence that the Bombe History is inaccurate in relation to the engineering problems is to be found in a summary of Op-20-G's signals for June–July 1943 in National Archives RG 457 Box 705; one signal implies that the first production bombe was expected to be delivered soon after 23 June 1943. Burke gained access to the documents relating to the American bombes pursuant to a Freedom of Information Act request passed to the National Security Agency in America. Many of the crucial documents are filed in the Message File for Op-20-G/Op-20-2, US Navy. The file is labelled 'Communication Supplementary Activities, Washington To Navy Computing Machine Laboratory.

13 History of Hut Eight pp. 87–8.

14 Alexander, *Naval Enigma History*, p. 57.

15 Questions asked by the Americans are in the 24 April 1942 note handed to Colonel Tiltman, and GC&CS' answers are in a 15 May 1942 note. Both are filed in National Archives, Washington in RG 457 Box 1283. The anecdote about Turing's views on the number of bombes being planned is in the Bombe History p. 7, and in Alan Turing's report concerning his visit to the National Cash Register Corporation on 21 December 1942. The latter document was found by Ralph Erskine in CNSG 5750/441 in RG 38 at the

National Archives, and was made available to me by Ralph Erskine and Frode Weierud. The September 1943 correspondence between Wenger and Travis is in National Archives RG 457 Box 705.

16 History of Hut Eight pp. 88–92 describes Op-20-G's criticized practice in relation to cribs and their bombes.

17 The Bombe History pp. 9–11. The reference to the British production of four-wheel bombes being 'extremely unsatisfactory' appears on p. 10 of an early draft of the Bombe History which is filed in the National Archives RG 457 Box 705.

18 Hinsley vol. 3 Part 1 p. 75 states that the Army Enigma key Albatross was broken after 2 June 1943 about 50 per cent of the time.

19 PRO ADM223/626.

20 *ibid.*

21 *ibid.*

22 *ibid.*

23 *ibid.*

24 A copy of these orders is held by NHB, MOD. It was given to the author by Tony Fabricius, an officer on *Roebuck* during Operation Covered.

25 The first report came in to *Roebuck's* commander at about 3.04 local time. The reports of the *Brake* sinking are in PRO ADM199/1388, and the author has also relied on the report by the commander of *Roebuck* given to him by Tony Fabricius.

26 The story about the weather man's analysis being given as a reason for going to the rendezvous was mentioned to the author by E. V. B. Morton who served as a Surgeon-Lieutenant on *Battler* during Operation Covered.

27 PRO ADM223/626.

28 *ibid.*

29 Addendum to BDU KTB 15 March 1944.

30 Mentioned in Blair vol. 2 p. 529.

31 Mentioned in Blair vol. 2 p. 537 and Hinsley vol. 3 p. 231.

32 National Archives in Washington RG 457 Box 623.

33 The convoy which was being escorted by Escort Group C2 was the HX280. The ships which became involved in the hunt were the destroyers *Icarus* (British) and the *Chaudière* and *Gatineau* (Canadian), the Canadian frigate *St Catherines*, the Canadian corvettes *Chilliwack* and *Fennel*, and the British corvette *Kenilworth Castle*. *Gatineau's* Asdic operators were the first to identify the U-boat, and *St Catherines* was the first to drop depth charges in an attempt to sink it. Times specified are according to GMT.

This account of the hunt for and the sinking of the *U-744* is based on the following sources: PRO ADM186/809, ADM199/2061 and ADM199/2029; report by Lieutenant T. H. Dunn, who was in charge of *Chilliwack's* boarding party, as well as a report by the senior officer in the C2 Escort Group. Both of these documents are in PRO ADM217/95; author's 1998–9 interviews with Wilfred Jenkins and Robert Martin who were members of *Chilliwack's* boarding party; author's 1998–9 interviews with Willi Brauckmann, Josef Hansen and Karl Erath who were on *U-744* on the day she was sunk.

34 There is some uncertainty as to what happened to the Enigma machine. After the war Friedo Spanjol, one of *U-744's* crew, told his U-boat comrades that he had thrown the Enigma or part of it into the U-boat's bilge under the inner deck. However the boarding party from *Chilliwack* noticed a machine which looked like a typewriter in the radio room. They presumed it was the coding machine. In view of these two conflicting accounts, I have come to the view that Spanjol probably merely threw the Enigma wheels – which, after all, were the most important elements inside the machine – into the bilge, leaving the typewriter-like shell in place in the radio room.

35 The two officers from *Chilliwack* who went down into the U-boat were Lieutenant Atherton and Lieutenant Hearn.

36 *Chaudière*'s commander was Lieutenant-Commander C. P. Nixon.

37 The article from the *Daily Telegraph* which was reprinted in a Canadian newspaper was brought to the author's attention by Terry Govier of Naval Network UK.

Chapter 26 The Last Hiccough (pp. 286–303)

1 Paillole p. 244 mentions that Menzies was told about the Poles' arrest.

2 The sources for this account are the author's 1998–9 interviews with Jerzy Palluth, the son of Antoni Palluth, and a report by Kazimierz Gaca, one of the Polish codebreakers who was with Antoni Palluth in the concentration camp.

3 Palluth's prisoner number appears on his correspondence with his family via their friend Stanislaw Guzicki.

4 This is from a translation of Langer's post-war Memoirs which are filed in the Polish Institute and Sikorski Museum in London.

5 The plan was approved by the Allies' Combined Chiefs of Staff on 26 February 1944.

6 'Fish' was the name given to the non-morse code that was sent by teleprinter impulses. The Fish messages were sent by people who were more senior to those using the Enigma. Hinsley vol. 3 Part 1 p. 481 states that the Army Enigma messages were transmitted by people communicating within Armies, or occasionally between Armies, but rarely above Army level.

7 The account of Bertrand's escape from France is taken from Bertrand pp. 194–204.

8 This account of Bertrand's interrogation by Paillole and of Bertrand's escape from the Abwehr is based on: Paillole pp. 245–9; Bertrand pp. 159–85 and 205–9; the anecdote about Otto Brandle comes from Bertrand pp. 80–3.

9 Masuy was the alias for Monsieur Defrasne, a Belgian who, according to Paillole p. 245, had been recruited by the Abwehr in 1941.

10 The sources for this account of Daniel Gallery's hunter-killer group's exploits, including the capturing of *U-505*, come from the following sources: reports of destroyers in the hunter-killer group about the sinking of *U-505*, together with the transcripts of messages sent to and from aeroplanes and destroyers during the action, and correspondence between Gallery and Dudley Knox, the commander of the *Chatelain*, all of which were made available to the author by the U-boat Archiv in Altenbruch near Cuxhaven, Germany. The warships in question were the *Chatelain*, *Flaherty*, *Jenks*, *Pillsbury* and *Pope*, as well as the aircraft carrier *Guadalcanal*. The logs for the *Pillsbury* and *Guadalcanal* for 4 June 1944 were provided by Wayne

Pickels, one of the *Pillsbury*'s crew on that day. Other sources included: the author's 1998–9 interviews with Earl Trosino who was on *Guadalcanal* on 4 June 1944, and with Gordon Hohne, Zenon Lukosius and Wayne Pickels who were in the boarding party sent over from *Pillsbury* to capture *U-505*; the author's 1998–9 interviews with Hans Göbeler, Werner Reh, Wolfgang Schiller, and Albert Weinhold who were on *U-505* when she was captured; Blair vol. 2 pp. 548–55.

11 The memo and other documents which specify the items captured are held by the Museum of Science and Industry in Chicago according to Blair vol. 2 p. 555. NHB, MOD documents specify that Offizier settings for June 1944 were recovered from *U-505* as well as the general settings. The documents also specify the date when the Enigma documents reached Bletchley Park: on 20 June 1944.

12 Blair vol. 2 p. 553 refers to King's furious reaction to the capture of *U-505*. Shortly before Clay Blair died during 1999 he told the author that Allan Rockwell McCann mentioned this story to him during an interview.

13 This account of what Hinsley was doing on 5–6 June 1944 is based on the Steinberg Hinsley interview and the author's 1997 interview with Hinsley. Times mentioned are in Double Summer Time, i.e. GMT+2 hours.

14 Alexander, *Naval Enigma History*, pp. 64–5 and History of Hut Eight, pp. 90–1.

15 Alexander, *Naval Enigma History*, pp. 68–72 and History of Hut Eight, pp. 100–102.

16 Alexander, *Naval Enigma History*, p. 56 states that there were 152 3-wheel bombes and 180 4-wheel bombes in Britain and the US by the end of the war. It is likely that he has misstated the correct number of 4-wheelers: The History of Hut Eight p. 5 appears to state that there were 64 4-wheelers in Britain in May 1945, and the Americans manufactured 121 4-wheelers as described in chapter 25. The American total of 121 was made up of the original 96 plus 25 of the 50 requested by Hugh Alexander as mentioned in chapter 25; the order for the remaining order of 25 was cancelled in September 1944 as is confirmed by the Chief of Naval Operations' 8 September 1944 memorandum to that effect in National Archives RG 457 Box 705. One reason for the cancellation was that a pluggable reflector had been introduced on an Air Force Enigma net, and because there was concern that it would be introduced on other nets, it was more important to manufacture a machine which could deal with the pluggable reflector than to make the additional 25 bombes. This is mentioned in a draft of the Bombe History in National Archives RG 457 Box 705.

17 *ibid.*, p. 53 and Hinsley vol. 3(2), p. 784.

18 PRO ADM223/195.

Epilogue (pp. 304–309)

1 Paillole pp. 239–43.

2 Goebbels Diaries, 10 May 1943.

3 Paillole pp. 251–8.

4 The information in this section comes from Dilly Knox's son, Oliver, and from Penelope Fitzgerald's *The Knox Brothers*, 1977.

5 This information is taken from Hodges' *Alan Turing, the Enigma*, and Alexander, *Naval Enigma History* pp. 42–3, which states that although Turing did not officially leave Hut 8 until after November 1942, he never worked for the Naval codebreaking section again.

6 Alexander, *Naval Enigma History*, pp. 42–3.

7 *Breaking The Code* used information taken from Hodges' *Alan Turing, the Enigma* which was published in 1983.

8 The information in this section is extracted from the History of Hut Eight. Alexander, *Naval Enigma History* specifies when Shark was mastered, and Hinsley vol. 2 pp. 663–4 specifies when Dolphin was mastered.

9 History of Hut Eight p. 114.

Appendix 1 (pp. 324–328)

1 This description is based on Rejewski's explanation in Kozaczuk, *Enigma* pp. 263–4 and 284–7.

2 This description is based on Rejewski's explanation in Kozaczuk, *Enigma* pp. 266–7.

Appendix 2 (pp. 329–340)

1 The explanation of the bombe in this Appendix has been made with the assistance of Professor Jack Good and Richard Pendered, both of whom worked in Bletchley Park's Hut 8 during the war, and Professor David Rees, who worked in Hut 6.

2 I have assumed that the middle wheel is not turned over by the right wheel as the settings change from AAA to AAG.

3 Deduction 4, which states that the G socket is connected to the A socket, would provide some evidence that the set of assumptions being tested was the correct set. But the cryptographers would not have felt that the deduction provided enough evidence to persuade them to try out the assumptions manually. As a rule of thumb the cryptographers sought three similar pieces of evidence before they were convinced that the set of assumptions was one to be shortlisted and should be tested further.

Appendix 3 (pp. 341–353)

1 This description was compiled with the assistance of Gilbert Bloch, the French expert on Enigma, and author of *Enigma Avant Ultra, 1930–1940*.

2 History of Hut Eight p. 26 specifies that by the end of March 1941 the reconstruction of the bigram tables was 'more or less complete'.

3 History of Hut Eight p. 95.

4 I have written this description of how the bigram tables were reconstructed with the assistance of Richard Pendered, who worked in Hut 8 during the war.

5 This detailed description of Banburismus is based on the example laid out in pp. 16–20 of The History of Hut Eight. However the contents of 'The History of Hut Eight' have been explained to me by Jack Good, Richard Pendered and Rolf Noskwith, all of whom worked in Hut 8 during the war.

Appendix 4 (pp. 354–356)

1 This Appendix was drawn up after obtaining guidance from Professor David Rees, who used cillis at Bletchley Park.

2 Hinsley vol. 3(2) pp. 953–4. Professor David Rees in his 1999 interview with the author stated that cillis were being used to help break the Enigma prior to 1 May 1940. Some codebreakers refer to them as 'cillies'.

3 Rejewski noticed before the war that the Germans were using obvious message settings. However he does not appear to have exploited his knowledge as mentioned in this Appendix.

Appendix 5 (pp. 357–367)

1 This Appendix has been prepared with assistance from Richard Pendered, who used rodding in Huts 6 and 8 during the war, and from other cryptographers who used it to break Italian Naval Enigma messages.

Appendix 6 (pp. 368–373)

1 This Appendix has been prepared after consultation with Professor Jack Good and Richard Pendered, both of whom helped to break Offizier messages in Hut 8. The text also relies on the descriptions of how the Offizier was broken in History of Hut Eight pp. 51–4, and Alexander, *Naval Enigma History* pp. 14–15 and 32–4.

Bibliography

Abbreviated titles used in the endnotes are supplied in square brackets for reference.

Published sources

BOOKS

Agar, Augustus, *Footprints in the Sea*, London, 1961.

Barnett, Correlli, *Engage the Enemy More Closely*, London, 1991.

Beesly, Patrick, *Very Special Admiral: the Life of J. H. Godfrey*, London, 1980.

    Very Special Intelligence, London, 1977.

Bertrand, Gustave, *Enigma, ou la plus grande énigme de la guerre*, Paris 1973. [Bertrand]

Blair, Clay, *Hitler's U-Boat War: the Hunters 1939–1942*, London, 1997. [Blair, vol. 1]

    Hitler's U-Boat War: The Hunted 1942–1945, New York, 1998. [Blair vol.-2]

Boutilier, James, ed., *The Royal Canadian Navy in Retrospect 1910–68*, Canada, 1982. Chapter quoted: Douglas W. A. B. and Rohwer, Jürgen, 'The Most Thankless Task Revisited: Convoys, Escorts and Radio Intelligence in the Western Atlantic 1941–3'. [Douglas and Rohwer 'Thankless Task']

Broome, Jack, *Convoy Is To Scatter*, London, 1972.

Budiansky, Stephen, *Battle of Wits: The Complete Story of Codebreaking in World War II*, US and UK, 2000.

Burke, Colin, *Information and Secrecy*, Metuchen, New Jersey, 1994.

Connell, G. G., *Arctic Destroyers: The 17th Flotilla*, London, 1982.

    Fighting Destroyer: The Story of HMS Petard, London, 1976. [Connell, Petard]

Doenitz, Karl, *Memoirs: Ten Years and Twenty Days* (Germany, 1958), London 1990.

Fitzgerald, Penelope, *The Knox Brothers*, London, 1977.

German, Tony, *The Sea Is At Our Gates: the History of the Canadian Navy*, Toronto, 1991.

Gilbert, Martin, *Finest Hour, 1939–49*, vol. VI of his biography, *Winston S. Churchill*, London, 1989. [Gilbert, *Finest Hour*]

Grant, Donald, *A Working Holiday*, Gisborne, New Zealand, 1992.

Hancock, W. Keith, ed. of *Statistical Digest of the War*, London, 1975.

Hinsley, F. H., Thomas, E. E., Ransom, C. F. G., and Knight, R. C., *British*

Bibliography

Intelligence in the Second World War, vols 1, 2 and vol. 3, part 1, London, 1979–84. [Hinsley]

Hinsley, F. H., Thomas, E. E., Simkins, C. A. G. and Ransom, C. F. G., *British Intelligence in the Second World War*, vol. 3, part 2, London, 1988. [Hinsley]

Hinsley, F. H. and Stripp, Alan, editors of *Codebreakers*, Oxford, 1993. Chapters quoted: by Joan Clarke, and by Christopher Morris.

Hodges, Alan, *Alan Turing, the Enigma*, London, 1992 [Hodges]

Hyde, H. Montgomery, *The Quiet Canadian: the secret service story of Sir William Stephenson*, London, 1962.

Irving, David, *The Destruction of Convoy PQ17*, London, 1968. [Irving]

Kahn, David, *Seizing the Enigma*, London, 1996. [David Kahn]

Kennedy, Ludovic, *Pursuit: The Sinking of the Bismarck*, London, 1974.
  Menace: The Life and Death of the Tirpitz, London, 1979.

Kozaczuk, Władysław, *Enigma: How the German Cipher Machine Was Broken, and How It Was Read by the Allies in World War Two*, London, 1984. [Kozaczuk, *Enigma*]

Lewin, Ronald, *Ultra Goes To War*, London, 1978.

MacDonald, Callum, *The Lost Battle: Crete 1941*, London, 1995.

Middlebrook, Martin, *Convoy: the Battle for Convoys SC122 and HX229*, London, 1976. [Middlebrook]

Mohr, Ulrich, *Atlantis – The Story of a German Surface Raider*, London, 1955.

Padfield, Peter, *War Beneath the Sea: Submarine Conflict 1939–45*, London, 1995.

Paillole, Paul, *Notre Espion Chez Hitler*, Paris, 1985. [Paillole]
  L'Homme Des Services Secrets: entretiens avec Alain-Gilles Minella, Paris, 1995.

Rohwer, Jürgen, *U-Boote, Eine Chronik in Bildern*, Germany, 1962. [Rohwer]

Roskill, Stephen, *The War At Sea, 1939–1945*, London, 1954–61. [Roskill]
  The Secret Capture, London, 1959. [Roskill, *Secret Capture*]

Santoni, Alberto, *Il Vero Traditore*, Milan, 1981. [Santoni]
  Storia E Politica Navale Dell'eta contemporanea, Rome, 1993.

Smith, Bradley F., *The Ultra-Magic Deals And The Most Secret Special Relationship 1940–1946*, 1993, US and UK.

Smith, Michael, *Station X*, London, 1998.

Turner, L. C. F., Gordon, H. R. and Betzler, J. E., *War in the Southern Oceans, 1939–1945*, London, 1961.

Warren, C. E. T. and Benson, James, *Will Not We Fear*, London, 1961.

Welchman, Gordon, *The Hut Six Story*, London, 1982. [Welchman]

Winton, John, ed., *The War At Sea, 1939–45*, London, 1994.
  Cunningham: the greatest admiral since Nelson, London, 1998.

Woodman, Richard, *Arctic Convoys*, London, 1994.

Wouk, Herman, *The 'Caine' Mutiny*, London, 1951.

JOURNALS

Beesly, Patrick and Jürgen Rohwer, 'Special Intelligence und die Vernichtung der Scharnhorst, Marine Rundshau, October 1977, pp. 556–68.

Erskine, Ralph, 'The Breaking of Heimisch and Triton', *Intelligence and National Security* 3(1), 1988, pp. 162–183.
  'Naval Enigma: a Missing Link', *International Journal of Intelligence*

and Counter-Intelligence vol. 3 no. 4, 1989, pp. 493–508, [Ralph Erskine, 'Missing Link']

'First Naval Enigma Decrypts of World War 2', *Cryptologia*, January, 1997, pp. 42–5.

'Kriegsmarine Short Signal Systems – And How Bletchley Park Exploited Them', *Cryptologia*, January, 1999, pp. 65–92.

'The Holden Agreement on Naval Sigint: The First BRUSA?', *Intelligence and National Security vol. 14 no. 2, 1999, pp. 187–197*.

Erskine, Ralph and Frode Weierud 'Naval Enigma: M4 and its Rotors', *Cryptologia*, October 1987, pp. 235–44.

Mulligan, Timothy, 'The German Navy Evaluates Its Cryptographic Security, October 1941', *Military Affairs* 49, April, 1985, pp. 75–9.

Rejewski, Marian, 'Remarks on Appendix 1 to *British Intelligence in the Second World War*, vol. 1 by F. H. Hinsley, *Cryptologia*, January, 1982 [Rejewski on Hinsley].

Welchman, Gordon, 'From Polish Bomba to British Bombe: the Birth of Ultra,' *Intelligence and National Security* 1, January 1986, pp. 71–110.

Unpublished sources

Alexander, Hugh, 'Cryptographic History of the Work on the German Naval Enigma', written after the war. [Alexander, Naval Enigma History]

Bloch, Gilbert, Enigma avant Ultra (1930–1940), privately printed, Paris, 1988.

Danilewicz, Leonard, untitled undated account describing the part played by AVA engineers in the Enigma story, sent to Marian Rejewski in 1975.

Esterer, Rainer, his account of the sinking of *U-13*.

Gaca, Kazimierz, untitled undated account written after the war about the part he played in the Enigma story.

Grandjean, Hans, his account of the sinking of *U-13*.

Hinsley F. H., 'The Influence of Ultra in the Second World War', London, 1992.

Langer, Gwido, 'Report on the work of Lieutenant-Colonel Langer's team during the French Campaign from 1 October 1939 to 24 June 1940'. ['1 October 1939–24 June 1940' Langer Memoirs]

Mahon, Patrick, 'The History of Hut Eight, 1939–1945', written after the war.

Rejewski, Marian, 'Memoirs', part of which was completed in 1967. [Rejewski, 'Memoirs']

Richardson, Richard, his account of the sinking of *U-13*.

Różycki, Basia, undated post-war account of her and her husband's escape from Warsaw in 1939.

Schulte, Max, his account of the sinking of *U-13*.

Suszczewski, Tadeusz, a post-war account of his escape from Warsaw in 1939.

Taylor, Telford, memorandum about the early E [Enigma] history, written in 1944.

Turing, Alan, 'Treatise on the Enigma', said to have been written between 1939–42. [Turing's Treatise]

Index